DISTRIBUTION OF INCOME AND WEALTH IN ONTARIO: THEORY AND EVIDENCE

Charles M. Beach

with the collaboration of
David E. Card and Frank Flatters

Distribution of Income and Wealth in Ontario: theory and evidence

PUBLISHED FOR THE ONTARIO ECONOMIC COUNCIL BY
UNIVERSITY OF TORONTO PRESS
TORONTO BUFFALO LONDON

꙳

Canadian Cataloguing in Publication Data

Beach, Charles M.
    Distribution of income and wealth in Ontario
    (Ontario Economic Council research studies, ISSN
    0708-3688 ; 22)
    ISBN 0-8020-3369-5
    1. Income distribution – Ontario. 2. Ontario –
    Economic conditions. I. Card, David E. (David
    Edward), 1956-   II. Flatters, Frank. III. Ontario
    Economic Council. IV. Title. V. Series.
    HC117.06B42   339.2'09713   C81-094439-1

This report reflects the views of the author and not necessarily those of the Ontario
Economic Council or of the Ontario government. The Council establishes policy
questions to be investigated and commissions research projects, but it does not
influence the conclusions or recommendations of authors. The decision to sponsor
publication of this study was based on its competence and relevance to public policy
and was made with the advice of anonymous referees expert in the area.

Contents

vi Contents

Acknowledgments

I should first of all like to thank the Ontario Economic Council for suggesting and financing the project on which this monograph is based, and Queen's University for providing research facilities and release time so that the project could be carried out. I also wish to express my particular appreciation to David Card for providing the effort to bring the project to completion and to Frank Flatters at Queen's for help in the organization and direction of the study.

A project such as the present one relies heavily on research assistance and indeed would never have come to fruition without the amiable, dependable, and energetic efforts of a number of persons. Special thanks are due to Ian Ladd for his good humour and for programming most of the computations in Part Three. I also wish to thank Ross Finnie, Martin Hellsten, David Prescott, Doug Snetsinger, and François Vaillancourt as well for their programming assistance. John Andrew helped write the basic computer program for calculating the inequality statistics used throughout the study. Françoise Grégoire and Tom Beasley did much of the work on the material of Chapters 13 and 12 respectively. I also wish to express my appreciation to A.B. Atkinson, Alan Harrison, Michael Wolfson, Constantine Kapsalis, and several anonymous referees who provided many helpful comments on an earlier draft of the study, and to members of the Ontario Economic Council for their comments during preliminary presentations of the present work at research seminars.

I wish to thank Gail Oja and Allison Paoliello at Statistics Canada for their assistance with our data requirements for the project, and Freya Godard for editorial assistance. Finally, I wish to acknowledge my indebtedness to Ellen McKay for her dependable pleasantness and excellent typing of large volumes of material, often under deadlines.

DISTRIBUTION OF INCOME AND WEALTH IN ONTARIO: THEORY AND EVIDENCE

1
Introduction

The last several decades have seen governments become heavily involved in the functioning of the Canadian economy through macroeconomic controls, expenditures on goods and services, taxes, subsidies, transfers, social security programs, and various forms of regulation. These activities can have important implications, whether intended or not, for the distribution of resources amongst individuals. Public debate has been concentrating more and more on the distributive consequences of public policies, and governments have recently been engaging in general reviews of goals and programs in the distribution area (see e.g. Lalonde, 1973; Ontario Economic Council, 1976). Such a review should begin with an evaluation of the economic environment in which the policies operate, and in particular with a detailed examination of the current inequalities in the distribution of economic resources. That is the purpose of this study. It aims to point out where distributional problems might exist and to quantify the principal aspects of the distributions of income and wealth.

In recent years also the interest in distributional questions has broadened from the determinants of poverty and characteristics of the poor to a much more general concern with over-all distribution and with the principles of equity underlying various aspects of government economic activity. The present study is written in the latter vein and examines income and wealth distribution as a whole in the light of recent theoretical work. I hope it will provide useful background information and broaden the horizons of current debate.

Almost all the research done in Canada on distribution has been based on annual money income receipts. But if one is interested in the economic well-being of the population, the proxy measure of current money income is deficient in many respects. It may be affected by underreporting of incomes, and it excludes income in kind or imputed benefits from home ownership. It does not reflect family size and composition or regional cost of living differences. And it does not take into account personal wealth holdings, capital gains, or expected social security benefits. We need a more accurate measure of distribution of economic well-being. The present study thus 'adjusts' the distribution of current money income for these inadequacies and examines the resulting distribution of adjusted real income to see how great a disparity there is between adjusted real incomes and conventional money incomes and to what extent the latter can be said to represent the former.

The seminal study of the distribution of income in Canada is Podoluk (1968). However, since its publication substantial changes have taken place in the quantity and detail of distributional data available and in the theoretical models of distribution of income and wealth. We now have annual income distribution surveys with sufficiently large samples to allow fairly detailed regional breakdowns, as well as publicly available micro data tapes from these surveys. Furthermore, the 1971 Census provides a wealth of new distributional detail. At the same time, substantial progress has been made in economic theory. Elaborate models of life-cycle behaviour in wealth accumulation, human capital investment, and work-leisure time allocation and of employers' behaviour in hiring, training, and remuneration policies have been developed as partial explanations of the distribution of income and economic well-being. These theories give us a framework in which to assemble the distributional data, and a perspective on the interpretation and evaluation of the more detailed information now available. The theories also provide a useful framework for analysing the potential distributional effects of changes in government policy. Consequently, they allow us to update the work of Podoluk.

Distributional research in Canada has been almost entirely at the national level. Analysis of interregional disparities has concentrated almost exclusively on mean income differences between regions or provinces with very little consideration given to the structure of inequality within regions. This is due partly to data limitations, which were severe until the release of micro data tapes began in 1975, and partly to a prevalent wish to see the total picture rather than only its separate components. Yet the regional heterogeneity of the Canadian economy suggests that the patterns of inequality differ regionally too. Consequently the present study takes a step towards regional comparisons in Canada by analysing the distribution of income and wealth in a major economic region of the country.

In general, then, the present study has four objectives. First, it reviews some recent theoretical work on distribution as background. Second, it reviews the data already available on the distribution of income and wealth in Ontario, outlining the basic distributional pattern, much as Podoluk did for Canadian income distributional patterns in the early sixties. Third, it addresses limitations in these data and by a series of adjustments seeks to make the estimated distribution of economic well-being in Ontario more accurate, while at the same time evaluating the adequacy of conventional income measures as proxies for the real distribution. Fourth, it seeks to provide a step toward analysis of a broad range of questions about government social security programs whose distributional aspects vary with time.

Several distinguishing features of the present study should be highlighted. First, it begins with an unusually extensive theoretical discussion, particularly of the theory of life-cycle income and wealth behaviour. I strongly believe that empirical analysis should be based explicitly on a theoretical framework and that such a framework is necessary to the intelligent evaluation of empirical findings. Second, heavy emphasis is placed on detailed micro data of individual families and income recipients. Micro data tapes from the 1971 Census and from several Surveys of Consumer Finances have only recently become available in Canada, presenting a degree of detail not formerly available. These new sources are used to make our analysis in depth of a region. Third, unlike much previous research this study emphasizes disaggregative analysis of distributional results. Earlier distribution studies usually expressed their results in a small number of summary inequality measures such as Gini coefficients and coefficients of variation. But such aggregative measures often hide a good deal of detail, suggest misleading distributional inferences, and implicitly contain odd schemes of weighting individual welfares. The distributional analysis here is often disaggregated by such factors as family size and age and sex of family head and is further broken down into detailed income-group components. The result is a much more complete picture of distributional inequality in Ontario than has formerly been available.

In outline, the study proceeds as follows. Part One provides the theoretical background for the study. Chapter 2 focuses on supply-side (life-cycle) theoretical considerations; Chapter 3 emphasizes demand-side aspects of income determination; and Chapter 4 brings the two sides together along with demographic considerations. Part Two presents the empirical background of the study. Chapter 5 provides a brief review of several types of inequality measures and different ways of characterizing inequality. Chapters 6 to 8 review the current distribution of income and wealth in Ontario and are mainly descriptive. Chapter 6 looks at individuals' incomes, Chapter 7 at incomes of family units, and Chapter 8 at net worth and asset distributions of family units. Part Three, containing the more analytic portions of the study, considers a number of adjustments to compensate for limitations in the conventional money income figures. Chapter 9 looks at adjustments for underreporting, home-ownership, and income-in-kind receipts and at the relative importance of personal income taxes and transfer receipts as components of the distribution of income. Chapter 10 examines the consequences of adjusting incomes for family size and composition and for regional cost-of-living differences. Chapter 11 turns to adjustments for capital gains receipts and Chapter 12 to adjustments for family net worth holdings. Chapter 13 presents a framework for analysing intertemporal distributional aspects of social security programs as illustrated by the Canada Pension Plan. Finally, Chapter 14 summarizes the study and highlights its principal findings.

The three principal micro data sources employed represent some of the most recent and detailed data available by region. The first, the Survey of Consumer Finances (SCF) 1974 micro data tape on Canadian census family units, is the main data source, from which a subfile of 7473 Ontario family units was generated. Upon these data the various adjustments and imputations in Part Three are performed, and from them the results in Chapter 7 are obtained. The second source of data employed, the Public Use Sample Tape (PUST) of individuals from the 1971 Census, contains a much larger sample of Ontario individuals, allowing a more disaggregated investigation of particular earnings relationships to supplement the smaller but richer SCF file. Results from the PUST file are used in Chapter 6 and in the construction of life-cycle earnings profiles used in Chapter 13. The third source of data, a set of summary tables on assets, debts, and net worth from the 1970 Survey of Consumer Finances, was assembled especially for this project by the Consumer Income and Expenditure Division of Statistics Canada; it serves as the basis for Chapter 8 and for all asset and net worth calculations in Chapters 11 to 13. Details on how these data sources were used are presented in various technical appendices. All calculations were done on the Burroughs B6700 computer at Queen's University and were based on computer programs generally available to the public (such as the SPSS package) or were written specifically for the project (see Appendix D for more details).

PART ONE: EXPLANATION OF INEQUALITY

This part presents a theoretical overview of some of the principal determinants of the distribution of income. Since distribution theory has advanced so rapidly and in so many directions in recent years, it seemed useful to pull together in a brief review several of its basic themes. The next three chapters thus outline the theoretical background of the study. They show (1) the way underlying determinants and behaviour interact with each other, (2) the distributional environment in which government activity and policy-making must be carried on, (3) the rationale for the analytical perspective pursued in later chapters, and (4) the basis for the interpretation and evaluation of empirical results that occur throughout. Readers interested only in the empirical portions of the study, however, may wish to skip directly ahead to Parts Two or Three.

The present study is not a comprehensive survey of recent work on distribution theory. It is restricted to positive economic theories, excluding normative theories from its outlook. The review is also limited in the time frame of the theories considered. Neither very long-run theories of intergenerational behaviour and mobility nor theories of the short-run distributional effects of cyclical macroeconomic fluctuations are considered. The analysis focuses instead on various aspects of the life-cycle behaviour of households and the labour market behaviour of firms. This study centres on the distribution of resources among individuals and households; that is, we do not address theories of factor shares, functional distribution of income, or regional differences in income. Since the aim is not to analyse particular government programs, such matters as distributional incidence theory or the effects of minimum wage laws are not discussed. The theoretical survey presented here should complement other recent surveys of distribution rather than replace them. Finally, much of the material reviewed below is of quite recent vintage and of some technical sophistication. The goal, however, is not theoretical rigour or mathematical detail but to present the basic ideas verbally and (where useful) in diagrams. Readers may seek further analytical detail in the sources cited.

In traditional microanalysis, economics has theories of the supply of factors by individual microeconomic units on the one hand, theories of the demand for such factors by individual firms or producers on the other, and (except where factor prices are determined by legislation or collective bargaining) theories of equilibrium behaviour linking the two at the market level. Accordingly, our theoretical discussion is divided into three chapters. Chapter 2, immediately following, examines a number of supply-side factors determining the distribution of income and wealth, and carries out the analysis in a life-cycle framework of individual choice and household activity. Individuals receive income from wealth holdings and remuneration from work effort, as reflected in hours of work and acquired training and job experience. These factors are open to long-run or life-cycle choice by individuals according to their tastes and endowment constraints. Chapter 3 turns to demand-side considerations (such as discrimination and screening) in the distribution of earnings, examining employer behaviour in the labour market and its implications for wage differentials between individuals and groups of workers. The analysis in Chapter 3 is thus more short-run than that of Chapter 2 and more focused on group-specific (as opposed to individual) differences in wage rates and employment opportunities. Chapter 4 then brings in demographic factors to derive an over-all distribution of income as observed in conventional data sources. It thus tries to show how a number of important factors become integrated in the total distribution of income.

2
Supply determinants and life-cycle behaviour

The subject of this study is the size distribution of income and its associated structure of inequality; that is, it examines differences in income among individual income recipient units. Consequently, we begin by looking at the economic behaviour of these individual recipient units, emphasizing the choices available to them, the constraints they face, and the implications of their decisions. Households and individuals are remunerated according to the productive factors they offer to the market. The present chapter considers the various supply-side factors affecting income difference and the distribution of income.

Analysis of the supply-side determinants of the distribution of income emphasizes the availability of individuals' talents and abilities to the process of production. Since some talents are highly rewarded on the factor market, a person will seek to acquire them either through capital investment, formal education, built-up job experience, or perhaps greater work effort. These involve making decisions often over fairly lengthy time horizons that have implications for one's entire earning career. Thus the framework of analysis in this chapter is the life-cycle theory of individual and household decision-making. The three key components of the life-cycle models employed are the abilities the individual possesses either through birth or upbringing, his tastes in leisure, consumption, and education, and the access he has to capital funds and endowments to support his desired career and consumption plans. 'If native talents were the same for all individuals; if they all had the same tastes and could obtain capital for training purposes on the same terms, then in long-run equilibrium earnings would be the same for all' (Reder, 1969, 224). Differences in incomes on the supply side thus reflect differences among individuals principally in these key factors.

Much recent research has been devoted to developing a life-cycle theoretical framework for distribution analysis. It is appropriate for analysing the effects of pensions, government medical and health insurance, and social security programs such as those considered in Chapter 13. It highlights the long-term nature of the many income differences and background factors that go into these differences. It permits inferences on the distribution of economic well-being from current income and wealth figures such as those considered in Chapter 12. It helps to determine when the low income of a group calls for transfer policies rather than job opportunities or policies to increase productivity. A life-cycle framework also helps in the interpretation of recent trends in summary inequality statistics associated with changing age, occupational structure, and labour force participation patterns in the economy.

There are several basic features or stylized facts of the life cycle. The early years are characterized by dependence upon parents or guardians, and most important decisions about education and upbringing are made by them. Talents and abilities are inherited or acquired from them, and one's socioeconomic background is provided by them. In the second stage one reaches adulthood and economic independence in the sense that the chief economic decisions are now made by oneself, perhaps along with a spouse. Given one's ability, resources, background, and preferences, an occupation or career is selected; choices are made to cease or continue further education in high school, university, or technical school; and decisions are made about work effort on the job. In principle one can also choose the number and timing of children so that household development can also be planned. And along with household development go life-cycle consumption, saving, and net worth accumulation patterns. These reveal relatively heavy expenses in the early years of family formation and perhaps also later on with education costs, but eventually tailing off as the children themselves become independent and leave home. In the third stage of economic life, one stops working because of retirement or infirmity and becomes dependent again either upon past accumulation of capital or upon transfer support from one's children or the state. This review treats the first stage as given, and focuses on the principal economic decisions made in the second and on their distributional implications for incomes in the second and third stages.

The next section of this chapter examines life-cycle consumption, saving, and wealth accumulation. The third section looks at human capital investment models as determinants of earnings. The fourth section extends the analysis to incorporate life-cycle labour supply as well. The fifth section considers several aspects of occupational choice. Household activity and labour supply behaviour of wives are discussed in the sixth section, along with family background and bequests. Implications of these principles are reviewed in the concluding section.

LIFE-CYCLE SAVING AND WEALTH ACCUMULATION

The factor or primary income Y_f that an individual or household receives in return for supplying productive inputs to the factor market comes from several principal sources. Wage and salary income YW, by far the largest component, is received by those who work as part-time or full-time employees. Capital income YK consists of rent, dividends, and interest income. Proprietory income YP includes farm proprietary income received by farmers and business and professional proprietary income received by self-employed businessmen and professionals such as medical doctors and lawyers. More formally, one may write

$$Y_f = \text{YW} + \text{YK} + \text{YP}.$$

However, the third component may be thought of as a return jointly to work effort and professional expertise of self-employed workers on the one hand and to the stock of capital or equipment they use in their work on the other hand. Consequently, in this chapter YP will be subsumed under the other main sources of factor income, YW and YK.

In addition, income may be received in the form of government transfers YT; and at the same time, government taxes T must be paid. Thus disposable income may be expressed as

$$Y_d = Y_f + (\text{YT} - T).$$

Part One of this study focuses on the determinants of the distribution of primary or factor income Y_f, while the distribution of disposable family income is considered at a later stage in the empirical work of Part Three. The present section examines some of the determinants of income from wealth holdings YK, while the following several sections look at earned income YW.

Although capital income is not as widespread a source of income as earnings, it is nonetheless a useful point at which to start a review of life-cycle theory because it is an important source of inequality at the top end of the distribution and because it introduces the basic neoclassical model of life-cycle decision-making, the distinction between flow of income and stock of wealth, and the role of wealth as such. Human capital theory is discussed in the next section, and the similarities in framework between the two sections can be noted. Capital income is made up of rents, dividends, and interest income that arise from ownership of different forms of real or financial assets. But the rest of this section assumes for convenience that there is only one homogeneous form of wealth that can be accumulated.

Life-cycle models of consumption and savings behaviour have a fairly long lineage compared to the recent contributions on life-cycle labour supply and human capital investment. Preliminary thoughts on the subject go back at least to Fisher (1907; 1930). But with the advent of Keynesian economics, interest shifted away from the savings–interest rate relationship towards the consumption-income relationship. However, by the early 1950s research interest was turning to longer-run models as theoretical underpinnings for a macro consumption function. Along with Friedman's permanent income model and Duesenberry's relative income approach came the Modigliani and Brumberg (1955) life-cycle hypothesis later extended by Ando and Modigliani (1963). The impetus for development of a life-cycle theory of consumption and saving thus lay in a reformulation of the theory behind aggregate consumption functions and macroeconomic analysis; but the main interest for our purposes now lies in its implications for a microeconomic analysis of the distribution of capital income across individuals in the population.

Outline of the life-cycle savings model
The main ideas of life-cycle analysis can be seen in a simple Fisher two-period formulation. Suppose that an individual has a two-period lifetime horizon ('present' and 'future') and given earnings in the two periods of YW_0 and YW_1 respectively. If he can borrow or lend at the given market rate of interest r, he faces consumption possibilities that lie anywhere on or below the market opportunities line AB (through the endowment point A and with slope $-(1+r)$) in Figure 1. At the same time, he is assumed to have a utility function $U(C_0, C_1)$, which indicates his relative preference or tastes for alternative combinations of current and future consumption in the form of a map of indifference curves (one of which is drawn) in Figure 1. The individual is assumed to maximize his utility subject to the market opportunities available to him by choosing that point B along the opportunities line that allows him to reach his highest possible indifference curve $\bar{U}$. Thus the individual consumes at point B with savings or capital accumulation of S_0 in the current period and dissavings or capital decumulation of S_1 in the future period. Savings act as a buffer as consumption is shuffled

Figure 1:
Two-period consumption-savings model

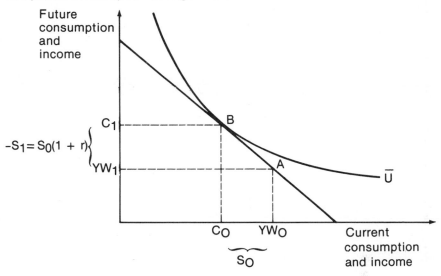

across time to maximize lifetime utility. Consumption depends not directly on current earnings but rather on the longer-run concept of lifetime earnings or what might be called the individual's discounted net worth. In the illustrated example, wealth is accumulated in the first period and depleted in the second.

Turning now to a more general formulation of the model in a continuous time framework with a T-period horizon, we shall assume an individual begins his 'economic life' (i.e. his economic age t equals zero) when he reaches the stage of economic independence referred to above and makes his consumption-savings decisions for the remaining portion of his life, which terminates when he dies at economic age T. The individual is assumed to have a known earnings profile $YW(t)$ over his economic life and to start off with some initial wealth endowment of K_0 perhaps left by his family. He in turn seeks to leave a terminal capital stock K_T to his own heirs. As before, the individual is assumed to be able to borrow or lend as much as his resources allow at a given interest rate r, so that one can in effect characterize an entire lifetime earnings stream by a single number, its discounted present value. The timing of the earnings receipts becomes irrelevant so long as the present value of the earnings stream remains the same.

Tastes are characterized by a utility function defined on consumption over the life cycle and assumed for convenience to be of the (time-invariant and separable) form $U(C(t))e^{-\rho t}$, where utility in period t is discounted at a subjective rate of time preference ρ, indicating one's preference, other things equal, of current over future consumption.[1]

Given an exogenously determined lifetime earnings profile and the borrowing-lending opportunities available in the capital market, one is assumed to select a lifetime consumption and savings profile that will maximize discounted lifetime utility. More formally, the individual is assumed to choose a lifetime consumption profile $C(t)$, a corresponding savings profile $S(t)$, and net worth profile $K(t)$ so as to maximize

$$\int_0^T U(C(t))e^{-\rho t}dt, \tag{1}$$

subject to the accumulation constraint that the accumulation of wealth at any period in time must equal one's savings at that time,

$$dK(t)/dt \equiv \dot{K}(t) = S(t), \tag{2}$$

a budget constraint that at any period the uses of income (consumption plus saving) must equal total available income, wages $\text{YW}(t)$ plus interest on wealth holdings $rK(t)$,

$$C(t) + S(t) = \text{YW}(t) + rK(t), \tag{3}$$

and a condition that the initial and terminal capital stocks must be K_0 and K_T respectively.

Solution of this problem, for example by Atkinson (1971) or Blinder (1974), yields the first-order optimality condition for consumption that over the life cycle,

$$dC(t)/dt \equiv \dot{C}(t) = (r - \rho) \cdot U'(C)/-U''(C). \tag{4}$$

With positive but decreasing marginal utility from consumption (i.e. $U' > 0$ and $U'' < 0$), the sign of the change in consumption over the life cycle

---

1 More technical details on the exact specifications of the life-cycle consumption-saving model may be found, for example in Tobin (1967), Becker (1971), Somermeyer and Bannink (1973), and Blinder (1974).

depends on the difference between the market rate of interest and the rate of time preference $(r - \rho)$. Intuitively, this should make some economic sense. Suppose there is a just-attainable consumption profile that is constant over the full life cycle. Then if the market rate of interest r exceeds one's subjective rate of time preference ρ, one could increase lifetime utility by postponing some consumption and accumulating assets to finance increased future consumption, so that the optimal consumption profile would start off relatively low and then build up over the life cycle (i.e. $\dot{C}(t) > 0$). Conversely, if the market makes present resources available more cheaply than the individual demands in terms of forgone future consumption (i.e. $r < \rho$), he will maximize lifetime utility by borrowing present resources, enjoying a high consumption level, and then steadily reducing future consumption to repay the debt, so that in this case the optimal consumption profile will decline over the life cycle.

If we further constrain the form of the utility function to the iso-elastic family

$$U(C) = C^{1-\delta}/(1 - \delta) + \text{constant}, \qquad \text{for } 0 < \delta \neq 1$$

and $\qquad\qquad\qquad\qquad\qquad\qquad\qquad\qquad\qquad\qquad\qquad\qquad$ (5)

$$U(c) = \log C + \text{constant}, \qquad \text{for } \delta = 1,$$

where $-\delta$ is the (constant) elasticity of the marginal utility curve with respect to consumption (and determines the degree of curvature of the indifference curve in Figure 1),[2] equation (4) can be simplified to

$$\dot{C}(t)/C(t) = (r - \rho)/\delta, \qquad\qquad\qquad\qquad\qquad (6)$$

which has the explicit solution for the consumption profile

$$C(t) = C_0 e^{gt},$$

---

2 If the utility function is of the isoelastic form (5), it can be shown that the slope of the indifference curves such as the one illustrated in Figure 1 is given by $- (1 + \rho)$ $(C_1/C_0)^\delta$. Thus along the 45° ray from the origin, the indifference curves have slope $- (1 + \rho)$ dependent solely on ρ. The second derivative of the indifference curve along this ray, however, can be shown to vary proportionally with δ and inversely with C_0. Thus if δ is large, the indifference curves are very convex toward the origin; while if δ is small, they are much less sharply bent.

where $g \equiv (r - \rho)/\delta$ is the constant rate of growth of consumption over the life cycle and C_0 is the initial consumption level. In particular, if V denotes the discounted present value of lifetime earnings,

$$V = \int_0^T \text{YW}(t) e^{-rt} dt,$$

then the optimal consumption profile $C(t)$ can be written as

$$C(t) = (K_0 + V - K_T e^{-rT})/N \cdot e^{gt} \tag{7}$$

where N is a constant depending on the parameters $r-g$ and T. The expression in the numerator of (7) is simply the present value of lifetime net worth. Thus, at each moment of time consumption absorbs a certain fraction of one's lifetime net worth, a fraction depending on one's (economic) age, lifespan, consumption tastes, and the market interest rate (Blinder, 1974, 27). Given the optimal consumption profile, the stock of accumulated net worth holdings $K(t)$ can be obtained from the buildup of initial endowments and the cumulation of savings (i.e. that part of income which was not consumed) over the worker's lifetime.[3]

Diagrammatically, the solution may be illustrated for various different parameter values of the model. In particular, if the rate of growth of consumption g is positive, as would seem to be reasonable empirically, and if the earnings profile were assumed constant for convenience, a set of consumption, net worth, and capital income ($\text{YK}(t) = r \cdot K(t)$) trajectories as illustrated in Figure 2 may be obtained.

Implications of the life-cycle savings model
What, then, are the main conclusions or implications that can be drawn from the standard life-cycle model of consumption-saving behaviour from the point of view of the distribution of capital income? First, since $\text{YK}(t) = rK(t)$, the distribution of capital income for a given market rate of interest r depends on the underlying distribution of wealth stocks. Thus, in order to understand an income distribution, one has to examine the basic determinants of the accumulation of the underlying stocks of wealth. As will be seen in the next section, an exactly analogous conclusion holds with respect to the distribution of earnings. Indeed, if the rate of return on wealth differs

---

3 More specifically, the profile of the stock of net worth holdings is given by $K(t) = K_0 e^{rt} + \int_0^t [YW(\tau) - C(\tau)] e^{r(t-\tau)} d\tau$ and the profile of the flow of capital income, $YK(t) = rK(t)$, in proportional to $K(t)$.

Figure 2:
Illustrative life-cycle trajectories for consumption, net worth and capital income

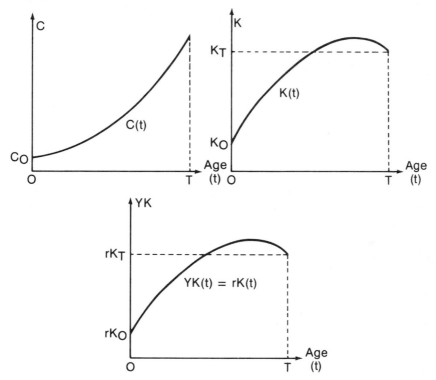

across individuals and is positively correlated with wealth holdings, the distribution of YK across individuals will be even more unequal than the distribution of K alone.

Secondly, savings and capital income act as buffers between earnings, which may move unevenly over time, and consumption, which tends to adjust more smoothly and slowly from one period to another. In the absence of savings, capital income, or borrowing-lending opportunities consumption would be tied to the earnings profile; but with this extra source of income a greater range of consumption possibilities is made available, and consumption adjusts according to the longer-run concept of discounted lifetime net worth.

Thirdly, it can be seen from Figure 2 that capital income varies systematically with age. Since the optimal level of YK changes with age over the life cycle and since consumption tends to follow wealth rather than earnings in any period, it may not be appropriate as a measure of individual economic well-being to examine income differences among individuals taken at different points of the life cycle. A more appropriate distribution for inequality analysis would perhaps be that of (broadly defined) lifetime net worth:

$$\text{KN} = K_0 + V - K_T e^{-rT},$$

or even the present value of lifetime earnings V. Lacking data on these, however, one should at the least compare people at similar points within the life cycle, since age-specific income distributions are more meaningful for analysis than a single over-all cross-sectional distribution.

The life-cycle model of consumption-savings behaviour just presented, while suggestive, is too simple in a number of respects, and the rest of this chapter is devoted to relaxing some of the simplifying restrictions and adding further complications. In the present model, consumption follows a very restrictive pattern, and the lifetime profile of earned income was treated as exogenously given to the individual. We turn next to an analysis that endogenizes the earnings profile and makes it also subject to individual choice through human capital investment behaviour and life-cycle labour supply. The present model is basically one of individual choice and does not explicitly recognize the role of the household in consumption and accumulation decisions. Finally, life-cycle considerations are not likely to be able to explain adequately wealth holdings and net worth inequality at the extreme top end of the distribution, where other factors such as inheritances, chance, entrepreneurial activity, and rent of ability are likely to have a more critical role.

HUMAN CAPITAL INVESTMENT AND EARNINGS

In the preceding section attention was focused on the determination of wealth stocks and capital income YK over the life cycle. The present and next sections turn to determinants of wage and salary or earned income YW over one's working life. In the earlier discussion capital income was seen to be determined by the stock of wealth one had accumulated and the supply of savings to build up the stock. In the present discussion it is argued that earned income is basically explained (given market-determined factor prices) by the supply of labour services over the life cycle. More specifically, the amount of earned income received in any year,

$$\text{YW}(t) = w(t) \cdot H(t),$$

can be thought of as being the product of one's hourly wage rate and the number of hours worked on the job per year. The second factor may be thought of as representing the time or quantity dimension of labour supply, while the first factor may be thought of as representing the degree of labour skill or the quality dimension of labour supply. Conceptually, then, the supply of labour over the life cycle is viewed as involving two sets of decisions – the acquisition of skills and the length of time worked. We shall now consider the first set of decisions in the human capital model of earnings determinations, and following that the second set in the theory of life-cycle labour supply.

The human capital framework
The general framework of human capital analysis is very similar to the earlier analysis of income from real or financial capital. Human capital, however, may be thought of as 'an individual's productive skills, talents, and knowledge' (Thurow, 1970, 1) used to produce earnings in the labour market. Assume for convenience in this section that the number of hours worked in the labour market within a year $H(t)$ is uniform across all individuals and age groups. Earnings then depend only on skill level or what is referred to as one's stock of human capital, which is in turn built up by investment in acquiring productive skills. Analysis thus focuses on optimal patterns of life-cycle human capital investment. As in the earlier discussion of capital income, the analysis is carried on in a long-run optimization framework involving a life-cycle tradeoff of expected future income gains against present income opportunity costs.

Human capital skills are built up through formal schooling (primary, secondary, university, and technical and trade school), through experience acquired working and learning on the job, through expenditures to maintain and improve one's general health, through efforts to learn an additional language for job market purposes, as well as through expenditures to migrate to regions that offer greater job opportunities. Only the first two sources of human capital investment will be considered explicitly here, although they will be viewed as special cases of a somewhat more general model.

While the human capital investment decision has obvious similarities to investment decisions on non-human capital, there is also a significant difference. Both kinds of decisions require a current sacrifice to increase future available resources and thus involve an intertemporal weighting of current costs against future returns. But in the absence of slavery human capital can only be rented and not purchased. The market is for the *services* of human capital rather than for the human capital itself. The wage is thus reviewed as a rental rate on the stock of human capital.

Consider now some of the details of the standard human capital model of Becker (1964) and Mincer (1958; 1962; 1970). Two forms of human capital are explicitly considered: formal education or schooling, and on-the-job training. The latter is divided between specific and general training. Specific training consists of knowledge useful only to a particular employer, who must thus pay for its acquisition. General training is widely useful on the labour market. Since this raises one's opportunity earnings, an employee would be willing to pay for its acquisition himself in currently forgone earnings. This general type of on-the-job training is the focus of our analysis, while some implications of specific training will be considered in the following chapter.

Applying our life-cycle saving and consumption framework, we assume that the period of 'economic independence' in one's life is entered at about age eighteen, say, or at 'economic age' zero. At that point one has the choice of continuing formal education and choosing a career or job profile with varying amounts of on-the-job training until retirement, assumed to occur T_R years in the future. Under the continuing assumption of perfect capital markets, the training investment decision can be treated independently of the consumption-saving decision considered above. Individuals are now assumed to choose their human capital investment profiles so as to maximize their discounted present value of lifetime earnings. In terms of Figure 1, they invest in a training program that will move their market opportunities line up to the right as far as possible.[4]

It will be convenient in the analysis that follows to distinguish between several income concepts instead of the single term YW(t) used so far. Accordingly, let $E(t)$ represent the 'gross earnings' an individual receives at economic age t, and let CE(t) denote the net human capital investment

4 For a discussion of education as a consumption good and its corresponding demand, see, for example, Lazear (1977) and Oniki (1968). In general, if the stock of human capital has positive utility for an individual, he will choose to acquire more of it than would be implied by the pure investment model. On the other hand, if the learning process is distasteful as Lazear appears to find, he will choose to acquire less.

costs an individual pays in the form either of direct out-of-pocket costs such as tuition, books, and equipment purchases or of indirect opportunity costs in the form of forgone earnings from staying in school or taking time to learn general skills on the job. Thus the 'net earnings' an individual receives are

$$\text{YE}(t) = E(t) - \text{CE}(t).$$

If $\text{CE}(t)$ consists solely of forgone earnings, then $\text{YE}(t)$ may be identified with the empirically observable $\text{YW}(t)$. In addition, let $X(t)$ represent the 'raw' earnings the individual would receive at economic age t if he invested in no further human capital beyond high school. And denote the proportional return to the individual at economic age t on human capital investment made a years earlier by $r(t - a)$. From the definitions of these terms, then, it can be seen that current gross earnings are composed of the earnings one would receive in the absence of any human capital investment beyond schooling at economic age zero plus the returns received on the investments (some of which may be zero) made each year since then, that is,

$$E(t) = X(t) + \sum_{\tau=0}^{t-1} r(\tau)\text{CE}(\tau) \quad \text{for } 1 \geqslant t \geqslant T_R. \tag{8}$$

Consequently, what determines $E(t)$ (and thus $\text{YE}(t)$) is the pattern of human capital investments (i.e. the $\text{CE}(t)$'s) over one's working life. Given an investment profile (and the corresponding rate-of-return profile) over the life cycle, one obtains a life-cycle trajectory of annual earnings.

The human capital decision thus becomes one of choosing an optimal profile of $\text{CE}(t)$'s. Optimality, however, as just pointed out, is defined in terms of the maximum discounted present value of lifetime earnings. Skill acquisition is valued solely for its income-producing ability and not as a consumption good having utility in its own right. It will be recalled from the preceding section that the principal constraint on the life-cycle consumption choice with perfect capital markets was exactly the present value of life-cycle earnings. Consequently, the maximum present value criterion for skill acquisition can be seen as a first step toward maximizing one's life-cycle consumption potential. For the moment, though, we turn aside from the problem of optimally choosing the $\text{CE}(t)$'s to analyse some of the consequences of optimally chosen investment profiles.

Implications of the human capital model
The first special case of the human capital model to be considered is Mincer's schooling model (1958; 1970), obtained by inserting several

specific assumptions into the general earnings function (8) above. In particular, assume the following: (i) Human capital investment occurs only through formal schooling that is assumed to continue for S years beyond age zero. For the first S years of one's economic life, one remains completely out of the labour force; and for the remaining $T_R - S$ years, one works full-time (investing no further in one's stock of human capital). (ii) There are no out-of-pocket investment costs, so that the only investment costs over the schooling period are the forgone earnings of staying out of the labour force (i.e. $\text{CE}(t) = E(t)$ for $0 \leqslant t \leqslant S$). (iii) The rate of return on acquired skills remains constant as one gets older. And (iv) one's raw earnings also remain constant over time (i.e. $X(t) = E_0$ for $0 \leqslant t \leqslant T_R$). It follows from these four assumptions that (8) can now be written as

$$E(t) = E_0 + r \sum_{\tau=0}^{S-1} E(\tau), \qquad \text{for } t \geqslant S. \tag{9}$$

Since $E(t) = E(t-1) + r\text{CE}(t-1)$ from (8), recursive substitution into (9) yields

$$E(t) = E_0 (1+r)^S$$

or approximately,

$$\log E(t) = \log E_0 + r \cdot S. \tag{10}$$

Several results follow immediately from this formulation. Looking across individuals in the population at a particular moment, one notes that, first, people's ability and access to finances (via r) and educational attainment (via S) interact multiplicatively to affect earnings exponentially. Secondly, even if distributions on rates of return and schooling levels are symmetrical across individuals, the resulting distribution on earnings will be skewed, which in fact it is. Thirdly, inequality in earnings among individuals will tend to be greater: the larger the dispersion in the distribution of schooling levels across the population, the larger the dispersion in the distribution of ability and resource availability across members of the population, and the more highly that r and S are positively correlated across members of the population. And fourthly, looking across time for given individuals, one notes that the life-cycle earnings profile predicted by (10) is horizontal. Thus earnings differences among individuals in the population do not arise because of earnings variation over the life cycle in this particular model. As we shall see in Part Two, though, actual wage profiles over the life cycle are not horizontal. Consequently, this model must be modified to allow for earnings differences both across individuals and over the life cycle for each individual.

The on-the-job training (or OJT) model provides such a generalization of the simple schooling model by relaxing assumption (i) listed above. Human capital investment can now occur while one is working in the labour force after having completed S years of formal schooling. Work thus has a dual role of generating current earnings and contributing to future productivity. In particular, suppose that the proportion of one's earning capacity (or available working time) devoted to further improving one's productive skills is $k(t)$. Therefore

$$\mathrm{CE}(t) = k(t) E(t),$$

$$k(t) = 1 \text{ for } 0 \leqslant t \leqslant S, \ k(t) < 1 \text{ for } S < t \leqslant T_R. \quad (11)$$

In general, the proportional investment profile $k(t)$ will be assumed to decline as one gets older (as illustrated in Figure 3) because later investment has a shorter payback period in which to recoup the forgone earnings from investment, and the market value of time tends to increase with the amount of human capital accumulated, so that one becomes less willing to sacrifice time for further human capital investment. The optimal choice of $k(t)$ will be discussed below.

If now (11) is substituted into (8), one obtains

$$E(t) = E(t-1) + r(t-1) \, k(t-1) \, E(t-1)$$

$$= E(t-1) \, [1 + r(t-1) \, k(t-1)],$$

which, by recursive substitutions back to period zero, may be written

$$E(t) = E_0 \, \Pi_{\tau=0}^{t-1} \, [1 + r(\tau) \, k(\tau)]$$

or

$$\log E(t) = \log E_0 + \sum_{\tau=0}^{t-1} \log \, [1 + r(\tau) \, k(\tau)].$$

Again, this can be rewritten approximately as

Figure 3:
Profiles of proportional investment in human capital
and earnings over the life cycle
Investment ratio k(t)

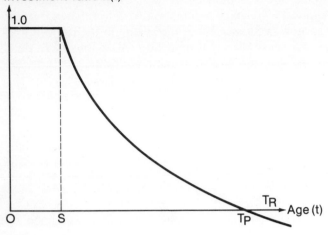

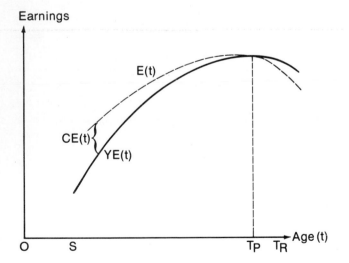

$$\log E(t) = \log E_0 + \sum_{\tau=0}^{t-1} r(\tau) \, k(\tau)$$

$$= \log E_0 + r_S \cdot S + r_J \sum_{\tau=S}^{t-1} k(\tau)$$

$$= \log E_0 + r_S \cdot S + r_J \cdot J(t), \tag{12}$$

where the rates of return r_S and r_J are again assumed constant over one's earning life and $J(t)$ represents the cumulative amount of time spent on on-the-job training. Total human capital investment thus consists of $S + J(t)$ years of year-equivalents.

The conclusions that follow from the OJT model extend those of the earlier schooling model. Across individuals in the population at a particular moment in time, the first three conclusions above still hold and indeed are augmented by on-the-job skill acquisition $J(t)$ and ability (through r_J) also interacting multiplicatively to affect earnings exponentially as well as by a positive correlation between ability and on-the-job training or between job skill acquisition and schooling increasing earnings inequality across members of the population. Across time for a particular individual, however, the life-cycle earnings profile is no longer flat, but slopes upwards with age so long as $k(t)$ is positive up to a peak earnings age T_P when investment falls to zero. If $k(t)$ and $CE(t)$ are declining over one's working life, the earnings profiles will also be concave, as in Figure 4. At a given age, earnings profiles grow more quickly for higher levels of human capital investment; and the earnings of larger investors tend to peak and decline later in life. Consequently, earnings profiles tend to fan out noticeably with later age and work experience. Among young workers, however, the opposite occurs. Those with larger amounts of schooling start full-time work later than otherwise, but their earnings tend to grow much more quickly, so that after a short while an overtaking period occurs when the more recent but steeper profiles overtake the longer-running and flatter ones. Thus among relatively young workers earnings inequality tends to decline with age. Consequently, across all age groups the inequality (as measured by the variance, for example) in earnings tends to have a U-shape, first declining with age and then increasing. In sum, the on-the-job training model predicts systematic earnings differences not only between individuals at the same stage of the life cycle, but also between different stages of the working life.

Optimal human capital investment
Consider now the problem of how the optimal investment profile of $k(t)$ is determined over the life cycle, and along with it the theoretical profiles of

Figure 4:
Illustrative life-cycle trajectories for human capital investment, stock of
human capital, and net earnings

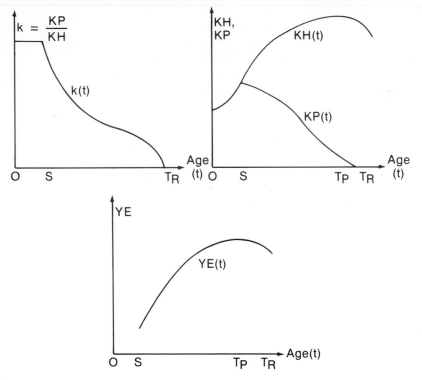

$\mathrm{KH}(t)$, the accumulated stock of human capital, and $\mathrm{YE}(t)$, the flow of net
earnings. This problem has been investigated by, among others, Ben-
Porath (1967), Lillard (1973), Wallace and Ihnen (1975), Haley (1973;
1976), Rosen (1973; 1976), and Hotz (1977). The basic ideas are that earnings capacity is the return to a cumulated stock of human capital

$$E(t) = R \cdot \mathrm{KH}(t),$$

where R is the constant rental rate on human capital; the stock of human
capital is built up through a production process involving investment of
time and effort by the individual; and the individual chooses the pattern of
lifetime human capital investments that maximizes the present value of his

discounted net earnings subject to his ability, endowments, and access to capital markets.

The production process by which the stock of human capital is built up involves the individual using a portion of his already accumulated human capital, $KP(t) = k(t) KH(t)$, and his ability, as represented by an index A, to produce further human capital according to some simple production process. For example, Haley (1973) suggests the simple specification

$$Q(t) = A \cdot KP(t)^\beta, \qquad 0 < \beta < 1, \tag{13}$$

where $Q(t)$ is the gross addition to human capital, the ability index appears as a multiplicative shift parameter, and the parameter β provides for decreasing returns to scale in the production of human capital. At the same time, however, the stock of human capital is worn down through deterioration and obsolescence at a constant exponential rate δ, so that the resulting net change in the stock of human capital is

$$K\dot{H}(t) = Q(t) - \delta\, KH(t). \tag{14}$$

Net earnings, as before, are the difference between earnings capacity and investment costs through forgone earnings,

$$YE(t) = E(t) - CE(t)$$

$$= E(t) - R \cdot KP(t). \tag{15}$$

The individual is assumed to choose an optimal investment path $KP(t)$ and the corresponding human capital trajectory $KH(t)$ so as to maximize the discounted present value of net earnings

$$\int_0^{TR} e^{-rt}\, YE(t)\, dt,$$

subject to constraints (13) to (15) and an initial human capital stock KH_0 with which he starts his period of economic independence.

While ignoring the technical details of the solution, one can show that the optimal investment trajectory goes through at least two stages. In each period the amount of human capital produced is determined by the equality of the marginal value of additional human capital and the associated marginal cost of the forgone earnings involved in producing it, subject to $KP(t) \leq KH(t)$, i.e. $k(t) \leq 1$. As the payback period shortens, the marginal value of additions to human capital declines over the life cycle until it eventually becomes zero at retirement T_R. Over the initial periods of one's economic life, however, the return to human capital investment may be so high that the optimal $KP(t)$ would exceed $KH(t)$ were it not physically impossible. Thus during this first stage of skill acquisition one spends all one's time investing in human capital with $k(t) = 1$. Once the marginal value of investment has declined far enough for the optimal $KP(t)$ not to exceed $KH(t)$, the second stage of investment is reached, and human capital production declines monotonically as in Figure 4. The first stage of complete specialization in human capital production can thus be interpreted as the period of full-time schooling, while the subsequent stage of part-time skill acquisition can be viewed as the period of on-the-job training. There may also be, as in Hotz's (1977) formulation, a third stage of no human capital investment ($k(t) = 0$) and full-time work on the job at the end of the working life just before retirement at age T_R. Finally, given optimal profiles of $KH(t)$ and $KP(t)$, one can obtain the corresponding trajectory for net earnings

$$\text{YE}(t) = R[\text{KH}(t) - \text{KP}(t)] \tag{16}$$

over the period from S to T_R as in Figure 4. The earnings trajectory during the working period of one's life is increasing at a declining rate; and if, as illustrated, the individual eventually ceases investing in human capital, the depreciation of the stock of skills takes over, and the earnings trajectory peaks and turns down.

General conclusions
The general conclusions are like those above on the importance of underlying capital stocks in the determination of income flows and on the problems of comparing income receipts at different stages of the life cycle. But note the overly simple way in which schooling and training are assumed to affect earnings. Although they are assumed to increase individuals' work productivity, the underlying mechanism, for example between schooling and on-the-job performance, is not spelled out or indeed generally known (Welch, 1975). Do schools actually teach productivity-related skills, or do they essentially identify pre-existing skills and abilities? (More will be said about this in the next chapter.) Furthermore, are the skills they teach essentially cognitive or (as suggested by Gintis, 1971) largely affective? And to what extent does quality of schooling or of the learning environ-

ment matter? According to a recent study by Wise (1975b), for example, 'the evidence suggests that college education is not only a signal of productive ability, but in fact enhances this ability,' 'although the findings of this study do not minimize the importance of non-academic traits, they suggest that affective traits do not dominate academic aptitude and knowledge in their effect on the productivity of these college graduates,' and 'the relation between college quality and grades on the one hand and ... job performance on the other is not only statistically significant but is quantitatively important' (Ibid., 363). While such findings are far from conclusive, they at least suggest the rather complex relation between schooling, on-the-job training, job performance, and earnings.

Secondly, the analysis does not explain fully how ability, family background, and access to resources for purposes of human capital investment affect the generation of human capital and hence earnings. What are the relevant dimensions of ability for earnings purposes; what are the roles played by determination, persistence, and aggressiveness; and how do ability and family background interact with schooling and job training? In the analysis of this section, the parameters KH_0 and A may be thought of as two channels by which ability can affect skill acquisition and the generation of earnings. In particular, it can be shown that a larger KH_0 reduces S, the period of investment specialization, shifting upwards the entire earnings profile by a constant amount, and that a larger A lengthens the period of investment specialization and shifts the earnings profile up to a steeper angle corresponding to a higher growth rate of net earnings (Hotz, 1977). But as the empirical research of Griliches and Mason (1972), Hause (1972), Taubman and Wales (1974), and Taubman (1977a), for example, shows, ability and background are difficult to characterize empirically and have complex structural effects on earnings over the life cycle that have yet to be fully understood.

Thirdly, human capital investment can take place in forms other than schooling and on-the-job training. Acquiring proficiency in a second language can be worthwhile in a bilingual work environment such as Quebec or other parts of Canada (Vaillancourt, 1980). Investment in health can also be viewed in this life-cycle framework, as suggested by Grossman (1972) and Cropper (1977). Health investment, for our purposes, can be viewed as determining the maximum number of hours available $\bar{H}$ within any given period for either working or acquiring skills. Thus health investment and other forms of human capital investment can be viewed interdependently. At the same time the maximum hours that can be worked or spent acquiring skills is clearly also a determinant of market labour supply.

LIFE-CYCLE LABOUR SUPPLY AND EARNINGS

As pointed out earlier, the earned income an individual receives (by far the most important single component of total personal income) can be usefully viewed as the outcome of two sets of factors, $YW(t) = w(t) H(t)$, where $w(t)$ represents the hourly earnings the individual receives on the basis of his education, skills, knowledge, and experience, and $H(t)$ is the number of hours he works in the labour market over the span of, say, a year. It has so far been assumed that the number of hours worked in the market was an exogenously given constant, uniform across all individuals, so that workers differed in the income they received because of differences in their stocks of human capital and thus in $w(t)$. We now turn to the other principal determinant of earnings, the number of hours worked per period or, stated differently, the lifetime pattern of labour supply among individuals. At first it will be assumed for convenience that the life-cycle wage profile $w(t)$ is now exogenously given, and the focus will be upon the determination of an optimal profile for $H(t)$ over an individual's life cycle. Later, both $w(t)$ and $H(t)$ will be treated endogenously, leading to a more general interpretation of the determinants of earned income over the life cycle.

Model of life-cycle labour supply
The time or quantity dimension of labour supply traditionally incorporates several factors or decisions about one's activity in the labour force. First, of course, is the participation decision, whether or not to enter the labour force by seeking employment. Secondly, one has to decide whether to work full-time, part-time, overtime, or even whether to hold a second job. There may be relatively little flexibility in the hours one can work on a particular job, but there is a considerably wider range of choice over the span of a year as to the total hours one may choose to work. Thirdly, one may choose between full-year employment and part-year employment through one's choice of job or region of employment. Fourthly, the length of working life until retirement must be decided. Clearly, rather different factors may enter into the decisions in the four different cases. However, for simplicity and ease of development it will be assumed that these four factors are embodied in a single labour supply decision as to the total number of hours to supply for work over a given period.

The theory of intertemporal labour supply can be traced back at least to Ramsey (1928), although the distributional implications of the theory have only recently been addressed. Principal contributions in the current theory of life-cycle labour supply have been made by Becker (1965),

Blinder (1974), Heckman (1974), and Weiss (1972b); the development in the first portion of this section essentially follows the formulations of Blinder and Weiss. The individual is now assumed to be given an exogenous wage profile $w(t)$ over his working life and an initial non-human capital endowment K_0, and is assumed to leave a terminal period bequest K_T at death in period T. Income at time t comes from earnings $w(t)H(t)$ and the return on capital holdings $rK(t)$. It is either spent on consumption $C(t)$ or put into savings $S(t) = \dot{K}(t)$ to build up one's (non-human) capital holdings. Consumption yields utility $U(C(t))$ with a decreasing marginal utility curve, while work effort is assumed to yield disutility $V(H(t))$ with a positive and increasing marginal disutility curve as hours worked approach the maximum number of hours that one's health allows $\bar{H}$. From the utility of consumption the individual now subtracts his disutility of work[5] and thus chooses a lifetime consumption profile (and associated savings and net worth profiles) and a profile of lifetime work effort so as to maximize discounted lifetime utility:

$$\int_0^T e^{-\rho t}\left[U(C(t)) - V(H(t))\right]\,dt, \tag{17}$$

subject to the given wage profile and the borrowing-lending opportunities provided by his endowments in a perfect capital market.

Assuming that the objective function is separable between consumption and hours of work, the optimal consumption profile has the same shape as in the original model and is unaffected by the life-cycle timing of labour supply and work effort.[6] Again, consumption follows the profile given by

$$\dot{C}(t) = (r - \rho) \cdot U'(C)/-U''(C), \tag{18}$$

as in the earlier model.[7] At the same time, however, the marginal rate of substitution (at an interior optimum) between consumption and work effort, or alternatively leisure, should equal their relative market prices:

---

5 More generally, the critical assumption is that the utility function is (additively) separable in leisure and consumption.

6 The *shape* of the consumption profile is unaffected although the *level* of the profile in general will be affected.

7 For a consideration of factors such as capital market imperfections, income uncertainty, and interdependence in utility as determinants of less simplistic and more realistic lifetime consumption profiles, see, for example, Nagatani (1972), Thurow (1969), and Heckman (1974).

$$V'(H)/U'(C) = w(t)$$

or

$$V'(H) = w(t) U'(C), \qquad \text{for } 0 \leq H(t) < \bar{H}, \tag{19}$$

where $w(t)$ is the real wage, $V'(H)$ is the direct marginal disutility of work effort, and $w(t) U'(C)$ can be interpreted as the corresponding indirect marginal utility of consumption. Logarithmic differentiation of this condition with respect to time yields the adjustment equation for work effort over the individual's working life:

$$\dot{H}(t) = [g_w - (r - \rho)] \cdot V'(H)/V''(H),$$

where $g_w = \dot{w}/w$ represents the rate of growth of wages over the life cycle. If, as before, one simplifies by assuming isoelastic marginal utility functions, and let $-\delta$ represent the (constant) elasticity of marginal utility of consumption and ϵ the corresponding (constant) elasticity of marginal disutility of labour, the two adjustment equations can be rewritten as

$$\dot{C}(t)/C(t) = (r - \rho)/\delta, \tag{20}$$

$$\dot{H}(t)/H(t) = (1/\epsilon)\,[g_w(t) - (r - \rho)]. \tag{21}$$

These are essentially the intertemporal conditions equivalent to the optimal utility conditions (18) and (19).

The slope of the intertemporal allocation of work effort thus depends on three basic factors (Weiss, 1972b), 1297). A high rate of time preference induces postponement of work effort since future effort appears at time zero to be much less burdensome, thus resulting in a growth of hours worked over one's life. A high rate of interest on the other hand induces greater early work effort to produce income that can be very productively invested, thus resulting in a decline of hours worked as one gets older. Finally, a rapid growth in wage rates results also in longer working hours as greatest effort is transferred to periods that will yield the highest earnings capacity.

If consumption is increasing over time, the marginal utility of consumption is falling over time. If condition (19) is to be maintained and wages are constant over the life cycle, the marginal disutility of labour supply must also be falling over time; that is, hours worked must be declining until one

Figure 5:
Determination of optimal consumption and work effort trajectories with
constant wages

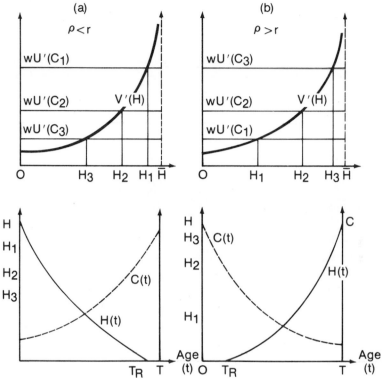

completely retires from the labour force in period T_R. The resulting paths
of consumption and work effort are seen in the lower panel of Figure 5(a).
Conversely, when consumption steadily declines over the life cycle the
marginal utility lines in Figure 5(b) rise over time. If condition (19) is to
hold for constant wages, marginal disutility of labour must also be rising
over time; that is, hours worked must be increasing as indicated in the
lower panel of the figure. More generally, for a constant wage rate, consumption of goods and leisure move together over the life cycle. Further,
someone with a (relatively) low rate of time preference may work hard
while young and then choose retirement as he becomes old. Someone with
a high discount rate, however, may choose to take a period away from the
labour force before he even begins work and while still young, and make up

Figure 6:
Determination of work effort trajectory with a concave wage
profile and $\rho < r$

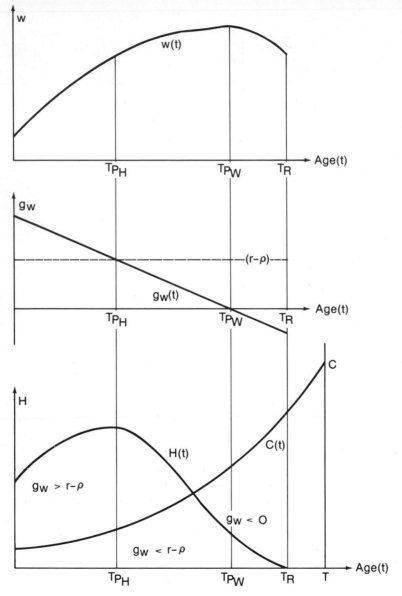

for it by working longer hours as he gets older. The model thus views retirement and 'dropouts' from the labour force as part of the over-all labour supply decision.

However, if wages are changing over the life cycle another consideration is introduced. If wages are increasing rapidly relative to rising consumption, $w(t) U'(C)$ will rise, and from (19) the marginal disutility of labour must be increasing, so that hours of work must also increase. On the other hand if wages fail to rise as fast as increases in consumption, thus bringing down $w(t) U'(C)$, marginal disutility of labour will decline, and hours of work must thus be decreasing. Conditions (20) and (21) express this pattern in the intertemporal context. Consider Figure 3, for example, where wage rates are a (single-peaked) concave function of age. Then the profile of optional work effort will also be single-peaked. As in the likely more empirically relevant case of $\rho < r$ in Figure 6, the early steep rise in the wage profile more than counteracts the declining marginal utility of consumption $g_w(t) > r - \rho$, and thus from (21) hours of work are increasing. But as the $w(t)$ profile rises less steeply and then falls off, the rate of growth of wages $g_w(t)$ declines over the life cycle (eventually becoming negative after T_{P_w}) and falls below $r - \rho$, so that from (21) work effort is reduced over the remainder of one's working life until retirement is reached in period T_R. In general, the peak in hours worked then will precede the peak in the wage profile if $\rho < r$ (and lag it if $\rho > r$). The peak in total earnings receipts $\mathrm{YW}(t) = w(t)H(t)$ will thus lie between the corresponding peaks in w and H, and the earnings profile will look like Figure 7, with the concavity in earnings reflecting concavity in both wage profile and work effort profile over much of its length.

Joint determination of labour supply and human capital investment
So far this section has been examining labour supply patterns over the life cycle given an exogenous wage profile, whereas the preceding section centred on life-cycle skill accumulation patterns assuming a constant work effort. But clearly these two factors seem to be jointly determined, and indeed recent research by Ghez and Becker (1975), Blinder and Weiss (1976), Heckman (1975; 1976), and Ryder et al. (1976) has been directed at integrating human capital and labour supply theory in a life-cycle framework. The models have become rather complex, but many of their basic results are quite similar to those already obtained here. Consequently, we shall provide only a brief sketch of one such model (Heckman, 1976) and review some of its main findings using our diagrams.

Figure 7:
Optimal earnings trajectory with a concave wage profile and $\rho < r$

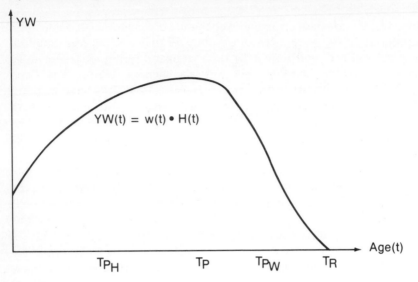

The individual now faces a three-way division of his available time into that devoted to leisure $L(t)$, to human capital investment either at school or on the job $I(t)$, and to work time in the labour market beyond that associated with skill acquisition $(H(t) = \bar{H} - L(t) - I(t))$. He gains utility from consumption and leisure; but leisure is weighted according to the amount of human capital possessed, so that those with larger amounts of human capital are assumed to enjoy their leisure more intensely:

$$U[C(t), L(t)\text{KH}(t)].$$

The human capital stock is again postulated to grow with human capital investment and also depreciates exogenously over time:

$$\text{K}\dot{\text{H}}(t) = Q(t) - \delta\text{KH}(t),$$

where $Q(t)$ is a standard production function with inputs of time devoted to human capital accumulation (weighted proportionally by the stock already possessed) and market goods (e.g. books) $D(t)$:

$$Q(t) = F[I(t)KH(t), D(t)].$$

Wages vary proportionally with the stock of human capital $w(t) = R \cdot KH(t)$, and non-human capital stock is again accumulated through saving according to

$$\dot{K}(t) = rK(t) + w(t)H(t) - (D(t) + C(t)),$$

where $rK(t)$ is capital income. The individual then chooses his time allocations $(L(t), I(t),$ and $H(t))$ and expenditure profiles $(C(t)$ and $D(t))$ to maximize his discounted lifetime utility subject to initial endowments $(KH_0$ and $K_0)$ and the opportunities provided by a perfect capital market.

The typical life-cycle profiles that emerge from this model are not unlike those already discussed. Restricting our consideration to the more interesting case where $r > p$, prices of goods are assumed constant over the life cycle, and goods and time are normal, while consumption of goods $C(t)$ and effective leisure $L(t) \cdot KH(t)$ increase monotonically over the life cycle. Inputs to the human capital investment process $(D(t)$ and $I(t)KH(t))$ on the other hand decline, so that additions to human capital stock $Q(t)$ also decline steadily and the human capital profile thus has the expected shape, first rising in concave fashion, eventually peaking, and then declining. The wage profile $w(t)$ thus has a similar shape. Investment time $I(t)$ generally declines. If on-the-job training occurs, measured hours of work $(H(t) + I(t))$ will also rise in concave fashion, peak before the market wage rate, and then decline as well. Consequently, $H(t)$ will have a generally similar concave profile, and earned income will have a shape generally similar to that in Figure 7.

What are the effects of different critical parameter values on the results of the model? Heckman shows that higher ability coefficients in the production of human capital corresponding to A in (13) result in greater investment in human capital, faster growth in wage rates, steeper age-earnings profiles, and a peak in the hours-of-work profile at a later age. Higher initial non-human capital endowments K_0 do not affect the acquisition of human capital but lead to lower earnings by inducing greater consumption of leisure (if leisure is a normal good). Higher initial endowments of human capital KH_0 shift up the entire human capital profile but decrease its rate of growth and induce longer initial hours of work but a flatter labour supply profile that peaks earlier. Finally, access to capital markets only at higher interest rates reduces investment in human capital, lowers the rate of growth of the human capital stock, and (under certain conditions) flattens the age-earnings profile.

One factor in the determination of lifetime incomes that we have not yet adequately addressed is the relationship between earnings and occupation. It seems overly simple to assume that people choose lifetime or career profiles of work effort and training without reference to any concomitant occupational choice as well. Yet the selection of an occupation can raise a number of considerations that are fairly important in determining earnings success but have not yet been touched upon; they are the topic of the next section. Secondly, the analysis so far in this chapter has basically dealt with a one-person decision unit. This may be appropriate for individuals, but does not adequately reflect the situation of married persons whose training and labour supply decisions are closely linked to family considerations. Consequently I shall discuss below the role of the family in life-cycle behaviour. Finally, mention has already been made of some of the effects of differences in endowments of human and non-human capital and in ability and background. These can in fact be viewed as channels for transmitting resources or benefits from one generation to the next. Since these factors clearly can have important distributional effects they will be briefly dealt with as well.

OCCUPATIONAL CHOICE AND EARNINGS DIFFERENTIALS

The primary investment decision an individual has been assumed to make so far in the analysis is that of skill acquisition through education and on-the-job training. While it is no doubt useful to highlight one problem at a time, the discussion of human capital investment behaviour can be viewed as somewhat unrealistic in the way it abstracts from a range of issues associated with occupational choice. Education and job training are not homogeneous forms of human capital but differ in type as well as quantity. They yield skills that may be specific to particular lines of work or quite general in their applicability. Consequently, the choice of the type and quantity of education and training is closely bound up with the choice of occupation. One may first choose broad occupations and then follow through on an investment plan to bring the choice to fruition. Indeed, Wilkinson (1966) has found that the amount of on-the-job training varies substantially with the occupation chosen: 'the amount of training appears to depend more upon the occupation one enters than on the level of education one achieves.' Within an occupation, additional education does not necessarily increase discounted lifetime earnings, while at the same time a certain level and type of education may represent a 'union card' for entrance into an occupation. Thus a more realistic model of skill acquisition would recognize the occupational choice dimension.

Much has been written on occupational earnings differentials that reflect factors on both demand and supply sides of the labour market. The present discussion, however, concerns only those supply-side factors that complement our life-cycle income framework. Some demand-side considerations are touched upon in the following chapter.

As Fleisher (1970) has observed, the choice of an occupation is usually the result of a series of related decisions. The effective choices among several broad occupational categories and associated types of education are often made fairly early in life and seldom changed later on. Choices among narrow categories of occupations and associated on-the-job training on the other hand often occur later in one's career and may well change with market conditions and opportunities depending on one's experience and ability. When relatively little human capital is required for entrance into an occupation and the human capital required is of a general nature, the costs of shifting from an occupation to a related one will be relatively small. One may then change occupations several times over one's working career, and the associated occupational earnings differentials would tend to be fairly small. But when large accumulations of highly job-specific types of human capital are needed for admittance into an occupation, the costs of changing become extremely high for an individual. He will then tend to continue along a single path of professional development (Weiss, 1971a), and the associated occupational earnings differentials will tend to be much larger.

Occupational choice, however, can be approached in a framework similar to that for human capital investment. Suppose, for convenience, that human capital is job-specific and no shifting occurs between occupations. Then, following Weiss (1971b), one chooses a single occupation along with an associated optimal profile of human capital investment so as to maximize the present value of lifetime earnings. In particular, the individual follows a two-stage optimization procedure. First, he determines the optimal profile of human capital investment in each occupation on the basis of his own ability, background, and access to resources. Thus for each occupation there is a corresponding earnings trajectory that the individual could conceivably follow. Secondly, the individual then chooses the particular occupation and associated earnings profile that yield him the highest discounted lifetime earnings over-all. The individual thus chooses an occupation and then obtains the education and training that will advance his earnings career within it. Occupational earnings differentials will thus arise on the supply side because the abilities and temperaments required for different occupations vary from person to person and because there is differential access to the resources to undertake the investment necessary for entering or succeeding in various occupations.

Future earnings, however, are not usually known with certainty. Instead, one may have not only an expectation of future earnings but also a degree of uncertainty or dispersion associated with the occupational earnings. Such uncertainty may arise from unforeseen unemployment and business conditions or simply from purely random factors. Some occupations have higher expected returns but higher risk of failure as well. Assuming individual behaviour to be characterized by some degree of risk aversion, one can model occupational choice in terms of a conventional mean income-risk analysis (Johnson, 1977), where individuals trade off some risk for a lower expected earnings profile. The optimal occupation (and associated education level) can be chosen to yield the most desirable combination of expected lifetime earnings and risk. Indeed, if most people are risk-averse and some occupations, such as certain kinds of entrepreneurial activity, have highly risky outcomes or yields, these occupations are going to have to provide very high remunerations for those that succeed, thus resulting in large income differentials at the top end of the distribution (Friedman, 1953).

As first pointed out by Adam Smith, occupations also differ in a number of non-pecuniary benefits and disadvantages, which in a competitive labour market would lead to differences in wages to compensate for them. The human capital model, which predicts that occupations requiring a higher investment of time and other resources must enjoy higher returns, is in fact a special case of this more general proposition. Regional cost-of-living differences are usually reflected in rates of pay, so that urban incomes, for example, are usually higher than incomes in rural areas. Instability of employment, uncertainty of success, and occupational health hazards have to be compensated for to attract workers to an occupation.

Tastes for the non-pecuniary benefits of a job can play an important role in the choice of an occupation or career. Some jobs involve work in comfortable environment; others may require very repetitive work in noisy surroundings. Some lines of work offer challenges and 'personal fulfilment,' while others are humdrum. Individuals may behave not just to maximize money income in choosing an occupation but in light of the over-all utility package of benefits across an available occupation set (Sattinger, 1977). Indeed if such non-pecuniary benefits are normal goods, greater wealth and non-wage income increases the propensity to choose pleasant low-paying work activities rather than higher-paying less pleasant ones (Weiss, 1972a). Thus large expected wealth or inheritance, other things equal, would tend to direct young workers toward more comfortable or enjoyable occupations at a lower wage than otherwise and young household heads with little wealth endowments to higher-paying less pleasant work activities. In a recent empirical study on non-pecuniary rewards, Taubman (1977a) found that

those who were not worried about future financial success receive 17 percent less than those who were worried ... those who wanted to help others earn 8 percent less, those who wanted to have a challenge earn 17 percent more, and those interested in job security receive 13 percent less earnings ... The basic threads running through these findings are that people who are willing to work hard on difficult or risky projects will end up with substantially more earnings, while those who are more interested in the intrinsic rewards of the job will receive less ... The tradeoffs of earnings with nonpecuniary returns is quite large. (444)

HOUSEHOLD TIME ALLOCATION, PRODUCTION, AND BEQUESTS

Analysis of the behaviour of a one-person decision unit does not adequately represent the range of considerations involved in determining the earnings behaviour and labour market experience of married persons, particularly those with children. Family formation and household time allocation have important distributional implications. The timing and number of children affect the time spent by parents on raising a family and the household labour supply, job skill acquisition, and total family earnings. More specifically, household time allocation by parents and household production patterns affect both the time allocated by parents to market activities, and thus family earnings, and the distribution of what may be called home-produced human capital among the children (Leibowitz, 1974). The impact of these factors can be viewed in both life-cycle and intergenerational contexts. They influence the pattern of family labour supply and earned income over the life cycle. But they also affect the home environment and thus the ability, personality traits, and stock of initial human capital KH_0 of the children. They are therefore also a potential transmission mechanism of income and wealth from one generation to the next.

Household activity and earnings of spouses
The labour supply decision of married persons and, most significantly, married women has been shown by Mincer (1962b) and Cain (1966), among others, to depend on a number of household factors and should thus be analysed in a general family framework. More recently, the analysis of a number of aspects of family economic activity has been carried out in the framework of what is called household production theory. Market goods

and services do not themselves directly yield utility but are valued only when combined with other factors such as consumer's time to produce commodities that yield utility. According to this approach (Becker, 1965), households thus produce commodities, such as home life, recreation, health, and meals, which generate enjoyment for the family but which in turn require as inputs both goods purchased on the market and the time of parents. Thus the household must maximize its welfare subject to both a budget constraint on the income that can be spent on market goods and a constraint on the time that the parents can afford to allocate to such non-market or household production activities as alternatives to market work and leisure. Spouses' time in household production may be substitutes for each other for various activities and reflect their comparative advantages in the home production process and their relative opportunity costs in terms of their alternative market wages. Husbands' wage rates usually exceed wives'. 'Thus, we observe that, in general, husbands specialize in work in the market, while the wife specializes in the production of home goods' (Gronau, 1973). This general framework has been the basis of numerous studies on marriage, fertility, health, and family labour supply, but we shall focus here on its application to the labour supply behaviour of married women, as outlined, for example, by Gronau (1973; 1977), Gramm (1975), and Leibowitz (1975).

Formalizing the above discussion in a one-period framework, Gronau (1973) assumes that households gain utility from consuming market-produced goods M, home-produced goods Z, and the leisure time of husband L_h and wife L_w:

$$U = U(M, Z, L_h, L_w).$$

Z commodities can be produced either by husband or wife, $Z = Z_h + Z_w$, where

$$Z_i = Z_i(X_i, T_i), \quad i = h, w,$$

and where X_i is the quantity of market goods used and T_i is spouse i's time input, although the exact functions will generally be different for the two parents. The household then maximizes its utility with respect to leisure, consumption, and household production possibilities subject to a budget constraint where the spouses spend H_h and H_w hours in the labour market at wages rates w_h and w_w respectively, and a set of time constraints for husband and wife:

Figure 8:
Effect of age of first child on wife's labour supply
Source: Gramm (1975, 98)

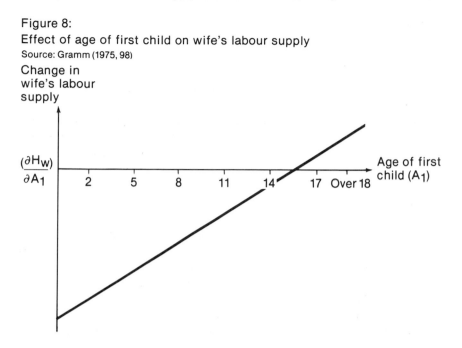

$$L_i + T_i + H_i = \bar{H}, \qquad i = h, w.$$

The resulting labour supply of the wife H_w (and indeed of the husband as well H_h) is a function of both husband's and wife's wages, household assets and non-labour income, the number and ages of the children in the house-hold (as reflected in the Z's), and the structure of the production and utility functions of the model. While predictions of the model can be fairly complex because of the separate income and substitution effects, empirical estimates reported by Gramm (1975) and Gronau (1977) for wife's labour supply indicate a negative effect of the husband's wage, a positive effect of the wife's wage, a weak negative effect of household assets and non-wage income inducing an increased demand for leisure, a negative effect for the number of children in the household, and a generally negative but attenu-ated effect of the age of the first child (Figure 8). On the other hand the husband's wage has a positive effect on the husband's labour supply to the market, the wife's wage has no effect, non-wage income a negative effect, and the number of children a positive effect on work time supplied to the market (Gronau, 1977).

The market work profiles of married women can be thought of as passing through three stages of market involvement: 'There is usually continuous market work prior to birth of the first child. The second stage is a period of non-participation related to childbearing and child care, lasting between 5 and 10 years, followed by intermittent participation before the youngest child reaches school age. The third stage is a more permanent return to the labour force for some, though it may remain intermittent for others' (Mincer and Polachek, 1974, S83). Since on-the-job training and the shape of wage profiles are related to job market experience, the shorter expected work experience and higher expected turnover rates for women weaken incentives to build up human capital. Also, the discontinuity of the work experience implies that the human capital investment profile will not continuously decline over the life cycle and yield a concave age-earnings profile as for men, but may even be negative (net depreciation) during childbearing years and then pick up on permanent re-entry into the market. Consequently the earnings profile for women are usually different from those for men. For women without children they are lower, less steep, and less concave than for males; for mothers the typical profile is double-peaked (Mincer and Polachek, 1974). To the extent that the first peak occurs when the household is fairly young and the husband's income relatively low, the wife's earnings reduce between-age-group inequality in family income. The second peak occurs much further on in later middle age when the husband's income would be higher, thus widening family age-income differentials. Over-all, Mincer (1974) found that including the wife's earnings in family income generally reduces inequality in family incomes compared to inequality in incomes of the male family earners.

Overview of household production and income
As can be seen from the above discussion, a number of household activities are interrelated over the family's life cycle. Cohen and Stafford (1974) have indeed developed a fairly elaborate household optimization model of life-cycle time allocation to market work, home consumption, and child care, the birth and spacing of children, life-cycle net worth accumulation, and life-cycle accumulation of human capital subsequent to formal schooling by husband and wife. According to the model the household is again assumed to maximize a lifetime utility function that depends upon family consumption associated with children $Z_1(t)$ and other family consumption $Z_2(t)$. Z_1 and Z_2 are home-produced commodities with Z_2, for example, generated by a CES production function,

$$Z_2(t) = F(X_2(t), L_w(t), L_h(t)),$$

with inputs X_2 representing market goods for non-children consumption and L_w and L_h the proportions of time spent by wife and husband on recreation activities. The determination of $Z_1(t)$ is somewhat more complex. Inputs of parents' time into child care, $T_h(t)$ and $T_w(t)$, combine with household expenditure on children $X_1(t)$ to produce child care

$$C(t) = G(T_h(t), T_w(t), X_1(t)),$$

where the relative intensity of use of time inputs compared to market expenditures varies with the average age of the children – young children requiring relatively heavy inputs of time and older children requiring relatively more market inputs. Finally, child care combines with the number of children in the household to produce $Z_1(t)$. Potential earnings capacity is generated by

$$\text{YE}_i(t+1) - \text{YE}_i(t) = G_i(H_i(t), \delta_i), \qquad i = w,h,$$

where the δ_i are rates of depreciation of human capital and the partial relationship of $\text{YE}_i(t)$ to $H_i(t)$ has the conventional concave shape in order to reflect the influence of work experience and learning by doing. Finally, the household faces a standard budget constraint and a set of time constraints on the spouses' use of their time.

Cohen and Stafford simulate the model and obtain the results reported in Table 1. Row 1 shows that total market expenditures have a moderate inverted-U shape essentially due to market expenditures on children. Secondly, because of the greater earnings potential of the husband (even in the absence of any differences in efficiency of home production by wife and husband), the latter spends more time working on the job and less time on child care than the former. As a result, depreciation effects on human capital further widen husband-wife earnings differentials over time as the wife keeps putting more time into the children as the household grows up. Third, the resulting labour market supply profile for the husband can be seen to follow the conventional single-peaked shape (row 6) along with potential earnings (row 4), so that actual earnings (row 8) of the husband also have a conventional humped shape over the life cycle, peaking in the late forties. The wife's labour supply profile, however, is much more influenced by the presence of children in the household and has a consequent double-peaked shape indicating where time is being withdrawn from the market for childcare. Finally, the net worth position of the family

TABLE 1
Illustrative life-cycle simulation for a household

Age of head	20-24	25-29	30-34	35-39	40-44	45-49	50-54	55-59	60-64	65-69
1 Expenditure on consumption and children $(X_1 + X_2)$ ($000/yr.)	8.0	9.2	10.4	12.5	11.0	10.1	9.1	6.0	6.0	6.0
2 Number of children present	0.8	1.3	1.8	2.8	2.0	1.5	1.0	0.0	0.0	0.0
3 Average age of children	2.0	5.1	7.8	8.8	10.6	13.6	17.0	–	–	–
4 Potential earnings of husband (YE_h) ($000/yr.)	9.9	11.9	14.2	16.6	18.9	20.3	19.6	15.6	8.6	0.1
5 Potential earnings of wife (YE_w) ($000/yr.)	6.0	7.2	8.7	10.3	11.8	12.6	12.2	9.9	4.2	0.0
6 Work time of husband (H_h) (% of time)	48.0	48.0	49.0	49.0	47.0	50.0	51.0	28.0	1.0	0.0
7 Work time of wife (H_w) (% of time)	43.0	41.0	40.0	34.0	29.0	34.0	35.0	8.0	0.0	0.0
8 Earnings of husband $(H_h \cdot YE_h)$ ($000/yr.)	4.75	5.71	6.96	8.13	8.88	10.15	10.00	4.39	0.09	0.0
9 Earnings of wife $(H_w \cdot YE_w)$ ($000/yr.)	2.58	2.95	3.48	3.50	3.42	4.28	4.27	0.79	0.0	0.0
10 Net worth at end of period ($000)	-3.6	-6.4	-6.6	-12.4	-6.3	18.2	52.4	57.4	33.5	4.7

SOURCE: Cohen and Stafford (1974, 457)

changes radically over the life cycle, troughing when family size is largest and then accumulating until a peak just prior to retirement. In summary, then, it can be seen that patterns of household production have potentially strong effects on family life-cycle earnings behaviour and thus on the overall distribution of family income across the population.

Household bequests and the transmission of economic status
A final aspect of household behaviour that should be at least mentioned in a study of distribution is the transmission of economic status from parents to children. The long-run consequences of such behaviour from one generation to the next are obviously significant from a distributional point of view, but they extend beyond the frame of reference of the present study and consequently will not be investigated here. However, I do wish to complement the analysis so far in this chapter by highlighting the various channels by which such a transmission can occur within the context of the current life-cycle discussion.

First, and perhaps most obviously, resources can be transferred directly by bequests, trusts, and gifts *inter vivos* of real and financial capital. Indeed, the optimal amount of capital a family may wish to leave to their heirs K_T can be readily generated from life-cycle models (for example, Yaari, 1964; Atkinson, 1971; Blinder 1974), and not surprisingly it depends critically on (1) the parents' relative preferences for bequests versus their own lifetime consumption and (2) their elasticity of marginal utility of bequest compared to their elasticity of marginal utility of consumption. Depending on the number of heirs and the distribution of the total bequest among the heirs, this can be thought of as determining the initial stock or endowment of non-human capital K_0 that has recurred in the various models of this chapter. Indeed, greater amount of wealth, at least in a world of imperfect markets, particularly for human capital, may mean greater access to financing for a human capital investment program as well.

Bequests of real and financial capital, however, are not the only vehicle for channelling economic status from parents to children within the household, and indeed they may not be nearly as important as the provision of family background, initial stock of human capital KH_0, health, and the influencing of the social and cultural inheritance and various personality characteristics of the children (Bowles, 1972, 1973). Ishikawa (1975), for example, has made a step toward extending the bequest motive to household determination of the amount of schooling and educational attainment of the children. In a 'general paternalistic household,' the parents choose consumption, bequests, and educational investment levels for their children during the latters' initial period of childhood and economic dependence on the household according to particular value norms ranging from 'parental self-satisfaction' (where children are viewed essentially as investment goods for the parents) to 'parental altruism' (where the parents seek to do 'what is best' for their children). Indeed, economists have only started examining ways to model parental influence on child development in a human capital and household production framework. Leibowitz (1974)) argues that human capital is built up over the life cycle not only through schooling and on-the-job training but also through home production of human capital by 'home investment' of parents in their children as outlined earlier in this section. The greater the quantity and quality of time inputs by parents (particularly the education level of the mother (Leibowitz, 1974) and of associated market good inputs, the greater the stock of human capital KH_0 that the young adult brings with him to the market when he attains his economic independence. Thus economic status can be maintained to some extent through differential access through family resources to educational and other opportunities. Upper-income parents tend to provide greater financial support for longer periods of education and for better schooling for their offspring. These are clearly forms of transmission of economic status from one generation to the next.

Indeed parents also influence important non-cognitive or affective skills such as leadership, social behaviour, and attitudes toward work, and psychological characteristics such as reaction to stress and achievement motivation in the development of their offspring. Moynihan (1967) and Kohn (1969), for example, have argued that families tend to transfer attitudes, aspirations, and non-cognitive traits from one generation to the next. Children from a low economic background may lack not only the economic resources to continue on to higher levels of education and occupational attainment but also the motivation and long-term horizons involved in continuing their schooling or in accumulating job experience.

Finally, the impact of ability A in human capital production processes may also reflect the roles of upbringing and family background as well as nature and innate ability. It is not the intention of this study to review the current work on the relative importance and distributional implications of nature versus nurture (see, for example, Taubman, 1976, 1977b). However, to the extent that ability of parents on average is positively correlated with that of offspring and that at least some portion of ability for purposes of job market productivity is influenced by family background and upbringing (Jencks, 1972), ability can also serve as a channel for transmission of economic status as well between parents and children. In the conclusion of a recent study, Taubman finds 'that education leads to large and statistically significant differences in earnings. These differences, however, are relatively small in comparison with those arising from the conglomeration of family background, attitudes, and non-pecuniary preferences, and are no larger than the differences which are the result of ability' (1977a, 446).

CONCLUSIONS AND IMPLICATIONS

Several general implications can be drawn from the discussion of this chapter. First, current income may not be a very good indicator of a family's economic well-being. According to the models discussed, economic well-being arises from household consumption and bequest activities very broadly defined, and these in turn are related to the long-run income and net worth status of the household. Current family income may adjust unevenly from one year to the next while following the systematic patterns outlined above, but lifetime consumption tends to be smoothed out, with savings and family labour supply acting as buffers. Consequently, family economic well-being may not be accurately represented simply by current annual income, particularly for those now at the peak (later middle age) or troughs (young family units and older retired family units) of their lifetime income trajectories. A more accurate representation of economic well-being would appear to be a longer-run measure of income status or 'permanent income' that abstracts from or averages out transitory components. To the extent that people actually are able to transfer resources through time according to perfect capital market conditions, discounted lifetime income or wealth broadly defined would be a useful indicator of long-run economic status of a household. Indeed, it would seem natural to consider a measure of permanent income status that lies somewhere between the two extremes of current annual income and one's full lifetime income experience. However, the main point for present purposes is that figures on the distribution of current income are only imperfect proxies for longer-run measures of economic status. More appropriate for drawing inferences with respect to economic well-being would be actual longitudinal income, wealth, and labour supply profiles for family units if they were available.

Secondly, some portion of inequality in observed current income figures may be due to individual choice and preferences, so that looking only at money income figures may again give a somewhat distorted view of the distribution of economic well-being. People may choose different occupations, human capital investment profiles, and work patterns at least partly because of their differences in tastes. This is particularly true of non-pecuniary benefits and earnings and of attitudes towards risk, leisure, and home production. Consequently, to the extent that these differences reflect meaningful choices, the distribution of money income may convey too pessimistic a view of inequality in the distribution of well-being. Since such choices, however, are likely to be more meaningful towards the upper portion of the distribution than at the bottom where poverty may be an ever-present constraint on horizons and opportunities, the degree of distortion in using money income figures as indicators of economic well-being may well differ over different regions of the distribution. For an analysis of poverty, an emphasis on choice would clearly be misplaced; but for a study of overall distributional inequality and an interpretation of what it involves, the role of choice and preferences subject to endowments, ability, and family background constraints would appear to be crucial.

The analysis of this chapter also underlines the important difference between inequality of opportunity and inequality of outcome. So long as life-cycle choices exist and people's tastes differ, even perfect equality of opportunity among children may result in rather marked differences in income receipts and wealth holdings. To know exactly what the limits of income concentration are that can result from such life-cycle choices (Fair, 1971) and how they would compare with actually observed distributions, however, we must await a substantially improved theoretical structure and better empirical information than are now available.

Thirdly, the life-cycle analysis highlights the fact that low incomes can be long-term in nature and characteristic of two quite different situations. On one hand they may occur during the prime-age period of one's working life because individuals may not have acquired (for reasons of opportunity or choice or changed market conditions) enough skill to maintain steady employment at a comfortable wage. Improving many situations of low and irregular income among prime-aged groups will entail effort to improve long-run productivity over a working life, to open up educational and occupational opportunities, and to induce steadier employment. On the other hand low-income situations may be a characteristic of the non-working population of disabled, elderly, and retired persons. These situations are better dealt with by transfer and insurance programs that may indeed seek to shift resources from periods of higher income over the life cycle to later periods of lower income.

Fourth, the theoretical models reviewed in this chapter have provided a fairly elaborate framework and detailed expectations for income patterns across age groups in the population. Capital income would tend to become more important with age, particularly towards retirement years when earnings fall off. Earned income reflects basically work effort, market skill acquisition, and family involvement. Among men, earned income would be expected to manifest a positively sloped but concave profile across ages until a peak in later middle age, with inequality generally increasing from early middle age until retirement. Since incomes are thus expected to vary systematically and rather markedly with age and family structure, empirical work on patterns of income inequality should make an effort to separate out these effects in order to evaluate their relative importance and the structure of inequality that still remains. Accordingly, the empirical parts of this study attempt some fairly elaborate disaggregations by age and family size in order to take account of life-cycle effects on the over-all structure of income and wealth in the population.

Fifth, economic policies should be made with such life-cycle behaviour in mind, and the distributional incidence of government programs such as educational subsidies, social security, and health insurance could usefully be analysed in this framework. Several examples can readily be cited. What, for example, are the long-run effects of minimum wage laws that differentially affect the employment opportunities of young and relatively unskilled workers at the beginning of their earning careers? What is the life-cycle incidence of the Ontario Student Assistance Program, which attempts to reduce capital market imperfections for human capital investment purposes, combined with a progressive personal income tax levied over one's working years to cover the expenditure? What is the life-cycle distributional incidence of the Canada Pension Plan combined with a fixed-rate payroll tax over career earnings, and what are its effects on the distribution of household private saving and the timing of retirement? What are the differences in distributional incidence between a daycare program for young children paid for out of progressive income taxes and tax deductions for personal daycare expenditures?

Finally, the presence of substantial life-cycle differences in income implies that demographic factors may have an important effect on the over-all structure of inequality in the distribution of income. More specifically, in order to transform a longitudinal age-income life-cycle trajectory such as that generated by the models of this chapter into an over-all cross sectional distribution of income such as that provided by census and survey data, we must find out the proportion of people in each age group of the population, or what is called the age distribution of the population. This will be considered in Chapter 4. Rather strong demographic shifts like those that have occurred in Canada since the Second World War would thus be expected to have fairly substantial distributional effects as well.

3
Selected demand-side determinants of the distribution of income

INTRODUCTION

As was pointed out in the introduction to Part One, theoretical analyses of the determinants of the size distribution of income have tended to emphasize supply-side considerations. Demand-side factors nonetheless can still have a considerable effect on the distributional structure through their impact on rates of factor remuneration and employment. The present chapter discusses some demand-side determinants of the distributional structure and their effects on wage rates and employment. The next chapter brings the supply and demand sides together in a discussion of market determination of factor prices, particularly in the labour market.

In the 1950s, substantial research occurred on the demand-side aspects of distribution, as the work of Kerr, Lester, and Reynolds focused on the structural characteristics of labour markets and types of market segmentation. In the 1960s, interest turned away to supply-side considerations with their emphasis on worker productivity and human capital investment models. But, more recently, concern with demand-side factors has returned, with an emphasis on dual labour markets and the employment situation of the working poor, as well as imperfect labour market information and manpower costs for a firm.

The present discussion of demand-side distributional considerations will be selective. It will be limited to the labour market, since that market has the most direct impact through employment and earnings on most individuals' incomes. It will also be confined to a number of topics that have been the subject of substantial recent work in the economics of information and market behaviour. Since the principal focus of this study is the life-cycle framework considered at some length in the previous chapter, the present discussion of demand-side considerations is necessarily brief and is meant to convey the flavour of some fairly recent advances in distribution analysis that complement the material outlined above.

The standard approach to the demand for productive factors in general, and for labour in particular, is based on the theory of marginal productivity according to which a factor is demanded by a firm for purposes of producing output up to the point where the market value of the output produced by a marginal increase in employment of a given factor just covers the additional cost of employing that factor. That theory will not be elaborated upon here[1] save to point out several important implications of it. First, it highlights the fact that demand for a factor is a derived demand dependent upon the demand for the firm's output in the product market. Consequently, different circumstances of demand for the firm's output, whether cyclical or secular, can have a substantial effect on differences in wage rates across various occupations, industries, and regions. Secondly, marginal productivity theory postulates that employer or firm behaviour (in the form of cost-minimization and profit-maximization) is central to the determination of factor demand, especially in making choices between very disaggregated forms of inputs that may be readily substitutable in the firm's production process. Thirdly, of course, the theory emphasizes the role of productivity in wage determination and employment behaviour. These points will recur in various guises through the discussion that follows.

Traditional emphasis in discussions of factor demand and distribution has focused heavily on the role of the firm in factor and output markets. At least one recent textbook (Bronfenbrenner, 1971) contains a detailed discussion of factor demand under various market conditions. In contrast, I shall focus on the distributional aspects of three sets of issues: the role of imperfect information about productivity and firm-specific human capital investment costs; the role of tastes and preferences in firm wage determination and employment policies; and the role of hierarchical structure and promotion policies of firms.

Accordingly, this chapter proceeds as follows. The next section examines some of the implications for wage structure of specific human capital as an alternative to the general human capital considered in the last chapter. The third section reviews some results on screening and signalling in the labour market and discusses an alternative explanation of the role of formal education and credentials in job access and remuneration. Some aspects of labour

---

1 For a fairly detailed discussion of marginal productivity theory of factor demand, see, for example, the textbooks of Bronfenbrenner (1971) and Ferguson (1969).

market discrimination are considered in the fourth section. Hierarchies and internal labour markets are touched upon after that, and the final section provides some brief concluding remarks.

SPECIFIC HUMAN CAPITAL AND WAGE PROFILES

Firm-specific human capital may be defined as that part of the human capital stock of the employees of a firm that has no value to any other potential employer. We shall treat specific human capital as a fixed training cost that must be paid before an employee can enter the productive labour force of a particular firm. I shall simply comment on the alternative situation of continuously accumulated specific human capital. Three cases will be examined where specific human capital has definite implications for the shape of the time profile of wages of employees, corresponding generally to the relaxation of any of several assumptions of the simplest perfectly competitive labour market. The introduction of labour turnover, non-homogeneous labour, or non-competitive labour supply with labour turnover is sufficient to generate a positively sloped wage profile, given optimizing behaviour on the part of the firm.

General framework
In the standard analysis of specific human capital, it is assumed that labour markets are perfectly competitive and that homogeneous, risk-neutral employees seek to maximize the expected discounted value of their earnings stream for a job. This implies that in equilibrium the expected discounted value of the earnings streams associated with any two jobs must be equal. Assume also that there exists a permanent market opportunity wage w^* offered by firms without training costs. Profit-maximizing firms are in equilibrium when the expected discounted value of the marginal revenue product of labour is equal to the expected discounted marginal cost of hiring and maintaining an additional worker. If T is the (fixed) cost of training per employee and w_t is the period wage rate, the discounted value of expected marginal hiring costs (in the absence of labour quits) is given by

$$\text{MC} = T + \sum_{t=1}^{\infty} w_t/(1+r)^t, \tag{22}$$

where r is the market rate of interest.[2] Under the competitive result that present values of alternative earnings streams are equal, the second term of (22) can be replaced by w^*/r and (22) rewritten as

2 For convenience it is assumed that employees have an infinite working life.

$$\text{MC} = T + w^*/r. \tag{23}$$

If marginal revenue product remains unchanged in future, it has a discounted present value per additional employee of $\text{MRP}(L)/r$. Equating the present values of marginal revenue and marginal cost yields the equilibrium condition that

$$\text{MRP}(L) = T \cdot r + w^*$$

analogous to that developed by Oi (1962) where labour is viewed as a quasi-fixed factor.

The implications of this condition for firms' labour force adjustment over the business cycle should be evident. In long-run equilibrium, employees who have been specifically trained by a firm are paid less on average than their marginal revenue product. In the short run, fluctuations in aggregate demand cause cyclical fluctuations in the marginal revenue product of labour. If there were no specific training costs, firms would immediately adjust their labour forces to bring wages and $\text{MRP}(L)$ back into line. However, firms with specific-training costs will not lay workers off until $\text{MRP}(L)$ falls by more than $T \cdot r$ below its long-run expected value. This suggests that there is a degree of fixity in the labour force of a firm with training costs, and this fixity increases with the amount of the training costs. It follows that the occupational incidence of layoffs will be negatively correlated with the level of fixed training costs for each occupation, and in particular that lower skilled workers will tend to suffer more cyclical variance in their employment than higher skilled workers (Oi, 1962).

Three illustrations
Some of the distributional implications of specific human capital can be shown by three separate cases. In each case a higher wage level is predicted in the post-training period than in the training period.

In the first case labour turnover is introduced into the discussion. Assuming that a firm stands to lose a portion of its training investment if a worker quits before the expected amortization period of the investment has elapsed, it is in the firm's interest to structure the wage profile so as to reduce the probability of turnover. If the probability of quitting in any post-training period is inversely related to the post-training wage, the firm can devise a two-step wage profile that indeed minimizes its turnover costs. In the training period the firm offers a wage somewhat less than w^*. Then in the post-training period the firm offers a wage greater than w^* so as to induce workers to stay on rather than return to the market. The shape of the wage profile thus results entirely from employers' desires to minimize turnover costs or maximize 'entrapment' (Donaldson and Eaton, 1976).

In the second case a non-homogeneous labour supply is introduced. Firms with turnover costs from employee training can use a two-step wage profile as a self-selection device to attract workers with a relatively low probability of quitting or a high probability of success in the training program. Following Salop and Salop (1976), suppose there are two classes of workers: slow quitters with probability q_s of quitting in any post-training period, and fast quitters with corresponding probability q_f. Employees know which group they belong to, but fast quitters will not reveal themselves voluntarily. Suppose the firm offers a two-step wage profile paying $w_1 < w^*$ in the training period and $\hat{w} > w^*$ after training. A prospective employee evaluates the alternative discounted expected earnings streams with the firm relative to that offered (w^*) on the market. If he is a slow quitter, the former will be higher than if he is a fast quitter. The firm can thus choose w_1 and $\hat{w}$ (within certain bounds) so that fast quitters will not apply but slow quitters will. In a competitive labour market, firms will bid up the present value of the income streams of slow quitters (i.e. increase $\hat{w}$) until firms are indifferent between hiring a fast or a slow quitter. The use of the wage profile as a self-selection device in this case results in the selected group (the slow quitters) forgoing at least the full costs of their training during the training period. However, the net effect of self-selection in a competitive labour market is to sort out employees and thereby increase the lifetime earnings of slow quitters to a point where they earn the full rents to their reliability.

A third case in which specific human capital has been shown to affect the wage profiles of employees is in an imperfectly competitive labour market. The supply of trainees to the firm is now an increasing function of the expected discounted value of the wage stream offered by the firm. Parsons (1972) considers a two-period model of a firm with a set of labour force options that include layoffs in either period, the hiring of trainees in the first period, and the rehiring of labour in the second period. The quit function of trained labour in each period is assumed to be a decreasing function of the wage rate of trained labour in that period, and the supply of trainees is an increasing function of the trainees' wage rate and the expected wage of trained labour. The firm then chooses wage rates and layoffs in each period to maximize the present value of its profits. If the quit function of trained workers is highly responsive to their wage rate, then the firm will pay relatively higher post-training wages and relatively lower wages during training and will concentrate on reducing turnover rather than increasing recruitment. On the other hand if the supply function of trainees is highly responsive to the wage offered during the training period, the firm will pay relatively higher wages to trainees and relatively lower wages to trained workers, thus hiring a large number of trainees in the first period while suffering a high rate of attrition of trained labour as a result of relatively low post-training wages.

Some aspects of the current analysis have been extended to the situation of continuously accumulated firm-specific human capital by Stiglitz (1975a) under the assumption that the cost of hiring a worker remains constant over time and the quit function is again negatively related to the current wage. The result is that wage rates offered to employees increase over time along with their specific training. In equilibrium the firm must be indifferent between hiring a new worker and retaining an older one. Since the costs of hiring a new worker are constant over time and the productivity of trained workers in terms of trainees is increasing over time, the firm must be willing to spend more in order to retain a worker as he gets older and more productive.

The preceding analysis suggests that, in general, the shape of the time profile of wages in the presence of firm-specific human capital is determined not only by the time profile of productivity but also by the behaviour of firms that must bear labour turnover costs whenever training is firm-specific. In a competitive and homogeneous labour market, for example, a sufficient condition to generate a positively sloped wage profile between the training and post-training periods is that the rate of turnover of trained workers be negatively related to their wage rate.

SCREENING, EDUCATION, AND THE DISTRIBUTION OF EARNINGS

General framework

In markets characterized by imperfect information, buyers and sellers engage in various activities with the goal of reducing uncertainty. For example, in the analysis of labour markets it is common to assume that employees know the quality of their labour services better than do potential employers. Processes that facilitate discrimination between otherwise homogeneous products are known as screening activities and can take two general forms: direct examination and the inference of product quality from sellers' behaviour. Where jobs are not paid piecerate, productivity may be measured only at some cost, if at all, because of the complexity of the jobs. Hence the first type of screening may be impractical, and the second may be adopted. The fact that buyers (employers) infer product quality from sellers' behaviour provides an incentive for sellers to modify their behaviour accordingly or 'signal.' By using sellers' behaviour as a guide to product quality, buyers force sellers to label themselves; hence, the second type of screening is commonly known as screening by self-selection.

Two forms of self-selection in the labour market may be identified (Spence, 1976). In both cases employers cannot observe the labour quality of applicants directly. If labour quality information is revealed to employers over time, they can offer potential employees a menu of alternative labour contracts, and the problem is formally similar to that of specific human capital and labour turnover (Salop and Salop, 1976; Spence, 1977) reviewed above. On the other hand if labour quality is not revealed over time, other screening processes must be adopted. An obvious self-selection device is educational attainment. Employers may infer labour quality from the education level of prospective employees, provided they believe that more highly educated workers are more skilled or productive than less educated workers, and prospective employees for their part can signal potential labour quality by choice of educational attainment. Obviously, for education to act as a signalling device it must be costly, and indeed the costs must be negatively correlated with labour quality. We shall concentrate entirely on signalling based on education, so that education is no longer viewed merely as increasing one's potential job productivity but also as a way of signalling labour quality to employers.

There are several important implications of screening and signalling activity for the distribution of earnings. First, compared to a situation with no screening, in which labour is undifferentiated, signalling usually reduces the earnings of those with lower quality labour services. In fact, signalling generally provides the same earnings for those with the lowest quality labour services as in a full-information competitive equilibrium (FICE). Secondly, in most cases, the returns to self-selection accrue to those who are more productive, although the absolute level of welfare of more productive individuals is not necessarily increased over a situation in which workers are undifferentiated, and it is reduced relative to a FICE. Thirdly, relative to an equilibrium without self-selection, a screening equilibrium implies a less equal distribution of earnings; on the other hand a screening equilibrium implies a more equal distribution of net earnings than a FICE. Fourthly, differentiation of the labour force through signalling may or may not be socially desirable, depending on the costs of signalling, the nature of production processes, and the social welfare criterion.

Three illustrations
These points can be illustrated by three simple models. The first model considers the simplest and limiting case where education has absolutely no

Figure 9:
Illustration of wage determination with education as a screen

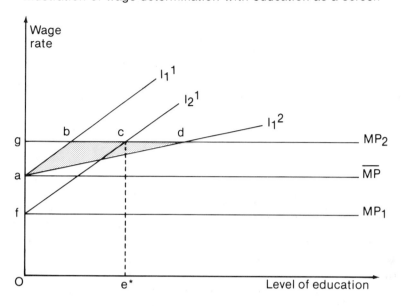

influence on output of workers (i.e. no productivity effects) and there is only one job involved in the production process of the firm (i.e. no allocative effects). These conditions are relaxed in the subsequent models. For simplicity, assume also that there are only two groups ($i = 1, 2$), which differ in some innate labour quality trait that we shall label as 'ability,' and also that markets are perfectly competitive. Let MP_2 represent the marginal productivity of members of the high-ability group and MP_1 that for the low-productivity group, so that $MP_2 > MP_1$. At the same time, assume that average and marginal costs of education are negatively correlated with ability, so that for example $MC_2(e) < MC_1(e)$ for any level of education e. Employers can observe educational attainment, but not ability; and individuals with the same education level who are allocated to the same job are paid the same wage. Education serves only a signalling and screening role, and individuals accordingly choose e_i's so as to maximize their expected earnings net of education costs.

This situation is illustrated in Figure 9, where $\overline{MP}$ is the weighted average productivity of the two groups. $I_1{}^1$ and $I_2{}^1$ (with superscripts corresponding to group 1) are lines along which net wages (i.e. gross wages less costs of education) are constant, so that individuals of group 1, for example, are indifferent between no education and gross wage 0 or e^* education and gross wage $0g$. Points on I_1^1, however, are clearly preferred to points on the lower I_2^1 curve. Similarly, I_1^2 is an 'indifference curve' along which net wages are constant for individuals of group 2, and the I^2 curves generally lie below the corresponding I^1 curves, reflecting the condition that education costs are lower for the higher-ability workers. From a no-screening situation at point a, in which neither group invests in education and all workers receive wage $0a = \overline{MP}$, it is clear that some firm could make a profit by introducing an education requirement and offering a wage rate that jointly lie in the shaded region abd. This would attract group 2 workers who find it profitable to invest in education since the offer would lie above the I_1^2 curve, and competition among firms to hire group 2 workers would drive up group 2's wages to $0g$. Group 1 workers would find their wages reduced to $0f$ in·the absence of unidentified group 2 workers. However, group 1 workers still have an incentive to invest in education and to imitate group 2's signals if the firm's offer lies above the indifference curve I_2^1. Consequently, the level of education that will be compatible with identifying higher-ability workers and will be at minimal cost to group 2 is e^* (Spence, 1974). Thus at the screening equilibrium, higher-ability workers identify themselves by investing in e^* level of education and receive wage $0g$, while lower-ability workers do not invest in education and receive the lower wage $0f$.

From a distributional point of view, this model has several characteristics. Since education is not productive, efficiency requires that neither group invest in education. Nonetheless, there are private returns to members of the higher-ability group to signal by making such an investment. Compared to a no-screening situation, screening reduces the relative and absolute earnings of those with lesser abilities, increases the relative earnings of those with higher abilities, and increases inequality in the distribution of earnings. The absolute level of welfare is increased compared to a no-screening equilibrium if point c lies to the left of point d. Screening reduces the net income of society by the amount of the education costs incurred by group 2; it also provides the same net earnings for lower-ability workers as in a FICE, lower net earnings for higher-ability workers, and a more equal distribution of net earnings than in a FICE (Stiglitz, 1975b).

Clearly the above model represents an extreme case; education has no productive effect and serves only as a means by which higher-ability workers can identify themselves. We now consider a second screening model that allows for the allocative effects of education. Suppose that there are a number of jobs to which a worker can be allocated within the firm, some of them more productive than others. Education is thus productive if it allows employers to identify the ability level of workers and improve the allocation of workers to jobs. A signalling equilibrium, if established, will provide a unique correspondence between educational attainment and ability (Spence, 1974). Each employee will be optimally allocated, and each ability group will be paid a wage equal to its maximum productivity across jobs. Given the optimal allocation of ability levels across jobs, the distributional characteristics of a screening equilibrium if established are similar to those for the simpler model above. The principal difference between this model and the earlier one is that, since there are productive returns to the allocation of workers to jobs, screening now increases the gross income of the economy. Aggregate *net* income may thus be either reduced or increased by screening, and as education costs rise for all groups the former case becomes more likely (Arrow, 1972b). As in the first model, screening provides the same earnings for lower-ability workers as in a FICE, lower net earnings for higher-ability workers, the same gross earnings for all ability groups, and a more equal distribution of net earnings than in a FICE.

The final model of interest is one in which education contributes directly to productivity. For simplicity, we now suppress the issue of job allocation and return to the two-group case where we also assume that the higher-ability group 2 is small compared to group 1.[3] The marginal productivity of workers now increases with education level, though (for convenience) with diminishing returns, and with $MP_2(e)$ still greater than $MP_1(e)$ for any level of education. The analysis of screening and signalling behaviour is essentially similar to that in the first model above, except that the marginal productivity curves in Figure 9 are now increasing concave functions of education level. In a FICE, the two groups choose levels of education $\hat{e}_1$ and $\hat{e}_2$ at which their respective marginal costs and returns to education are equalized, implying that $\hat{e}_2 > \hat{e}_1$. In the absence of employer information on abilities, however, the screening equilibrium is characterized by group 2 again overinvesting in education by choosing an education level $e^* > \hat{e}_2$ that allows group 2 to differentiate itself from group 1 at minimal cost while providing no incentive for group 1 to imitate them. Group 1 then continues to invest optimally in $\hat{e}_1$ level of education. As in the previous models, screening provides the same earnings for lower-ability workers as in a FICE, lower net earnings for higher-ability workers, and thus a more equal distri-

---

3 This last assumption is made to avoid discussion of subsidized screening equilibrium situations (Spence 1977).

bution of net earnings. The principal difference from the two previous cases, however, is that gross earnings for group 2 and thus for society are no longer the same as in a FICE but are now larger because the overinvestment in education is producing higher output.

Distributional implications
The models described in this section illustrate several important points. First, they point out the important role of the information available to employers in determining job access and wage differentials. Compared to an 'uninformed' market solution without screening, a screening equilibrium increases inequality in the distribution of earnings. Compared to a full-information competitive equilibrium, net earnings in a screening equilibrium are likely to be more equally distributed as a result of the signalling costs incurred by the higher-ability groups. In similar vein, Reder (1968) has noted that if there is general consensus that one worker is more productive than another, employers will bid up the former's wages in comparison to the latter's; whereas if there is little or no consensus as to the ranking of workers there will be relatively small differences between workers' wages.

Secondly, the models indicate the important role of firms' production processes and signalling costs in determining group wage differentials (for example, between $\hat{e}_1$ and e^*). In particular, if firms screen on the basis of educational attainment and if the costs of education for some young workers are lower than for others because of more ready access to capital markets or family funds for education purposes, the effect can be to screen out some higher-ability workers and admit some less able ones to higher-paying jobs and occupations. Such a screen may thus be far from perfect. If markets are perfectly competitive, it was seen above that a screen such as education can identify higher-ability workers in a screening equilibrium. Thus the degree to which a screen such as education is an imperfect identifying device depends in part upon the degree of market imperfection. The distributional costs of market imperfections therefore extend well beyond the simple concepts of monopoly and monopsony gains discussed in standard texts. Indeed, screening and credential requirements are often used to restrict entrance to jobs that may determine a life-long career, so that the long-run effects of such behaviour may be substantial.

Thirdly, in this framework the private returns to education are not completely related to productivity gains as they are in the human capital framework. They may include some return to the identification of members of one labour group from another. Finally, it should be clear that screening need not be done only on the basis of education. It can also be based on sex, race, ethnic background, language, and personality traits. This brings us to the theory of discrimination in general.

LABOUR MARKET DISCRIMINATION

So far we have seen that earnings differences can arise from labour suppliers' (life-cycle) choices and from firms' labour investment and screening behaviour in response to workers' productivity differences. We now examine how earnings differences can arise between equally productive members of different groups. The work on labour market discrimination has yielded a number of models of discriminatory behaviour that emphasize different aspects of the process, but no single theory is generally accepted. Consequently, I shall highlight several principal contributions but leave broader reviews to several recent surveys of the literature (Marshall, 1974; and Welch, 1975). We begin with the taste-based theories of 'pure discrimination' by Becker and Arrow, and then to place them in perspective we consider several alternatives, including 'statistical discrimination.'

Neoclassical models of pure discrimination

The starting point of modern theories of labour market discrimination is the work of Becker (1957), in which discrimination is viewed as a result of people's tastes. Individuals are said to have a 'taste for discrimination' if they are willing to pay or to forgo income so as not to be associated with some group.[4] At the market level, discrimination is manifested in terms of a market discrimination coefficient,

$$D = (w_W - w_B)/w_B,$$

where w_B is the equilibrium wage rate of those disciminated against and w_W for those not discriminated against. Becker's principal contribution lay in identifying the main factors on which D would depend. More recently, his analysis has been formalized in a general equilibrium framework by Arrow (1972a, 1974).

To focus solely on the direct effects of discrimination, Arrow abstracts from differences in productivities between groups of workers and assumes

---

4 This may be a result of aversion to being associated with members of another group, of envy or malice toward the other group (Alexis 1974), or of status-consciousness in which discriminators object to certain groups of workers because they feel they would lower the job-status of the work done by the former (Marshall 1974).

them to be perfect substitutes in production. In accordance with the general neoclassical framework, factors are assumed to be fully employed in a world of competitive markets. In the simplest case, that of employer discrimination, Arrow assumes that employers have a subjective tradeoff between profits π and the relative mix of their work force, so that they maximize a utility function $U(\pi, B/W)$ where the firm's profits in the short run are given by

$$\pi = f(B + W) - w_B \cdot B - w_W \cdot W,$$

where $f(\cdot)$ is the firm's production function and B and W are the firm's employment levels of the discriminated and preferred groups. Optimally, then, each firm will choose its employment levels so that the workers' marginal productivities are just equal to their 'net price' to the employer

$$MP_B = w_B + d_B,$$

$$MP_W = w_W + d_W,$$

where the second terms are the employer's discrimination coefficients with $d_B > 0$ and $d_W \leq 0$ indicating that the employer acts as if the B wage were larger than w_B by the amount d_B and the W wage less than w_W by the amount d_W. But with B and W workers acting as perfect substitutes in production, their marginal products must be equal, so that in equilibrium the market wages are

$$w_W - w_B = d_B - d_W > 0,$$

and a discriminatory wage differential arises with W workers paid above their marginal product and B workers paid below it:

Under this model, it is clear that [B] workers incur a definite loss, as compared with the competitive level in the absence of discrimination. On the other hand, [W] workers are likely gainers relative to the nondiscriminatory level. It can be shown that aggregate output is unaffected if all employers discriminate equally; otherwise there may be some efficiency loss in total output. (Arrow, 1972a, 87).

Discrimination can also arise with coworkers. Consider the case of complementary factors where foremen F dislike working with members of the discriminated group and choose among jobs on the basis of B/W as well as wages. In this case the equilibrium wage for foremen will be a relation,

$$w_F = w_F\,(W/L),$$

where the total number of floor workers, $L = B + W$. The lower the ratio W/L, the more the foremen must be paid to compensate for their discriminatory tastes. Even if the employers have no such tastes for discrimination and simply seek to maximize profits, discriminatory wage differentials will again arise

since an increase in W decreases the wages and therefore the cost of F, while an increase in B increases the cost of F. Hence, a W worker is worth more than his marginal product, while a B worker is worth less, exactly as in the case of employer discrimination. Further, the extent of the premiums over or deficits from marginal product depends only on the ratio of W to B ... W workers are paid more than their marginal product, B workers less. If all firms wind up with the same levels of W and B, then the results are entirely parallel to those for employer discrimination: production remains efficient, and the entire incidence of the foremen's discrimination falls negatively on the B workers and positively to an equal extent on the W workers. (Ibid., 11)

The actual extent of the wage differential between B and W workers is shown to be

$$(w_W - w_B)/\text{MP}_L = -\ w'_F/w_F \cdot S_F/S_L,$$

where w'_F/w_F is the proportional rate of change of the foremen's demanded wage rate with respect to W/L, S_F and S_L are total payments to foremen and floor workers respectively, and MP_L is the latter's wage level in the absence of discrimination. The relative wage differential thus depends on the strength of the foremen's discriminatory tastes and on the importance of foremen's incomes as a component of the firm's factor payments. The analytics of this solution, however, are quite independent of the discriminatory roles of foremen and labourers. The floor workers may in fact be represented by F and different types of foremen by B and W, in which case one would expect fairly substantial differences in remuneration between, say, white and black supervisors or male and female managers.

In summary, then, it is seen that the taste-based neoclassical theories of Becker and Arrow can yield two short-run explanations for the existence of wage differentials between perfect substitutes in production – employers' tastes for discrimination and the discriminatory tastes of complementary workers. Wage discrimination by workers against other workers who are perfect substitutes for them can be shown to result only in segregation of the workers and not wage differentials in a competitive market. These results, however, have been obtained in a rather restrictive framework, and it would be useful to evaluate them in some perspective.[5]

Critique of the models and alternative approaches
The above models are only short-run. Yet market discrimination should be analysed as a long-run phenomenon. The principle of competition works to eliminate discriminatory wage differentials in the long run as firms that act with little or no discrimination expand and drive the discriminating firms out of business. To attenuate this effect, recourse is had to manpower training and adjustment costs and to market imperfections in a rather makeshift fashion. The models are thus not entirely convincing as explanations of observed long-run phenomena.

Secondly, the above analysis does not take account of the role of various institutions such as labour unions and government in affecting discrimination. Labour unions are considered in the next chapter, but it may be noted here that historically there has been a substantial difference in the treatment of blacks, for example, between industrial unions and craft unions in the United States. In general, unions tend to equalize wages across skill categories among their members but at the same time to create union–non-union wage differentials. Consequently, the effects of unions on the average relative wages of a discriminated group will depend on the effectiveness of unions in creating such union–non-union differentials and the extent to which the members of this group are admitted to unions. On balance, Ashenfelter (1972) concludes from empirical analysis that

in 1967 the ratio of black to white male wages might have been 4 percent higher in the industrial union sector and 5 percent lower in the craft union sector than they would have been in the absence of all unionism. The average of these two effects is positive, however, so that the ratio of black to white male wages may have been some 3.4 percent higher in 1967 than it would have been in the absence of unionism. Finally, combining the effect of the presence of unionism on the wages of black males relative to white males with its effect on the wages of black females relative to white females suggests that the ratio of the wages of all black workers relative to all white workers might have been 1.7 percent higher in 1967 than it would have been in the absence of unionism. (Ibid., 463)

5 See, for example, the recent critiques by Stiglitz (1974), Welch (1975), Marshall (1974), and Cain (1976).

More generally, though, economic discrimination may not be restricted to the labour market; it may take various non-market forms as well. As emphasized by Welch (1973), there may be discrimination in the government provision of education between groups such as blacks and whites. This leaves members of the discriminated group less well prepared to compete for jobs than the better-educated group and allows employers to practice less overt forms of discrimination by using educational requirements as a screening device in deciding on what workers to hire for which jobs. It also lowers the resulting rate of return that a victim of discrimination can earn on his schooling investment and thus (according to the human capital model) leads him to spend a shorter time in formal education than his more privileged colleagues, to lower his lifetime earnings profile, and to restrict the occupational choices available to himself.

Thirdly, employer discrimination need not be attributed to discriminatory tastes at all but can be ascribed to the employers' 'perceptions of reality' in the presence of imperfect and costly information on workers' true abilities. Not knowing the true productivity of a worker, the employer may use proxy information such as sex, race, ethnic background, native language, or age, which is much more cheaply available as an initial screening device, and may discriminate on the basis of these characteristics if he believes them to indicate productivity. Arrow (1972a) and Phelps (1972) have formalized these ideas in a 'statistical theory of discrimination.' Suppose, for example, that there are two kinds of complementary labour, skilled and unskilled, but only some workers are qualified for skilled positions. The true productivity of any worker is unknown at first to the employer and can only be determined after some personnel evaluation and investment costs are incurred. The employer does, however, have a prior opinion of the distributions of the different types of workers. If a worker is found to be unskilled, he is paid at the marginal product of unskilled labour, and the employer gains nothing on his personnel investment. If the worker is indeed found to be skilled he is paid a wage w somewhat less than the marginal product of skilled workers MP_S, so that the employer can earn a return on his personnel investment costs. The expected return on W workers then is $(MP_S - w_W)\, p_W$, where p_W is the employer's subjective probability that a worker will indeed be qualified, and the expected return for B workers is correspondingly $(MP_S - w_B)\, p_B$. For these returns to be the same across the two groups, it follows that in equilibrium

$$w_W = qw_B + (1 - q)\, MP_S,$$

where $q = p_B/p_W$. Thus if the employer believes $p_B < p_W$ or $q < 1$, the resulting skilled wage of W workers will exceed the skilled wage of B workers. The model can thus be viewed in terms of the specific human capital framework discussed earlier. Each individual of a group is treated according to the perceived average for the group.

A fourth point is that the simple neoclassical models of discrimination fail to address adequately the problem of job or occupational segregation as an integral part of discriminatory behaviour. With imperfect labour markets, discrimination may take the form not of wage differences for the same job, but of exclusion from any (higher-status) occupations. According to Bergmann (1971), this unequal access to such jobs tends to crowd the members of a group that is discriminated against, such as women, into a limited number of occupations, thereby reducing their marginal productivity and corresponding wages. Conversely, the reduced supply of workers to the excluded jobs or occupations raises the marginal productivity and wages of the non-discriminated workers there. The size of this effect clearly depends on the relative number of qualified candidates that have been excluded from such occupations. Indeed, if some of the latter obtain employment in a limited-access job, there may also be paid less than a non-discriminated worker because the opportunity wage they could earn elsewhere (in the crowded sector) would be less. According to this form of discrimination, then, the workers in the excluded occupations gain at the expense of the workers in the crowded sector. More generally, one would expect the degree of segregation within an occupation to vary simultaneously along with the wage differential in response to the degree of discrimination in the occupation, while both are manifestations of the same phenomenon.

This analysis shows the need of some detailed study of the various restrictions on occupational and job choice. What are the institutional barriers present, and to what extent are credentials and licensing actually used as discriminatory devices to restrict supplies and increase earnings in the restricted occupations or jobs? Indeed, to what extent does the government itself have a role in this process? The above analysis also suggests that the labour market may to some extent be viewed as segmented into a number of relatively non-competing groups of jobs or occupations between which mobility may be low.[6] Clearly, discrimination in its various forms and screening can both be used to restrict workers' job choices between such

6 Substantial discussion has in fact recently appeared in the literature under such headings as dual and segmented labour markets. See, for example, Doeringer and Piore (1971) and Cain (1976).

groups, and consequently both affect earnings differentials. Job access and earnings, however, are also very much affected by traditional hiring and promotion policies of firms and by the degree to which there are separate labour markets and definite promotion tracks in the firm.

INTERNAL LABOUR MARKETS AND HIERARCHY MODELS

Internal labour markets

An 'internal labour market' in a firm arises when workers are hired at only a few points of entry well down in the hierarchy of job positions, and the jobs above these are then filled by promotions of workers along lines of career development. Thus, within the firm, many jobs are protected from close outside competition, and wage differentials within the firm do not rigidly reflect external competitive forces, which serve rather to establish upper and lower bounds on the wage rate for different job positions (Doeringer and Piore, 1971).

Internal labour markets develop within a hierarchical organization essentially to capture the returns to firm-specific training that employees obtain on the job. The typical hierarchical system is built up of fixed job slots in which earnings are related to job assignment. If the jobs are characterized by specific training, experienced employees acquire a comparative advantage in performing these jobs and hence are not strictly competitive with other prospective employees outside the firm. This fact induces firms to retain employees (e.g. by seniority preference and pension benefit), reduce labour turnover, and promote from within.

At the same time, however, this 'first-mover advantage' introduces a bilateral bargaining problem for the firm, since employees with experience are the monopoly sellers of their specific training. Thus there is an incentive for firms with jobs in which workers acquire firm-specific human capital to avoid market-like negotiations with labour sellers and thereby capture a greater share of rents to specific training (while also avoiding negotiation costs). Harris, Wachter, and Williamson (1975) argue that the desire to avoid bargaining problems induces firms to establish a hierarchical manpower structure of fixed job slots that internalizes labour markets and eliminates the need for recontracting with the labour force. In such a hierarchy, where earnings are tied to job classification, employees have little opportunity to exert their monopoly power in salary negotiations since the salary for any particular job is more or less fixed. On the other hand individual incentives to act in the firm's interests are retained, since job performance is a key determinant of the rate of promotion to higher paying jobs.

Earnings distributions and hierarchies

The distributional implications of a hierarchical manpower organization depend on two sets of factors: the number of employees in consecutive levels of the hierarchy, and the earnings in consecutive levels of the hierarchy. Consider, for example, a hierarchy of R levels, indexed by $r = 1, ..., R$, with n_r employees in each level, and in which employees of the rth level earn Y_r per period. This distribution of earnings within the hierarchy will be more skewed the greater the number of supervisees per supervisor (what may be called the employment structure or degree of control) $- n_r/n_{r+1}$. Similarly, the distribution of earnings within the hierarchy will be more skewed the greater the ratio of supervisors' salaries to those of their supervisees (what may be called the salary structure) $- Y_{r+1}/Y_r$. We now turn to a discussion of some of the determinants of the earnings structure of a hierarchy. The ratio n_r/n_{r+1} will be referred to as α_r and the ratio Y_{r+1}/Y_r as β_r.

Lydall (1968) has worked out the distributional characteristics of a hierarchy characterized by two rules: a fixed α_r for all r, and a fixed $\beta_r > 1$ for all r. These rules give rise to an earnings distribution that is approximately Pareto, similar to the upper tail of typical income distributions. However, this approach is rather mechanical and does not explain how assumed rules evolve as the consequence of underlying economic behaviour.

A more satisfactory model of hierarchical earnings has recently been advanced by Beckmann (1975). Applicants are assumed to accept employment with the firm if the expected utility of employment exceeds that available from other employment. In particular, prospective employees consider only the utility of the earnings they expect to receive $U(Y_r)$ once they reach their highest level in the hierarchy, and accept employment if this exceeds a given market certainty-equivalent wage. The firm in turn minimizes total labour costs given the n_r's and the above labour supply function of applicants. The resulting hierarchical earnings structure approximately satisfies the condition that

$$U'(Y_r)/U'(Y_{r+1}) = \alpha_r \cdot p_r, \tag{24}$$

where p_r is the applicant's subjective probability of promotion from the rth level to the $(r+1)$th level. Given well-behaved concave utility functions on the part of employees, the left-hand side of (24) increases with the ratio $\beta_r = Y_{r+1}/Y_r$. Thus, the ratio of the salaries in the $(r+1)$th and rth rank, β_r, is an increasing function of α_r and p_r. That is, if individuals believe that they have a high probability of promotion to higher ranks (a higher p_r for each r), they will be willing to work for relatively low salaries at the start of their career in expectation of higher salaries at the end of their career.

The model also admits of screening by self-selection. Hierarchical firms could offer contingent contracts specifying a base salary (for the first level of the hierarchy) and a set of Y_r's. Individuals who estimate that they have a relatively high probability of success would choose to work for firms with a lower base salary and a greater increment to salaries between grades of the hierarchy.

Elsewhere, Beckmann (1977) has examined the determination of the employment structure α_r given the salary structure β_r. Ideally, one should treat both α_r and β_r as simultaneously determined by the firm, but this method becomes analytically complex. Within the framework of the simpler analysis above, it has been found that the technical structure of a hierarchy and the promotional mobility within a hierarchy are of substantial importance in determining the distribution of earnings that results. In particular, the distribution of earnings will tend to be more highly skewed the greater the degree of individual mobility through the hierarchy and the greater the degree of control within the hierarchy.

CONCLUDING REMARKS

The principal conclusion that follows from the analysis above is that the behaviour and structure of firms or hierarchical organizations in general can have systematic effects on workers' earnings quite distinct from the individuals' behaviour discussed in the previous chapter. Supply-side theories of the distribution of income tell only part, although admittedly a very important part, of the story. However, the desire of firms to minimize costs, particularly in the presence of very imperfect information on employees' productivity, can have marked effects on access to various jobs and occupations and on the wage rates that are paid. Clearly, the demand and supply sides must be linked in the market.

4
Distributional aggregation

INTRODUCTION

Chapter 2 examined in some detail the supply of factors of production by individuals and households in a life-cycle framework with particular emphasis on the age-income trajectories generated by the life-cycle models. Chapter 3 then turned to the demand-side of the labour market and considered some of the implications for distributional inequality of employer behaviour in the market with particular emphasis on specific human-capital investment and cost-minimization in the face of imperfect information about employees' productive characteristics. In each case the discussion focused on one side of the factor market. We now try to bring the two sides together and look at some broad influences on the market for factor services and the aggregate cross-sectional distribution of income.

More specifically, this chapter examines three different but related problems: the matching up of demand- and supply-side factors in the labour market, the importance of cohort effects in the total distribution, and the role of the age structure of the population upon the aggregate distribution. Accordingly, the following two sections examine equilibrium of demand and supply in the labour market, first in a competitive framework and then in recognition of institutional constraints such as labour unions. The fourth section turns to the relation between age-income cross-sections and longitudinal life-cycle income trajectories. The fifth section considers the generation of an over-all distribution from age-income cross-sections. Concluding remarks are presented in a final section.

MATCHING UP DEMAND AND SUPPLY IN THE LABOUR MARKET

In traditional microanalysis, economics offers theories of the supply of factors by individuals and households on the one hand, theories of the demand for such factors by firms and producers on the other hand, and (except where factor prices are determined by legislation or collective bargaining) theories of equilibrium behaviour linking the two at the market level. With the above exceptions, it is the interaction of demand- and supply-side factors at the market level that determines the prices paid and received for different factors and the quantities of those factors that are employed. Clearly, all these considerations affect the incomes that factor owners receive. While these remarks may appear elementary, they should serve to indicate that the standard micro theories of distribution such as life-cycle savings, labour supply, and human capital investment are essentially supply-side analyses and not in themselves complete theories. They take the array of factor prices as given to individuals by the market. But as Tinbergen (1959) has pointed out, they incorporate only the availability of productive capacity and not the degree to which the economy demands this capacity. In Chapter 3 on the other hand firms and producers are assumed to provide a demand for labour. Together with a model of market behaviour, supply and demand jointly determine market wages and employment in various occupations, industries, and skill categories. Since the general topic of market wage determination goes beyond the focus of the present study and is covered in standard labour economics texts (for example, Fleisher, 1970; Ostry and Zaidi, 1972; and Rees, 1973), it will not be dealt with here. I wish simply to place in perspective the general blocks of theories discussed in the two preceding chapters.

Certainly the most important factor market from the point of view of inequality in the personal income distribution is the labour market. Yet the theories of labour demand and supply reviewed in the preceding chapters have been fairly cavalier about exactly what they mean by demand for and supply of a factor called labour. On one hand firms offer jobs with certain characteristics; on the other hand workers offer various talents to the market. Exactly how then are job characteristics and worker talents matched up in the labour market? Tinbergen (1959) suggested that labour be regarded as a composite commodity and that the wage rate be regarded as a hedonic price index defined over a set of relevant attributes such as intelligence and the ability to work with others.

More recently, this approach has been extended by Rosen (1974, 1978) and Sattinger (1975) to make clear the process of co-determination of the characteristics of a job, the allocation of individuals to jobs within the production process, and the corresponding wage rates across individuals. According to this approach, the basic unit of analysis is the 'task.' A worker's abilities or talents are expressed in terms of the number of specific tasks that he can perform in a given time. These talents can be augmented in a life-cycle framework by human capital investment and work effort, and workers can be ranked in terms of their comparative advantage or productivity relative to certain tasks. On the other hand firms bundle productive tasks into job assignments and occupations to maximize output and then assign workers to particular job slots on the basis of their comparative advantage.

Together, the demand for and supply of task performance determine a hedonic wage function that associates a wage rate with each labour supplier and with each job. An individual and a firm trade when the firm chooses to demand the same set of characteristics or task-performance levels that the individual chooses to supply at a given hedonic wage. At any moment the prevailing hedonic wage function is derived from the interaction of market demand and available supply. In the short run the important influence on the market wage structure is demand, as many of the attributes that an individual offers to the market are in fixed supply. The market wage function influences investment decisions and earnings expectations of individuals and thereby the nature of supply in future periods.

In contrast to the view of the labour market as a set of largely noncompeting groups, the hedonic framework emphasizes the substitutability between groups of workers with different characteristics. The task requirements of jobs are not exogenously fixed but are endogenous, along with relative rates of remuneration. In general, then, the hedonic framework provides an extension of the model of competitive market behaviour for very non-homogeneous commodities such as labour.

INSTITUTIONAL RESTRICTIONS IN THE LABOUR MARKET:
LABOUR UNIONS

While the competitive framework can be useful for analysing labour market behaviour, as it is for other sectors of the economy, the labour market is also characterized by numerous imperfections, which in this case are likely to be very significant. A few large employers face large unions over negotiated wage settlements. A complex tax system discriminates between different types of incomes and earning activities. Labour is a very nonhomogeneous factor, and labour productivity is often difficult to measure. In comparison with capital markets, employment and wage information is very imperfect, and search costs are high. Minimum wage laws and wage-price controls restrict market behaviour and remuneration rates. Seniority and discrimination, legislated job conditions, licensing, and union-employer restrictions on access to particular jobs or occupations place further constraints on the free functioning of the market. To examine each of these imperfections would take several studies. To illustrate some of the considerations involved, I look at one form of labour market institutional restriction, labour unions, and their effects on market wage rates and returns to labour. To distinguish the discussion from the standard textbook treatment, I shall follow the general equilibrium approach of Johnson and Mieszkowski (1970).[1]

Unions of course have many objectives and their influence extends from working conditions to rates of advancement and overtime bonuses (Rees, 1973). We look here only at their effect on wage and employment. Extending the work of Lewis (1963) for the United States, Johnson and Mieszkowski set up a two-sector (unionized and non-union), two-factor (labour and capital), general equilibrium model to analyse the relative wage effects of unionization that occurs in one sector of an economy. In particular, unionization is represented by introducing a proportional differential of wages in the unionized sector over those in the non-unionized sector.

This differential between wages in the two sectors of the economy introduces both output and factor substitution effects that have to be taken into account. First, the wage differential introduces a production inefficiency, so that total output in the economy is less than in the absence of unionization, total income is less, and the demand for output of the unionized sector will, under normal conditions, be less too. The higher costs of production in the unionized sector also result in a higher output price, further restricting demand for the product of this sector. The public's consumption tastes between products of the two sectors thus have an effect on the final gains and losses by the different factors in the two sectors. Secondly, the higher cost of labour in the unionized sector induces firms to shift away from labour and toward heavier use of capital, thereby releasing labour to the non-unionized sector and attracting capital from that sector. The increased supply of labour to the non-unionized sector lowers the non-unionized wage there, and the bidding away of capital raises the return to capital there:

unionization is in effect a tax on the labor of the unionized industry and therefore has the effect of shifting demand away from that industry. If such a tax is imposed on a capital-intensive industry, the result is a fall in the demand for and price of the services of capital and an increase in the demand for labor, from which both sectors of the labor force may gain. If the unionized industry is labor-intensive, the result is

1 For more extensive discussions of this general area, see also Johnson (1973), Jones (1971), and Magee (1973).

a rise in the demand for capital and a fall in the demand for labor, from which both sectors of the labor force may lose. (Johnson and Mieszkowski, 1970, 547)

Assuming that the unionized sector is labour-intensive, and accepting Lewis's (1963) results that unions raise money wages by 10 to 15 per cent relative to non-union wages, Johnson and Mieszkowski estimate roughly that in the United States 'most, if not all, of the gains of union labor are made at the expense of non-unionized workers, and not at the expense of earnings on capital ... and in large measure this distribution of gain and loss occurs because decreases in the level of employment in the union sector depress wages in the nonunion sector' (Johnson and Mieszkowski, 1970, 560). Thus unionization of only part of the economy benefits only part of labour, chiefly at the expense of the rest of labour. Indeed, the benefit within the unionized sector may also be very unevenly distributed, with labourers gaining relatively more than operatives (Boskin, 1972) and blacks gaining different amounts than whites (Ashenfelter, 1974).

Diewert (1974) disaggregates Johnson and Mieszkowski's analysis to a four-factor economy with some rough Canadian estimates. The factors now consist of unionized blue-collar labour, non-unionized blue-collar labour, white-collar workers, and capital. Unions are viewed as inducing a reduction in union blue-collar employment in the unionized sector, and the analysis attempts to determine the unions' equilibrium wage-employment tradeoff (i.e. the percentage change in the union wage and real income resulting from a marginal employment restriction in the unionized sector). Using sectoral employment and output data for Canada in 1961 and several different assumptions about factor substitutability in production and consumers' preferences for the outputs of the two sectors, Diewert solves the model for full general equilibrium responses to the union input restriction. Two general findings result. First,

if elasticities of substitution both in production and consumption are small, the union can increase its nominal wage tremendously while suffering only a small loss in employment. Due to higher prices, the union's increased nominal wages get deflated somewhat to yield a somewhat smaller increase in real income for union members who remain employed ... Capitalists *invariably* bear at least a part of the 'incidence of collective bargaining' ... while white collar workers and blue collar workers *generally* lose in terms of real income. (Diewert, 1974, 488).

Secondly, Diewert remarks upon 'the relatively large size of the various elasticities, that is, a relatively small barrier to entry in the union sector generates relatively large changes in prices, outputs, factor rewards, and real incomes' (Ibid). For example, with high substitutability in both production and consumption, a 1 per cent decrease in union blue collar employment is estimated to yield a 7.9 per cent increase in unionized workers' real income, while with low substitutability in both cases the estimated increase is 37.1 per cent. Certainly, such results are based on strong assumptions and some rather crude calculations. But they convey the flavour of fairly recent general equilibrium analyses of factor market distortions and suggest the need for a more complete set of social accounts in order to estimate and draw conclusions from the theoretical models.

AGE-INCOME CROSS-SECTIONS AND COHORT EFFECTS

How does an income distribution observed from standard cross sectional data sources relate to the longitudinal income trajectories generated by the life-cycle models of Chapter 2? Rates of payments to factors of production are assumed determined in the market, as discussed in the preceding sections, and we shall now study some of the implications of combining that discussion with the life-cycle material of Chapter 2. To simplify for the moment, I abstract from all differences between individuals, so that individuals of a particular cohort are assumed to have identical patterns of earnings, saving, wealth accumulation, labour supply, and so on over the life cycle. The only source of variation in income between individuals is that, at any given time, different persons are at different stages of their life cycle. This will allow us to isolate theoretically the relationship between typical age-income trajectories and corresponding age-income cross-sections, and then reintroduce differences in income within cohorts to account for the pattern of variation in inequality across age groups in the population.

Inequality and the lifetime income trajectory
How life-cycle effects produce inequalities in income can be illustrated simply with the aid of some stylized diagrams. The theoretical discussion of Chapter 2 suggests that the typical individual will enter the labour market with certain raw labour skills that incorporate inherited ability and skills obtained through education before full-time participation in the labour force. The level of wages at this stage will depend on the amount and quality of human capital, expectations of career advancement and job training, the technological characteristics of production, market structure, and output demand. From the time of entry into the labour market, incomes will rise as a result of increased productivity due to on-the-job training, techno-

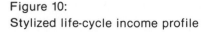

Figure 10:
Stylized life-cycle income profile

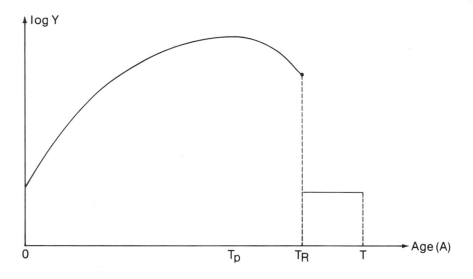

logical change over the worker's lifetime, and further educational investments, possibly increased work effort, and increased capital income from
cumulated savings. Income will then peak at or some time before retirement and fall to a substantially lower level during the retirement period.
Such a pattern is illustrated in Figure 10, where for convenience it is
assumed that (the log of) income is a concave function $g(A)$ of age A from
economic age zero to time of retirement T_R and then drops to a constant
amount during retirement until death at age T. If all individuals are identical in the sense that they follow the same pattern of lifetime income,
incomes will still be distributed unequally, since at any time the population
will be spread over different points along this profile.

A simple set of predictions is obtained by assuming also that no cohort
effects exist, so that the lifetime income trajectories are the same for all
cohorts, and the population is stable and constant, so that individuals are
uniformly distributed across all ages. In this case, the distribution of income
will depend solely on the shape of the income profile in Figure 10. For
example, if members of the labour force have higher incomes than retired
workers, the extent of inequality will depend on the vertical difference

Figure 11:
Longitudinal profile and two income cross-sections

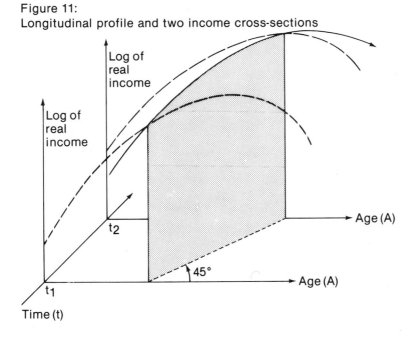

between the two income segments. Inequality will also increase with the steepness of the $g(A)$ curve as life-cycle income differences become more marked. An increase in life expectancy T for a given time of retirement will increase inequality by lengthening the period over which lowest income is received. A decrease in the length of working life T_R, however, has mixed effects, lengthening the period of (low) retirement income but also cutting off some upper-income receipts around the peak of the income profile.

Figure 11 shows the relationship between the longitudinal income profile and an age-income cross-section. The age-income cross-sections are essentially slices across incomes in the population taken at particular moments, while the shaded profile at 45° to the age and time axes is the lifetime income trajectory or longitudinal profile one would actually follow through time. Where there are no cohort effects, the longitudinal profiles are all the same shape, as are all the cross-sectional age-income slices. Time as such has no separate effect upon incomes.

The longitudinal income paths can be viewed as geometrically constructed from two components parallel to the age and time axes: the dashed age-income cross-section, which illustrates income differences associated with different productivities and labour market experiences between age groups in the population at a given period in time; and shifts (usually upward) in the cross-section profile parallel to the time axis, which show age-specific changes in productivities, rates of remuneration, and labour market opportunities. Longitudinal income experience thus reflects static cross-sectional income differences (an age effect) as well as dynamic changes in these differences over time (a time effect). Different cohorts pass through the distribution in different periods and thus at any given age benefit differently, resulting in what may be called cohort effects. These incorporate both general productivity gains, which can affect more or less all groups uniformly, and changing discrimination, screening, and other labour market practices, which affect different groups quite unequally.

Cohort effects and age-income cross-sections
Consider now the consequences of relaxing the simplifying assumption of no cohort effects on the lifetime income profiles for different cohorts. Suppose instead that the incomes of the working population all increase by a constant percentage of δ a year and retirement incomes are tied by a constant proportionality factor $0 < c < 1$ to total income at the time of retirement t_R, but do not increase beyond that. Incomes are thus now represented by

$$\log Y(A,t) = g(A) + \delta t, \quad \text{for } 0 \leq A \leq T_R, \quad t \leq t_R,$$

and

$$\log Y(A,t) = \log c + \log Y(T_R, t_R), \quad \text{for } A > T_R.$$

Increases in real income can be thought of as taking the form of steady technological progress that benefits everyone in the working population by a uniform proportional amount per year. Figure 12 shows how this affects the longitudinal income profiles and age-income cross-sections.

The longitudinal income trajectory now slopes upwards more steeply than before, because of the time or cohort effect, and peaks later, so that absolute income differences along the profile are now larger. The cross-sectional profiles up until retirement age, however, retain their shape but now shift up a constant δ per cent a year. Once retirement is reached incomes no longer rise. Since, in the cross-section, older persons to the right of T_R reached retirement before younger ones, their retirement incomes are correspondingly lower. Thus it can be seen that when a cohort

Figure 12:
Longitudinal income profile and age-income cross-section with
technological cohort adjustment

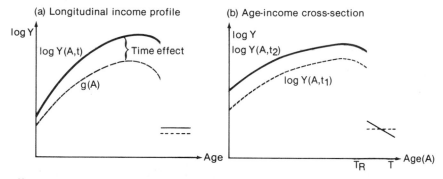

(a) Longitudinal income profile

(b) Age-income cross-section

effect in the form of constant technological change occurs, the age-income
cross-section no longer has the same shape as the age-income trajectory.
The cross-section profile is now flatter than the longitudinal trajectory, and
its retirement segment has a downward slope. The effect of the cohort
adjustment on the age-income cross-section is thus to introduce inequality
into the distribution of retirement incomes, to increase the absolute dollar
gap between pre-retirement and post-retirement incomes, and to increase
absolute inequality over time.

A different situation occurs when the cohort effect takes the form of a
pure vintage effect, where the incomes of all the members of a cohort are
proportionally greater by a constant amount δ than the incomes of the
previous cohort. The cohort effect is embodied immediately in each new
vintage of worker, but does not have any effect upon his longitudinal
income gradient. The effect on the age-income cross-sections is to reduce
their slopes, flattening out the upward-sloping segment, steepening any
downward-sloping segment, and again inducing a negative slope over the
retirement segment. The influence of such a vintage effect on income
inequality is mixed. The lowest-income workers (i.e. the youngest) receive
the greatest benefits, but income inequality is again introduced into the
distribution of the retired population. In general, such vintage effects
benefit the young workers more than the older members of the population,
particularly the retired.

Moss (1978, 124) found for United States men over the period 1947–72
'that the difference between the rate of growth in income of the average
cohort and that of the cross-section is equal to about 3 percent per year for

the prime ages. This is approximately equal to the rate of productivity growth in the economy in the 1947–72 period.' For the older group aged 55 and over, however, the difference in growth rates was close to 2 per cent. Consequently, average longitudinal income profiles for prime age men resembled cross-sectional profiles blown up by a constant productivity growth factor with a lower adjustment factor for older and retired workers, a situation roughly similar to the first one discussed above. This should not be taken as the case for any particular year or group of individuals in the economy. To find out information such as this for Canada would require longitudinal income files that are not available.

So far, income inequality within age groups has been assumed away. But as we have seen, income differences within age groups can occur both because of differences in individuals' tastes and preferences in work effort, consumption, and various non-pecuniary benefits and because of differences in resources and endowments and differential access to capital markets. Consequently, for each age group or cohort there is in fact a whole distribution of incomes, which for convenience we shall treat as being characterized by a mean and a measure of inequality. The age-income cross-section can thus be thought of as representing the cross-sectional profile of mean incomes over age groups in the population. At the same time the human capital model implies that earnings differentials are expected first to narrow with age until an overtaking period is reached and then widen in middle and later age. Capital income differences are usually small in young age groups, but they widen markedly with age. Consequently, while the age–mean income cross-section would be expected to have a general inverted-U shape, the pattern of within-cohort income inequality would be expected to have a J or U shape over age groups in the cross-section (Figure 13). These two relationships, the age–mean income cross-section and the age-inequality cross-section, together help generate a total income distribution in the following section.

DEMOGRAPHIC EFFECTS ON OVER-ALL DISTRIBUTION

The next thing to be considered in the construction of an over-all distribution of income is the consequence of relaxing the simplifying assumption of a uniform age distribution for the population and allowing for population growth. The distribution of income will now depend on the combined effects of two distributions: the distribution of income by age (as approximated by the age-income cross-sectional profile) and the age distribution of

Figure 13:
Illustrative age-inequality profile

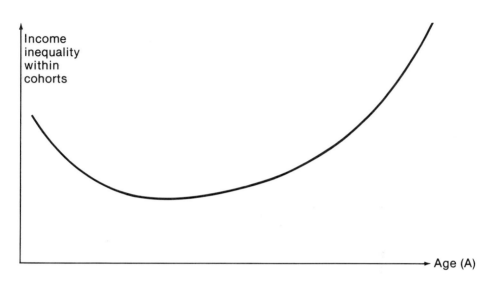

the population. A constant positive net rate of population growth distributes the population at any moment most heavily at the youngest age, with geometrically declining frequency up the age spectrum. Among the working population, this of course increases the relative representation of the lowest-income recipients and decreases that of the higher-income recipients, thus tending to skew the distribution to the right. But it also decreases the relative representation of the retired population, who are also assumed to be low-income recipients, thus having an offsetting skew effect.

Constructing an over-all income distribution
Figure 14 demonstrates a simple geometric technique that could be used to examine the combined effects of the distribution of income over the life cycle and the age distribution of the population. Again, we can simplify the discussion for the moment by assuming away any within-cohort income inequality and represent life-cycle income differences solely by an age-income cross-section at a particular moment. The curve *ABCD* in the northeastern quadrant of Figure 14 illustrates a hypothetical age-income cross-section (with the vertical axis now in level rather than log form). The curve *PP'* in

Figure 14:
Generating an income distribution from an age-income cross-section

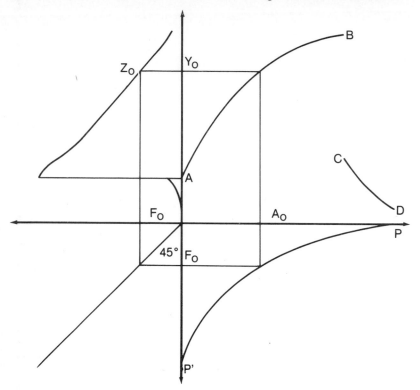

the southeastern quadrant represents the age distribution of the population and indicates for any given age interval the proportion of the population that lies in that interval. The ordinate on this curve is measured southwards from the age axis. The straight line in the southwestern quadrant is simply a 45° ray from the origin and maps each ordinate of the age distribution into the northwestern quadrant. If age-income differences are represented by the cross-sectional profile $ABCD$, the resulting over-all distribution of income with age distribution PP' is constructed in the northwestern quadrant by geometrically combining the two distributions. For instance, all persons of age A_0 have income Y_0 (from $ABCD$), while the frequency of persons of that age is F_0 (from PP'). Therefore, the frequency with which income Y_0 occurs in the population is F_0, and this gives the point Z_0 on the income distribution curve in the northwestern quadrant. We can repeat this process for all income levels, thereby mapping out the curve of the over-all distribution of income as viewed from the income axis looking west.

Clearly, variations in either of the underlying cross-sectional profile *ABCD* or age distribution of the population will change the shape of the over-all distribution of income; and the way in which a change in the life-cycle income trajectories (and thus the age-income cross-sections) affects the distribution will depend on the age structure of the population. The resulting distribution is skewed to the right, with people in late middle age and just before retirement at the top end of the distribution and low-income retired persons at the bottom end. The steeper the age-income cross-section over its rising portion, the further up the final distribution will extend and the greater will be the resulting degree of over-all inequality.

Figure 14 represents a rather stylized situation. The tail at the upper end of the distribution does not extend very far, suggesting that life-cycle considerations do not account very well for the typical long right-hand upper tail; and the lower portion of the distribution appears to be fairly heavily bunched around its mode, essentially reflecting the large number of young workers in the population. Suppose, though, that we again introduce within-cohort income inequality. At the upper end of the distribution, among workers in late middle age, income inequality is expected to be fairly large, thus extending the upper-income tail of the distribution. Among very young workers, before the 'overtaking' period of their incomes, inequality is again expected to be fairly large, thus diffusing the rather sharp peak of the distribution around its mode and extending the lower tail of the distribution as well. In addition, the discussion so far has ignored transfer income in its emphasis on the determination of the distribution of factor or primary income. However, if transfers are received largely by (low-income) retirees and those with only a weak attachment to the labour force, their inclusion in the analysis will tend to raise the lower end of the distribution and thus reduce over-all income inequality. In summary, then, reasonably shaped income distributions can indeed be generated from an underlying basis of the life-cycle relationships.

Some distributional effects of demographic change
Now consider how the relationships in Figure 14 can be used to analyse some effects of demographic changes on the over-all distribution of income. Two of the most significant modern demographic changes in Canada have

Figure 15:
Age distribution of the population

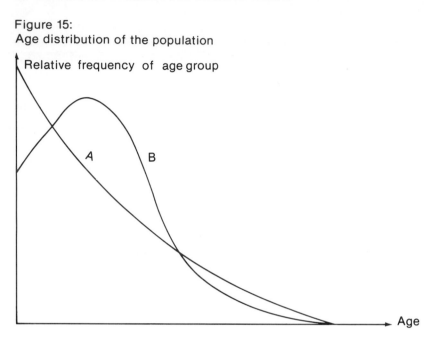

been the baby boom after the Second World War, and more recently a substantial decline in the birth rate. Consider a flat or uniform age distribution for all but the aged population, a situation characteristic of countries with a fairly low population growth rate (e.g. Sweden). The resulting income distribution will also be flat except for the income overlap between young and old individuals in Figure 14 and any within-cohort inequality differences across ages. The introduction now of a sudden faster birth rate so that the age distribution of the population acquires a steep slope at its young end skews the distribution more heavily, because a larger proportion of the population consists of young workers with low incomes in the region of the mode; over-all income inequality is generally increased by the relative increase, at one end of the distribution, in workers who have relatively large within-age-group inequality.

As the bulge of workers in the young cohort progresses through the age distribution and is followed by a marked drop in birth rates, the age distribution may gradually change in shape from curve A to B in Figure 15. When these two curves are mapped through the age-income cross section in Figure 14, it can be seen that the shift in the peak of the age distribution corresponding to the baby boom reaching young middle age lowers the skewness of the over-all income distribution, shifts up the mode of the distribution towards the mean, and thus reduces the over-all degree of inequality in the distribution. Thus important demographic changes can have marked and systematic effects on the structure of income inequality in the population.

Major demographic changes may also affect the distribution of income indirectly by cohort effects on the underlying age-income trajectories. A rapid inflow of young workers may lower the returns to education for their cohort and those immediately following, resulting in lower age-income trajectories than otherwise for those groups. This could lower the bottom end of the age-income cross-section and thus temporarily increase the degree of inequality slightly. But the demographic shifts can also have fairly substantial effects on asset values, particularly the market values of houses. As young workers form families they drive up the price of family houses. Capital gains on asset holdings, whether realized or not, are included in the returns to assets and thus represent an increase in income broadly defined. To the extent that the incidence of home ownership generally increases with age until retirement, the increasing portion of the age-income cross-section may be temporarily steepened by the initial surge of family formation among young workers. As has been already seen, such a steepening of the cross-sectional profile stretches out the income distribution and further raises the degree of income inequality in the distribution of broadly defined income. In summary, then, demographic effects and associated cohort effects can have fairly marked influences on the structure of income inequality in the distribution. Indeed, we shall see later that the distributional effects of accrued capital gains on home ownership have at times been very strong.

CONCLUDING REMARKS

This chapter has examined a number of aggregate distributional considerations affecting the general structure of inequality in the over-all distribution of income. The functioning of factor markets (and particularly the labour market) and various institutional and government-imposed constraints on the market can have an important role in the distribution of incomes among groups in the population. The later portions of the chapter then considered how over-all distributions can be built up from life-cycle income patterns combined with the age distribution of the population. The principal conclusions are that important distributional effects on the aggregate structure of income inequality may result from the large demographic changes that have been occurring and that cohort effects exist between different age groups in the population. Clearly, these factors need to be recognized in evaluating the empirical results of this study.

PART TWO: DATA ON DISTRIBUTION OF INCOME AND WEALTH

Part One reviewed some of the current theory of the principal determinants of distribution in the population. Part Two turns to recent data on the distribution of income and wealth in Ontario to present necessary background information for the more analytic portions of the study to follow in Part Three. It also sets out the magnitude and importance of various dimensions of distributional inequality. What follows is a detailed study of Canadian distribution based on micro data files that have recently become available. It provides the first compendium of distributional data for Ontario from several different sources. Thus, although the descriptive statistics presented in the next four chapters serve as input for later analysis in this study, they should also be of considerable interest in themselves. Consequently, some of the descriptive material is presented in fairly substantial detail. Readers interested only in the analytical portions of the study, however, may wish to skip ahead to Part Three.

Because large micro data files are used, it was too costly to perform comparative analyses between Ontario and other provinces or regions in Canada and too difficult to obtain meaningful comparisons of Ontario-specific distributional statistics over several years. So we are restricted to relatively recent distributional data for Ontario alone.

Chapter 5 outlines various ways of describing distributions and measuring inequality and discusses how to interpret summary inequality statistics. Just as there are different ways of characterizing inequality in a distribution, there is also no accepted 'distribution of income' in which inequality should be analysed. Should one look at inequality of incomes among individual workers or among families in the population? Should one look at distributions of income or of wealth? Since every distribution makes its own useful contribution to the total picture of inequality, we have attempted to touch upon each of these. Chapter 6 looks at the distribution of incomes across individuals in the province; Chapter 7 extends the analysis to distributions of incomes for family units; and Chapter 8 focuses on distributions of wealth. By examining the distribution of resources in Ontario from several different angles we can identify some of the principal characteristics and patterns of inequality in the province.

5
On measuring inequality

We shall be using various methods for describing distribution of income and wealth and for measuring the inequality in the distribution. Since the emphasis will be on the effects on measured inequality of various adjustments to income and wealth data, it is important that the reader have some familiarity with the principal statistics that characterize the important features of a distribution. Such distributional measures will include Gini coefficients, Lorenz curves, coefficients of variation, and Atkinson's inequality index. This chapter briefly explains what is meant by a distribution and how inequality in a distribution can be characterized and interpreted. The discussion is largely geometric in emphasis, with technical details relegated to an appendix. Further discussion may be found in Atkinson (1975) and Cowell (1977).

WHAT IS A DISTRIBUTION?

The distribution of income is a relationship indicating the proportions of individuals or families in the population that have different levels of income. Distributional data are usually provided, by Statistics Canada, for example, in a form such as Table 2, which shows estimates of the proportions of families, say, with incomes within a set of intervals. In Figure 16 each percentage figure in Table 2 is represented by the *area* of a corresponding rectangle.

How can we characterize a number of the salient features of such a distribution by a few summary statistics? Several statistics are often used for this purpose. One measure of central tendency for the distribution is the 'mean,' or 'average,' income (usually represented by μ). Another candidate for the most 'typical' income is the 'median' (represented by μ_d), that

TABLE 2
Percentage distribution of families by income class
(hypothetical distribution)

Income class ($)	Percentage
0–1999	6.7
2000–2999	3.8
3000–3999	4.2
4000–4999	4.4
5000–5999	4.7
6000–6999	4.9
7000–7999	5.0
8000–8999	5.3
9000–9999	5.8
10000–10999	6.0
11000–11999	5.9
12000–12999	5.3
13000–13999	4.9
14000–14999	4.7
15000–16999	7.4
17000–19999	8.4
20000–24999	6.7
25000 and over	5.9
Total	100.0

is, the income level such that half the families have incomes less than it and the other half have incomes greater than it. (For a formal definition of the terms presented in this chapter, the reader may look at Appendix A). In a distribution that has a relatively small number of very-high-income units so that it has a long tail to the right (or is said to be skewed to the right, or positively skewed), the mean income level of a distribution will exceed the median.

How concentrated the distribution is around its middle or how spread out it is can also be characterized in summary fashion. The 'variance' (represented by σ^2) measures the mean squared deviation of the individual income levels from the over-all mean, and the 'standard deviation' σ is the square root of the variance. That is, if we take any family at random in the population, calculate the difference between its income and the mean income μ, square this difference, and average this figure over the whole population, we obtain the variance of incomes. As Figure 17 shows, a small value of σ^2 corresponds to the distribution that is more tightly centred on

Figure 16:
Illustrative income distribution

Source: Table 2

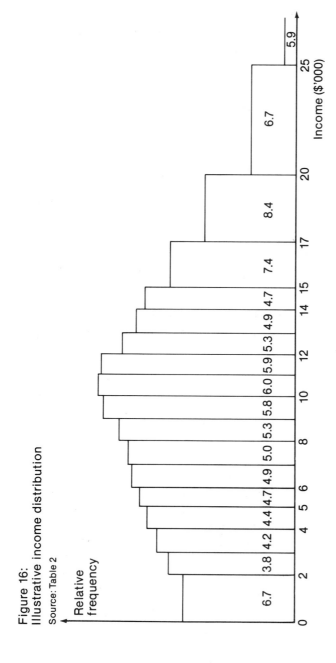

Figure 17:

(a) Distribution with small variance (b) Distribution with large variance

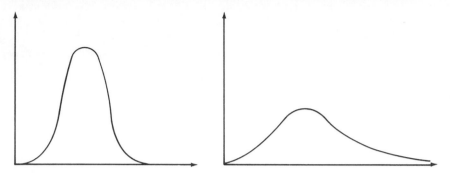

μ, whereas a large value of σ^2 corresponds to a much more dispersed distribution. Dispersion of a distribution may also be captured by the 'mean difference' Δ between incomes over the distribution. That is, if we take two families at random in the population, calculate the positive difference in their incomes, and average this difference over the whole population, we obtain the mean difference in incomes for the distribution. Again a small value of Δ corresponds to the situation in Figure 17a, while a large value corresponds to Figure 17b.

As should be apparent from this discussion, there is more than one way to measure the salient aspects of a distribution. This will be a recurrent theme throughout this study, and consequently the analysis and description will be based on several different types of distributional measurements.

CHARACTERIZING INEQUALITY

Closely related to dispersion in a distribution is the concept of inequality. If incomes vary widely across the population, then one might characterize income inequality as being fairly substantial. But what is 'substantial'? Does a standard deviation of income of $7500 show a wide dispersion or not? If the mean income were only $1000 that deviation would be very large; if the mean were $100000, such a deviation would represent a very small degree of inequality. Consequently, one of the simplest ways to characterize inequality is in terms of the *relative* dispersion in a distribution. Two of the most frequently quoted measures of inequality are the coefficient of variation (to be denoted by V), which is the standard deviation divided by the mean ($V = \sigma/\mu$), and the Gini concentration ratio (denoted by R), which is the mean difference normalized relative to the mean ($R = \Delta/4\mu$). Since these are dollar ratios, they themselves have no units. As indicated in Appendix A the Gini ratio has the added feature of lying between zero and one-half, the former corresponding to complete equality and the latter to complete inequality in a sense to be explained shortly. Consequently, a figure such as 0.187, for example, represents moderate income inequality somewhere between two extremes.

By its very nature, however, any summary measure of inequality also hides a great deal of information. For example, one might wish to know whether inequality is more extreme in some sense at the bottom end of the distribution or at the top end, or what portion of a distribution contributes more than another to over-all inequality. In a classic paper on measuring inequality, Bowman (1945) argued that summary measures of inequality, by aggregating or averaging over many important details, may be quite misleading and thus ought not to be used. She proposed instead that inequality be characterized in disaggregated form by means of a table or graph showing the degree of inequality over the entire range of a distribution. For example, Table 3 shows the shares of income received by each 20 per cent (or 'quintile group') of the population ranked from the lowest-income fifth to the highest-income fifth, and also the income shares for each five percentage income group (or 'vigintile group'). If there were perfect income equality, each quintile group would receive 20 per cent and each vigintile group 5 per cent. As is evident, the bottom and top shares differ quite substantially in their incomes. Such detail is very useful if one wishes, for example, to compare inequality patterns in two distributions that differ in some respect. Clearly some shares may go up and others go down, so that the resulting inequality change may be rather complex.

Of course, as Bowman also pointed out, any single graph or table may also be a less than adequate representation of the over-all pattern of inequality in a distribution. This is simply a return to the theme that there is not just one way of measuring inequality even when over-all curves or detailed tables are concerned. Consequently, just as several summary measures of inequality have been considered, one can also look at several different tabular or graphical representations of disaggregated inequality over a distribution.

Perhaps the device used most frequently to illustrate inequality over a distribution is the Lorenz curve, shown in Figure 18. Along the horizontal axis is cumulated the percentage of family units in the population ranging from the lowest-income group to the highest-income group. Along the ver-

TABLE 3
Hypothetical example of vigintile and quintile income shares

	Share (%)
Vigintile	
First (lowest)	0.4
Second	0.8
Third	1.1
Fourth	1.6
Fifth	2.0
Sixth	2.5
Seventh	3.0
Eighth	3.5
Ninth	4.0
Tenth	4.4
Eleventh	4.8
Twelfth	5.2
Thirteenth	5.7
Fourteenth	6.1
Fifteenth	6.6
Sixteenth	7.2
Seventeenth	7.8
Eighteenth	8.7
Nineteenth	10.1
Twentieth	14.5
Quintile	
First (lowest)	3.9
Second	11.0
Third	18.4
Fourth	25.6
Fifth (highest)	41.1

tical axis is measured the cumulative share of total income received by those on the horizontal axis. That is, Figure 18 has been drawn simply by cumulating the vigintile share figures in Table 3, so that the share of the bottom 5 per cent is only 0.4 per cent, that of the bottom 10 per cent is 1.2 per cent, that of the bottom 15 per cent is 2.3 per cent, etc.

The Lorenz curve is a useful graphical device for several reasons. First, as a descriptive tool it implicitly compares the actual Lorenz curve to two extreme standards. If there were perfect mathematical equality of incomes among families, each vigintile group would receive 5 per cent of total income in the population, and the corresponding Lorenz curve would coin-

Figure 18:
Lorenz curve for an income distribution

Source: Cumulative figures in Table 3

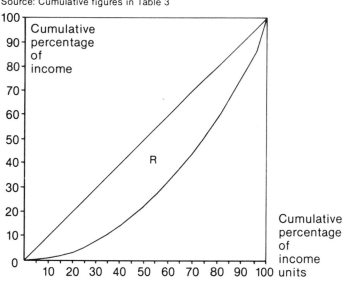

cide exactly with the diagonal line in the diagram. At the other extreme, if all families but one had no income at all and that one received the total amount of income in the population, the resulting Lorenz curve would exactly coincide with bottom and right-hand side axes. The actual Lorenz curve lies somewhere between these two hypothetical extremes.

Second, it also turns out that the total shaded area in the diagram between the actual Lorenz curve and the equality diagonal is simply a graphical representation of the Gini ratio R introduced earlier (Kendall and Stuart, 1969, 49). Since the Lorenz curve lies between the two limiting equality and perfect inequality curves, R must take on values between zero and one-half, as mentioned earlier. Closely related to the Gini ratio is Gini's concentration coefficient (denoted by G), which is simply twice the value of the Gini ratio and is thus bounded between zero and one. Geometrically, it is the area between the actual Lorenz curve and the equality diagonal relative to the whole triangle below the equality diagonal. Analytically, it also has the interpretation of the expected average gain in income (relative to the mean) if each family in the population had the choice of its own income or that of another's drawn at random (Pyatt, 1976).

Figure 19:
Two intersecting Lorenz curves

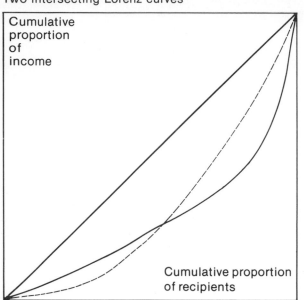

Cumulative
proportion
of
income

Cumulative proportion
of recipients

Third, the Lorenz curve allows comparisons of over-all inequality between two distributions. Under fairly broad conditions, it can be said that one distribution is unambiguously more equal than another if the Lorenz curve for one of the distributions lies completely inside the other (Atkinson, 1970).[1] If the two curves intersect as shown in Figure 19, however, different summary measures of inequality can lead to different conclusions. Consequently, a Lorenz curve is a useful indicator of whether it can be said that one distribution is unambiguously more or less unequal than another.

Another useful characterization of inequality is a relative mean income curve. If the upper bound for each vigintile group is referred to as the corresponding vigintile income level, then a distribution can be character-

1 It should be remarked that the Lorenz curve is not being used to indicate whether one distribution is preferable to or better than another since distributions can differ in their mean income levels as well. If, of course, two distributions have equal means and one Lorenz curve uniformly inside the other, one may be said to be preferable to the other. If, however, the inside Lorenz curve corresponds to a lower mean income, then a choice between distributions must reflect preferences for equality (or inequality) as well as efficiency (or mean income levels).

Figure 20:
Relative mean income curve

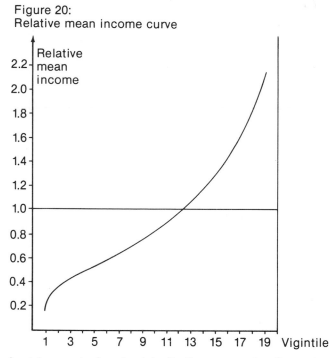

ized by a set of such vigintile figures ranging from those for the bottom 5 per cent, 10 per cent, etc. to those for the upper income groups. The tenth vigintile level, for example, is the median. Each of these vigintile income levels can then be divided by mean income for the distribution and plotted (in Figure 20) as a relative mean income curve that shows the degree to which various incomes across the distribution deviate from the mean by indicating the degree to which the relative mean income curve deviates from the absolute equality line drawn horizontally at unity. The relative mean income curve is in fact the slope of the Lorenz curve (see Appendix A). Hence the point of intersection of the relative mean income and absolute equality line in Figure 20 corresponds exactly to the vigintile level in Figure 18 where the Lorenz curve is just parallel to the equality diagonal. The relative mean income curve is a particularly useful device for comparing inequality between distributions when the corresponding Lorenz curves intersect as in Figure 19. In this case (illustrated on Figure 21) the relative mean income curves will intersect twice, so that one can see over what ranges of the distributions one curve dominates in being closer to the equality line. A relative mean income curve reveals more clearly than a

Figure 21:
Two intersecting relative mean income curves

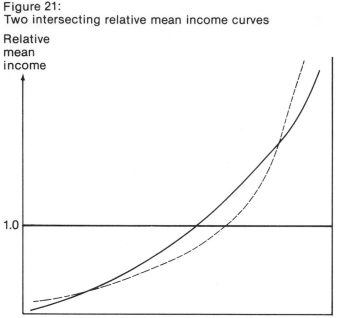

Relative
mean
income

1.0

Cumulative proportion of recipients

Lorenz curve the various portions of a distribution over which disaggregated inequality is greater or less between two distributions. Together the
relative mean income curve and Lorenz curve thus provide complementary
information for comparing inequality between distributions.

EVALUATING INEQUALITY

As early as Dalton (1920) it was recognized that in ranking distributions on
the basis of some measure of inequality, one is essentially making a value
judgment that one distribution is better than another. As mentioned earlier,
one can unambiguously rank inequality patterns under fairly weak conditions if the corresponding Lorenz curves do not intersect. Where the
Lorenz curves do intersect, however, one cannot rank inequality patterns
without some stronger rules on how to compare the well-being of some
people in one part of the distribution who may be better off to that of some
others elsewhere in the distribution who may be worse off. Consequently,
in providing some over-all measure of inequality, one is obliged to make
interpersonal comparisons and (implicitly at least) place particular weights

on different individuals over different parts of the distribution. Any aggregate inequality measure is inevitably based on subjective value judgments, and such judgments should be recognized.[2] This raises a number of questions about the implied value judgments incorporated in such standard inequality measures as the Gini coefficient or coefficient of variation. The Gini coefficient, for example, attaches more weight to income changes affecting the middle portion of the distribution, while the coefficient of variations attaches equal weight to transfers in different parts of the distribution. It is enough to recognize that the different standard measures of inequality used in this study do not always yield the same result in ranking inequality patterns precisely because they are ranking on the basis of different social value judgments, and the choice between such measures is a subjective one. That is why we have relied on several different inequality measures instead of just one.

Atkinson (1970) has explored this relationship between inequality measurement and social value judgments by developing an aggregate inequality measure (denoted by I) that explicitly incorporates social valuations. Instead of examining the social welfare judgments implicit in the traditional inequality measures, he explicitly chose a set of desirable social welfare properties and thence derived a new inequality measure based on them (see Appendix A for technical details). This is best illustrated by use of a diagram (Muellbauer 1974). In Figure 22 the population is represented by two people with incomes Y_1 and Y_2. CAD is then a social indifference curve representing the various distributions of Y_1 and Y_2, which a given social welfare function ranks equally. If point C represents the actual distribution of income, point A indicates the level of income $(2Y_A)$ that, if equally distributed, would yield the same level of social welfare as achieved at C. Point B represents the maximum social welfare achievable given total income available $(Y_1 + Y_2)$. The inequality index is thus defined to be

$$I = 1 - Y_A/Y_B = (OB - OA)/OB,$$

2 The literature in this area has rapidly become voluminous. Several of the principal contributions are Atkinson (1970), Sheshinski (1972), Dasgusta et al. (1973), Sen (1973), and Kolm (1976a and b). One of the principal questions addressed in this literature is that of finding an inequality measure or way of ranking alternative distributions that is substantially more powerful than the Atkinson criterion of non-intersection Lorenz curves and at the same time is based on some broadly acceptable assumptions on the comparison of incomes of different individuals. To date, however, there does not appear to be any general consensus on a most acceptable ranking criterion.

Figure 22
Illustration of Atkinson's inequality index

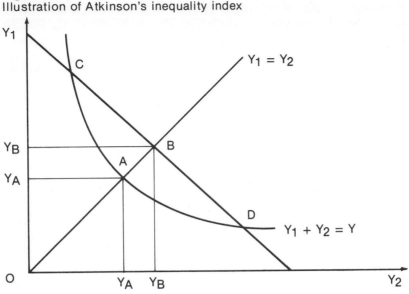

which represents the proportional loss in attainable social welfare for the population associated with the present inequality at *C*. Alternatively, it represents the proportional amount by which total income could be reduced at an equal distribution of this income so as to leave the same level of social welfare as at *C*. Clearly, the index *I* must lie between zero (perfect equality) and one (perfect inequality), just as the Gini coefficient and its value will depend on the curvature of the social indifference curve, or what Atkinson calls the 'degree of inequality aversion' (denoted by ϵ). If the degree of inequality aversion is large (ϵ in the range of 2.5 for example), the curve *CAD* is very concave or bent and *I* assumes large values. If the social welfare function is not characterized by much aversion to inequality (ϵ around 1.0, say), the curve will be fairly flat with little bend in it, and *I* will take on fairly small values, indicating a willingness to trade off only a small amount of total output for a more equal distribution of this output. Consequently, *I* is an explicit function of ϵ, $I(\epsilon)$, and one can analyse how the rankings of alternative inequality patterns change as ϵ varies over a continuum of values. The rankings given by the Gini coefficient and the coefficient of variation, for example, appear to correspond to a relatively low degree of inequality aversion (ϵ around 1.0). Use of this measure, for various values of ϵ, should thus help to keep in mind the social valuation aspects of the aggregate measures of inequality that will be relied upon throughout the study.

6

Incomes of individuals

INTRODUCTION

The distribution of income among *individuals* across the province is for a number of reasons a logical place to start a review of empirical patterns of inequality. For most sources of earnings and self-employment, pension, and investment income, the individual is the basic income-receiving unit, and the amount he receives depends on his own particular characteristics (e.g. his productivity and wealth-holdings) as evaluated by the market system; it is some of these characteristics that we wish to highlight. Much of the theory of the size distribution of income considered in Part One focuses on the individual as the basic subject of analysis and decision-making unit, and on behavioural differences among individual income recipients. Since families on the other hand are groups of individuals with differing characteristics, the distributions of individual incomes serve as one of the basic building blocks out of which family distributions are constructed. For several reasons, therefore, the distribution of individual incomes is logically prior to that of families, and our empirical review of income inequality in Ontario begins with an examination of individual incomes.

The data source for the analysis of individual incomes is the 1971 Census 'Public Use Sample Tape,' a micro data tape of about 54000 individuals in Ontario, provided by the Census Division of Statistics Canada (1975a).[1] Such a large data set allows a fairly detailed analysis of individual income

1 Technical details on sample design and characteristics of the Public Use Sample microdata base for individuals are presented in Statistics Canada (1975a). It should be noted, for example, that individual incomes above $75000 in 1970 have been entered as exactly $75000 so that income shares, particularly at the very top end of the distributions, may be biased slightly by the high income exclusions. It should also be pointed out that all tables in this chapter are based on the Public Use Sample Data derived from the 1971

patterns for the year 1970. However, this chapter is not intended to be a comprehensive empirical review, but rather it highlights selective results that are of particular interest in their own right and that will be of use in later portions of this study. Specific terms on income components and individual characteristics used in this chapter are defined in Appendix B to the chapter. Technical details on how various summary statistics on inequality have been calculated from the data are available in Appendix D. The chapter procedes by first looking at differences in individual incomes by sex and age, then considering various characteristics by age and income class, and finally examining specific educational and occupational differences in income.

DIFFERENCES IN INCOME BY SEX AND AGE

One would expect from the discussion in Part One that incomes among individuals would vary substantially between different sex and age groups because of life-cycle behaviour and various demand-side considerations. Consequently, we begin the empirical review with an examination of these differences.

Tables 4 and 5 present the figures for the distribution of income across all income recipients in Ontario in 1970. The mean and median income levels were $5537 and $4434, respectively. The distribution tends to decline over most of its range; this illustrates the fact that there is a large proportion of individuals with low incomes (29.6 per cent with incomes less than $2000) and a rather small proportion with fairly high incomes (1.1 per cent with incomes above $25 000). Correspondingly, the income share of the bottom ten per cent of income recipients is substantially less than one per cent, while that of the top ten per cent of the distribution is over thirty per cent. This rather substantial inequality in shares is also reflected in the fairly high values of the various inequality measures.

Such aggregate figures, however, hide as much as they reveal. Actually, the distribution for all income recipients can be broken down into its component parts in several different ways. For instance, an examination of the separate distributions for male and female income recipients reveals some substantial differences. Not only do the median incomes for men ($6644) and for women ($2312) differ radically, but so also do the shapes of their distributions. As illustrated in Figure 23, the distribution for female income recipients has a very pronounced declining shape, while that for men has a

Canadian Census of Population supplied by Statistics Canada. The responsibility for the use and interpretation of these data is entirely that of the authors.

TABLE 4
Distribution of income among individual income recipients by sex, Ontario 1970 (percentages)

Income ($)	Men (%)	Women (%)	Total (%)
Less than 500	4.0	13.6	8.1
500–999	4.0	10.9	6.9
1000–1499	5.1	14.3	9.1
1500–1999	3.8	7.7	5.5
2000–2999	6.2	11.2	8.3
3000–3999	6.0	11.6	8.4
4000–4999	6.6	10.6	8.3
5000–5999	8.3	7.0	7.8
6000–6999	9.3	4.8	7.3
7000–7999	9.9	2.9	6.9
8000–8999	8.4	1.8	5.6
9000–9999	6.9	1.1	4.4
10000–11999	8.8	1.1	5.5
12000–14999	5.9	0.7	3.7
15000–24999	5.0	0.5	3.1
25000 and over	1.8	0.2	1.1
Number in sample	24804	18714	43518
Median income ($)	6644	2312	4434

SOURCE: Based on Public Use Sample Data for Ontario derived from the 1971 Canadian Census of Population supplied by Statistics Canada.

TABLE 5
Income inequality measures among individual income recipients by sex, Ontario 1970

Measure	Men	Women	Total
Shares			
Bottom 10%	0.8	0.6	0.6
Top 10%	27.1	29.6	30.7
Gini coefficient	0.394	0.466	0.467
Atkinson index			
$\epsilon = 1.05$	0.321	0.413	0.420
$\epsilon = 1.55$	0.502	0.607	0.618
$\epsilon = 2.55$	0.770	0.837	0.846
Coefficient of variation	0.73	0.86	0.88
Mean income ($)	7298	3092	5537

SOURCE: See source to Table 4.

Figure 23:
Distribution of income for male and female income
recipients, Ontario 1970

Source: Table 4

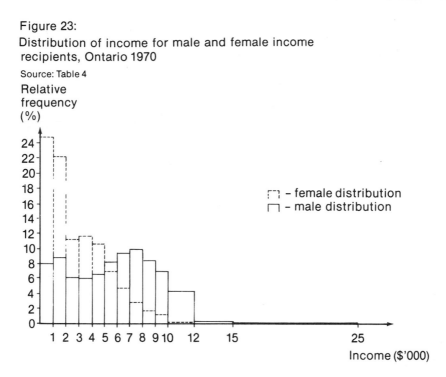

more humped pattern including a much higher proportion of recipients at
middle and upper income levels. That finding is not peculiar to Ontario, but
is a common result of the differences between men and women in pay
rates, the proportion of part-time workers, life-cycle work patterns, and
occupational roles in the labour market. Clearly these factors will bear more
detailed investigation. Their effect on inequality measures is also quite
marked with the distribution of income for female recipients being consistently more unequal than that for males – both at the bottom and top ends
of the distributions. The results highlight the substantial differences between
the distributions for male and female income recipients and point out the
need to treat these two distributions separately and to disaggregate by sex in
any further analysis of income distributions of individuals.

The distributional differences by sex are even more substantial when
differences in income recipient status are taken into account. In Table 4 and

TABLE 6
Income recipient status by age and sex, Ontario 1970 (percentages)

Age	Men		Women	
	Recipients (%)	Nonrecipients (%)	Recipients (%)	Nonrecipients (%)
Under 25	72.45	27.55	61.91	38.09
25–34	98.12	1.88	62.06	37.94
35–44	98.79	1.21	61.20	38.80
45–54	98.79	1.21	65.22	34.78
55–64	97.57	2.43	65.02	34.98
65–69	98.46	1.54	93.24	6.76
70 and over	99.53	0.47	98.53	1.47
All ages	91.76	8.24	67.29	32.71
Number in sample	27030		27809	

SOURCE: See source to Table 4.

Figure 23, the distributions of individuals' incomes include only those individuals who actually received some income. Among prime-aged men, virtually everyone does receive some income and is thus included in the income distribution. This is not so, however, for secondary workers. Table 6 shows the proportions of all individuals by sex and age groups who are income recipients and thus included in the income distribution. As can be seen, a much higher proportion of women (32.7 per cent) than men (8.2 per cent) had zero incomes, reflecting the fact that a much higher proportion of married women work in the home and do not receive a market wage. Thus the income distributions for *all* men and women differ even more than suggested in Tables 4 and 5 in that the distribution for men covers a much larger proportion of all men and omits a much smaller proportion of individuals at the lower end of the distribution.

One may observe from Table 6 that the income recipient ratios differ by age as well as sex. Many young people are in school and do not have jobs, so that only 72.4 per cent of young men and 61.9 per cent of young women receive income. Among those 65 and over, however, almost everyone receives some income (often in the form of annuities, pensions, or government old-age security).

Figure 24:
Median income age cross-section for income recipients by sex,
Ontario 1970

Source: See source to Tables 7 and 8

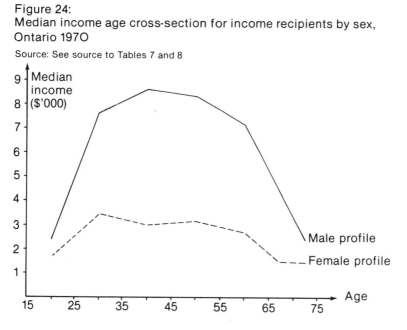

A general prediction of the theoretical literature on the size distribution of income is that incomes should differ systematically with age over the life cycle. Direct estimation of such age-income profiles requires the use of longitudinal or time-series data on individuals over time (see Chapter 4). Lacking such data, however, we look instead at age-income cross-sections of income recipients in a given period (1970). While such cross-sectional relationships are interesting because they show a slice of the income distribution at a particular period, they nonetheless differ from longitudinal profiles because of demographic factors and changing economic behaviour over time. Consequently, the present cross-sectional patterns should be interpreted with some care.

Tables 7 and 9 give complete distributions for seven age groups for male and female income recipients separately. As can be seen, the distributions vary substantially with age. Median incomes for men in the cross-section follow a pronounced concave age-income profile (see Figure 24) with a peak in the 35–54 age interval, while the median age-income profile for women is much lower and flatter and reaches a peak earlier – in the 25–34 age interval – and then again later – in the 45–54 age interval. Figure 25

TABLE 7
Distribution of male income recipients by age, Ontario 1970 (percentages)

Income ($)	Under 25	25–34	35–44	45–54	55–64	65–69	70 & over
Less than 500	15.7	1.2	0.8	0.9	1.7	1.3	0.5
500–999	13.7	1.2	0.7	0.9	2.2	2.7	4.1
1000–1499	8.9	1.7	1.2	1.5	3.0	11.2	24.1
1500–1999	7.3	1.7	1.2	1.3	2.3	7.7	13.6
2000–2999	10.2	3.4	2.8	3.3	4.9	10.4	18.3
3000–3999	8.5	4.5	3.6	4.1	5.5	11.9	11.3
4000–4999	8.3	6.5	4.5	4.5	7.7	10.7	7.8
5000–5999	8.2	9.2	7.1	8.2	10.6	9.3	5.2
6000–6999	7.9	11.6	9.1	9.7	10.3	9.5	3.7
7000–7999	5.3	14.0	11.4	11.6	11.7	6.6	2.2
8000–8999	2.8	11.5	12.1	10.9	8.4	4.8	1.8
9000–9999	1.5	9.7	10.1	9.2	6.7	2.9	2.1
10 000–11 999	1.3	12.2	14.1	12.0	8.8	3.6	1.6
12 000–14 999	0.3	6.9	9.8	9.6	5.7	3.4	1.3
15 000–24 999	0.2	3.9	8.6	9.0	7.2	2.4	1.2
25 000 and over	0.0	0.6	2.8	3.4	3.4	1.6	1.1
Total number	5046	5168	4661	4156	3050	1021	1702
Percentage by age	20.3	20.8	18.8	16.8	12.3	4.1	6.9
Median income ($)	2435	7635	8623	8371	7157	4448	2417

SOURCE: See source to Table 4.

TABLE 8
Income inequality measures among male income recipients by age, Ontario 1970

Measure	Under 25	25–34	35–44	45–54	55–64	65–69	70 & over
Shares							
Bottom 10%	0.5	2.1	2.3	2.0	1.3	1.6	2.0
Top 10%	27.5	21.5	24.9	26.0	28.8	30.9	35.4
Gini coefficient	0.474	0.279	0.309	0.330	0.376	0.423	0.460
Atkinson index							
$\epsilon = 1.05$	0.449	0.162	0.176	0.198	0.262	0.295	0.314
$\epsilon = 1.55$	0.654	0.261	0.268	0.299	0.397	0.413	0.415
$\epsilon = 2.55$	0.866	0.485	0.461	0.507	0.645	0.591	0.556
Coefficient of variation	0.83	0.51	0.56	0.60	0.71	0.83	0.99
Mean income ($)	3263	8081	9831	9768	8514	5600	3698

SOURCE: See Table 7.

TABLE 9
Distribution of female income recipients by age, Ontario 1970 (percentages)

Income ($)	Under 25	25–34	35–44	45–54	55–64	65–69	70 & over
Less than 500	21.1	12.8	14.9	15.2	15.8	4.8	0.5
500–999	14.4	8.9	8.5	7.1	10.0	18.1	11.8
1000–1499	10.4	7.2	8.0	8.2	9.4	29.1	42.0
1500–1999	7.1	5.6	6.1	5.3	6.5	9.8	16.2
2000–2999	10.2	10.1	12.5	12.2	11.3	11.7	11.6
3000–3999	12.6	12.2	13.6	13.5	11.5	6.9	6.4
4000–4999	11.9	13.6	11.0	12.9	10.2	5.0	4.3
5000–5999	6.5	10.1	8.5	8.1	6.8	3.7	2.3
6000–6999	3.7	7.4	5.4	6.2	5.6	2.7	1.0
7000–7999	1.2	5.0	3.6	3.9	4.2	1.6	0.7
8000–8999	0.5	2.9	2.5	2.6	2.5	1.6	0.7
9000–9999	0.1	2.0	1.8	1.4	1.1	1.4	0.5
10000–11999	0.2	1.1	1.7	1.3	2.2	1.4	0.5
12000–14999	0.1	0.7	0.8	1.3	1.1	1.1	0.7
15000–24999	0.0	0.2	0.8	0.6	1.2	0.8	0.5
25000 and over	0.0	0.1	0.2	0.3	0.4	0.4	0.4
Total number	4246	3242	2852	2764	2045	1145	2420
Percentage by age	22.7	17.3	15.2	14.8	10.9	6.1	12.9
Median income ($)	1788	3438	2995	3151	2725	1465	1448

SOURCE: See source to Table 4.

TABLE 10
Income inequality measures among female income recipients by age, Ontario 1970

Measure	Under 25	25–34	35–44	45–54	55–64	65–69	70 & over
Shares							
Bottom 10%	0.5	0.5	0.5	0.5	0.4	1.4	1.8
Top 10%	27.3	25.4	29.7	27.9	32.5	38.3	34.4
Gini coefficient	0.472	0.421	0.461	0.445	0.496	0.502	0.418
Atkinson index							
$\epsilon = 1.05$	0.450	0.394	0.431	0.423	0.467	0.374	0.281
$\epsilon = 1.55$	0.656	0.610	0.644	0.642	0.672	0.491	0.388
$\epsilon = 2.55$	0.867	0.853	0.869	0.871	0.879	0.650	0.585
Coefficient of variation	0.82	0.74	0.87	0.80	0.96	1.10	0.94
Mean income ($)	2388	3711	3586	3590	3623	2750	2202

SOURCE: See source to Table 9.

Figure 25:
Distributions of income for male income recipients by age, Ontario 1970

Source: Table 7

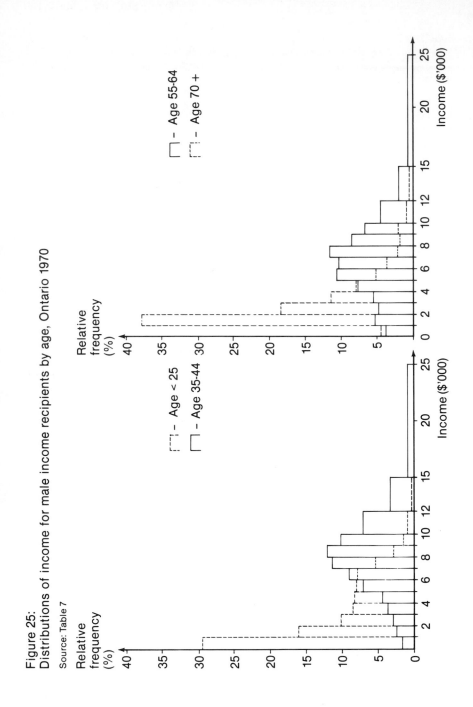

Figure 26:
Gini inequality coefficients across ages for income recipients by sex,
Ontario 1970

Source: See source to Tables 8 and 10

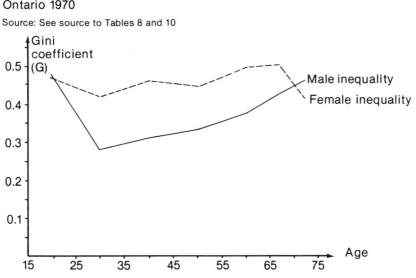

illustrates graphically the transformations in shape of the age-specific distributions for male income recipients. The distributions start off highly unequal with a declining shape because there are a large number of low-income recipients from part-time and part-year work among the young workers. Then gradually the centre of gravity of the distributions shifts to the right as the distributions become more humped shaped in the middle age. Finally, the centre of gravity of the distributions shifts back toward the left-hand axis and inequality again increases as many recipients' incomes fall off markedly at retirement. In the case of women, much the same pattern recurs though less markedly, and the general declining shape tends to persist across all ages.

Looking at the summary inequality figures in Tables 8 and 10, one can see that income inequality among men is greatest among the very young and old; and beyond the first age group, inequality increases steadily with age (see Figure 26). In the case of female income recipients except for the first and last age groups, inequality also generally increases with age, although not so markedly as for men. For both men and women, however, inequality is concentrated more at the bottom end of the distribution

Figure 27:
(a) Bottom income shares for male income recipients by age

Source: See source to Table 8

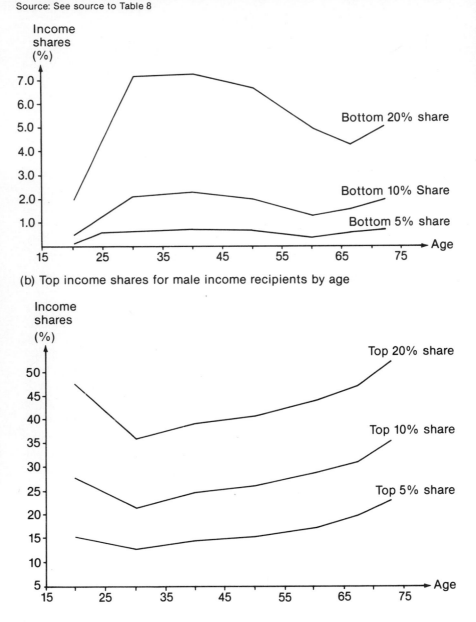

(b) Top income shares for male income recipients by age

among the young and more at the top end among the old. This is further illustrated in Figure 27, where it can be seen that bottom income shares for male income recipients start off very low, peak in the 35–44 age interval, and then decline somewhat until the oldest age group; top income shares, on the other hand, trough in the 25–34 age interval, and then increase steadily with age beyond there. Consequently, one would expect rather different factors to affect income inequality for different age groups. More generally, as both theory and data suggest, income distributions differ substantially by age, so that in the subsequent analysis such distributions will be separated by age as well as sex.

CHARACTERISTICS BY AGE AND INCOME

What are the characteristics of the income recipients who belong to different income classes? Tables 11 and 12 throw some light on this question. Percentage figures for each characteristic sum vertically to a hundred, and the figures in parentheses are the average percentages across all income classes. Turning first to the age composition of each income class, one can see that very young workers predominate at the bottom end of the distribution and are underrepresented elsewhere, particularly in the case of men as illustrated in Figure 28. Older and retired income recipients are most noticeable in the next-to-bottom group, probably because of uniform old-age security transfers in this range. The upper-income classes are filled largely with middle-aged recipients, who are near the peak of the (cross-sectional) age-income profiles.

Turning to major source of income of the recipients,[2] one can see that government transfers are most important in the next-to-bottom income group coincident with the concentration of old and retired recipients noted above. As illustrated for men in Figure 29, wages and salaries, which are by far the most important source of income, are most dominant in the middle-

2 In Chapter 9 it is noted that certain income sources tend to be under-reported more than others. In particular, for the Survey of Consumer Finances data, it appears that some transfer payments are seriously under-reported. Transfer payments in total, however, are less seriously under-reported than investment income and self-employment income, which suffer most from this shortcoming. One would perhaps expect that reported income figures would be rather more biased than a simple statement of which income source is the major one for an individual. Nonetheless, it is probable that the wage and salaries major-source-of-income percentages in Tables 11 to 14 are biased upwards somewhat, and the percentages for particularly investment income are biased downwards. The percentages for self-employment income and transfers as major sources of income are probably not affected as much by such biases.

TABLE 11
Characteristics of male income recipients by income, Ontario 1970

Individual characteristics	Under $1000	$1000–1999	$2000–4999	$5000–7999	$8000–11 999	$12 000–24 999	$25 000 +
Age							
Under 25 (20.3)	74.6	36.8	29.4	15.8	4.7	0.9	0.5
25–34 (20.8)	6.2	7.8	16.2	26.4	28.9	20.7	7.0
35–44 (18.8)	3.5	5.2	10.9	18.8	28.4	31.6	29.9
45–54 (16.8)	3.8	5.3	10.6	18.0	23.3	28.4	31.7
55–64 (12.3)	5.9	7.2	11.9	14.6	12.2	14.5	23.3
65–69 (4.1)	2.1	8.7	7.3	4.8	1.9	2.2	3.6
70 and over (6.9)	4.0	28.9	13.7	2.8	1.6	1.6	4.1
Major source of income							
Wage and salary (81.9)	76.0	48.0	68.6	91.4	94.2	89.2	63.1
Non-farm							
self-employment (4.5)	2.4	2.9	5.4	3.6	3.2	7.1	26.0
Farm self-employment (1.8)	2.1	2.4	3.9	1.1	0.9	1.1	3.2
Government transfers (6.8)	13.4	43.7	9.0	0.5	0.1	0.1	0.0
Investment income (2.3)	4.7	1.4	5.3	1.4	0.9	1.2	5.4
Retirement pensions and							
other income (2.6)	1.4	1.6	7.7	1.9	0.7	1.4	2.3
Class of worker							
Wage earners (81.6)	78.9	52.3	70.3	90.7	92.4	84.7	54.8
Self-employed (9.1)	5.2	7.5	12.4	6.7	6.3	14.0	42.3
Others (9.3)	15.9	40.2	17.3	2.6	1.3	1.3	2.9

Labour force status							
Employed (80.8)	51.5	44.2	69.0	90.1	95.1	95.1	94.1
Unemployed (4.4)	13.3	6.6	7.1	3.3	1.4	0.9	0.2
Not in labour force (14.9)	35.2	49.2	24.0	6.6	3.5	4.0	5.7
Marital status							
Single (23.9)	78.7	48.7	32.3	17.4	7.4	5.0	1.4
Married (69.7)	18.3	37.1	59.3	76.8	87.8	90.5	93.2
Other (6.4)	3.0	14.2	8.4	5.8	4.8	4.5	5.4
Mother tongue							
English (73.5)	81.0	73.6	71.2	70.4	73.5	79.6	81.9
French (6.4)	6.1	7.3	6.6	6.6	6.7	4.8	2.5
German (3.1)	2.1	2.9	2.8	3.0	3.6	3.5	3.4
Italian (5.0)	3.0	3.7	6.0	6.9	4.8	2.1	2.0
Other (11.9)	7.8	12.5	13.4	13.1	11.4	10.1	10.2
Number in sample	1984	2219	4642	6831	5978	2708	442
Percentage of sample	8.0	8.9	18.7	27.5	24.1	10.9	1.8

NOTE: Figures in parentheses are percentages.
SOURCE: See source to Table 4.

TABLE 12

Characteristics of female income recipients by income, Ontario 1970

Individual characteristics	Under $1000	$1000–1999	$2000–4999	$5000–7999	$8000–11999	$12000+
Age						
Under 25 (22.7)	32.9	18.0	23.6	17.6	4.5	2.2
25–34 (17.3)	15.3	10.1	18.7	26.6	25.9	11.1
35–44 (15.2)	14.6	9.8	16.9	18.2	22.6	19.3
45–54 (14.8)	13.5	9.0	17.0	18.3	19.4	22.6
55–64 (10.9)	11.5	7.9	10.8	12.4	15.6	20.7
65–69 (6.1)	5.7	10.8	4.3	3.3	6.6	10.0
70 and over (12.9)	6.5	34.3	8.6	3.5	5.3	14.1
Major source of income						
Wage and salary (67.4)	55.1	42.7	80.1	91.2	85.5	67.0
Non-farm self-employment (1.6)	1.7	1.1	1.5	1.7	3.2	4.1
Farm self-employment (0.3)	0.5	0.2	0.2	0.2	0.0	0.0
Government transfers (18.1)	18.7	50.2	7.2	0.6	0.7	0.4
Investment income (9.8)	21.0	4.1	7.4	4.2	7.3	24.8
Retirement pensions and other income (2.8)	2.9	1.8	3.7	2.2	3.4	3.7
Class of worker						
Wage earners (69.2)	56.2	45.9	82.1	92.9	86.8	68.2
Self-employed (2.1)	1.6	1.7	2.1	2.2	3.7	8.9
Others (28.7)	42.2	52.4	15.7	5.8	9.5	23.0

Labour force status						
Employed (55.4)	32.2	33.8	69.0	86.5	82.8	70.0
Unemployed (3.9)	5.2	3.8	4.2	1.9	1.6	0.7
Not in labour force (40.7)	62.6	62.4	26.8	11.6	15.6	29.3
Marital status						
Single (22.2)	28.2	17.9	18.7	23.8	28.8	30.0
Married (56.7)	62.4	48.5	59.8	56.4	47.1	43.3
Other (21.1)	9.4	33.7	21.4	19.8	24.1	26.7
Mother tongue						
English (78.1)	80.1	77.2	75.2	81.3	82.3	81.5
French (5.5)	5.2	5.9	5.7	5.0	4.9	4.8
German (3.0)	2.7	3.2	3.1	2.8	2.9	3.7
Italian (3.5)	2.8	2.8	5.5	2.1	0.9	1.5
Other (9.9)	9.3	10.9	10.5	8.8	9.0	8.5
Number in sample	4583	4113	6248	2744	756	270
Percentage of sample	24.5	22.0	33.4	14.7	4.0	1.4

NOTE: Figures in parentheses are percentages.
SOURCE: See source to Table 4.

Figure 28:
Age group shares of male income recipients by income class, Ontario 1970
Source: Table 11

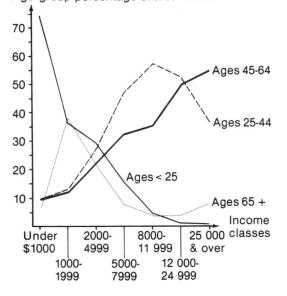

upper income ranges and slightly less so in the top group and bottom two groups. Farm self-employment income occurs largely in the mid-bottom ranges of the distribution, although a few high-income male farm-income recipients appear as well. Non-farm self-employment income is concentrated somewhat at the top end of the distribution where highly paid professionals tend to appear. Investment income appears more frequently at the bottom and top ends of the distribution. Retirement pensions and other income occurs mostly in the lower-middle range for men, but is much more evenly spread across the distribution for women. In general, then, the pattern that emerges as one moves up the distribution is that the importance of government transfers at the bottom end dies away and wage and salary income becomes overwhelmingly important and then falls off somewhat as non-farm self-employment and investment income gain some importance.

Turning next to the distribution according to class of worker, one sees that wage earners are again most prominent in the middle-upper portion of the distributions, the self-employed appear most noticeably at the top end, and unemployed and those not in the labour force are highly concentrated

Figure 29:
Major source of income shares of male income recipients by
income class, Ontario 1970

Source: Table 11

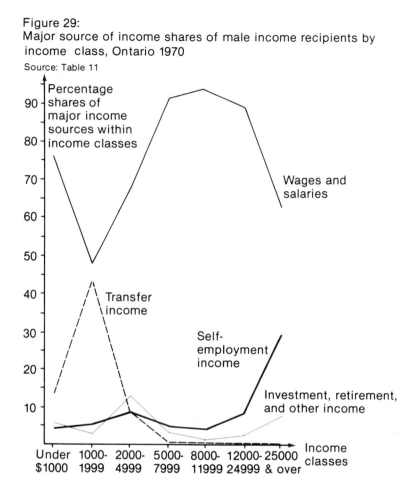

near the bottom end. These findings are reinforced further by the figures for labour force status by income class. Note, however, the much higher proportion of women who are not participating in the labour force as compared to men throughout the full range of the distribution.

Marital status characteristics by income class, however, are quite different for men and women. In the case of men, single income recipients predominate at the bottom end of the distribution, while high-income recipients are almost entirely married. In the case of women, married per-

TABLE 13
Major income source and labour force status shares of male income recipients by age, Ontario 1970

	Under 25	25–34	35–44	45–54	55–64	65–69	70 & over
Major source of income							
Wage and salary	94.8	93.4	88.6	86.2	77.6	40.6	12.9
Non-farm self-employment	1.6	3.3	6.2	6.4	7.6	3.2	2.5
Farm self-employment	0.3	0.8	2.4	2.9	3.6	3.0	1.4
Government transfers	1.7	1.9	2.0	2.8	4.7	26.6	52.2
Investment income	1.0	0.3	0.4	1.0	3.8	10.4	13.2
Retirement pensions and other income	0.5	0.4	0.4	0.6	2.8	16.1	18.0
Labour force status							
Employed labour force	76.4	93.0	93.6	92.1	83.3	38.1	14.8
Unemployed labour force	9.1	3.6	3.0	3.2	3.4	3.7	1.5
Not in labour force	14.6	3.4	3.5	4.8	13.3	58.2	83.7
Number in sample	5046	5168	4661	4156	3050	1021	1702
Percentage of sample	20.3	20.8	18.8	16.8	12.3	4.1	6.9

SOURCE: See source to Table 4.

TABLE 14

Major income source and labour force status shares of female income recipients by age, Ontario 1970

	Under 25	25–34	35–44	45–54	55–64	65–69	70 & over
Major source of income							
Wage and salary	92.9	85.3	80.7	75.0	59.5	16.9	5.0
Non-farm self-employment	0.7	1.7	2.7	2.5	2.2	0.9	0.4
Farm self-employment	0.1	0.2	0.6	0.3	0.5	0.0	0.3
Government transfers	3.7	6.3	5.6	6.3	9.4	59.7	75.1
Investment income	1.6	4.8	8.9	13.6	23.7	14.5	13.3
Retirement pensions and other income	1.0	1.6	1.6	2.3	4.7	8.0	5.8
Labour force status							
Employed labour force	67.6	67.4	72.1	67.2	54.8	14.2	4.6
Unemployed labour force	7.1	4.6	3.4	4.2	1.9	1.3	0.3
Not in labour force	25.3	28.0	24.5	28.6	43.3	84.5	95.0
Number in sample	4246	3242	2852	2764	2045	1145	2420
Percentage of sample	22.7	17.3	15.2	14.8	10.9	6.1	12.9

SOURCE: See source to Table 4.

sons occur most frequently among the low-income recipients, while singles appear with highest frequency at the top end. The widowed, separated, and divorced ('other') category is also larger among women than men, particularly in the next-to-bottom income class, where there are many older persons receiving government transfers.

As regards mother tongue, it can be seen that English predominates; in the case of men, this is particularly so at the two ends of the distribution. The bottom group, however, is likely to comprise young workers still in school, while the top group probably includes prime-age income recipients much farther along on their life-cycle income profile. Those with German mother tongue tend to be slightly overrepresented at the top end of the distribution, those with Italian mother tongue overrepresented in the lower-middle portion of the distribution, and those with French mother tongue near the bottom end of the distribution. In the case of women, the proportion where mother tongue is French tends to remain fairly stable across income classes and does not markedly decline at the top end of the distribution.

In summary, then, it is seen that individuals' characteristics differ systematically by income class. Most of those receiving incomes of less than $2000 are women, or men who are very young (students), old (retirees), or single. Many, particularly women, are not in the labour force at all, and others have a relatively weak attachment to the labour force (in the form of part-time or part-year work) and fairly high unemployment. Correspondingly, the low incomes received have a large transfer component and an above-average investment component. On the other hand, most of those with incomes above $25 000 are married, middle-aged men who have a very strong attachment to the labour force and virtually no unemployment. They include a relatively large number of (non-farm) self-employed and receive substantial income in the form of investment and self-employment income. Between these two extremes lies the majority of workers, most of whom are employees whose incomes consists mainly of wages and salaries.

Consider now the differences in income recipients' characteristics, which are presented in Tables 13 and 14 for men and women respectively. I shall concentrate here on two characteristics that show particularly interesting patterns across the different age groups; these are highlighted in Figures 30 and 31. In the case of major source of income, one should note the marked decline in wage and salary income as the major source of income as age increases. At the same time, government transfers, investment income, and pension income tend to rise in importance, reflecting in part an

Figure 30:
Major source of income shares of male income recipients by
age group, Ontario 1970
Source: Table 13

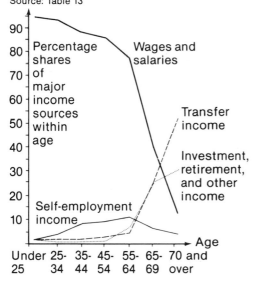

increased accumulation of wealth with age and decreased participation in the labour force. In other words there appears to be a fairly steady and marked shift in income sources over the life cycle toward non-wage income forms, very much as is to be expected on the basis of the life-cycle saving, capital accumulation, and labour supply behaviour discussed in Part One. This shift away from wage and salary income is further underlined by the figures on labour force status over the life cycle. In the case of men the employment and participation rates peak in early middle age and then fall with increasing age and retirement. A similar pattern is observed for women, except that substantially larger proportions of female recipients in all age groups are not in the labour force.

In summary, then, it is seen that there are very marked life-cycle patterns (particularly for men) of labour force experience and the relative importance of different income sources. Consequently, within different age groups, income inequality appears to be determined by rather different factors. Among the young, inequality patterns are critically affected by labour market attachment and unemployment; among middle-aged workers, by educational and occupational factors (as we shall see in the next section)

Figure 31:
Percentage of male and female income recipients not in labour force by
age, Ontario 1970

Source: Tables 13 and 14

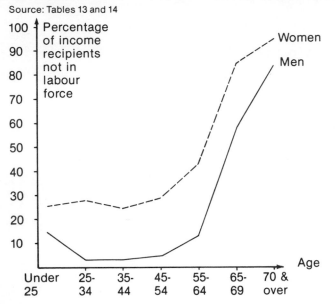

and by labour supply factors, particularly for women; and among the old, by
government transfer programs, pension provisions, and accumulated investment income.

EDUCATIONAL AND OCCUPATIONAL DIFFERENCES IN INCOME

According to the theory of human capital discussed in Part One, earnings
differences between individuals are to be expected because of differences in
the amount of formal education received and in the amount of work experience and on-the-job training acquired. Essentially, investment of time and
resources in education and training increases one's productivity on the labour market and thus results in higher wages. Educational credentials may
also serve as a screening device on the labour market and as entrance
requirements to particular occupations. Consequently, one would expect a
strong positive effect of education on earnings, and indeed a cumulative
effect if learning on the job is positively related to the level of formal education. And since earnings are the major source of income for most income
recipients, these expected patterns should also show through for total

TABLE 15
Distribution of male income recipients by education, Ontario 1970 (percentages)

Income ($)	Less than grade 5	Grades 5–8	Grades 9–11	Grades 12–13	Some university, no degree	University 3–4 with degree	University 5 + with degree
Less than 500	3.3	1.9	6.9	4.1	2.7	1.3	0.9
500–999	3.7	2.3	4.3	5.2	7.1	1.9	1.5
1000–1499	14.3	6.7	3.2	4.5	6.6	2.8	1.3
1500–1999	8.4	4.3	2.4	3.4	6.9	4.3	2.5
2000–2999	11.5	7.5	4.9	5.1	8.6	5.7	3.4
3000–3999	8.3	7.8	5.6	5.0	5.0	3.6	4.4
4000–4999	9.2	8.3	6.5	5.7	5.2	3.6	3.2
5000–5999	10.1	10.9	8.4	7.0	6.3	4.0	4.4
6000–6999	9.3	11.5	10.1	8.9	6.2	2.5	2.2
7000–7999	6.9	11.3	11.5	9.8	6.8	5.0	3.6
8000–8999	5.8	9.0	10.0	8.5	6.1	4.4	3.4
9000–9999	2.7	6.0	8.1	8.0	6.5	5.1	3.6
10000–11999	3.4	6.6	9.3	11.1	9.5	10.8	9.6
12000–14999	1.4	3.2	5.1	7.2	7.5	16.5	14.2
15000–24999	1.4	1.8	3.0	5.3	7.2	21.4	25.3
25000 and over	0.3	0.7	0.7	1.3	1.7	7.0	16.8
Percentage	5.06	25.76	31.19	23.08	7.07	3.76	4.07
Median income ($)	4054	6199	6771	7112	6258	11064	13298

SOURCE: See source to Table 4.

TABLE 16
Distribution of female income recipients by education, Ontario 1970 (percentages)

Income ($)	Less than grade 5	Grades 5–8	Grades 9–11	Grades 12–13	Some university, no degree	University 3–4 with degree	University 5+ with degree
Less than 500	7.4	9.9	17.2	14.3	13.4	9.8	5.5
500–999	11.8	11.8	10.7	10.5	11.8	10.2	5.5
1000–1499	34.0	23.3	11.9	9.3	8.6	8.1	5.5
1500–1999	11.8	10.8	7.3	5.6	6.9	7.6	4.4
2000–2999	12.8	14.2	12.2	8.5	8.9	9.4	8.8
3000–3999	9.8	13.1	12.9	10.9	6.9	6.5	8.1
4000–4999	6.2	8.2	11.7	12.9	7.5	6.1	9.2
5000–5999	2.2	3.7	6.9	10.1	8.6	4.8	5.5
6000–6999	1.2	2.1	3.9	7.6	7.5	5.0	4.8
7000–7999	1.1	0.9	2.2	4.2	6.4	6.7	4.4
8000–8999	0.7	0.6	1.2	2.3	4.7	7.8	5.9
9000–9999	0.3	0.3	0.6	1.3	3.3	5.2	7.0
10000–11999	0.2	0.3	0.6	1.1	3.5	4.3	8.1
12000–14999	0.2	0.3	0.4	0.6	0.9	5.7	6.6
15000–24999	0.1	0.2	0.1	0.5	0.7	2.6	9.9
25000 and over	0.0	0.2	0.0	0.4	0.4	0.4	0.7
Percentage	4.84	21.90	32.16	30.77	5.98	2.98	1.45
Median income ($)	1453	1728	2229	3165	3058	3768	5535

SOURCE: See source to Table 4.

TABLE 17
Income inequality measures among male income recipients by education, Ontario 1970

Measure	Less than grade 5	Grades 5-8	Grades 9-11	Grades 12-13	Some university, no degree	University 3-4 with degree	University 5 + with degree
Shares							
Bottom 10%	1.4	1.4	0.6	0.7	0.8	1.0	1.1
Top 10%	26.4	23.7	23.6	25.7	29.5	25.6	26.0
Gini coefficient	0.406	0.345	0.360	0.383	0.449	0.393	0.389
Atkinson index							
$\epsilon = 1.05$	0.297	0.238	0.331	0.324	0.379	0.308	0.294
$\epsilon = 1.55$	0.435	0.369	0.556	0.516	0.551	0.472	0.450
$\epsilon = 2.55$	0.651	0.601	0.845	0.786	0.770	0.716	0.702
Coefficient of variation	0.74	0.63	0.65	0.69	0.80	0.68	0.67
Mean income ($)	4690	6294	6844	7537	7373	12337	15559

SOURCE: See source to Table 15.

TABLE 18
Income inequality measures among female income recipients by education level, Ontario 1970

Measure	Less than grade 5	Grades 5–8	Grades 9–11	Grades 12–13	Some university, no degree	University 3–4 with degree	University 5+ with degree
Shares							
Bottom 10%	1.5	1.1	0.5	0.5	0.5	0.5	0.6
Top 10%	29.0	28.4	27.8	26.7	28.6	29.3	29.7
Gini coefficient	0.404	0.423	0.456	0.445	0.478	0.482	0.456
Atkinson index							
$\epsilon = 1.05$	0.275	0.321	0.423	0.423	0.458	0.454	0.399
$\epsilon = 1.55$	0.401	0.479	0.629	0.635	0.664	0.655	0.593
$\epsilon = 2.55$	0.625	0.727	0.856	0.862	0.873	0.864	0.830
Coefficient of variation	0.78	0.80	0.82	0.80	0.88	0.88	0.81
Mean income ($)	2117	2389	2794	3514	4043	5126	7296

SOURCE: Table 17

income receipts being considered in this chapter. Tables 15 and 16 show the distributions of income by education level for men and women respectively. In general, incomes rise with the education level from a median of $4054 for men and $1453 for women with less than a grade five education to a median of $13 298 for men and $5535 for women with graduate degrees. The distributions tend to shift to the right along the income axis with higher levels of education. One exception to this rising income pattern, however, is for those who start university but don't complete it; usually they are not quite as well off as those who enter the labour force immediately after completing high school, which suggests that there may well be some 'credentials effect' at the upper end of the educational distribution. Note also the predominance of persons with only grades 5–13 education (80 per cent for men and 85 per cent for women), and the markedly smaller proportions with university degrees (7.8 per cent for men and only 4.4 per cent for women). Tables 17 and 18 present the corresponding inequality statistics for the different education groups. For men it appears that the different inequality measures give conflicting impressions of how income inequality changes from one distribution to another; while for women the summary measures tend to increase with educational level except for the very top category.

On-the-job work experience is also expected to affect one's labour income and at a gradually decreasing rate as one gets older. Tables 19 and 20 show how median incomes change with age for given sex and education groups. In the case of men (Figure 32) the cross-section age-income profiles are generally concave; the higher-education profiles climb more steeply, peak later, and flatten out less than the lower-education profiles. Indeed, for those with university education, no downturn occurs in median incomes. More broadly, the income-generating effects of education and work experience appear to be strongly reinforcing. Thus educational differences in income across individuals tend to widen with age with a resulting tendency to increase inequality with age as well. In the case of women (see Figure 33) the cross-section age-income profiles have somewhat different shapes. The lower education profiles are again concave, while the upper education ones are bimodal, rising steeply during the periods of greatest labour force attachment and falling off during the period when more time is spent at home with children.

The incomes of individuals would also be expected to differ by occupation. Some occupations pay much more than others, and some have a much broader range of remuneration than others. This is illustrated in Tables 21–24 for selected groups of occupations for men and women sepa-

TABLE 19
Median incomes by education and age for male income recipients, Ontario 1970 (dollars)

Education	Under 25	25–34	35–44	45–54	55–64
Less than grade 5	1950	5 600	6 260	5 770	5 208
Grades 5–8	3756	6 402	7 343	7 048	6 260
Grades 9–11	2064	7 390	8 500	8 363	7 411
Grades 12–13	2757	8 114	9 799	9 835	8 400
Some university, no degree	1969	7 875	10 442	11 321	9 538
University 3–4, with degree	2471	10 156	14 903	16 753	19 259
University 5+, with degree	3417	10 008	17 778	20 775	20 781

SOURCE: See source to Table 4.

TABLE 20
Median incomes by education and age for female income recipients, Ontario 1970 (dollars)

Education	Under 25	25–34	35–44	45–54	55–64
Less than grade 5	1205	2125	2738	2529	1338
Grades 5–8	1981	2521	2583	2587	2130
Grades 9–11	1313	2758	2805	3166	2788
Grades 12–13	2383	4199	3513	3685	3608
Some university, no degree	1471	5083	5038	4300	5045
University, with degree	2368	5971	5300	5668	7334

SOURCE: See source to Table 4.

rately. Exact definitions of occupation titles are found in Appendix B. As can be seen in the case of male income recipients, the occupations, ranked from the lowest median income level to the highest, are farming and related services, clerical and related, construction trades, machining and fabrication, sales, engineering and related, medicine and health, and managerial and related. The median income level in the top occupational grouping is more than four times that of the bottom.

Figure 32:
Median income by age and education level for male
income recipients, Ontario 1970
Source: Table 19

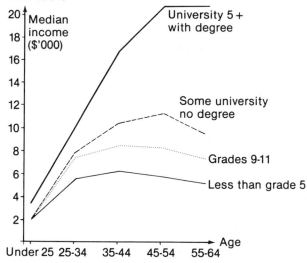

Figure 33:
Median income by age and education level for female income
recipients, Ontario 1970
Source: Table 20

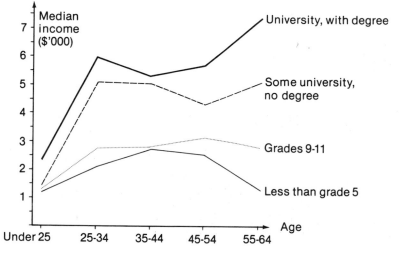

TABLE 21
Distribution of male income recipients by selected occupations, Ontario 1970 (percentages)

Income ($)	Farming & related	Services	Clerical & related	Construction trades	Machining & fabrication	Sales	Engineering & related	Medicine & health	Managerial & related
Less than 500	11.6	6.0	4.3	2.7	1.3	4.1	0.9	0.3	0.1
500–999	10.7	4.9	3.7	3.1	1.4	4.0	1.7	2.8	0.5
1000–1499	6.8	3.8	3.1	3.0	1.8	3.3	1.2	2.8	0.2
1500–1999	6.6	3.6	2.7	2.1	1.5	2.5	2.5	2.5	0.6
2000–2999	13.7	6.5	4.4	5.8	3.5	4.1	3.9	3.4	1.4
3000–3999	10.1	8.9	6.3	5.7	4.5	4.0	2.7	2.5	1.4
4000–4999	7.9	9.8	7.1	6.8	7.0	4.7	3.2	5.2	1.2
5000–5999	7.7	11.3	9.6	8.9	10.9	7.5	3.5	6.5	3.5
6000–6999	4.5	10.5	13.2	11.3	14.0	8.6	5.5	9.3	3.9
7000–7999	4.9	10.4	15.0	10.2	14.3	9.6	9.0	5.6	5.9
8000–8999	3.6	5.6	11.2	8.9	12.7	9.1	9.0	5.2	6.9
9000–9999	2.3	6.4	7.4	8.3	9.6	6.7	10.5	2.5	7.1
10000–11999	2.7	7.0	6.5	13.0	10.5	12.0	14.7	4.9	14.8
12000–14999	2.3	3.1	3.8	6.5	5.1	8.8	16.4	4.3	16.8
15000–24999	3.0	2.0	1.5	3.1	1.7	9.2	13.9	15.1	23.9
25000 and over	1.7	0.2	0.3	0.5	0.2	1.9	1.6	27.2	11.9
Percentage of all recipients	4.4	8.3	7.6	8.5	13.6	8.8	4.2	1.3	5.4
Median income ($)	3059	5575	6667	7059	7287	7750	9657	10571	12446

SOURCE: See source to Table 4.

TABLE 22

Income inequality measures among male income recipients by selected occupations, Ontario 1970

Measure	Farming & related	Services	Clerical & related	Construction trades	Machining & fabrication	Sales	Engineering & related	Medicine & health	Managerial & related
Shares									
Bottom 10%	0.5	0.7	1.0	1.2	2.2	0.7	1.5	0.8	2.7
Top 10%	36.9	24.1	20.9	22.2	18.9	26.7	23.3	28.6	24.3
Gini coefficient	0.523	0.369	0.309	0.325	0.251	0.382	0.316	0.453	0.323
Atkinson index									
$\epsilon = 1.05$	0.480	0.313	0.250	0.238	0.143	0.320	0.208	0.372	0.175
$\epsilon = 1.55$	0.671	0.513	0.433	0.394	0.239	0.518	0.335	0.540	0.255
$\epsilon = 2.55$	0.872	0.801	0.747	0.684	0.471	0.802	0.592	0.769	0.409
Coefficient of variation	1.06	0.66	0.55	0.58	0.45	0.67	0.54	0.80	0.57
Mean income ($)	4647	5908	6507	7381	7399	8665	10616	16056	15115

SOURCE: Table 21

TABLE 23
Distribution of female income recipients by selected occupations, Ontario 1970 (percentages)

Income ($)	Services	Sales	Processing	Machining & fabrication	Clerical & related	Medicine & health	Managerial & related	Teaching
Less than 500	20.7	16.9	13.7	4.5	6.9	5.3	5.4	5.6
500–999	14.6	14.0	7.8	7.4	7.6	6.4	1.8	5.8
1000–1499	12.0	10.1	10.9	7.0	6.7	7.7	2.9	4.9
1500–1999	9.1	9.3	5.6	6.1	5.5	5.6	2.5	3.6
2000–2999	15.0	13.8	11.5	16.1	10.0	10.0	6.5	6.6
3000–3999	13.2	14.9	17.1	24.9	14.5	12.7	6.5	5.7
4000–4999	7.7	8.6	15.8	18.1	18.5	14.5	14.4	6.0
5000–5999	3.0	4.1	9.0	9.3	13.5	9.1	13.3	10.1
6000–6999	1.5	3.1	4.0	3.7	8.3	11.0	9.0	12.3
7000–7999	1.2	1.6	2.8	1.1	3.9	8.3	11.5	11.2
8000–8999	0.7	1.2	0.6	0.7	2.0	4.4	4.3	10.5
9000–9999	0.6	0.4	0.0	0.5	1.2	1.4	3.2	6.7
10 000–11 999	0.5	0.7	0.6	0.1	0.7	1.8	5.4	5.8
12 000–14 999	0.1	0.6	0.3	0.3	0.4	0.7	5.8	3.0
15 000–24 999	0.1	0.6	0.3	0.0	0.1	0.5	6.5	2.3
25 000 and over	0.1	0.1	0.0	0.1	0.1	0.3	1.1	0.0
Percentage of all recipients	10.4	6.1	1.7	4.9	25.0	5.9	1.5	4.6
Median income ($)	1648	1984	3029	3357	3917	4159	5752	6138

SOURCE: See source to Table 4.

TABLE 24
Income inequality measures among female income recipients by selected occupations, Ontario 1970

Measure	Services	Sales	Processing	Machining & fabrication	Clerical & related	Medicine & health	Managerial & related	Teaching
Shares								
Bottom 10%	0.5	0.6	0.6	1.4	0.9	1.0	0.9	0.7
Top 10%	29.8	31.1	24.0	20.5	21.8	24.4	28.8	23.1
Gini coefficient	0.472	0.474	0.400	0.308	0.348	0.377	0.392	0.361
Atkinson index								
$\epsilon = 1.05$	0.428	0.425	0.366	0.213	0.285	0.295	0.313	0.316
$\epsilon = 1.55$	0.626	0.622	0.577	0.349	0.465	0.463	0.504	0.516
$\epsilon = 2.55$	0.850	0.846	0.835	0.612	0.749	0.729	0.804	0.797
Coefficient of variation	0.87	0.90	0.70	0.54	0.61	0.70	0.72	0.64
Mean income ($)	2201	2639	3073	3349	3865	4488	7037	6042

SOURCE: Table 23

TABLE 25
Proportions of male and female income recipients in different occupation groups,
Ontario 1970 (percentages)

Occupation group	Men	Women
Managerial, administrative, and related	5.4	1.5
Engineering, natural science, and mathematics	4.2	0.5
Social science and related	0.9	0.9
Religion	0.3	0.0
Teaching	2.3	4.6
Medicine and health	1.3	5.9
Artistic, recreation, and related	1.0	0.6
Clerical and related	7.6	25.0
Sales	8.8	6.1
Services	8.3	10.4
Farming and related	4.4	1.3
Other primary occupations	1.5	0.1
Processing	4.0	1.7
Machining and product fabrication	13.6	4.9
Construction trades	8.5	0.1
Transport equipment operating	5.0	0.2
Other occupations	7.1	2.5
Occupations not stated	6.8	5.9
Not employed	9.1	27.6

SOURCE: See source to Table 4.

In the case of women the ranking by median income is services, sales, processing, machining and fabrication, clerical and related, medicine and health, managerial and related, and teaching. What is of interest here is not so much the similarities in the two rankings as the differences. For women, teaching is a high-income occupation, whereas sales is much lower than for men (the latter, however, is a very broad category, and men and women may be selling rather different things). Within the same broad occupational groupings, women receive much lower incomes than men, ranging from a relative income ratio of 0.26 in sales to 0.59 in clerical (a rather more homogeneous category). At the same time, male and female income distributions differ also in their relative proportions in the various occupations (see Table 25). Women are relatively concentrated in teaching, medicine and health, clerical and related, and services, but are relatively underrepresented in managerial and related, machining and product fabrication, construction trades, and transport equipment operating for example (see Table

TABLE 26
Median incomes by occupation and age for male income recipients, Ontario 1970 (dollars)

Occupation / Age	Under 25	25–34	35–44	45–54	55–64
Managerial and related	5536	9772	13744	14686	14683
Engineering and related	3898	9257	11820	13143	11587
Social science and related	925	7499	14241	12374	11011
Teaching and related	4125	9122	14034	14348	11993
Medicine and health	2682	8336	22987	20794	11654
Recreation and related	1170	7255	9163	10555	8241
Clerical and related	3000	7195	8179	7960	7268
Sales	1879	8093	9315	9851	8970
Services	1361	6648	7618	6585	5692
Farming and related	768	4432	4827	4922	3639
Other primary	2438	7200	7954	8005	7298
Processing	4237	7692	7911	7922	7915
Machining and fabrication	4570	7445	8160	8298	7359
Construction trades	2943	7695	8485	7958	6923
Transport operating	3494	7028	8009	7832	7378

SOURCE: See source to Table 4.

TABLE 27
Median incomes by selected occupations and age for female income recipients,
Ontario 1970 (dollars)

Occupation groups	Under 25	25–34	35–44	45–54	55–64
Teaching and related	5415	6716	6214	6500	8250
Managerial and related	4077	5600	6000	7045	8000
Medicine and health	2648	4439	4341	4375	5107
Clerical and related	3151	4224	3914	4572	4881
Machining and fabrication	2692	3115	3598	3845	3710
Sales	814	1703	2109	3034	2969
Processing	1917	3400	3286	3393	3000
Services	706	2049	2063	2435	2535

SOURCE: See source to Table 4.

26). Thus male and female income differences are reflected not only by differences in incomes within occupations but also to some extent by occupational segregation of the labour force.

Just as in the case of education groups, occupational income distributions incorporate age effects as well. Tables 26 and 27 present (cross-sectional) median age-income profiles within occupations for men and women separately. There are again substantial differences in income across age groups, much the same as for education, except that the cross-sectional age-income profiles within occupations do not seem to diverge at higher age levels the way they do within education groups. It is clear, though, that some occupations offer much greater opportunities for long-run income growth than others; for that reason the question of occupational opportunities should be of some concern. Note also that age-income profiles for occupations with generally higher education and skill levels tend to peak later and reach higher income levels. Of course, not all individuals with a given education level remain in the same occupation throughout their lives; they may move up or down the distribution over time by changing occupations, particularly if the latter are narrowly defined. For example, one may start off in a services or clerical occupation and then move up to a managerial position later in one's working life. Such changes, however, are less likely to occur between very broad occupational categories.

GENERAL CONCLUSIONS

What can one conclude from the general findings of this chapter? First of all, there appears to be a very marked pattern in individual income over the life cycle: incomes vary with age according to labour market attachment and experience, educational attainment and occupation, transfer receipts, and investment benefits. Cross-sectional income profiles tend to be concave with respect to age, first rising and then flattening out or declining, so that in any cross-section of the distribution there is bound to be some degree of inequality simply because people are at different stages of their life cycle. Thus income inequality will depend a good deal on the age distribution of the population, as discussed in Part One. Indeed the large increases in recent years in the number of retirees and young entrants to the labour force would be expected to result in a trend toward higher inequality figures. To the extent that the trend simply reflects the movement of different sized cohorts along a given life-cycle income profile, one should not conclude that the distributional situation is worsening or that additional government policies are called for on this account. On the other hand, this does raise the question of the extent to which individuals within a cohort are mobile and can change their relative income positions. Do those at the bottom or top of age-specific distributions stay there, or do they in fact move around within their distribution? The question of mobility has very important implications for welfare and policy. If the same people remain at the extremes of the cohort-specific distributions as they proceed along their life-cycle path, inequality is much more undesirable than otherwise, and government policies may be called for to loosen this immobility. Unfortunately, however, we are not in a position to answer this question without detailed longitudinal income data, which are not available for Canada.

A second principal conclusion of this chapter is the crucial importance from a distributional point of view of individuals' labour market attachment. Those with low income tend to have weak and discontinued labour market experience; those with high incomes tend to have very strong and continuous market experience. Consequently, in evaluating various social security, educational, health, and transfer programs, governments should have particular concern for possible labour supply and employment effects and their corresponding distributional implications. This question will be discussed further in the next chapter.

Thirdly, the empirical results obtained so far appear to lend at least some support to the segmented labour market approach and the presence of marked occupational restrictions mentioned in Part One. Within broad occupation and education groups, incomes differ substantially between men and women – by as much as 50 per cent or more; and at the same time there appears to be a fair amount of occupational segregation and sex-typing of jobs.

Finally, it has been found that individuals' characteristics vary systematically across income classes particularly with respect to sex, labour market attachment, age, educational attainment, and occupation. Because, for welfare and policy purposes, we are interested in *family* income distributions, we now need to look at how the above characteristics are reflected in family income patterns.

7
Incomes of family units

INTRODUCTION

The distribution of family incomes is built up from the incomes of individuals considered in the last chapter. We now turn to family distributions as the principal focus for the rest of this study. Whereas individuals are the basic recipients of income, families may be viewed as the basic beneficiary units of income. Common resources and consumption bundles are shared within the family. Consequently, if income distributions are to be viewed as indicators of the distribution of well-being across the population, ultimately it is family income distributions that we ought to look at. According to the theoretical discussion in Part One (Chapter 2) many important economic decisions, particularly about labour supply and nonmarket uses of time, are made in the family. In addition, the only reasonably complete distributional data available for Ontario and Canada as a whole since the 1971 Census data, which were examined in the last chapter, are in the form of family income data collected from the (now annual) Surveys of Consumer Finances. The asset and wealth data to be discussed in the next chapter as well are collected essentially for families, and it is for a family framework that I shall combine income and asset data in later portions of the study.

The family unit used in this chapter is the 'census family' unit consisting of either a husband and wife (with or without children who have not married) or a parent with one or more children who have not married, living together in the same dwelling (Statistics Canada 1975b, 8). A person not in a family is an 'unattached individual,' who is living alone or with unrelated individuals (such as a lodger) or with relatives in other than a husband-wife or parent-unmarried child relationship (ibid). 'Family units' can thus be subdivided according to family size into families of two or more (which will

TABLE 28
Distribution of income among family units, Ontario 1973

Income ($)	Percentage
Zero or negative	2.0
1–999	1.9
1000–1999	5.8
2000–2999	7.2
3000–3999	4.5
4000–4999	5.2
5000–5999	4.4
6000–7999	9.0
8000–9999	9.5
10 000–11 999	10.6
12 000–14 999	14.6
15 000–24 999	20.8
25 000 and over	4.6
Number in sample	7624
Median income ($)	10 238

SOURCE: Based on data for Ontario from the 1973
Consumer Finance Micro Data Release Tape supplied by
Statistics Canada.

be referred to simply as 'families') and unattached individuals. The head of a
family is defined as the husband or (in his absence) the parent. The head of a
one-person family unit is the person himself (Statistics Canada 1976b, 27).

The data source for the present chapter and for much of the work following in Part Three is the 1973 Consumer Finance Micro Data Tape (Census
Families) of about 7600 family units for Ontario collected in the 1974
Survey of Consumer Finances and provided by the Consumer Income and
Expenditure Division of Statistics Canada (1975b). The chapter first looks
at income differences by family size and by age and sex of family head,
then examines different family characteristics including education and occupation of the head, and finally considers different sources of income by age
and income class.

Table 28 and Figure 34 show the distribution of income among all family
units in Ontario in 1973.[1] As can be seen, the distribution is substantially

1 All tables in Chapter 7 are based on the subsample of Ontario records from the 1973
   Consumer Finance Micro Data Release Tape provided by the Consumer Income and
   Expenditure Division of Statistics Canada. The responsibility for the use and interpre-
   tation of these data is entirely that of the authors.

Figure 34:

Distribution of income among family units, Ontario 1973

Source: Table 28

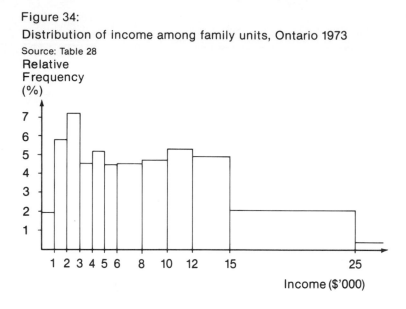

further right on the horizontal axis than those of individuals in 1970 reviewed in the last chapter. It should also be noted that it is customary for Statistics Canada to include family units with no income in family unit income distributions, whereas this was not the case for individuals. Virtually all family units, however, receive some income over a period of a year. Comparing Tables 29 and 5, one sees that the figures for income inequality among family units are markedly smaller than among individuals. It should also be observed that the distribution is slightly bimodal, as is often the case with a composite of several subdistributions that have very different shapes. In such cases it is more revealing to look at the underlying component distributions than the over-all one. This is indeed the case with the distribution of family units which, as was pointed out above, can be divided into separate distributions for 'families' (accounting for 73 per cent of family units) and for 'unattached individuals' (accounting for the remaining 27 per cent). This is done in Tables 30 and 31, and the resulting distributions graphed in Figure 35. There is a radical difference in the shape of the distributions for families and for unattached individuals. The former distribution has a much higher proportion in the upper income ranges and a

TABLE 29
Income inequality measures for family units, Ontario 1973

Shares	
Bottom 10%	1.2
Top 10%	24.5
Gini coefficient	0.374
Atkinson index	
$\epsilon = 1.05$	0.276
$\epsilon = 1.55$	0.420
$\epsilon = 2.55$	0.655
Coefficient of variation	0.66
Mean income ($)	11 091

SOURCE: Table 28

Figure 35:
Distributions of income for families of two or more and for
unattached men, Ontario 1973
Source: Table 30
Relative frequency (%)

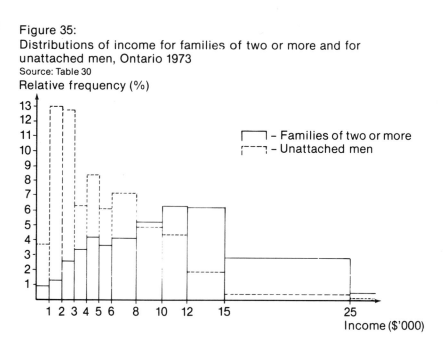

– Families of two or more
– Unattached men

Income ($'000)

TABLE 30
Distribution of income of family units by family size, Ontario 1973 (percentages)

Income	All family units	Families of two or more	Unattached individuals	
			Men	Women
Zero or negative	2.0	0.5	6.2	5.9
1–999	1.9	0.9	3.7	4.8
1000–1999	5.8	1.3	13.0	21.1
2000–2999	7.2	2.6	12.8	24.2
3000–3999	4.5	3.4	6.3	7.9
4000–4999	5.2	4.2	8.4	7.6
5000–5999	4.4	3.6	6.1	7.2
6000–7999	9.0	8.2	14.3	9.2
8000–9999	9.5	10.4	9.8	5.5
10000–11999	10.6	12.6	8.7	2.6
12000–14999	14.6	18.7	5.3	2.1
15000–24999	20.8	27.6	3.7	1.7
25000 and over	4.6	6.1	1.5	0.2
Total number in sample	7624	5563	805	1256
Proportion of family units	100.0	73.0	10.5	16.5
Median income ($)	10238	12338	·4934	2753

SOURCE: See source to Table 28.

TABLE 31
Income inequality measures for family units by size of family, Ontario 1973

Measure	All family units	Families of two or more	Unattached individuals	
			Men	Women
Shares				
Bottom 10%	1.2	2.1	0.3	0.5
Top 10%	24.5	22.4	29.9	31.1
Gini coefficient	0.374	0.306	0.456	0.453
Atkinson index				
$\epsilon = 1.05$	0.276	0.179	0.629	0.602
$\epsilon = 1.55$	0.420	0.275	0.994	0.993
$\epsilon = 2.55$	0.655	0.472	0.999	0.999
Coefficient of variation	0.66	0.52	0.85	0.87
Mean income ($)	11091	13198	6246	4039

SOURCE: Table 30

TABLE 32

Distribution of income among all family units by age of head, Ontario 1973 (percentages)

Income ($)	Under 25	25–34	35–44	45–54	55–64	65–69	70 & over
Zero or negative	7.2	1.2	0.9	1.4	2.7	1.8	0.7
1–999	5.4	1.7	0.7	1.1	2.6	2.9	0.2
1000–1999	9.1	1.5	1.2	2.7	6.0	9.2	18.8
2000–2999	5.5	1.8	1.1	1.6	4.7	17.7	30.6
3000–3999	6.0	3.2	1.7	2.0	4.0	9.6	10.3
4000–4999	8.4	3.5	3.6	2.3	3.7	9.0	11.2
5000–5999	8.0	3.6	2.7	2.2	4.6	7.2	6.6
6000–7999	12.5	10.0	7.5	6.3	9.5	12.3	8.1
8000–9999	12.0	11.8	8.9	10.0	9.7	8.4	4.4
10000–11999	9.7	14.9	12.2	10.8	11.8	6.0	2.4
12000–14999	9.4	20.3	19.6	16.7	15.0	6.4	2.9
15000–24999	6.8	23.7	32.6	33.1	19.7	7.4	2.8
25000 and over	0.0	2.7	7.2	9.9	6.0	2.1	0.9
Number in sample	763	1642	1372	1264	1085	513	985
Median income ($)	6463	11456	13370	13984	10430	4977	2988

SOURCE: See source to Table 28.

TABLE 33

Distribution of income among families of two by age of head, Ontario 1973 (percentages)

Income ($)	Under 25	25–34	35–44	45–54	55–64	65–69	70 & over
Less than 1000	2.8	1.5	4.3	1.2	1.3	1.6	0.0
1000–1999	1.9	2.6	1.7	1.6	2.0	2.4	2.5
2000–2999	3.2	2.0	3.5	2.0	3.5	9.8	13.4
3000–3999	4.5	1.7	3.5	3.6	3.9	10.6	16.3
4000–4999	4.5	2.0	1.7	1.6	3.1	11.0	20.2
5000–5999	2.3	2.6	4.3	2.0	3.3	9.0	13.1
6000–7999	11.3	7.3	7.8	5.2	11.1	15.1	13.6
8000–9999	15.8	4.9	13.0	14.2	11.8	12.2	8.5
10000–11999	16.3	10.8	10.4	17.4	15.8	8.2	3.8
12000–14999	19.0	20.9	13.0	18.6	19.5	8.6	4.4
15000–24999	18.6	39.8	30.4	26.3	19.3	9.4	3.3
25000 and over	0.0	3.8	6.1	6.1	5.5	2.0	1.1
Percentage of total	29.0	21.0	8.4	19.5	42.1	47.8	37.3
Number in sample	221	344	115	247	457	245	367
Median income ($)	10465	14088	11932	12176	11271	6644	4880

SOURCE: See source to Table 28.

TABLE 34

Distribution of income among families of three or more by age of head, Ontario 1973 (percentages)

Income ($)	Under 25	25–34	35–44	45–54	55–64	65–69	70 & over
Less than 1000	4.0	2.0	0.6	1.2	1.5	0.0	0.0
1000–1999	2.7	0.9	0.7	0.4	2.1	0.0	0.0
2000–2999	1.3	1.2	0.4	0.7	1.2	3.8	0.0
3000–3999	2.6	2.5	1.2	0.8	1.2	3.8	2.0
4000–4999	3.9	2.6	3.2	1.4	3.0	3.8	3.9
5000–5999	5.9	2.7	2.4	1.6	1.8	5.8	7.8
6000–7999	11.8	8.5	6.6	4.8	4.8	9.6	13.7
8000–9999	25.7	12.3	8.3	7.8	8.7	7.7	13.7
10000–11999	18.4	17.4	12.4	9.5	10.7	9.6	9.8
12000–14999	17.8	23.5	21.0	18.4	19.3	21.2	17.6
15000–24999	5.9	23.8	35.4	41.1	34.2	25.0	23.5
25000 and over	0.0	2.9	7.9	12.3	11.6	9.6	7.8
Percentage of total	19.9	61.4	82.6	66.1	31.0	10.1	5.2
Number in sample	152	1008	1133	835	336	52	51
Median income ($)	9367	12005	14035	15826	14338	12827	11795

SOURCE: See source to Table 28.

TABLE 35

Distribution of income among unattached men by age, Ontario 1973 (percentages)

Income ($)	Under 25	25–34	35–44	45–54	55–64	65–69	70 & over
Zero or negative	13.6	6.6	1.4	5.6	6.3	1.8	1.3
1–999	8.6	0.6	1.4	2.2	7.3	7.3	0.0
1000–1999	11.4	1.2	4.1	12.4	16.7	21.9	27.3
2000–2999	7.4	1.8	2.7	4.5	7.3	18.2	42.7
3000–3999	8.5	6.0	4.1	3.4	4.2	10.9	6.7
4000–4999	13.6	8.4	9.6	3.4	7.3	3.6	7.3
5000–5999	8.5	7.2	2.7	4.5	5.2	9.1	4.0
6000–7999	14.2	19.2	16.4	15.7	15.6	16.4	5.3
8000–9999	6.3	18.0	12.3	18.0	10.4	5.4	0.0
10000–11999	5.1	15.1	15.1	11.2	9.4	3.6	2.7
12000–14999	1.7	9.6	17.8	7.9	3.1	0.0	0.7
15000–24999	1.1	4.8	8.2	5.6	6.3	1.8	1.3
25000 and over	0.0	1.2	4.1	5.6	1.0	0.0	0.7
Percentage of total	23.1	10.1	5.3	7.0	8.8	10.7	15.2
Number in sample	176	166	73	89	96	55	150
Median income ($)	4036	7893	9300	7831	5182	3072	2500

SOURCE: See source to Table 28.

TABLE 36
Distribution of income among unattached women by age, Ontario 1973 (percentages)

Income ($)	Under 25	25–34	35–44	45–54	55–64	65–69	70 & over
Zero or negative	11.7	3.2	17.6	9.7	8.2	3.7	1.2
1–999	9.4	5.6	2.0	4.3	8.7	5.6	0.4
1000–1999	19.6	4.0	7.8	16.1	17.4	18.0	32.6
2000–2999	9.3	5.6	9.8	5.4	12.2	34.2	45.1
3000–3999	7.9	9.7	3.9	6.5	8.7	9.3	7.2
4000–4999	11.2	8.1	7.8	10.8	4.6	9.3	5.5
5000–5999	15.0	8.9	5.9	6.5	12.2	4.3	1.7
6000–7999	12.6	18.6	13.7	12.9	10.7	7.4	3.3
8000–9999	2.8	20.2	7.8	10.7	6.2	3.7	1.5
10000–11999	0.5	5.6	7.8	5.4	5.6	2.5	0.2
12000–14999	0.0	7.3	5.9	4.3	3.1	0.6	0.7
15000–24999	0.0	3.2	9.8	5.4	2.6	0.6	0.5
25000 and over	0.0	0.0	0.0	2.2	0.0	0.6	0.0
Percentage of total	28.0	7.6	3.7	7.4	18.1	31.4	42.3
Number in sample	214	124	51	93	196	161	417
Median income ($)	3000	6504	5168	4749	3413	2660	2348

SOURCE: See source to Table 28.

markedly lower level of inequality. Median incomes, for example, are
$12330 for families of two or more and only $4934 for unattached men and
$2753 for unattached women. As a consequence of these great differences
in shape, much of the further analysis in this study on income distributions
of family units will incorporate this disaggregation by family size.

DIFFERENCES BY SEX AND AGE OF HEAD OF FAMILY

As was shown in the previous chapter, the incomes of individuals follow
systematic age patterns, causing substantial income differences between age
groups. The same is true for family units. Tables 32–36 present summary
distributions by age for all family units disaggregated by family size. It can
be seen that the distributions tend to shift upward along the income axis
until middle age and then shift back somewhat until retirement, when
incomes fall off dramatically – much the same as for individual men. This is
illustrated in part in Figure 36, which shows the cross-section median
income profiles across age groups to be very distinctly concave. It also
shows, however, how different the profiles are for family units of different

Figure 36:
Median income by age of family head for different sized
family units, Ontario 1973
Source: Tables 32-36

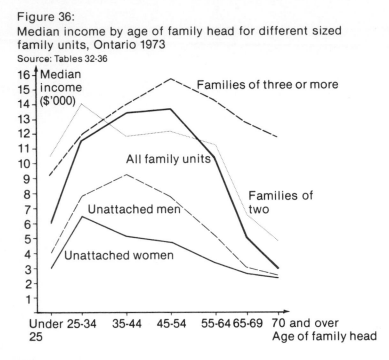

sizes. Young families of two tend to have higher incomes than other young family units. Among middle-aged family units, families with children tend to have higher incomes and unattached individuals relatively low incomes. Beyond middle age all the profiles decline, but again families receive substantially larger incomes than unattached individuals over sixty-four. Corresponding inequality figures for family units of different sizes are provided in Tables 37–41.

However, as family units do not remain the same size over the life cycle, any particular family unit is likely to move between distributions as it ages. This is illustrated in Figure 37 where it can be seen, for example, that the proportion of family units of three or more increases with age from 20 per cent among the youngest group to 83 per cent among the group 35–44, and then declines to only 5 per cent among the 70 and over group. The typical family tends to move from the lower to the upper profiles illustrated in Figure 36 as it increases in size during middle age and then to move back down to lower profiles as the family shrinks again. The result is a profile for all family units that is much more concave than the component profiles.

TABLE 37
Income inequality measures for all family units by age of head, Ontario 1973

Measure	Under 25	25–34	35–44	45–54	55–64	65–69	70 & over
Shares							
Bottom 10%	1.1	2.2	2.5	1.8	1.1	1.7	2.0
Top 10%	22.8	19.9	21.6	22.0	24.7	32.8	33.6
Gini Coefficient	0.369	0.276	0.282	0.306	0.370	0.458	0.438
Atkinson index							
$\epsilon = 1.05$	0.281	0.158	0.151	0.190	0.267	0.318	0.282
$\epsilon = 1.55$	0.440	0.253	0.232	0.305	0.431	0.438	0.391
$\epsilon = 2.55$	0.699	0.467	0.406	0.551	0.685	0.609	0.518
Coefficient of variation	0.63	0.47	0.50	0.54	0.66	0.95	0.92
Mean income ($)	7263	11939	14275	15016	11483	7052	4675

SOURCE: Table 32

TABLE 38
Income inequality measures for families of two by age of head, Ontario 1973

Measure	Under 25	25–34	35–44	45–54	55–64	65–69	70 & over
Shares							
Bottom 10%	1.6	1.7	1.0	1.9	1.8	2.2	3.0
Top 10%	21.6	19.2	22.6	21.8	23.3	28.4	27.2
Gini coefficient	0.306	0.280	0.349	0.300	0.323	0.386	0.338
Atkinson index							
$\epsilon = 1.05$	0.205	0.179	0.286	0.179	0.198	0.237	0.178
$\epsilon = 1.55$	0.341	0.298	0.501	0.285	0.304	0.333	0.246
$\epsilon = 2.55$	0.625	0.562	0.833	0.515	0.518	0.486	0.359
Coefficient of variation	0.51	0.47	0.59	0.52	0.56	0.70	0.67
Mean income ($)	11013	14651	13379	13825	12481	8723	6206

SOURCE: Table 33

TABLE 39
Income inequality measures for families of three or more by age of head, Ontario 1973

Measure	Under 25	25–34	35–44	45–54	55–64	65–69	70 & over
Shares							
Bottom 10%	1.5	2.3	2.6	2.7	1.8	2.0	3.0
Top 10%	19.0	20.8	20.7	21.6	22.7	23.7	23.4
Gini coefficient	0.260	0.278	0.279	0.279	0.311	0.336	0.317
Atkinson index							
$\epsilon = 1.05$	0.211	0.156	0.145	0.145	0.197	0.204	0.162
$\epsilon = 1.55$	0.418	0.250	0.221	0.222	0.317	0.308	0.231
$\epsilon = 2.55$	0.803	0.466	0.385	0.390	0.575	0.507	0.352
Coefficient of variation	0.46	0.47	0.48	0.48	0.54	0.58	0.55
Mean income ($)	9432	12928	15487	17359	16140	14277	13752

SOURCE: Table 34

TABLE 40
Income inequality measures for unattached men by age, Ontario 1973

Measure	Under 25	25–34	35–44	45–54	55–64	65–69	70 & over
Shares							
Bottom 10%	0.0	0.7	1.5	0.3	0.1	1.2	1.3
Top 10%	28.0	23.3	25.7	31.4	31.6	26.9	33.4
Gini coefficient	0.463	0.327	0.349	0.442	0.483	0.418	0.406
Atkinson index							
$\epsilon = 1.05$	0.797	0.547	0.237	0.655	0.664	0.321	0.294
$\epsilon = 1.55$	0.997	0.994	0.370	0.997	0.994	0.482	0.435
$\epsilon = 2.55$	0.999	0.999	0.629	0.999	0.999	0.735	0.702
Coefficient of variation	0.83	0.60	0.63	0.81	0.87	0.77	0.92
Mean income ($)	4329	8392	10202	8768	6257	4134	3362

SOURCE: Table 35

TABLE 41
Income inequality measures for unattached women by age, Ontario 1973

Measure	Under 25	25–34	35–44	45–54	55–64	65–69	70 & over
Shares							
Bottom 10%	0.0	0.6	0.0	0.0	0.1	1.3	1.4
Top 10%	24.6	23.5	31.8	33.5	30.4	30.9	28.0
Gini coefficient	0.437	0.350	0.509	0.498	0.479	0.413	0.344
Atkinson index							
$\epsilon = 1.05$	0.737	0.348	0.867	0.692	0.642	0.309	0.246
$\epsilon = 1.55$	0.993	0.661	0.998	0.988	0.986	0.475	0.394
$\epsilon = 2.55$	0.999	0.941	0.999	0.999	0.999	0.764	0.692
Coefficient of variation	0.74	0.63	0.91	0.94	0.88	0.86	0.71
Mean income ($)	3410	6768	6553	6168	4629	3642	2699

SOURCE: Table 36

One of the principal findings of the last chapter was the very great differences between individual men's and women's incomes. A similar pattern holds in the case of family units when classified according to the sex of the head. As can be seen in Tables 42 and 43 female-headed households constitute only about one-fifth of all family units, and their incomes are generally much lower than those for family units with a male head. The median income for the former is $3202 compared to $11 854 for the latter. It is apparent, then, that the economic role of the woman in a family is likely to have a substantial effect on the economic status of the family unit, and it is to this that we now turn in more detail.

DIFFERENT CHARACTERISTICS OF FAMILIES

Family units differ in a wide range of characteristics, one of the most important of which is the working status of the wife and other family members. Table 44 shows the median family incomes by number of income recipients within the family unit and by age of head. Not surprisingly, additional income recipients within the family on average result in a substantially higher family income, particularly in later middle age. Just as the family size varies systematically over the life cycle of the family, so also does the average number of income recipients. Table 45 shows the percentage of family units within given age groups that have different numbers of income recipients (within any age group, the percentages fall short of

Figure 37:
Percentage breakdown of family units by family size for
different ages of family head, Ontario 1973
Source: Table 32-36

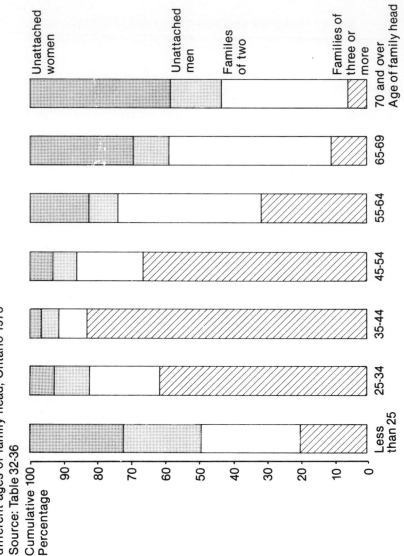

TABLE 42
Distribution of income among family units by sex of family head,
Ontario 1973 (percentages)

Income ($)	Male head	Female head
Under 1000	2.1	10.2
1000–1999	2.6	17.6
2000–2999	3.6	20.5
3000–3999	3.3	8.6
4000–4999	4.3	8.4
5000–5999	3.6	7.4
6000–7999	8.8	9.9
8000–9999	10.2	7.0
10000–11999	12.4	3.8
12000–14999	17.7	3.2
15000–24999	25.6	3.1
25000 or more	5.8	0.4
Percentage of total	78.6	21.4
Number in sample	5993	1631
Median income ($)	11854	3202

SOURCE: See source to Table 28.

TABLE 43
Income inequality measures for family units by sex of head, Ontario 1973

Measure	Male head	Female head
Shares		
Bottom 10%	1.4	0.6
Top 10%	22.6	31.9
Gini coefficient	0.337	0.464
Atkinson index		
$\epsilon = 1.05$	0.230	0.447
$\epsilon = 1.55$	0.366	0.756
$\epsilon = 2.55$	0.625	0.966
Coefficient of variation	0.58	0.89
Mean income ($)	12994	4779

SOURCE: Table 42

TABLE 44
Median income of family units by number of income recipients and age of family head,
Ontario 1973 (dollars)

Number of persons with income	Under 25	25–34	35–44	45–54	55–64	65–69	70 & over
One	4565	9184	10899	9047	6513	3283	2424
Two	11213	13999	14944	14638	12912	7621	5046
Three or more	n.a.	n.a.	17900	18905	17730	15436	13009
All family units	6068	11563	13445	13733	10423	4977	2988

NOTE: n.a. means reliable estimate not available.
SOURCE: See source to Table 28.

summing to one hundred by the proportion of family units with no income recipients). As can be seen in Figure 38, the average number of income recipients generally increases with age until age 45 to 54 and then declines. The greatest relative changes occur in the three-or-more-recipient category, which peaks in the 45 to 54 age group, while the proportion of family units with only a single income recipient (49 per cent of the total) troughs in the same age interval.

As expected, the working status of a wife in particular seems to be highly correlated with family incomes. Table 46 presents median income figures for husband-wife families by working status of the wife. About 60 per cent of such families did not have a working wife, while 40 per cent did in 1973. The median income for the first group was $11323, while that for the second was $14722, a difference of over $3000.

One of the principal factors related to a wife's labour market activity is whether or not the family has children at home. As shown in Table 47 the presence of children under 16 does tend to result in somewhat lower median family incomes (again among husband-wife families) although this difference diminishes with age and may even reverse itself among upper age groups.

What is the average contribution of a wife to a family's total income? The mean incomes of wives are shown in Table 48 along with the mean incomes of heads of family units by age. Mean incomes of wives can be seen to peak at about $2100 among young families and then decline (cross-sectionally) with age. Also presented are mean incomes for other family recipients (such as teenage children), and these can be seen to peak at

TABLE 45
Percentage of family units with different numbers of income recipients by age of family head, Ontario 1973

Number of persons with income	Under 25	25–34	35–44	45–54	55–64	65–69	70 & over	% Over-all
One	58.2	51.0	43.4	33.9	46.1	57.5	59.9	49.3
Two	34.7	47.7	39.6	32.7	34.4	34.9	34.9	38.8
Three or more	0.0	0.1	16.3	32.2	16.9	6.0	4.5	11.9
Total number	763	1642	1372	1264	1085	513	.985	7624

SOURCE: See source to Table 28.

TABLE 46
Median income of husband-wife families by working status of wife, Ontario 1973

	Median income ($)	Percentage
Wife employed	14 722	40.3
Wife not employed	11 323	59.7
Total	12 807	100.0

SOURCE: See source to Table 28.

TABLE 47
Median income of husband-wife families by age of head and children less than sixteen,
Ontario 1973 (dollars)

	Under 25	25–34	35–44	45–54	55–64	65–69	70 & over
With children under 16	9630	12 463	14 283	14 922	12 875	n.a.	n.a.
No children under 16	11 114	14 860	15 947	15 975	12 550	7352	4049

NOTE: n.a. means reliable estimates not available.
SOURCE: See source to Table 28.

TABLE 48
Mean income among husband-wife families of family head and wife by age of family head,
Ontario 1973 (dollars)

	Under 25	25–34	35–44	45–54	55–64	65–69	70 & over
Family head	5378	9740	11 749	10 932	8754	5363	3343
Wife	1354	2123	1843	1830	1332	896	741
Other family members	n.a.	n.a.	478	1775	1339	623	629
Total family income	6735	11 863	14 070	14 536	11 425	6882	4713

NOTE: n.a. means reliable estimates not available.
SOURCE: See source to Table 28.

Figure 38:
Proportions of family units with different number of income recipients by age of family head, Ontario 1973
Source: Table 45

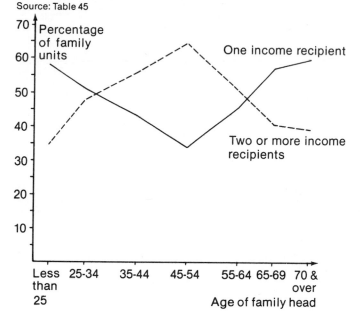

about $1800 in the age of family head interval 45 to 54 and decline thereafter as older children leave the family. It should be emphasized, however, that these figures are averages of quite varied incomes, including many zero-incomes and a few high incomes.

The incomes of family units also differ according to the class of worker to which the family head belongs (see Tables 49 and 50). The incomes of family units whose heads were self-employed at the time of survey or most recent job are less equally distributed than those headed by employees, as is shown by the higher proportions of incomes at both the top and bottom intervals of the former distribution. The median income of family units headed by employees ($12 374) is higher than that for family units with heads who are self-employed ($10 010). About 25 per cent of family units have heads who are not even in the labour force at the time of survey largely because they are very young and still in school or university or because they are older and retired, and as might be expected these family

TABLE 49
Distribution of income among family units by class of worker of family head,
Ontario 1973 (percentages)

Income ($)	Paid employee	Self-employed	Not in labour force
Under 1000	1.7	3.3	9.1
1000–1999	1.7	3.0	17.0
2000–2999	1.5	4.9	22.7
3000–3999	2.4	3.6	10.1
4000–4999	3.1	5.7	10.3
5000–5999	3.8	4.8	5.9
6000–7999	8.9	13.8	7.8
8000–9999	10.9	10.8	5.3
10000–11999	13.5	9.3	3.4
12000–14999	19.2	11.6	3.7
15000–24999	27.7	19.3	3.6
25000 and over	5.4	9.8	1.0
Percentage of total	66.3	8.0	25.6
Number in sample	5053	610	1954
Median income ($)	12374	10010	3113

SOURCE: See source to Table 28.

TABLE 50
Income inequality measures for family units by class of worker of head, Ontario 1973

Measure	Paid employee	Self-employed	Not in labour force
Shares			
Bottom 10%	1.9	1.1	0.7
Top 10%	21.6	27.0	35.0
Gini coefficient	0.308	0.403	0.480
Atkinson index			
$\epsilon = 1.05$	0.188	0.309	0.442
$\epsilon = 1.55$	0.300	0.481	0.723
$\epsilon = 2.55$	0.540	0.760	0.954
Coefficient of variation	0.53	0.71	0.97
Mean income ($)	13612	12580	4925

SOURCE: Table 49

TABLE 51

Distribution of income among family units by type of residence,
Ontario 1973 (percentages)

Income ($)	Non-farm	Farm
Less than 1000	3.7	5.7
1000–1999	5.7	8.2
2000–2999	7.0	9.8
3000–3999	4.4	5.3
4000–4999	5.1	6.3
5000–5999	4.4	4.9
6000–7999	8.8	11.4
8000–9999	9.5	9.2
10 000–11 999	10.7	8.1
12 000–14 999	14.8	11.4
15 000–24 999	21.3	13.6
25 000 and over	4.5	6.1
Percentage of non-farm and farm	93.6	6.4
Number in sample	7133	491
Median income ($)	10 251	7718

SOURCE: See source to Table 28.

TABLE 52

Income inequality measures for family units by type of residence,
Ontario 1973

Measure	Non-farm	Farm
Shares		
Bottom 10%	1.0	0.6
Top 10%	24.7	29.7
Gini coefficient	0.390	0.456
Atkinson index		
$\epsilon = 1.05$	0.313	0.409
$\epsilon = 1.55$	0.489	0.632
$\epsilon = 2.55$	0.758	0.888
Coefficient of variation	0.67	0.81
Mean income ($)	11 321	9926

SOURCE: Table 51

TABLE 53
Median income of family units by size of urban area, Ontario 1973 (dollars)

	Median income ($)	Percentage
Rural area	8869	19.3
Urban: 1000–14999	8599	12.2
Urban: 15000–29999	9182	4.2
Urban: 30000–99999	10914	8.4
Urban: 100000 and over	10842	55.8
Total	10103	100.0

SOURCE: See source to Table 28.

units have much lower incomes than family units with heads in the labour force.

The distinction between farm and non-farm family residence is also important. As Tables 51 and 52 show, incomes of farm family units are generally lower than for non-farm family units (median of $7718 and $10251 respectively). At the same time there is a slightly higher proportion of very high-income farming units than of non-farm units, so that over-all income inequality is higher for farm family units than for non-farm family units.

Finally, one may inquire into the differences in incomes according to the size of the urban or non-urban areas in which the family units live. Table 53 shows that in 1973 about one-fifth of family units lived in rural areas and had a median income of $8869, and the rest lived in urban areas of varying sizes and had generally higher incomes. Over half of all family units lived in cities of 100000 and had a median income of $10842. However, although incomes tend to rise with size of urban area, the increase is not uniform: for example, urban areas of 30000 to 100000 have a slightly higher median income than the largest cities.

EDUCATION AND OCCUPATION OF HEAD OF FAMILY

In the last chapter we saw that individual incomes varied quite substantially with education levels and occupation. A similar pattern also holds in the case of family income. Since these relationships have been discussed in some detail already, I shall simply sketch the general findings here.

TABLE 54
Distribution of income of family units by education level of family head, Ontario 1973 (percentages)

Income ($)	Less than grade 5	Grades 5–8	High school not completed	High school completed	Non-university some	Non-university[a] completed	University, some	University, completed
Less than 1000	5.9	4.1	4.0	3.1	7.7	2.5	4.1	1.3
1000–1999	18.3	9.1	4.1	3.6	8.7	2.2	5.9	0.3
2000–2999	21.6	12.3	5.5	3.6	4.3	2.8	2.6	1.7
3000–3999	7.4	5.5	5.1	2.9	4.3	4.6	1.9	1.6
4000–4999	7.1	7.1	5.4	2.7	4.3	4.6	4.1	3.2
5000–5999	5.2	5.2	4.4	4.5	3.0	5.7	1.9	2.0
6000–7999	7.7	9.4	9.8	8.9	8.2	11.1	9.2	4.9
8000–9999	6.6	9.6	11.0	8.9	8.7	11.4	10.0	6.1
10000–11999	6.0	9.8	12.0	11.2	10.8	10.9	10.0	9.3
12000–14999	7.7	12.3	16.8	16.1	13.9	15.8	17.0	13.5
15000–24999	6.6	13.6	19.3	28.5	21.6	24.7	26.3	36.3
25000 and over	0.0	1.9	2.6	5.9	4.3	3.7	7.0	19.8
Percentage of total	4.8	27.2	30.5	15.8	3.0	6.0	3.5	9.0
Number in sample	366	2073	2326	1210	231	457	270	691
Median income ($)	3573	7414	10116	11317	10129	10935	12052	16693

a A post-secondary educational institution that grants diplomas or certificates.
SOURCE: See source to Table 28.

TABLE 55
Income inequality measures for family units by education level of head, Ontario 1973

Measure	Less than grade 5	Grades 5–8	High school not completed	High school completed	Non-university some	Non-university completed	University, some	University, completed
Shares								
Bottom 10%	0.6	1.0	1.0	1.1	0.4	1.6	0.7	1.8
Top 10%	31.3	27.9	24.2	22.5	25.3	22.8	23.8	23.3
Gini coefficient	0.482	0.431	0.369	0.346	0.418	0.342	0.366	0.321
Atkinson index								
$\epsilon = 1.05$	0.441	0.342	0.290	0.265	0.432	0.226	0.313	0.198
$\epsilon = 1.55$	0.691	0.503	0.470	0.438	0.725	0.353	0.531	0.308
$\epsilon = 2.55$	0.932	0.734	0.764	0.738	0.949	0.595	0.839	0.531
Coefficient of variation	0.91	0.74	0.62	0.59	0.72	0.58	0.63	0.55
Mean income ($)	5814	8998	10941	13143	11016	12149	13107	18292

SOURCE: Table 54

Tables 54 and 55 describe the distribution of incomes of family units according to the education level of the family head. As we have seen, there is often more than one income recipient in a family and spouses do not always have similar education backgrounds; consequently, while incomes generally tend to increase with the educational attainment of the family head, the relationship is not quite so straightforward. As can be seen from Table 54, 62.5 per cent of family heads did not complete high school, and the 5 per cent with less than grade five education generally have very low incomes. Those with post-secondary non-university training tend to have slightly lower incomes than those who completed high school. Those with some (but not completed) university education receive incomes with about the same median level as those who completed high school, but with rather larger dispersion. Those who completed university again have substantially higher median family incomes ($16700) than those who only completed high school or did some university work ($12100).

Occupational income differences for family units also follow roughly similar patterns to those for individual men. Tables 56 and 57 provide summary distributions of incomes for family units by occupation group of the family head.[2] As can be seen, primary, clerical, and services generally tend to have somewhat lower median incomes (about $8000 to $10000), although the primary group has a substantial amount of income dispersion as well. Transportation, manufacturing, mining and processing, sales, and construction groups tend to fall in the intermediate income ranges (with median incomes of about $12000 to $13000), but sales shows a relatively large dispersion of incomes. At the top end occur professional services and managerial and administrative occupations, which have median incomes of about $13500 and $18000 respectively; professional services also has a fair amount of income dispersion. In summary, then, education and occupation of family heads can be seen to be associated with systematic and fairly substantial family income differentials across the population.

SOURCES OF INCOME BY AGE AND INCOME

Different income sources were shown in the preceding chapter to be distributed in markedly different fashions, and the same is true for incomes of

2 It should be noted that occupation categories refer to occupations of family heads at the time of the survey in 1974 or in the most recent job held. Income figures, on the other hand, refer to incomes of family units received during the previous calendar year, 1973. The same applies to the results in Tables 49 and 50 for class of worker.

TABLE 56
Distribution of income of family units by type of occupation of family head,
Ontario 1973 (percentages)

Income ($)	Managerial & administrative	Professional services	Construction	Sales	Mining & processing
Less than 1000	0.9	3.4	0.4	0.9	1.0
1000–1999	0.4	1.6	1.2	2.1	0.5
2000–2999	0.4	1.1	0.5	3.3	0.8
3000–3999	0.2	1.9	0.7	2.8	1.5
4000–4999	0.0	2.9	3.5	2.2	2.0
5000–5999	0.9	2.4	2.8	3.5	2.7
6000–7999	2.0	8.1	9.4	9.8	8.4
8000–9999	4.4	10.4	10.9	8.9	12.6
10000–11999	9.4	9.6	14.4	11.3	14.5
12000–14999	19.1	16.7	22.5	18.7	23.5
15000–24999	40.1	31.5	29.4	28.4	29.5
25000 and over	22.0	10.2	4.3	8.0	3.2
Percentage of total	5.8	10.9	7.4	7.1	8.7
Number in sample	446	832	564	539	664
Median income ($)	18041	13526	12826	12825	12778

SOURCE: See source to Table 28.

TABLE 57
Income inequality measures for family units by occupation of head, Ontario 1973

Measure	Managerial & administrative	Professional services	Construction	Sales	Mining & processing
Shares					
Bottom 10%	3.3	1.4	2.9	1.9	2.9
Top 10%	22.0	23.5	20.1	23.1	20.0
Gini coefficient	0.272	0.336	0.271	0.326	0.265
Atkinson index					
$\epsilon = 1.05$	0.129	0.250	0.134	0.196	0.129
$\epsilon = 1.55$	0.191	0.428	0.205	0.299	0.199
$\epsilon = 2.55$	0.318	0.760	0.355	0.501	0.351
Coefficient of variation	0.48	0.58	0.46	0.56	0.44
Mean income ($)	20023	15181	13930	14576	13807

SOURCE: Table 56

TABLE 56 (continued)

Manufacturing	Transportation	Services	Clerical	Primary	Not in labour force
1.4	0.9	3.9	2.5	5.5	9.1
2.5	0.7	3.4	3.5	6.3	17.0
1.2	1.0	3.2	3.2	6.7	22.7
2.0	1.9	6.4	3.9	5.6	10.1
2.8	3.1	8.0	4.8	6.7	10.3
2.8	4.4	5.5	9.4	6.3	5.9
9.5	9.9	9.2	14.7	14.8	7.8
10.9	12.4	10.5	15.1	13.0	5.3
15.8	16.5	13.8	14.2	8.9	3.4
21.9	19.4	14.2	12.3	10.0	3.7
27.0	27.0	20.8	14.2	11.9	3.6
2.5	2.7	1.1	2.2	4.4	1.0
8.6	7.7	6.9	7.7	3.5	25.6
653	588	528	585	270	1954
12170	11896	9983	9013	7735	3113

TABLE 57 (continued)

Manufacturing	Transportation	Services	Clerical	Primary	Not in labour force
2.1	2.7	1.2	1.5	0.7	0.7
20.6	20.6	23.9	24.8	28.6	35.0
0.287	0.281	0.364	0.344	0.421	0.480
0.168	0.144	0.277	0.231	0.368	0.442
0.270	0.219	0.450	0.366	0.600	0.723
0.501	0.377	0.750	0.635	0.884	0.954
0.48	0.47	0.60	0.59	0.75	0.97
13032	13129	10769	10279	9467	4925

TABLE 58
Distribution of income among family units by major source of income,
Ontario 1973 (percentages)

Income ($)	Wages & salaries	Self-employment income	Government transfers	Investment income	Pension, etc.
Less than 1000	1.0	2.4	5.5	4.9	0.5
1000–1999	2.1	3.6	25.5	3.8	2.5
2000–2999	1.5	4.5	34.0	12.8	12.0
3000–3999	2.3	5.4	12.2	10.5	10.5
4000–4999	3.1	8.1	11.4	10.9	15.5
5000–5999	3.7	4.8	5.6	10.9	10.5
6000–7999	9.4	15.6	3.9	10.5	20.5
8000–9999	11.5	9.3	1.0	9.8	12.0
10000–11999	13.5	8.1	0.6	5.3	7.5
12000–14999	18.9	12.3	0.3	8.6	3.5
15000–24999	27.3	16.9	0.1	7.1	4.5
25000 and over	5.6	8.7	0.0	4.9	0.5
Percentage of total	72.0	4.4	15.0	3.5	2.6
Number in sample	5488	332	1145	266	200
Median income ($)	12293	8907	2559	5650	5856

SOURCE: See source to Table 28.

TABLE 59
Income inequality measures for family units by major source of income, Ontario 1973

Measure	Wages & salaries	Self-employment income	Government transfers	Investment income	Pension, etc.
Shares					
Bottom 10%	2.1	1.2	2.5	1.2	2.8
Top 10%	21.6	27.9	23.2	32.7	24.8
Gini coefficient	0.306	0.412	0.316	0.448	0.324
Atkinson index					
$\epsilon = 1.05$	0.177	0.307	0.174	0.332	0.173
$\epsilon = 1.55$	0.275	0.465	0.261	0.474	0.249
$\epsilon = 2.55$	0.482	0.728	0.432	0.699	0.385
Coefficient of variation	0.52	0.73	0.58	0.85	0.61
Mean income ($)	13584	11866	2954	8209	6799

SOURCE: Table 58

TABLE 60
Proportions of family units with different major sources of income by age of family head,
Ontario 1973

Major source of income	Under 25	25–34	35–44	45–54	55–64	65–69	70 & over
No income (1.9)[a]	7.1	1.2	0.8	1.2	2.7	1.6	0.7
Wages and salaries (72.0)	87.2	91.3	88.6	86.1	72.8	26.7	9.4
Self-employment income (4.4)	1.3	2.9	5.9	6.9	5.5	4.5	2.4
Government transfers (15.0)	3.8	3.9	3.8	4.1	7.3	40.7	67.0
Investment income (3.5)	0.3	0.1	0.4	0.9	6.5	10.3	12.2
Pensions, etc. (2.6)	0.1	0.0	0.1	0.5	4.1	14.6	7.3
Other (0.7)	0.3	0.7	0.4	0.3	1.0	1.6	0.9
Total	100.0	100.0	100.0	100.0	100.0	100.0	100.0

a Figures in parentheses are average proportions over all age groups together.
SOURCE: See source to Table 28.

family units. Tables 58 and 59 presents distributions for each of five main
sources of income. Wages and salaries are the major source of income for
72 per cent of family units compared to 15 per cent for government transfers, 4.4 per cent for self-employment income, 3.5 per cent for investment
income, and 2.6 per cent for pension and other income. It is apparent that
the distributions of family income by major source of income are radically
different in shape. The distribution for those whose major source is self-
employment income has a substantially lower median and higher dispersion
than that for wage and salary income. The distributions corresponding to
investment income and to pensions and other income sources have similar
medians (substantially below those for wage and salary and self-employment income), but the latter distribution is much more evenly distributed
with a smaller dispersion. The distribution of income among those whose
major source of income is government transfers shows the greatest proportion in the lower income ranges and has a correspondingly low median
income of only about $2500.

Figure 39:
Percentage of family units with different major sources of
income by age of family head, Ontario 1973
Source: Table 60
Percentage of family units

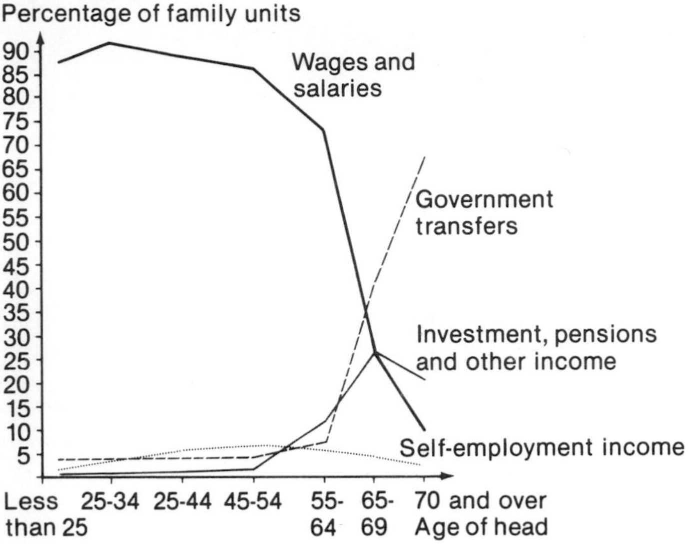

Not only do these distributions differ substantially in shape, but they also
contain very different mixes of age groups. This is illustrated in Table 60
and the corresponding Figure 39, which show how major income sources
differ across family units of different age groups. Wages and salaries as a
major source of income reach a peak of 91 per cent of family units for the
group aged 25 to 34 and then steadily decline to less than 10 per cent for
the elderly group 70 and over. Self-employment as a major income source
peaks later in the age interval 45 to 54, and then also declines as retirement
age is reached. Government transfers as a major source of income remain
fairly constant at about 4 per cent of family units until retirement age is
reached, at which time it shoots up above 50 per cent of family units.
Investments are also the principal source of income for an extremely small
proportion of family units until retirement age is reached when it rises to
10–12 per cent of family units. Similarly, pensions and other income peak
at about 16 per cent of family units in the 65–69 age interval, but then
decline among the 70-and-over group. Those with no family income at all
occur largely among the very young. The major income source can thus be
seen to change quite substantially over the life cycle of the family unit.

TABLE 61
Mean income sources by age and family size, Ontario 1973 (dollars)

Income source	Under 25	25–34	35–44	45–54	55–64	65–69	70 & over
Family size three or more							
Earnings	8607	11 736	13 937	15 208	13 993	9 047	n.a.
Transfers	518	500	558	529	505	2 241	n.a.
Investment	55	192	338	722	1 161	2 376	n.a.
Total income	9179	12 428	14 832	16 458	15 659	13 664	n.a.
Family size two							
Earnings	9926	13 452	12 020	12 178	10 167	3 290	1492
Transfers	276	234	387	381	362	2075	2697
Investment	110	226	355	795	1 843	2857	2088
Total income	10 312	13 912	12 762	13 353	12 372	8222	6277
Unattached men							
Earnings	3945	7849	9590	8198	5001	1338	518
Transfers	177	114	65	255	349	1425	1636
Investment	137	187	236	298	802	1317	1229
Total income	4259	8150	9891	8751	6152	4080	3383
Unattached women							
Earnings	3267	6141	5485	5348	2551	439	26
Transfers	51	142	145	224	478	1433	1606
Investment	23	273	447	385	1514	1737	1060
Total income	3341	6556	6077	5957	4542	3608	2692

NOTE: n.a. means reliable estimates not available.
SOURCE: See source to Table 28.

Another way of looking at changes in income from different sources across ages is to examine mean income from different sources tabulated according to age group as in Table 61 for different family sizes. As can be seen, earnings (i.e. wage and salary plus self-employment income) have their standard concave shape across age groups. Transfers are relatively unimportant until 65 and over. And 'investment income' (i.e., investment income in Table 60 plus pension and other income) starts very low and increases steadily until retirement age when it starts to decline by age 70 and over as accumulated assets are run down. Again, the same pattern emerges as in Figure 39.

Finally, what is the pattern of income source receipts by income class instead of by age? Results for this question are presented in Table 62,

TABLE 62
Percentage of income sources by income and family size, Ontario 1973

Income ($)	Mean total family income ($)	Earnings	Government transfers	Investment income
Family size three or more				
1–499	217	0.02	0.94	0.04
500–999	763	0.32	0.68	0.00
1000–1499	1181	0.64	0.31	0.05
1500–1999	1784	0.45	0.38	0.17
2000–2999	2599	0.50	0.43	0.06
3000–3999	3505	0.47	0.48	0.05
4000–4999	4472	0.59	0.35	0.07
5000–5999	5562	0.74	0.22	0.03
6000–6999	6536	0.85	0.12	0.03
7000–7999	7585	0.86	0.09	0.04
8000–8999	8500	0.88	0.08	0.04
9000–9999	9492	0.92	0.05	0.03
10000–11999	10975	0.93	0.05	0.02
12000–14999	13423	0.94	0.04	0.03
15000–24999	18685	0.95	0.02	0.03
25000 and over	32091	0.92	0.01	0.07
Family size two				
1–499	258	0.46	0.48	0.07
500–999	831	0.21	0.61	0.18
1000–1499	1231	0.50	0.39	0.11
1500–1999	1761	0.29	0.60	0.11
2000–2999	2488	0.15	0.74	0.10
3000–3999	3540	0.23	0.60	0.17
4000–4999	4466	0.21	0.54	0.25
5000–5999	5440	0.35	0.34	0.31
6000–6999	6444	0.59	0.19	0.22
7000–7999	7511	0.65	0.17	0.19
8000–8999	8524	0.74	0.10	0.16
9000–9999	9480	0.76	0.10	0.14
10000–11999	10924	0.85	0.05	0.10
12000–14999	13501	0.88	0.04	0.09
15000–24999	18452	0.91	0.02	0.07
25000 and over	33729	0.80	0.02	0.18
Unattached men				
1–499	184	0.26	0.11	0.63
500–999	708	0.32	0.44	0.24
1000–1499	1235	0.22	0.71	0.07
1500–1999	1795	0.41	0.52	0.07
2000–2999	2360	0.20	0.64	0.16

TABLE 62 (continued)

Income ($)	Mean total family income ($)	Earnings	Government transfers	Investment income
3000–3999	3550	0.60	0.21	0.19
4000–4999	4485	0.71	0.13	0.16
5000–5999	5444	0.79	0.10	0.11
6000–6999	6347	0.86	0.07	0.07
7000–7999	7520	0.87	0.04	0.08
8000–8999	8531	0.94	0.02	0.04
9000–9999	9455	0.97	0.01	0.02
10000–11999	10896	0.92	0.01	0.07
12000–14999	13335	0.92	0.01	0.07
15000–24999	17939	0.91	0.01	0.08
25000 and over	32195	0.89	0.01	0.11
Unattached women				
1–499	240	0.53	0.31	0.15
500–999	749	0.44	0.40	0.16
1000–1499	1235	0.19	0.74	0.07
1500–1999	1772	0.24	0.66	0.10
2000–2999	2349	0.13	0.65	0.22
3000–3999	3478	0.46	0.24	0.29
4000–4999	4528	0.56	0.17	0.26
5000–5999	5433	0.68	0.07	0.20
6000–6999	6454	0.75	0.07	0.17
7000–7999	7446	0.73	0.04	0.23
8000–8999	8413	0.73	0.04	0.23
9000–9999	9422	0.81	0.04	0.15
10000–11999	10745	0.75	0.03	0.22
12000–14999	13388	0.72	0.04	0.24
15000–24999	17077	0.62	0.04	0.34
25000 and over	28978	0.62	0.01	0.36

SOURCE: See source to Table 28.

which is disaggregated by family size as well. The first column gives the mean family income within each income class, and the remaining three columns give the proportions of that mean income that come from the three sources: earnings, transfers, and 'investment' income. Among all family sizes, transfers appear most predominantly at the bottom end of the distributions. Except for families of three or more, earnings proportions reach a trough (of between 13–20 per cent) in the $2000–3000 range; and except for unattached women, earnings proportions reach a peak (of over 90 per cent) at the upper end of the distributions (though peaking before they reach the very top income interval). 'Investment' income appears to be scattered across almost all income intervals with slight peaks in the 'investment' proportion occurring at the very bottom interval, very top interval, and various lower-middle income ranges between. In general, families of three or more tend to have higher proportions of income from earnings, while unattached women and families of two receive somewhat higher proportions from investment income. Transfers are received in higher proportions by low-income families than by unattached individuals or unattached men.

GENERAL CONCLUSIONS

A comparison of the patterns of income distribution among families and individuals shows that the family distributions tend to be more complex and less easily explained by simple economic theory. This arises quite naturally from the aggregation on varying individual characteristics to family units. In particular, two new dimensions of the distribution of income have been highlighted in this chapter: family size (or the distinction between families and unattached individuals), and the number of income earners in the family. As was described in Part One, the theory of income distribution concentrates on the behaviour of primary income recipients; i.e., family heads, and does not explain as well the markedly different income patterns of secondary income recipients in the family. Life-cycle patterns of labour supply and income differ substantially between primary and secondary income recipients within the family, and economic theory would do well to pay more attention to these differences. Models of family income and work behaviour raise a large number of complex issues, and they warrant much greater attention in the distributional literature.

The findings of this chapter also have several important welfare implications. Since the family unit is the basic group of individuals in the sharing of consumption and since consumption is assumed to be the basis of economic welfare, it is with the income distributions of *family units* that we ought to be concerned when making welfare judgments between different distributions of income. Consequently, in Part Three I shall deal almost exclusively with distributions for family units. Furthermore, since there are substantial differences in family size, it would be best wherever possible to compare distributions that are adjusted or normalized for the size of family units. For that reason, distributions will be disaggregated by family size as well as age of family head, and Chapter 10 will investigate in some detail the various adjustments for family size in order to examine distributions on a per-capita or individual-adult-equivalent basis. In general distributions of potential consumption bundles should be expressed in as comparable a fashion as possible.

Some important policy implications also follow from this chapter. One is the need to consider the labour supply effects of any policy or program, particularly on secondary earners in families. While the primary earner may not change his work patterns very much in response to various income support or social security programs (except perhaps very young and older workers), the labour supply response of secondary earners, particularly wives, may be much more sensitive. Since the potential distributional implications of such changes may be substantial, they deserve a good deal of attention. If wives in upper-income families, for example, were to spend more time in the labour market, the distributional effects would be much different than if a similar response occurred at the lower end of the distribution of family incomes.

Another thing that is clear is that low-income family units are not all the same. One important distinction is between those that have low long-run income status and little expectation of future income gains because of age, infirmity, discrimination, and structural changes that result in low market valuation of particular skills that are not easily changed; and those who will have higher incomes in the future but who have temporarily low incomes because they are going to school, or are between jobs, and so on. The first group has little or nothing to fall back on to meet short-run family needs, while the second is likely to have much greater resources to carry it through the current situation. If one were to distinguish between the long-run status of these two groups, policies suitable for each could be designed. What the second group needs are income insurance and improved access to capital markets so that temporary periods of low income can be more easily overcome. For the first group, however, such schemes are likely to be of little help because of the long-run nature of their situation; they would be helped more by direct transfers, income-support, manpower retraining, anti-discrimination programs, and a reduction in barriers to job entry. What is needed is different programs for the very different kinds of low-income family units.

This chapter has also raised a number of important questions for which we do not have answers. To what extent is there upward mobility within the distribution once a family head has left school and entered an initial occupation? If there is a great deal of opportunity for upward advancement within occupations or by shifting occupations and jobs, the argument for public provision of additional resources to young people (in the form of education grants and loans for example) or for various forms of affirmative action job policies (for women or minority groups, for example) is fairly weak. However, if upward mobility is very limited in some areas, and particular classes of individuals tend to get locked into low-paying jobs with little opportunity of advancement, such arguments become much stronger. We have little information on such mobility or on its determinants, and additional work in this area should be given high priority because of its social implications. A second set of questions on which we need to know much more in order to make better policy recommendations pertain to the behavioural responses (especially educational, savings, and labour supply) of different types of individuals (particularly married women and other secondary workers). How do the head's earnings or family wealth status affect the behaviour of such persons? A great deal more information along these lines is essential to the rational planning of distributional policies.

8
Distribution of family wealth

INTRODUCTION

So far our empirical investigation has been of the distribution of income among individuals and family units. As both the theory of life-cycle behaviour and the evidence of the previous two chapters show, one of the causes of income inequality is income from wealth. Inequality in the distribution of wealth can do much to cause and maintain income inequality: large quantities of wealth, whether from inheritance, past savings, or good luck, yield high capital income; furthermore, large incomes facilitate high savings levels and hence rapid accumulation of net worth. Consequently inequalities in income and in net worth might be expected to reinforce each other. Quite apart from its association with the distribution of income, inequality in the wealth distribution contributes directly to inequality in the distribution of economic well-being – large quantities of wealth provide social and economic power, greater control over one's economic environment and, often, reduced uncertainty. In order to understand the redistributive effects of many government policies, it is essential to examine their impact on and through family wealth holdings.

In this chapter we present some basic facts on the distribution of net worth across families in Ontario according to the composition of wealth and characteristics of families. In a later part of the study we integrate the wealth and income distribution data in order to improve our picture of the distribution of economic welfare, and in another chapter we examine the Canada Pension Plan in order to see how this particular social security scheme might affect our view of the distribution of wealth among Ontario families.

TABLE 63
Distribution of net worth among family units, Ontario 1970

Wealth class ($)	Percentage
Negative	10.7
None	3.0
1–999	12.5
1000–1999	5.2
2000–4999	8.0
5000–9999	9.9
10000–14999	9.6
15000–24999	17.4
25000–49999	17.6
50000–99999	4.8
100000–499999	1.3
500000 and over	0.0
Sample size	2550
Mean net worth ($)	17249
Median net worth ($)	10365
Shares	
Bottom 10%	−1.2
Top 10%	40.7
Gini coefficient	0.633
Coefficient of variation	1.24

SOURCE: Based on data for Ontario from the 1970 Survey
of Consumer Finances supplied in cross-tabular form by
Statistics Canada.

The source of data for this chapter and for later work in this study is the eleventh Survey of Consumer Finances (Statistics Canada 1973a), which collected information in May 1970 on assets, net worth, and indebtedness of family units at the time of the survey as well as 1969 incomes.[1] Much of

1 All tables in Chapter 8 are based on special cross-tabulations from the subsample of
   Ontario records from the 1970 Survey of Consumer Finances provided to the authors by
   the Consumer Income and Expenditure Division of Statistics Canada. The responsibility
   for the use and interpretation of these data is entirely that of the authors.
      Other Canadian studies of assets, debts, and net worth based on the 1970 SCF data are
   by Podoluk (1974), Wolfson (1977b), and Statistics Canada (1974a, 1977). Podoluk
   (1974) and Davies (1979), in particular, discussed some of the fairly substantial data
   deficiencies and reporting errors for this survey. Consequently, the main results in
   Chapter 8 should be evaluated with these limitations in mind.

the analysis specific to Ontario in this chapter, however, has been based on cross-tabulations from this survey especially run off by the Consumer Income and Expenditure Division of Statistics Canada for the current study, and thus has not been previously available.

DISTRIBUTION OF NET WORTH IN ONTARIO

Net worth holdings in Ontario, as elsewhere, are distributed very unequally across the population but systematically by age and income level of the family. Table 63 provides summary histogram data for the over-all distribution of net worth among family units in Ontario in 1970. As can be seen, the distribution has a long right-hand tail with a small number of very high wealth holdings, so that the mean net worth, $17 249, is substantially above the median, $10 365. The summary inequality figures in Table 63 also show that the distribution of net worth is much more unequal than that of income. The top 10 per cent of wealth holders have over 40 per cent of the net worth, while the corresponding group for income (see Table 29) receives about 25 per cent. Similarly, the Gini coefficient and coefficient of variation are markedly higher for net worth than income.[2]

Just as with income, however, net worth distributions differ substantially by family size. Table 64 shows, for example, that 48 per cent of unattached individuals had wealth of less than $1000 and only about 10 per cent had net worth in excess of $25 000 in 1970. For families of two or more, the corresponding figures are 19 and 28 per cent. Not surprisingly, then, the

It should also be pointed out that the family unit concept used in Chapter 8 is the 'economic family' unit consisting of persons sharing a common dwelling unit and related by blood, marriage, or adoption (Statistics Canada 1973, 69). 'Thus all relatives living together [are] considered to comprise one family whatever the degree of family relationship. Aside from single sons and daughters, other relatives most commonly found living in the household were married sons and daughters and widowed parents' (ibid.). The economic family definition is thus a rather broader one than that of the census family used in Chapter 7. Since many of the economic family members who would be considered as constituting separate census family units (e.g., married children or elderly parents) may have fairly low incomes, it would be expected that the income distributions for economic family units would have slightly less inequality than for census family units, particularly at the bottom end of the distribution.

2 It may be noted that the inequality tables for net worth distributions in Chapter 8 and elsewhere do not include figures for the Atkinson inequality indexes; this is a consequence of the Atkinson index being defined only for positive values. Since a fairly substantial proportion (about 11 per cent) of net worth holdings among family units are negative, the Atkinson index figures computed from conventional formulas are not meaningful and have thus been omitted.

TABLE 64
Distribution of net worth among family units by family size, Ontario 1970

Wealth class ($)	Unattached individuals	Family of two or more	Total family units
Negative or none	21.7	11.2	13.7
1–999	26.5	8.2	12.5
1000–1999	10.3	3.6	5.2
2000–4999	7.9	8.1	8.0
5000–9999	4.3	11.6	9.9
10000–14999	6.2	10.6	9.6
15000–24999	13.2	18.7	17.4
25000–49999	7.6	20.7	17.6
50000–99999	2.2	5.6	4.8
100000 and over	0.1	1.7	1.3
Sample size	495	2055	2550
Percentage by family size	19.4	80.6	100.
Mean net worth ($)	7915	20134	17249
Median net worth ($)	1175	13437	10365

SOURCE: See source to Table 63.

TABLE 65
Net worth inequality measures by family size, Ontario 1970

Measure	Unattached individuals	Family of two or more	Total family units
Shares			
Bottom 10%	−0.9	−1.0	−1.2
Top 10%	52.8	33.3	40.7
Gini coefficient	0.755	0.559	0.633
Coefficient of variation	1.67	0.99	1.24

SOURCE: Table 64

mean and median net worth figures for families are very much higher than for unattached individuals ($13437 compared to only $1175 for the median). Since about four-fifths of all family units are families, the family distributional pattern tends to predominate in Table 63. The inequality results in Table 65 reflect this as well: inequality is greatest for unattached individuals, least for families of two or more (though still substantial), and at an intermediate level for total family units.

The comparisons of inequality between income and net worth (both from the 1970 survey) are highlighted in Figure 40, which shows the respective Lorenz curves by family size category. In all cases, the net worth curves lie uniformly outside those of income. One can also see that the Lorenz curve for unattached individuals lies markedly outside that for all family units, which in turn lies outside that for families of two or more. This should not be surprising since families of two or more are much more homogeneous in age, being concentrated among middle-aged groups, while unattached individuals are spread more widely across ages and include particularly a high proportion of young and old. Because of data limitations, subsequent analysis in this section deals only with families of two or more and not with unattached individuals; but this incorporates 80 per cent of all family units.

As might be expected, distributional patterns in net worth also differ substantially by age of the family head. Table 66 shows that net worth holdings tend to increase with age until around 65 and then flatten out or decrease slightly. For example, the percentage of each age group with net worth less than $1000 declines with age from 68.7 to 33.3, 14.4, 10.7, 9.3, and then 6.1; while the percentage with wealth of $25000 or more moves from 0.0 to 6.8, 24.8, 39.0, 48.0, and 46.9. This pattern is illustrated in Figure 41, which shows the rapid growth and then flattening out of median wealth levels across age groups in the population in 1970.

Net worth inequality, however, shows a very different pattern across ages in the population. This is presented in Table 67 and illustrated in Figure 42. As can be seen, the coefficient of variation, for example, starts off very high among young families and then declines to a plateau at about age 55 and over. Young families can have very different accumulations of net worth: some run up heavy debts associated with family formation and education completion while others postpone having children and rapidly build up their equity in a house and consumer durables. By later middle age, however, these differences in net worth have had an opportunity to even out. Thus while net worth tends to rise with age and then level off with retirement, net worth *inequality* tends to decrease with age and then level off. This pattern of net worth inequality also contrasts with that for family income, which as we saw in the last chapter decreases initially with age and then increases rapidly in the higher age groups. Income and net worth inequality behave rather differently at the older end of the age distribution.

Consider now the distribution of net worth by income class. Again, as would be expected, net worth holdings and income are positively correlated. (It should be noted incidentally that, while net worth figures are for May 1970, the income figures are for 1969.) Table 68 shows, for example,

Figure 40:
Lorenz curves of income and net worth among family units
by family size, Ontario 1970
Source: See source to 63

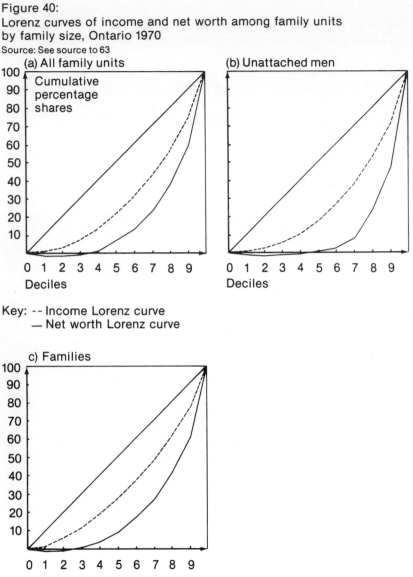

(a) All family units

(b) Unattached men

Key: -- Income Lorenz curve
— Net worth Lorenz curve

c) Families

TABLE 66
Distribution of net worth among families by age of family head, Ontario 1970

Net worth ($)	Under 25	25–34	35–44	45–54	55–64	65 & over	All ages
Negative or none	38.5	20.1	8.9	6.4	4.3	1.9	11.2
1–999	30.2	13.2	5.5	4.3	5.0	4.2	8.2
1000–1999	3.2	6.3	3.8	0.6	4.0	3.0	3.6
2000–4999	13.6	11.4	8.8	5.4	5.2	5.3	8.1
5000–9999	6.4	16.3	10.2	10.7	7.4	14.3	11.6
10000–14999	6.4	12.1	13.6	11.7	7.6	5.3	10.6
15000–24999	1.6	13.7	24.4	22.1	18.4	19.1	18.7
25000–49999	0.0	5.7	19.9	27.6	34.8	33.2	20.7
50000 and over	0.0	1.1	4.9	11.4	13.2	13.7	7.3
Sample size	124	467	513	418	273	260	2055
Percentage by age	6.0	22.7	25.0	20.3	13.3	12.7	100.
Mean net worth ($)	1689	8230	19092	26198	31162	30777	20134
Median net worth ($)	381	4715	14694	20008	23886	23368	13437

SOURCE: See source to Table 63.

TABLE 67
Net worth inequality measures among families by age of head, Ontario 1970

Measure	Under 25	25–34	35–44	45–54	55–64	65 & over	All ages
Shares							
Bottom 10%	−11.2	−3.1	−0.9	−0.5	−0.2	0.3	−1.0
Top 10%	71.0	41.9	30.6	29.1	27.5	27.5	33.3
Gini coefficient	n.a.	0.686	0.509	0.469	0.451	0.443	0.559
Coefficient of variation	2.33	1.31	0.89	0.81	0.77	0.76	0.99

NOTE: n.a. means reliable estimate not available.
SOURCE: Table 66

Figure 41:
Median net worth by age of family head, Ontario 1970
Source: Table 66

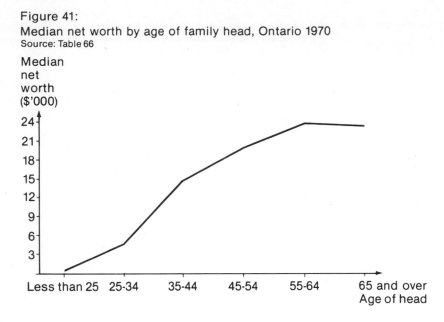

Median
net
worth
($'000)

24 –
21 –
18 –
15 –
12 –
9 –
6 –
3 –

Less than 25   25-34   35-44   45-54   55-64   65 and over
                                                                      Age of head

TABLE 68
Distribution of net worth among families by income class, Ontario 1970

Income ($) Net worth ($)	Under 4000	4000– 6999	7000– 9999	10000– 14999	15000 & over	Total
Negative or none	13.4	20.4	11.8	7.2	3.0	11.2
1–999	20.5	11.7	6.8	4.9	2.2	8.2
1000–1999	4.1	4.0	4.4	3.2	1.8	3.6
2000–4999	9.0	8.8	9.2	8.9	2.2	8.1
5000–9999	12.2	6.8	17.5	11.7	6.3	11.6
10000–14999	5.2	11.9	11.5	12.3	8.1	10.6
15000–24999	15.0	15.6	18.2	24.0	16.1	18.7
25000–49999	18.0	15.8	16.8	21.3	37.0	20.7
50000 and over	2.6	5.2	3.8	6.5	23.3	7.3
Sample size	243	404	550	589	269	2055
Percentage by income class	11.8	19.7	26.8	28.7	13.1	100.0
Mean net worth ($)	13503	14706	15674	20219	42254	20134
Median net worth ($)	6241	8846	10174	15727	31965	13437

SOURCE: See source to Table 63.

Figure 42:
Coefficient of variation for net worth by age of family head,
Ontario 1970
Source: Table 67

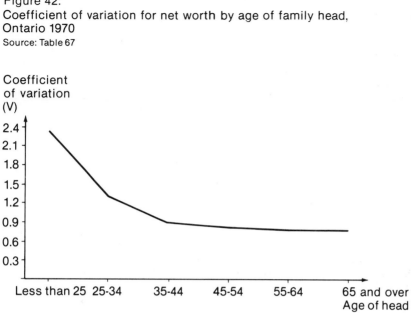

that the percentage of families that have net worth of less than $1000 declines by income class from 33.9 to 32.1, 18.6, 12.1, and 5.2, while the percentage with net worth above $25000 moves from 20.6, 21.0, and 20.6 to 27.8 and then 60.3. Figure 43 illustrates this pattern for median net worth; and as can be seen, net worth holdings increase relatively little over the lower three income groups, and then increase much more rapidly within the top two income classes.

Table 69, however, shows that net worth inequality decreases quite steadily with income class. The share of the top 10 per cent of wealth holders within each income class, for example, declines from 40.3 per cent to 38.6, 34.7, 30.4, and then 25.6 per cent. As illustrated in Figure 44, the

Figure 43:

Median net worth by family income class, Ontario 1970

Source: Table 68

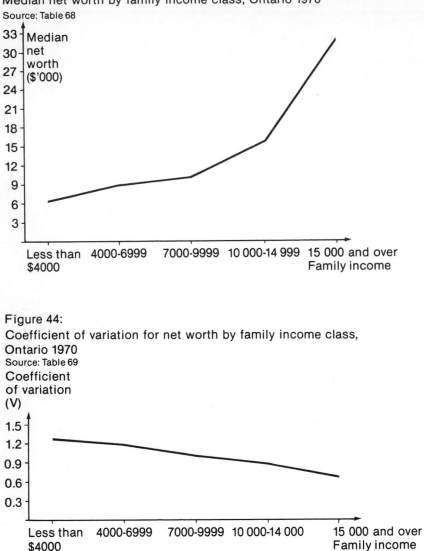

Figure 44:

Coefficient of variation for net worth by family income class, Ontario 1970

Source: Table 69

TABLE 69
Net worth inequality measures among families by income class, Ontario 1970

Measure	Under $4000	$4000–6999	$7000–9999	$10000–14999	$15000 & over	Total
Shares						
Bottom 10%	−6.0	−1.5	−1.4	−0.8	0.1	−1.0
Top 10%	40.3	38.6	34.7	30.4	25.6	33.3
Gini coefficient	0.729	0.647	0.570	0.501	0.396	0.559
Coefficient of variation	1.29	1.18	1.02	0.88	0.68	0.99

SOURCE: Table 68

TABLE 70
Median net worth among families by age and income class, Ontario 1970

Income ($)	Under 25	25–34	35–44	45–54	55–64	65 & over	All ages
Less than 4000	n.a.	351	958	2874	5030	15989	6241
4000–6999	n.a.	711	10440	11650	14416	30268	8846
7000–9999	n.a.	6160	11334	19355	18862 ⎞		10174
10000–14999	n.a.	6145	17327	20749	25076 ⎬	35897	15727
15000 and over	n.a.	13386	28041	34512	41651 ⎠		31965
All income groups	381	4715	14694	20008	23886	23368	13437

NOTE: n.a. means reliable data not available.
SOURCE: See source to Table 63.

TABLE 71
Mean net worth among families by age and income class, Ontario 1970

Income ($)	Under 25	25–34	35–44	45–54	55–64	65 & over	All ages
Less than 4000	n.a.	505	10283	23194	13216	17622	13507
4000–6999	n.a.	4614	10539	15577	19374	34094	14706
7000–9999	n.a.	8098	15225	21608	25489 ⎞		15674
10000–14999	n.a.	9364	20436	24975	29690 ⎬	52015	20219
15000 and over	n.a.	16922	36194	41667	64588 ⎠		42254
All income groups	1689	8230	19092	26198	31162	30777	20134

NOTE: n.a. means reliable estimates not available.
SOURCE: See source to Table 63.

TABLE 72
Distribution of assets by family size, Ontario 1970

Assets ($)	All family units	Families of two or more	Unattached individuals
None	3.7 ⎱	4.1	28.8
1–249	6.2 ⎰		
250–999	9.3	7.8	14.3
1000–1999	7.7	6.5	11.6
2000–4999	9.1	8.7	10.4
5000–9999	6.8	7.5	4.5
10000–14999	5.6	5.7	5.4
15000–19999	7.9 ⎱	18.0	11.7
20000–24999	8.6 ⎰		
25000–29999	9.6 ⎱	32.2	10.5
30000–49999	17.6 ⎰		
50000–99999	6.4	7.6	2.4
100000 and over	1.5	1.9	0.3
Percentage of family units	100	81.1	18.9
Sample size	2550	2067	483
Mean assets ($)	21165	24848	8946
Median assets ($)	16047	20398	1588

SOURCE: See source to Table 63.

TABLE 73
Asset inequality measures by family size

Measure	All family units	Families of two or more	Unattached individuals
Shares			
Bottom 10%	0.1	0.1	0.0
Top 10%	34.7	32.9	50.6
Gini coefficient	0.563	0.513	0.724
Atkinson index			
$\epsilon = 1.05$	0.698	0.587	0.855
$\epsilon = 1.55$	0.910	0.832	0.956
$\epsilon = 2.55$	0.983	0.962	0.988
Coefficient of variation	1.06	0.94	1.58

SOURCE: Table 72

coefficient of variation behaves correspondingly. Once again, therefore, net worth holdings and net worth inequality move in opposite directions, this time across family income classes. But then, this might be expected since income, net worth, and age all tend to be positively correlated up until about age 65. Thus the results in Figures 41–44 are different reflections of the same pattern of income growth and wealth accumulation across ages in the population.

Because of the correlation between age and income it is useful to examine net worth patterns according to age and income class not only separately as we have just done, but also jointly. Tables 70 and 71 summarize median and mean net worth holdings by both age and income class together. In general, the pattern of net worth rising with either income or age persists rather strongly here even when controlling for the other variable. Consequently, there indeed appears to be a mutually reinforcing positive correlation between cross-sectional income and net worth holdings even without any age effects.

DISTRIBUTION OF ASSETS

A family's net worth is the difference between its assets and its debts. In order to examine in more detail the pattern of wealth holdings across Ontario families, we shall deal with the two components separately.

As in the case of net worth, asset holding patterns differ substantially according to family size. Tables 72 and 73 show that families of two or more generally hold very much greater stocks of assets than do unattached individuals, while the distributions of asset holdings are more equal among the former. For example, median asset holdings were only $1588 for unattached individuals as compared to $20398 for families in Ontario in 1970; while the shares of the top 10 per cent of asset holders were 50.6 and 32.9 per cent respectively. Relative inequality by family size is highlighted in Figure 45, which shows the Lorenz curves of asset holdings for all family units, for unattached individuals, and for families. If these were plotted on the same diagram, the curve for unattached individuals would lie completely outside that for families, and that for all family units would lie between the two.

The figures also show that, in each of these three cases, the Lorenz curves for asset holdings lie inside those for net worth, so that there is less inequality in the distributions of assets than those of net worth. Since inequality in net worth is attributable to differences in both asset holdings and debt obligations among family units, we can conclude from this that

Figure 45:
Lorenz curves of assets and net worth among family units by family size,
Ontario 1970
Source: See sources Tables 64 and 72

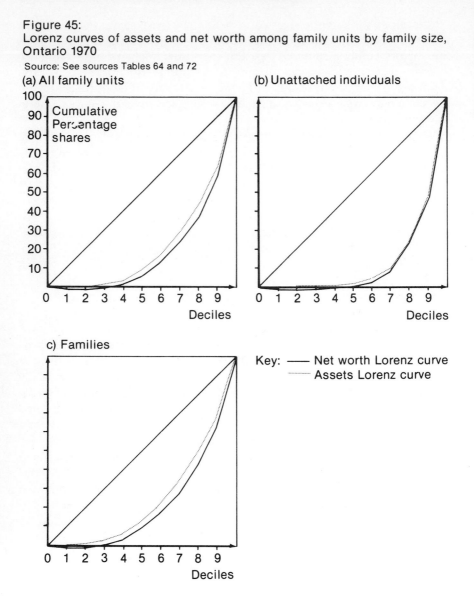

(a) All family units

(b) Unattached individuals

c) Families

Key: —— Net worth Lorenz curve
.... Assets Lorenz curve

TABLE 74
Distribution of assets among families by age of head, Ontario 1970

Assets ($)	Under 25	25–34	35–44	45–54	55–64	65 & over	All ages
Less than 250	12.5	4.8	4.1	2.5	2.8	3.1	4.1
250–999	30.3	13.5	5.6	3.8	3.5	3.0	7.8
1000–1999	17.9	11.2	4.6	2.3	6.0	3.8	6.5
2000–4999	18.0	15.5	7.4	4.8	5.3	4.8	8.7
5000–9999	8.2	8.0	4.3	7.0	6.9	13.9	7.5
10000–14999	1.6	5.2	7.6	7.0	3.5	4.7	5.7
15000–24999	4.9	15.5	20.1	22.6	16.2	18.9	18.0
25000–49999	6.6	24.2	37.1	35.4	41.3	34.0	32.2
50000–99999	0.0	2.2	7.5	12.3	10.2	10.5	7.6
100000 and over	0.0	0.0	1.7	2.3	4.1	3.3	1.9
Percentage by age	6.0	22.7	25.0	20.3	13.3	12.7	100.0
Sample size	124	467	513	418	273	260	2055
Mean assets ($)	4931	14336	26223	30810	33761	30940	24848
Median assets ($)	1402	8146	23176	24995	28411	23848	20398

SOURCE: See source to Table 63.

TABLE 75
Asset inequality measures among families by age of head, Ontario 1970

Measure	Under 25	25–34	35–44	45–54	55–64	65 & over	All ages
Shares							
Bottom 10%	0.2	0.2	0.2	0.3	0.2	0.3	0.1
Top 10%	59.4	33.2	30.3	30.4	31.6	32.6	32.9
Gini coefficient	0.720	0.575	0.464	0.448	0.462	0.479	0.513
Atkinson index							
$\epsilon = 1.05$	0.732	0.652	0.527	0.438	0.491	0.483	0.587
$\epsilon = 1.55$	0.860	0.844	0.805	0.704	0.752	0.739	0.832
$\epsilon = 2.55$	0.949	0.953	0.962	0.933	0.941	0.941	0.962
Coefficient of							
variation	1.74	1.08	0.84	0.80	0.84	0.88	0.94

SOURCE: Table 74

TABLE 76
Distribution of assets among families by income class, Canada 1970

Income ($) Assets ($)	Under 4000	4000– 6999	7000– 9999	10000– 14999	15000 & over	Total
Less than 250	17.7	7.5	2.2	0.9	0.0	5.5
250–999	13.8	15.1	9.4	3.8	0.6	9.3
1000–1999	5.5	9.0	8.5	4.7	1.9	6.5
2000–4999	10.8	11.0	13.0	11.8	4.9	11.0
5000–9999	14.4	11.9	9.3	7.7	6.4	10.1
10000–14999	9.1	9.6	9.0	5.4	3.6	7.8
15000–19999	8.4	9.6	11.2	9.9	3.9	9.3
20000–24999	5.6	8.5	12.6	13.0	5.7	9.8
25000–49999	12.6	13.2	21.2	35.3	42.3	23.4
50000 and over	2.1	4.6	3.5	7.5	30.8	7.4
Percentage by income class	19.0	24.5	25.7	21.5	9.3	100.0
Sample size	1508	1937	2035	1699	740	7919
Mean assets ($)	11260	13845	17149	24129	51738	20747
Median assets ($)	5781	8108	14170	22215	38329	14931

SOURCE: Based on data for Canada from the 1970 Survey of Consumer Finances supplied in cross-tabular form by Statistics Canada.

TABLE 77
Asset inequality measures among families by income, Canada 1970

Measure	Under $4000	$4000– 6999	$7000– 9999	$10000– 14999	$15000 & over	Total
Shares						
Bottom 10%	0.0	0.1	0.3	0.4	0.9	0.1
Top 10%	40.0	38.1	31.0	26.5	23.9	32.4
Gini coefficient	0.622	0.589	0.502	0.429	0.351	0.531
Atkinson index						
$\epsilon = 1.05$	0.844	0.689	0.535	0.417	0.282	0.617
$\epsilon = 1.55$	0.995	0.894	0.757	0.641	0.464	0.856
$\epsilon = 2.55$	0.999	0.979	0.922	0.872	0.754	0.971
Coefficient of variation	1.18	1.10	0.88	0.74	0.60	0.94

SOURCE: Table 76

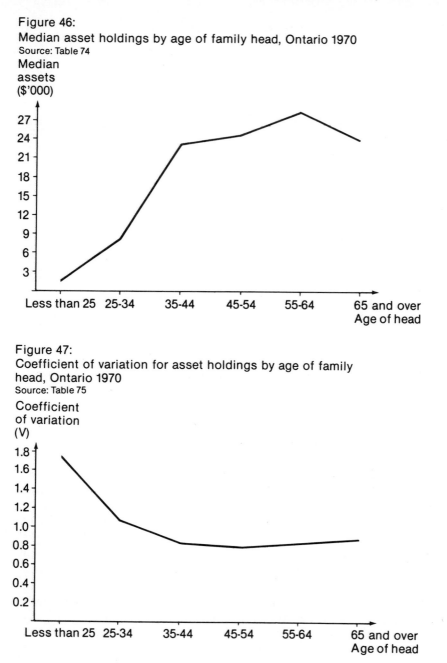

Figure 46:
Median asset holdings by age of family head, Ontario 1970
Source: Table 74

Figure 47:
Coefficient of variation for asset holdings by age of family
head, Ontario 1970
Source: Table 75

Figure 48: Median asset holdings by family income, Ontario 1970
Source: Table 76

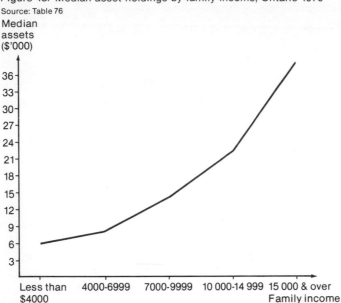

debts are less equally distributed than assets. But since the assets and net worth curves lie so close together, it would be expected that the asset component contributes the major share of inequality in net worth.

Asset holdings also vary substantially according to the age of the family head and family income class. Focusing now just on family units of two or more (or families), one can see from Table 74 that assets tend to increase with age of the family head up to age 55–64 and then to decline somewhat during retirement. This pattern is illustrated in Figure 46 for median asset holdings. It may be remarked that, whereas asset holdings tend to decline over the oldest age interval, net worth simply flattens out so that the decrease in assets must be matched by a corresponding reduction of debts during retirement.

While the profile of asset holdings across age groups in the population is concave, the corresponding pattern of asset inequality (see Table 75) tends to be convex. Figure 47, for example, illustrates that the coefficient of variation declines with age until later middle age and then increases slightly. The Atkinson indices, however, give more mixed results.

Similar patterns in the distribution of assets hold across family income classes. Table 76 shows that asset holdings tend to increase with family

TABLE 78
Mean assets among families by age of head and income class, Ontario 1970 (dollars)

Income ($)	Under 25	25–34	35–44	45–54	55–64	65 & over	All ages
Less than 4000	n.a.	1 180	12 501	24 721	14 991	17 899	14 360
4000–6999	n.a.	8 305	15 657	18 493	21 211	34 638	17 557
7000–9999	n.a.	14 676	21 962	27 127	27 277 ⎫		20 977
10 000–14 999	n.a.	16 514	27 880	29 904	33 718 ⎬ 52 944		26 249
15 000 and over	n.a.	27 355	48 430	47 442	69 778 ⎭		50 942
All income groups	4948	14 489	26 363	30 944	34 202	31 291	25 004

NOTE: n.a. means reliable estimates are not available.
SOURCE: Table 76

TABLE 79
Distribution of assets among families by employment status of head, Ontario 1970

Assets ($)	Employer	Employee	Not in labour force	Total
Less than 250 ⎫		2.9		4.1
250–999 ⎬ 9.0		8.8 ⎫ 23.4		7.8
1000–1999 ⎭		7.3 ⎭		6.5
2000–4999	9.5	9.2	5.0	8.7
5000–9999	7.0	7.0	10.4	7.5
10 000–14 999	5.5	5.8	5.1	5.7
15 000–24 999	14.4	18.9	16.4	18.0
25 000–49 999	29.3	33.3	28.9	32.2
50 000–99 999	15.9	6.3	7.8	7.6
100 000 and over	9.4	0.5	3.1	1.9
Percentage by group	11.3	74.8	13.9	100.0
Sample size	201	1576	290	2067
Mean assets ($)	43 063	21 649	26 781	24 848
Median assets ($)	28 895	19 763	18 753	20 398

SOURCE: See source to Table 63.

income, although less rapidly over lower income intervals than at the top end of the income range.[3] This is illustrated in Figure 48 for median asset

3 Since results specific to Ontario were not available, Tables 76 and 77 are for Canada as a whole.

TABLE 80
Asset inequality measures by employment status of head, Ontario 1970

Measure	Employer	Employee	Not in labour force	Total
Shares				
Bottom 10%	0.3	0.2	0.2	0.1
Top 10%	33.1	29.5	36.1	32.9
Gini coefficient	0.514	0.492	0.548	0.513
Atkinson index				
$\epsilon = 1.05$	0.518	0.547	0.615	0.587
$\epsilon = 1.55$	0.741	0.780	0.831	0.832
$\epsilon = 2.55$	0.921	0.936	0.953	0.962
Coefficient of variation	0.93	0.89	1.02	0.94

SOURCE: Table 79

TABLE 81
Median asset holdings among families by age and employment status, Ontario 1970 (dollars)

Employment status	Under 25	25–34	35–44	45–54	55–64	65 & over	All ages
Employer	n.a.	16216	29848	34794	32559	21889	28895
Employee	1582	8316	23231	24732	28736	22954	19763
Not in labour force	489	200	246	13956	20431	24564	18753
All employment groups	1402	8146	23176	24995	28411	23848	20398

NOTE: n.a. means reliable data not available.
SOURCE: See source to Table 63.

holdings. Inequality in the distribution of family asset holdings, however, decreases across income classes. This is the case for all the inequality measures in Table 77 and is illustrated as well in Figure 49. Thus as one moves up the income scale, asset distributions tend to move up but with reduced relative dispersion or inequality.

Corresponding to Table 71, which showed the distribution of mean net worth figures jointly according to age and income class, similar figures for mean asset holdings are presented in Table 78. The main patterns across age and income classes that have been pointed out already can be seen to persist simultaneously across the joint sets of intervals. Even when one controls for age there is a marked reinforcing effect between income and asset holdings.

Another factor associated with different asset holding patterns is the employment status of the family head. One would expect in general that employers would hold larger stocks of assets than employees, and Table 79 shows that this is indeed the case. Mean assets of employer-headed families were $43 563 in Ontario in 1970 compared to $21 649 for employee-headed families; the proportions with assets over $50 000 were 25.3 and 6.8 per cent respectively. Asset holdings of families with a head not in the labour force at all, however, were much more dispersed than in either of the other two groups. The mean and median asset figures are roughly similar to those for employee-headed families, but the proportions with very small (less than $2000) and very large ($100 000 and over) assets are rather greater. As a result, the not-in-labour-force inequality figures in Table 80 are greater than for the other two categories. Between the employer and employee categories, however, the results are mixed.

One reason for expecting employers to have larger asset holdings on average than employees is that employers are generally older, and we have seen that assets are strongly correlated with age of the family head. Table 81 looks at median asset holdings according to employment status within age groups. As can be seen, except for the youngest and oldest groups, employer-headed families still have higher asset holdings than employee-headed families, which in turn are markedly higher than for those not in the labour force. Within the oldest age group, 65 and over, however, exactly the reverse ranking occurs. The relative importance of each of the three groups within each age interval is shown in Table 82; and as expected, employees occur in greatest proportion among younger households, employers among older middle-aged households, and the not-in-the-labour-force category among older families, particularly those 65 and over. The latter group thus consists largely of elderly plus some very young families, so that in light of Figures 46 and 47 one would expect a relatively high degree of asset inequality within such a disparate group of age extremes. In short, then, one finds that employment status is associated with fairly marked differences in asset holdings within middle-aged families, and that high asset inequality among the non-labour-force group appears to be largely consistent with the age-heterogeneity of the group.

COMPOSITION OF ASSETS

Not only the total value of asset holdings but also their composition differs across families in the population. Assets can vary according to such characteristics as yield, risk, and liquidity, all of which can be desired in different combinations according to a family's tastes, needs, and constraints. An

TABLE 82
Percentage of family heads with different employment status by age of head, Ontario 1970

Employment status	Under 25	25–34	35–44	45–54	55–64	65 & over	All ages
Employer	0.0	7.7	11.3	16.1	15.0	11.4	11.3
Employee	92.2	88.5	85.3	78.5	73.0	16.4	74.8
Not in labour force	7.8	3.7	3.4	5.4	12.0	72.2	13.9

SOURCE: See source to Table 63.

TABLE 83
Composition of assets among families by age of family head, Ontario 1970

Asset type	Under 25	25–34	35–44	45–54	55–64	65 & over	All ages
Financial assets	17.8	16.2	13.4	24.3	32.0	44.2	24.8
Liquid	13.9	9.3	8.3	15.5	16.0	28.8	14.9
Cash on hand	0.6	0.4	0.2	0.2	0.2	0.4	0.3
Savings deposits	6.2	4.7	3.1	6.4	5.8	7.9	5.4
Other deposits	5.7	2.8	3.2	3.8	5.0	9.7	4.7
Can Sav Bonds	1.1	0.9	1.3	3.6	3.2	7.1	3.1
Other bonds	0.4	0.4	0.5	1.4	1.8	3.8	1.5
Non-liquid	3.9	6.9	5.1	8.8	16.0	15.4	9.9
Stocks	2.6	2.2	2.6	3.8	7.4	6.6	4.3
Mortgage invmt	1.1	3.9	1.7	4.0	6.2	8.1	4.4
Misc invmt	0.3	0.9	0.8	1.1	2.4	0.7	1.2
Non-financial assets	82.2	83.8	86.6	75.8	68.0	55.8	75.2
Mkt value of home	60.2	70.9	72.3	58.7	53.5	46.1	61.0
Mkt value of vac home	0.0	1.4	2.5	4.4	4.9	1.8	3.1
Invmt in other real estate	3.8	4.3	7.6	8.0	5.5	5.4	6.5
Mkt value of car	18.2	7.2	4.2	4.7	4.1	2.4	4.6

SOURCE: See source to Table 63.

analysis of asset portfolio composition can provide some indication of the effects of these factors across age, income, and asset classes in the population. Since the value of different assets grows at different rates according to the general level of economic activity and since certain assets might be treated differently under government tax and subsidy programs, a knowledge of the patterns of portfolio composition will be important in determining the distributional effects of macroeconomic policies and of different tax and social security systems. This section examines the principal patterns in asset portfolio composition.

Several points can be observed immediately from Table 83, which provides a detailed breakdown of asset holdings of families in Ontario by age of family head. First, by far the largest single component in asset portfolios is the market value of owner-occupied housing. On average across all ages, market value of homes represents 61 per cent of total family assets while other nonfinancial assets represent about 14 per cent of the total. This leaves about 25 per cent for financial assets – 15 per cent in liquid assets in the form of bonds and deposits of various kinds and 10 per cent non-liquid assets such as corporate stock, mutual funds, and mortgage investment. The second main point to note is that this composition changes quite markedly over the life cycle. The proportion of housing and of total nonfinancial assets reaches a peak during the age interval 35–44 when families are rapidly growing, and then falls off as older families invest more in financial assets such as savings and other deposits, bonds, and mortgages. The share of financial assets increases from 13.4 per cent in the 35–44 age interval to 24.3, 32.0, and finally 44.2 in the 65 and over interval. Between these intervals, liquid assets' share rises from 8.3 to 28.8 per cent, and non-liquid financial assets' share from 5.1 to over 15 per cent. In contrast, the share of cars in total family assets declines across ages from 18.2 per cent for young families to only 2.4 per cent for families 65 and over.

The share of owner-occupied houses is so important in these results that it deserves further comment. Even for the youngest age group, it constitutes 60 per cent of asset holdings; it rises to 72.3 per cent for the 35–44 age group, and then declines to less than 50 per cent for the oldest age group. This pattern reflects two main factors: incidence of home-ownership, and investment in financial assets during later middle age. Incidence of home-ownership (Table 84) increases with age of family head until the age interval 45–54, and then flattens out at a level that is about fifteen percentage points higher among non-metropolitan-area families than among metropolitan-area families. In general, non-metropolitan-area families have a higher incidence of home-ownership than their metropolitan-area cohorts. Beyond middle age, however, home-ownership incidence stabilizes for families: families have grown up, the burden of mortgage payments has eased, and the family then puts a larger proportion of savings into non-housing forms of investment. For both these reasons, then, the share of home-ownership in total assets generally declines with age after middle age.

TABLE 84
Incidence of home-ownership among family units by area of residence and age of head, Canada 1970 (percentages)

	Under 35	35–44	45–54	55–64	65 & over	All ages
All family units	27.5	66.2	69.8	67.6	63.6	55.0
Metro areas	19.9	59.0	62.7	60.4	52.3	45.8
Non-metro areas	44.2	79.5	79.6	77.7	75.9	69.9
Families of two or more	38.0	72.0	78.3	76.3	78.6	65.2
Metro areas	30.0	66.3	73.2	70.0	69.8	57.6
Non-metro areas	52.3	81.8	85.2	85.3	87.2	76.5

SOURCE: Statistics Canada (1973a, Table E, 33)

Asset-holding patterns also differ substantially according to family size. Table 85 shows portfolio breakdowns into major components for Canada separately for families (size two or more), unattached individuals, and all family units. The principal patterns are shown in Figures 49–52. The patterns for families of two or more and for all family units are rather similar to each other and to what has been discussed. The pattern for unattached individuals, though, is quite different. For them, financial assets have a greater proportion than market value of home and vacation home for all ages. In particular, liquid assets have a much greater share for all ages, and non-liquid financial assets and cars are more important among younger and middle-aged groups. Once again, then, rather marked differences in behaviour are observed between families and unattached individuals. For reasons of data limitations and economy of presentation, the rest of this section will deal mainly with families and not with unattached individuals.

Asset composition also would be expected to differ according to family income. Table 86 and Figure 53 present results for Canadian families for all age groups. As can be seen, the share of homes reaches a peak (of 69.1 per cent) in the middle-income interval $7000–$9999 and then steadily declines with higher family incomes (down to about 36 per cent), while the share of financial (and particularly non-liquid) assets reaches a trough (of 5.3 per cent) in this interval and then rises with income to 26.3 per cent for the top interval of $25 000 and over.

However, this is not the pattern *within* all age groups. Table 86 shows the distribution of major asset components by income class, and within particular age groups. It can be seen that the share of houses and vacation homes in total assets tends to increase with income across top income intervals for

Figure 49:
Coefficient of variation for asset holdings by family income class, Ontario
1970 Source: Table 77

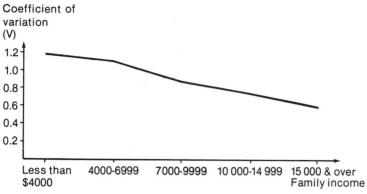

Figure 50:
Percentage shares of asset holdings among all family units by age of
head, Canada 1970 Source: Table 85

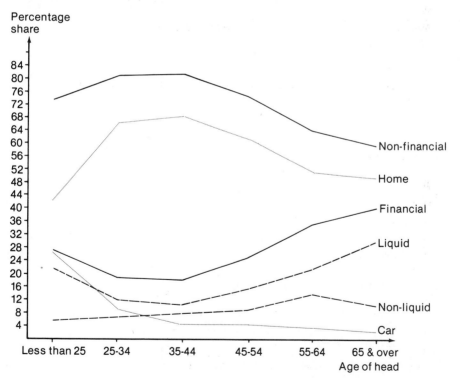

Figure 51:
Percentage shares of asset holdings among unattached individuals by age, Canada 1970 Source: Table 85

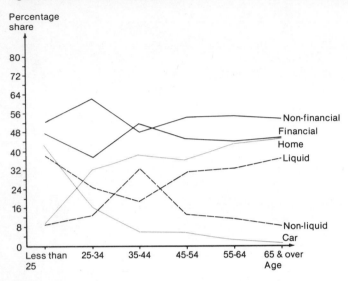

Figure 52:
Percentage share of asset holdings among families of two or more by age of head, Canada 1970 Source: Table 85

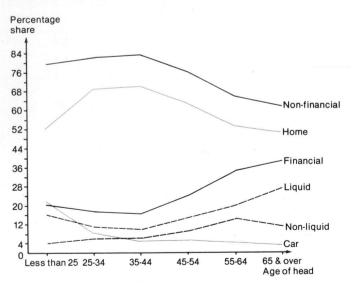

TABLE 85

Composition of assets among family units by family size and age of head, Canada 1970

	Under 25	25–34	35–44	45–54	55–64	65 & over	All ages
All family units							
Liquid assets	21.7	12.0	10.7	15.8	21.8	30.0	18.1
Nonliq fin assets	5.2	6.8	7.6	9.4	14.0	10.6	9.7
Total financial assets	26.9	18.8	18.3	25.2	35.8	40.6	27.8
Mkt value of home & vac home	42.7	66.8	68.7	61.5	51.4	49.3	59.3
Invmt in other real estate	4.1	5.5	8.2	8.5	8.9	7.9	7.9
Mkt value of car	26.4	8.9	4.8	4.9	3.9	2.3	5.0
Total non-financial assets	73.2	81.2	81.7	74.9	64.2	59.5	72.2
Unattached individuals							
Liquid assets	38.6	24.7	18.9	31.8	33.0	37.2	32.9
Nonliq fin assets	8.9	13.1	32.9	13.5	11.7	8.9	12.9
Total financial assets	47.5	37.8	51.8	45.3	44.7	46.1	45.8
Mkt value of home & vac home	9.6	32.5	38.6	36.6	43.6	45.9	41.8
Invmt in other real estate	1.3	13.8	3.8	12.5	9.0	6.9	8.0
Mkt value of car	41.6	15.9	5.8	5.6	2.7	1.1	4.4
Total non-financial assets	52.5	62.2	48.2	54.7	55.3	53.9	54.2
Families (two or more members)							
Liquid assets	16.5	11.1	10.2	14.8	19.9	27.0	16.0
Nonliq fin assets	4.0	6.4	6.1	9.1	14.4	11.3	9.3
Total financial assets	20.5	17.5	16.3	23.9	34.3	38.3	25.3
Mkt value of home & vac home	52.7	69.2	70.5	63.0	52.7	50.6	61.7
Invmt in other real estate	5.0	4.9	8.4	8.2	8.9	8.3	7.9
Mkt value of car	21.8	8.4	4.7	4.9	4.1	2.8	5.0
Total non-financial assets	79.5	82.5	83.7	76.1	65.7	61.7	74.7

SOURCE: See source to Table 76.

TABLE 86
Composition of assets among families by age and income class, Canada 1970 (percentages)

Asset type	Under $4000	$4000–6999	$7000–9999	$10000–14999	$15000–24999	$25000+
Age under 25						
Liquid assets	19.5	16.4	24.6	13.9	8.4	n.a.
Nonliq fin assets	4.0	5.8	3.0	3.3	2.3	n.a.
Total financial assets	23.5	22.2	27.6	17.2	10.7	n.a.
Mkt value of home & vac home	38.8	46.1	38.0	61.4	66.5	n.a.
Invmt in other real estate	5.7	8.8	2.4	1.6	15.0	n.a.
Mkt value of car	30.9	21.8	32.1	19.9	7.7	n.a.
Total non-financial assets	75.5	76.8	72.5	82.9	89.3	n.a.
Age 25–34						
Liquid assets	15.6	11.6	10.0	10.0	18.0	9.7
Nonliq fin assets	1.9	3.5	4.3	8.6	9.4	6.4
Total financial assets	17.5	15.1	14.3	8.6	27.4	16.1
Mkt value of home & vac home	64.7	70.7	72.4	69.1	57.2	69.2
Invmt in other real estate	4.8	5.8	4.5	4.1	7.5	9.9
Mkt value of car	12.6	9.4	8.9	8.1	7.8	4.7
Total non-financial assets	81.6	85.9	85.8	81.3	72.5	83.9
Age 35–44						
Liquid assets	9.7	9.3	8.4	8.5	13.5	17.0
Nonliq fin assets	4.7	4.5	2.9	4.9	10.8	11.1
Total financial assets	14.3	12.9	11.3	13.4	24.3	28.1
Mkt value of home & vac home	76.9	77.4	80.1	72.4	63.5	39.8
Invmt in other real estate	2.5	2.3	3.3	9.4	7.7	29.8
Mkt value of car	5.3	6.3	5.3	4.9	4.6	2.3
Total non-financial assets	84.7	86.1	88.7	86.7	75.8	71.9
Age 45–54						
Liquid assets	18.7	12.6	13.2	13.8	15.1	19.7
Nonliq fin assets	7.5	3.2	5.1	7.0	10.6	26.0
Total financial assets	26.8	15.9	18.3	20.8	25.7	45.7
Mkt value of home & vac home	65.0	65.2	69.5	67.7	59.0	38.7
Invmt in other real estate	5.4	13.3	7.8	5.7	10.2	11.8
Mkt value of car	2.4	5.8	4.5	5.7	5.1	3.9
Total non-financial assets	73.7	84.2	81.8	79.2	74.3	54.4

TABLE 86 (continued)

Asset type	Under $4000	$4000–6999	$7000–9999	$10000–14999	$15000–24999	$25000+
Age 55–64						
Liquid assets	23.6	22.7	19.6	18.6	24.0	15.6
Nonliq fin assets	4.0	6.2	8.0	11.2	12.6	40.7
Total financial assets	27.6	28.9	27.6	29.8	36.6	56.3
Mkt value of home						
& vac home	63.9	63.7	58.1	58.0	45.8	30.5
Invmt in other real estate	5.4	3.9	9.5	7.2	13.5	11.1
Mkt value of car	5.1	4.5	4.9	5.0	4.2	2.0
Total non-financial assets	72.4	72.1	72.5	70.2	63.5	43.7
Age 65+						
Liquid assets	21.2	32.9	31.6	27.6	23.9	44.0
Nonliq fin assets	5.9	11.1	10.9	14.1	22.1	32.0
Total financial assets	27.2	43.9	42.5	41.7	46.0	76.0
Mkt value of home						
& vac home	64.4	4.8	48.2	45.5	30.5	11.1
Invmt in other real estate	5.3	6.8	5.6	8.7	20.6	11.0
Mkt value of car	2.2	2.6	3.7	4.0	3.0	1.8
Total non-financial assets	71.7	56.0	57.5	58.3	54.1	24.0
All age groups						
Liquid assets	19.9	20.4	14.0	13.5	17.5	18.5
Nonliq fin assets	5.7	6.5	5.3	7.9	12.1	26.3
Total financial assets	25.7	27.0	19.3	21.4	29.6	44.8
Mkt value of home						
& vac home	65.4	61.2	69.1	65.9	54.7	35.8
Invmt in other real estate	5.1	6.5	5.8	6.9	11.0	16.7
Mkt value of car	3.8	5.3	5.9	5.8	4.8	2.7
Total non-financial assets	74.4	73.0	80.7	78.6	70.5	55.2

NOTE: n.a. means figures not available or unreliable.
SOURCE: See source to Table 76.

the youngest age group, that it has an inverted U-shaped pattern across income intervals for middle-aged families, and that it generally decreases with higher incomes for the oldest age group, 65 and over. Not surprisingly the pattern of the proportion of financial assets is just the converse. In the youngest age group it tends to fall off with upper incomes; among middle-

Figure 53:
Percentage shares of asset holdings among families of two or more by
income class, Canada 1970 Source: Table 86

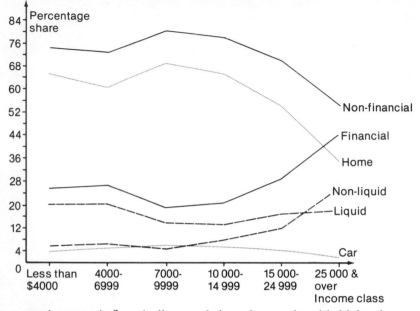

aged groups it first declines and then rises again with higher incomes; and
for the oldest age group it generally rises with income, particularly at high
income levels.

Now consider the figures in Table 86 from a different perspective: what
happens to asset shares across ages for families that are consistently at one
extreme of the income distribution or the other? Figures 54–56 graph the
proportions for liquid assets, non-liquid financial assets, and market value
of house and vacation home for the lowest income group (less than $4000),
the highest income group ($25000 and over), and an upper-middle income
group ($10000–$14999). In the case of the market value of home and vacation home, it can be seen that for low-income families the proportion first
rises and then flattens out beyond middle age; it generally declines with age
for high income families; and first rises slightly and then declines for upper-
middle-income families. In the case of liquid assets, the proportion first
declines and then generally increases with age beyond the interval 35–44
for both low-income and upper-middle-income families. For high-income
families, the liquid assets' proportion is fairly stable for most of the life
cycle, and then rises dramatically for the age group 65 and over. In the case

Figure 54:
Percentage share of liquid asset holdings among families of two or more by income class and age of head, Canada 1970 Source: Table 86

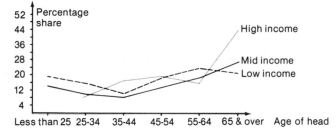

Figure 55:
Percentage shares of non-liquid financial assets out of total assets among families of two or more by income class and age of head, Canada 1970 Source: Table 86

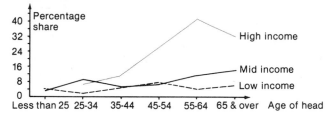

Figure 56:
Percentage shares of market value of home and vacation house out of total asset holdings among families of two or more by income class and age of head, Canada 1970 Source: Table 86

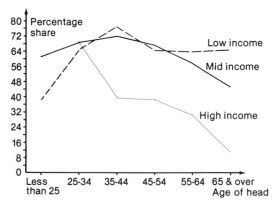

TABLE 87

Incidence of home-ownership among family units by place of residence and income, Canada 1970 (percentages)

	Under $3000	$3000–3999	$4000–4999	$5000–5999	$6000–6999	$7000–9999	$10000–14999	$15000–& over	All income classes
All family units	43.1	45.9	47.8	45.7	51.4	57.9	67.1	78.2	55.0
Metro areas	23.2	26.0	29.8	29.8	36.8	50.5	63.9	75.8	45.8
Non-metro areas	62.2	70.3	69.2	67.7	73.7	71.9	75.4	86.1	69.9
Families of two or more	63.6	60.6	59.2	56.4	61.1	62.0	70.3	80.3	65.2
Metro areas	38.8	39.8	41.1	39.8	49.0	55.4	67.2	77.9	57.6
Non-metro areas	77.6	76.2	74.3	73.2	76.0	74.0	78.4	88.1	76.5

SOURCE: Statistics Canada (1973a, Table D, 31)

TABLE 88
Percentage composition of assets among family units by asset holding class, Canada 1970

Asset type	Under 1000	1000–1999	2000–4999	5000–9999	10000–14999	15000–19999	20000–24999	25000–29999	30000–49999	50000–99999	100000 & over	All asset classes
Financial assets	53.1	45.3	44.7	35.4	21.9	18.2	15.8	14.1	21.7	36.5	49.7	27.8
Liquid	49.6	41.1	39.2	29.5	17.3	14.9	12.8	11.2	16.3	21.9	20.0	18.1
Cash on hand	8.7	3.7	1.8	1.0	0.6	0.5	0.6	0.3	0.3	0.2	0.1	0.4
Savings deposits	16.7	16.7	14.1	12.6	6.5	6.0	4.8	4.3	6.2	7.0	4.0	6.2
Other deposits	21.5	16.8	16.9	10.2	6.5	4.7	4.6	3.8	4.7	6.3	6.1	5.8
Can Sav Bonds	2.4	3.7	4.3	4.5	2.8	2.4	1.7	2.3	3.9	5.2	5.2	3.8
Other bonds	0.2	0.3	2.0	1.2	1.0	1.3	1.0	0.5	1.3	3.1	4.5	2.0
Non-liquid	3.6	4.2	5.6	5.8	4.7	3.3	3.0	2.9	5.4	14.7	29.7	9.8
Stocks	1.6	2.9	3.1	2.7	2.7	1.6	1.5	1.4	2.6	8.1	13.5	4.8
Mortgage Invmt	0.3	0.3	1.3	1.6	1.3	1.1	1.1	1.2	1.9	5.2	12.5	3.7
Misc Invmt	1.7	1.0	1.2	1.5	0.7	0.6	0.4	0.3	0.9	1.4	3.7	1.3
Non-financial assets	46.9	54.7	55.3	64.6	78.1	81.8	84.2	85.9	78.3	63.5	50.3	72.2
Mkt value of home	1.9	7.4	19.2	48.0	65.6	72.8	75.2	77.4	67.2	44.9	24.6	57.2
Mkt value of vac home	0.1	0.1	0.8	2.2	1.4	0.7	0.7	1.7	2.0	3.1	3.7	2.1
Invmt in other real estate	0.5	0.4	1.9	3.1	4.0	3.4	3.5	2.6	5.5	12.8	20.7	7.9
Mkt value of car	44.4	46.9	33.4	11.4	7.0	5.0	4.8	4.1	3.7	2.7	1.3	5.0

SOURCE: See source to Table 76.

Figure 57:
Percentage shares of asset holdings among all family units by asset class, Canada 1970
Source: Table 88

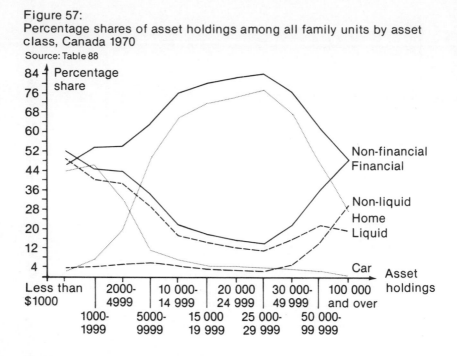

of non-liquid financial assets, low and upper-middle income shares remain fairly stable (although the latter rises somewhat in the oldest two age groups), in contrast to that for high income families, where the share rises very markedly from the 25–34 year age interval. In summary, then, the share profiles in Figure 52 for all families are roughly indicative of life-cycle asset composition patterns across ages, but at the same time they hide a fair amount of variation in these patterns associated with different income classes.

Just as home ownership varies with age, it also varies systematically with family income (see Table 87). The incidence of home ownership for metropolitan area families increases fairly steadily with income, while for non-metropolitan families, it is again at a higher level but first decreases with income and then increases at the higher end of the income scale. It can also be seen that the incidence of home-ownership is somewhat lower for all family units than for families of two or more, particularly at lower income levels; but this difference is smaller at higher income levels.

One may also expect asset compositions to vary with the actual level of asset holdings. Table 88 gives a detailed component breakdown for eleven asset holding classes; the principal results are shown in Figure 57. As can be seen in the diagram, the share of market value of home and vacation home increases from 2.0 per cent in the lowest asset class to 79.1 per cent in the asset class $25000–$29999, and then falls to 28.3 per cent in the top asset class. Financial assets' share on the other hand, (particularly that of liquid assets) declines rather steadily with total asset holdings from 53.1 per cent to 14.1 per cent in the $25000–29999 class, and then (spurred by non-liquid asset accumulation) climbs back to 49.7 per cent in the $100000-and-over asset class. Not unexpectedly, cars' share falls as total asset holdings increase, while investment in other real estate increases, particularly over the very top asset intervals. In short, the patterns of asset composition across asset classes are somewhat similar to those across income classes but rather more pronounced.

Finally Table 89 shows differences in asset composition according to whether the family head is an employee, employer, or not in the labour force. Since the third category applies largely to older families, it is not surprising to find that the shares of market value of home and vacation home and of all nonfinancial assets are relatively small, while the shares of both liquid and non-liquid financial assets are relatively large. Secondly, it can be seen that employers hold relatively larger proportions of financial assets and other real estate, while employees have proportionately larger investments in their own homes and automobiles.

Both the value and composition of asset holdings can thus be seen to differ according to life cycle and other principal factors. For that reason, there are many economic forces such as changes in social security or in the inflation rate that could be expected to have far-reaching distributional effects on asset account.

DISTRIBUTION OF DEBTS

The net worth over which a family has command is the difference between the assets it possesses and the debts it owes. Asset holdings have been examined in some detail in the last two sections. We turn now to the distribution of debts.

Once again, one may start by examining the different distributions of debt by family size. Table 90 shows that a higher proportion (73.8 per cent) of families of two or more have debts than do unattached individuals (only 35.1 per cent), and the mean and median debts are much higher for the former than the latter. Almost 20 per cent of families have debts of more

TABLE 89
Composition of assets among families by employment status of head, Canada 1970

Asset type	Employee	Employer	Not in labour force
Financial assets	20.7	29.7	39.5
Liquid	13.5	18.1	24.9
Cash on hand	0.4	0.5	0.3
Savings deposits	4.9	5.3	8.1
Other deposits	4.7	6.1	7.3
Can Sav Bonds	2.8	3.3	5.7
Other bonds	0.8	2.8	3.5
Non-liquid	7.2	11.6	14.6
Stocks	3.8	5.0	8.0
Mortgage Invmt	2.8	4.1	5.4
Misc Invmt	0.6	2.5	1.2
Non-financial assets	79.3	70.3	60.5
Mkt value of home & vac home	67.2	53.2	47.9
Invmt in other real estate	6.1	12.8	9.8
Mkt value of car	6.0	4.3	2.8

SOURCE: See source to Table 76.

TABLE 90
Distribution of debts by family size, Ontario 1970

Debts ($)	All family units	Families of two or more	Unattached individuals
None	35.0	26.2	64.9
1–249	8.8	8.4	10.2
250–499	3.4 ⎫	9.0	9.4
500–999	5.7 ⎭		
1000–1999	8.7	8.7	8.6
2000–4999	12.3	14.6	4.5
5000–9999	10.5	13.4	0.6
10000–14999	8.6	10.9	0.7
15000–19999	4.0	4.9	1.0
20000–24999	1.7 ⎫	3.8	0.1
25000 and over	1.3 ⎭		
Size of sample	2550	2077	473
Percentage of family units	100.	81.5	18.5
Mean debts ($)	3917	4880	653
Median debts ($)	740	1728	0

SOURCE: See source to Table 63.

than $10000, while fewer than 2 per cent of unattached individuals do. In both cases, however, debts are highly concentrated in a small number of family units. The proportion of total debts owed by the largest 10 per cent of debtors is 41.3 per cent for families and 77.9 per cent for unattached individuals. This phenomenon is also captured by the rather high values of the various inequality indices in Table 91, with the figures for unattached individuals slightly larger than for families of two or more.

Since for most people debts are associated largely with family formation and mortgages, one would expect the distribution of debts to change substantially across age groups in the population. This is indeed the case as shown in Table 92. Mean and median debts have an inverted-V shape across age groups; it peaks at $7241 and $4960 respectively in the interval 35–44, and then declines to virtually nothing in the retirement period of 65 and over (see Figure 58). Inequality of debts by age, on the other hand, has the opposite pattern (see Figure 59): it reaches a trough in the interval 35–44 and peaks at both ends. The inequality measures, however, disagree substantially on the degree to which inequality varies with age.

Debts would also be expected to vary with the income of the family, and this is shown to be the case in Table 94 – debts rise steadily with family income from $853 for the income class of less than $4000 to $8099 for the top income class, $15000 and over. It can also be seen that the peaked pattern of mean debts across ages holds within each income class, and the steady increase in debts across income classes also holds within each age class. By comparing Tables 71, 78, and 94, one can also examine the breakdown of mean net worth into mean assets and debts by age and income jointly.

Finally, Table 95 shows the general composition of total debts for families across age groups. Mortgages are the largest component of debts, and they reach their relative peak in the 35–44 age interval along with the share of home and vacation home in total assets for all but top income groups. The share of consumer debt peaks among very young families that are just setting up households and borrowing in order to make large investments in consumer durables, and among older families who have paid off most of their mortgages and have very few debts left. In general, then, one observes the pronounced effect of life-cycle family development on debt components as well as on total family debts.

GENERAL CONCLUSIONS

Comparing the data in this chapter to those on family income in the last chapter, one notes that asset holdings and net worth are substantially more

TABLE 91
Debt inequality measures by family size, Ontario 1970

Measure	All family units	Families of two or more	Unattached individuals
Shares			
Bottom 10%	0.0	0.0	0.0
Top 10%	47.5	41.3	77.9
Gini coefficient	0.718	0.661	0.869
Atkinson index			
$\epsilon = 1.05$	0.999	0.964	0.995
$\epsilon = 1.55$	1.000	0.999	0.999
$\epsilon = 2.55$	1.000	0.999	0.999
Coefficient of variation	1.45	1.26	2.83

SOURCE: Table 90

TABLE 92
Distribution of debts among families by age of head, Ontario 1970

Debts ($)	Under 25	25–34	35–44	45–54	55–64	65 & over	All ages
None	16.8	14.0	14.2	23.4	33.3	73.5	26.2
1–249	11.5	7.6	5.7	8.2	11.4	11.1	8.4
250–999	14.8	10.0	8.8	8.9	9.0	5.3	9.0
1000–1999	22.9	11.2	6.3	8.6	8.8	2.0	8.7
2000–4999	18.2	19.6	15.1	13.8	13.8	4.6	14.6
5000–9999	4.7	10.5	18.2	19.0	14.2	3.5	13.4
10000–14999	4.0	13.3	18.2	12.1	5.0	0.0	10.9
15000–19999	5.6	7.0	7.5	3.0	3.3	0.0	4.9
20000 and over	1.6	6.9	5.9	2.9	1.1	0.0	3.8
Sample size	126	472	516	424	278	261	2077
Percentage by age	6.0	22.7	25.0	20.3	13.3	12.7	100.0
Mean debts ($)	3302	6336	7241	4734	3085	473	4880
Median debts ($)	1300	3109	4960	2189	687	0	1728

SOURCE: See source to Table 63.

unequally distributed than family income; this is due in large part to the cumulative nature of asset acquisition with age. Even though net worth inequality within age groups tends to decline slightly with age (in the cross-section) as early differences in net worth holdings are worn down, net

TABLE 93
Debt inequality measures among families by age of head, Ontario 1970

Measure	Under 25	25–34	35–44	45–54	55–64	65 & over	All ages
Shares							
Bottom 10%	0.0	0.0	0.0	0.0	0.0	0.0	0.0
Top 10%	53.2	37.4	32.3	37.0	47.3	89.7	41.3
Gini coefficient	0.693	0.611	0.549	0.622	0.709	0.900	0.661
Atkinson index							
$\epsilon = 1.05$	0.908	0.889	0.878	0.946	0.976	0.996	0.963
$\epsilon = 1.55$	0.997	0.998	0.998	0.999	0.999	0.999	0.999
$\epsilon = 2.55$	0.999	0.999	0.999	0.999	0.999	0.999	0.999
Coefficient of variation	1.48	1.13	0.97	1.18	1.47	2.84	1.26

SOURCE: Table 92

Figure 58:
Median debts of families of two or more by age of family head,
Ontario 1970
Source: Table 92

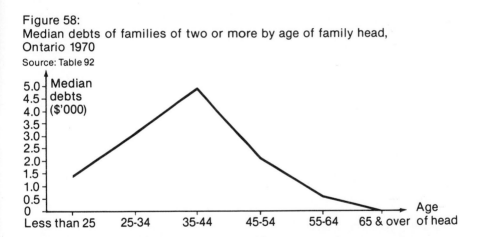

worth differences between age groups become much larger. Whereas cross-sectional income receipts tend first to rise with age, to peak around later middle age, and then to decline markedly, family net worth holdings generally increase with age right up until retirement, and then flatten out during early retirement. These strong positive age effects on net worth reflect simultaneously life cycle patterns in both asset holdings and debts associated with family investment in housing, then gradual repayment of mortgage, and finally a gradual shift toward more financial assets in preparation for retirement. These strong life-cycle patterns in asset holdings, debts, and

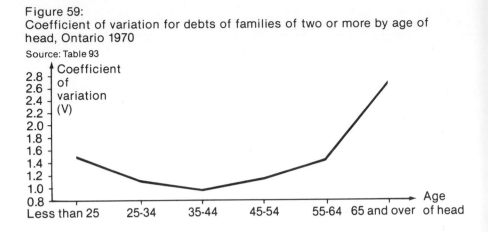

Figure 59:
Coefficient of variation for debts of families of two or more by age of head, Ontario 1970

Source: Table 93

TABLE 94
Mean debts among families by age of head and income class, Ontario 1970 (dollars)

Income ($)	Under 25	25–34	35–44	45–54	55–64	65 & over	All ages
Less than 4000	n.a.	675	2217	1527	1775	277	853
4000–6999	n.a.	3691	5118	2917	1838	544	2847
7000–9999	n.a.	6578	6738	5519	1788		5304
10000–14999	n.a.	7150	7444	4929	4028	} 929	6031
15000 and over	n.a.	10433	12236	5775	5191		8099
All income groups	3260	6259	7271	4745	3041	513	4870

NOTE: n.a. means data not available.
SOURCE: See source to Table 63.

net worth position also reinforce earlier arguments for the need to disaggregate by family size and age of head in any further analysis of distributional structure.

The findings of this chapter also have several important welfare implications. In the first place, since wealth holdings make consumption possible, measures of inequality and welfare should be based on family net worth position as well as income. The resulting measures for young families may not differ much from those already calculated in Chapter 7, since the young tend to have little wealth. But for retired families, for example, who usually have relatively low incomes and fairly high net worth positions, estimates of their level of well-being may differ substantially. In Chapter 12 we

TABLE 95
Composition of debts among families by age of head, Canada 1970 (percentages)

	Under 25	25–34	35–44	45–54	55–64	65 & over	All ages
Personal debt	57.6	31.4	24.9	31.0	39.8	40.3	30.8
Consumer debt	51.6	26.4	16.8	22.6	28.0	24.7	23.1
Charge accnts &							
instlmt debt	7.3	4.8	3.4	4.9	6.1	6.0	4.5
Selected loans							
from banks	25.9	12.3	6.8	9.3	10.9	10.7	10.0
Loans from small							
co, credit unions	18.5	9.3	6.5	8.4	11.0	8.0	8.6
Other personal debt	6.0	5.1	8.1	8.4	11.9	15.6	7.8
Home impvmt loans,							
bank loans against							
securities	1.7	1.1	2.2	4.0	4.0	5.9	2.5
Other debt	4.3	4.0	5.9	4.4	7.9	9.7	5.3
Mortgage debt on home							
& vac home	42.4	68.6	75.1	69.0	60.2	59.6	69.2

SOURCE: See source to Table 76.

attempt to incorporate both income and net worth jointly in an improved measure of family economic welfare in order to examine to what extent the over-all pattern of inequality described in the last chapter is changed. Secondly, net worth holdings also provide a source of potential consumption in the form of capital gains on the assets. Once again, measures of economic well-being (on which inequality measures are based) should be constructed to reflect this, particularly in an inflationary period when asset prices may change substantially over time. This issue is also examined in Chapter 11. It is clear that both these net worth effects could be expected to change fairly substantially the over-all structure of inequality across age groups. More generally, the findings of this chapter highlight the need to broaden the measures of inequality and welfare to reflect wealth holdings as well as income flows.

Some important policy implications also follow from this chapter. One is that, for the various government welfare or support programs that use means tests, consideration should be given not only to current family income but also to the family assets and net worth. A family with a modest stock of capital to fall back on is much better able to get through a period of temporarily low income than one with virtually nothing to fall back on.

Secondly, it may be remarked that the federal and provincial governments tax income rather than wealth, that is, potential capital accumulation rather than current capital holdings. Yet wealth holdings are obviously a source of potential well-being of a family, they are strongly correlated with income particularly at the upper end of the distribution, and they are more unequally distributed than total family income. There are certainly other considerations (such as administrative aspects and incidence effects on factor supplies) in a decision to replace or supplement income tax with a wealth tax. Nonetheless, the pros and cons of a direct tax on wealth deserves more consideration and public debate.

Thirdly, since wealth is such an important aspect of inequality across families, it is necessary to consider in some detail the net worth effects of government policies and programs. For example, policies that result in later retirements, particularly in fairly high-income positions, may be expected to increase somewhat the degree of inequality in the distribution of wealth because of the strong and increasing (cross-sectional) age-income profile up until retirement. Similarly, different tax treatments of family mortgage payments and different urban land zoning laws would be expected to affect the market prices of houses, and thus the resulting distribution of equity in home ownership among families.

This chapter also raises a number of basic questions to which we have remarkably few answers in spite of their importance. One is the detailed relationships between assets, debts, and family labour supply, particularly over the family's life cycle. Debt and asset acquisition are closely linked with home ownership (i.e., mortgages) and consumer durable purchases (particularly cars), and the labour supply of secondary workers in the family may well be sensitive to the levels of such assets and debts. For example, a wife may take a job for a couple of years to help meet the mortgage payments on a house. On the other hand, the time when a worker may choose to retire may be related to the real value of his stock of wealth. Consequently, there may be significant interactions between the labour supply of family members and the family asset and debt position, and such relationships may become more important in future as more workers exercise greater choice over their labour market involvement; and as we have seen in the last two chapters, the wealth holdings and labour supply dimensions are two critical aspects in the over-all structure of inequality among families.

A second important issue is the degree to which compulsory social security pensions like the Canada Pension Plan are viewed by the public as rights to a publicly provided capital stock, and thus considered as a component of the expected net worth of families. One aspect of this is how figures on family net worth inequality may change when expected net benefits from public pensions are taken into account; this is the subject of Chapter 13. Another aspect is the extent to which public pensions may be considered as substitutes for or complements to private pensions and other forms of private capital formation. That is, does the Canada Pension Plan result in reduced family savings and private capital accumulation, or does it make families more aware of a need to provide for future retirement and thus increase their rate of private capital formation? Indeed, could these different effects dominate over different portions of the income or wealth distribution? Certainly a good deal more information is needed on issues such as these.

PART THREE: IMPUTATIONS AND ADJUSTMENTS TO THE DISTRIBUTION OF INCOME

In Part Two we reviewed recent evidence on the general structure and patterns of family economic inequality in Ontario as revealed by standard data on income and wealth from the Canadian census and surveys. The reason for examining these distributions, of course, is that they are observable proxies or estimates of the distribution of economic well-being across families in the province. But family income, for example, is an overly simple and imperfect approximation because it ignores many important factors or does not take them into account. Part Three, therefore, attempts to adjust conventional family income figures for a number of such factors in order to move at least a few steps closer to more complete empirical measures of family economic well-being and their corresponding distributions. I hope that some of the adjustments, which are based on the life-cycle theoretical framework of Chapter 2, make some contributions to methodology. Ultimately, though, I wish to use these empirical measures to evaluate and interpret the results of Part Two in order to discover whether the inequality picture revealed in Part Two is indeed a reasonably accurate representation of the distribution of economic well-being; to find out which family groups in the population are better or worse off than indicated in Part Two; and to suggest which groups need special assistance. Government policies can then be better directed toward the most pressing distributional problems.

Four general types of adjustments to the standard family income data will be examined in Part Three. The first group of adjustments, considered in Chapters 9 and 11, will focus on omitted sources of income such as income-in-kind from home ownership, underreporting of various income sources, and omission of capital gains. The second group of adjustments concerns the measurement of income relative to family need and circumstances as reflected by location, age, size, and composition of the family unit; this is addressed in Chapter 10. The third set of adjustments relate to the accounting period over which the flow of income is measured, such as annual, 'permanent,' or lifetime income, which, for life-cycle reasons, may all be quite different; these are considered in Chapter 13. Finally, the fourth set of adjustments reflects different basic concepts of income and family resources, and attempts to integrate income, asset, and wealth accounts for the family as discussed in sections of Chapters 11–13.

Adjustments for a number of the above factors have been considered in some detail with both United States and British data in studies by Morgan and Smith (1969), Stark (1972), Taussig (1973), Smith (1975) and Moon and Smolensky (1977). Until very recently, though, little work of this type had been done for Canada. But within the past couple years, a number of Canadian studies by Irvine (1976), Health and Welfare Canada (1977),

Love and Wolfson (1976), Kapsalis (1977), Wolfson (1977a), Henderson and Rowley (1977), and Cloutier (1978) have addressed at least some of the issues listed above. The present study considers more adjustments than the above studies, and it deals entirely with Ontario rather than all of Canada. At the same time, though, it is also much more disaggregative in its empirical analysis and representation of inequality differences across the population. More specific comments on the differences in technique, methodology, and empirical findings between this and other Canadian studies will be made within the discussion of the relevant chapters.

Several caveats and limitations of the present study should, however, be noted. In the first place, the adjustments being considered are accounting adjustments only and do not pretend to represent the behavioural effects of changing some aspects of the economic environment. In looking at the distributional differences between family income receipts and disposable income after direct taxes, for example, we are not analysing the distributional impact of the taxes, but only describing how inequality figures change when we look at one measure of income rather than another. We are not changing the economic environment, but rather changing the way of measuring economic well-being within a given environment. Secondly, the present study is not intended to be complete or exhaustive in its coverage of possible adjustments. Consequently we have not constructed a combined adjusted distribution that includes all of the separate adjustments considered. Rather, the study is intended to suggest several different ways of improving empirical approximations of the distribution of well-being and to illustrate how much the apparent structure of family income inequality is changed with the use of each of these improved proxies.

The main source of data used in Part Three is the Survey of Consumer Finances 1974 micro data tape, from which was made a subfile of family unit records for Ontario, the same subfile from which the figures reported in Chapter 7 were computed. The various adjustments and transformations of family incomes discussed in the following chapters were performed on each of the individual records of this subfile with the various inequality measures computed after each adjustment (for details, see Appendix D).

9
Disposable income, under-reporting, and omitted receipts

INTRODUCTION

This chapter examines the ways in which the structure and pattern of inequality change when the conventional basis for inequality comparisons, total family income reported, is adjusted to reflect the disposable real income resources available. It is clear that the distribution of economic well-being depends partly upon income other than that reported, imputed and non-pecuniary real income benefits, and tax payments that must be paid out of any given level of income. This chapter reviews the pattern of inequality in the distribution of total family income, and compares it to that of non-transfer income receipts and disposable family income; examines the effects of adjusting reported total income figures for under-reporting of several sources of income; and considers the distributional effects of imputing income for home-ownership and farm income-in-kind receipts.

PRIMARY, TOTAL, AND DISPOSABLE INCOME

The starting point of analysis in this and further chapters is the measured inequality in the distribution of reported total family income. This was discussed in Chapter 7, and some summary results are reproduced in Table 96. The various measures have been explained and illustrated in Chapter 5. Relative poverty characteristics of a distribution are indicated by lower income shares, while summary degree of inequality is represented by the Gini coefficient, coefficient of variation, and a particular value of the Atkinson index (corresponding to the inequality aversion index ϵ equal to 1.5). By way of review, one may note the 'inverted U' pattern of mean or median income across ages, and the U-shaped pattern of summary inequal-

Figure 60:
Lorenz curves for all family units of primary, total, and disposable
incomes, Ontario 1973

Source: Table 99

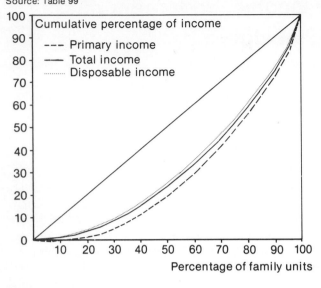

Figure 61:
Relative mean income of all family units for primary, total, and disposable
income, Ontario 1973

Source: Table 100

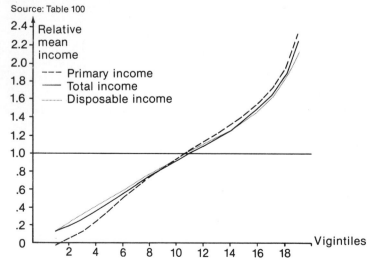

TABLE 96
Inequality measures among all family units by age of head for total family income, Ontario 1973

Measure	Under 25	25–34	35–44	45–54	55–64	65 & over	All ages
Shares							
Bottom 10%	1.1	2.2	2.5	1.8	1.1	2.1	1.2
Bottom quintile	3.8	7.0	7.4	6.4	4.0	5.4	4.0
2nd quintile	11.3	14.6	14.4	13.7	11.7	8.5	11.0
3rd quintile	18.1	19.4	18.8	18.6	18.3	13.3	18.4
4th quintile	26.6	24.3	23.5	24.0	24.9	21.7	25.6
Top quintile	40.2	34.7	35.9	37.3	41.2	51.0	41.0
Top 10%	22.8	19.9	21.6	22.0	24.7	33.5	24.5
Top 5%	12.6	11.3	12.8	13.0	14.4	21.0	14.4
Gini coefficient	0.369	0.276	0.282	0.306	0.370	0.447	0.374
Coef of variation	0.63	0.47	0.50	0.54	0.66	0.93	0.66
Atkinson index ($\epsilon = 1.55$)	0.440	0.253	0.232	0.305	0.431	0.391	0.420
Mean income ($)	7263	11939	14275	15016	11483	5482	11091
Median income ($)	6463	11456	13370	13984	10430	3704	10238

SOURCE: Based on data for Ontario from the 1973 Consumer Finances Micro Data Release Tape supplied by Statistics Canada.

ity figures across age groups. Bottom income shares are greatest for the groups aged 25–44 and least for the ages less than 25 and 55–64. Top income shares are greatest for ages less than 25 and 55 and over, and least for age group 25–34. In general the distribution for all ages together is very similar to that for the age group 55–64. The Lorenz curve and relative mean income curve for total family income of all family units are illustrated by solid lines in Figures 60 and 61 respectively.

For purposes of comparison, it may be useful to look also at the distribution solely of factor income receipts (or 'primary income'), obtained by subtracting all direct government transfer receipts from total income of family units. This provides a rough approximation to the distribution of factor market income and may be viewed as representing the direct or first-round effects of current transfer payments. The resulting distribution figures presented in Table 97 describe the structure of inequality in the distribution of factor payments in the 1973 Ontario economy. Comparing the summary inequality measures in Tables 96 and 97, one can see that inclusion of transfers results in a moderate reduction in the Gini coefficients and coefficients of variation, but that this reduction is not at all uniform across different age groups. Over-all, the Gini coefficient, for example,

TABLE 97

Inequality measures among all family units by age of head for primary income receipts, Ontario 1973

Measure	Under 25	25–34	35–44	45–54	55–64	65 & over	All ages
Shares							
Bottom 10%	0.6	1.3	1.5	1.1	0.3	−0.8	−0.07
Bottom quintile	2.9	5.9	6.1	5.5	2.4	−1.2	1.3
2nd quintile	10.4	14.2	14.1	13.4	10.6	1.2	9.8
3rd quintile	17.3	19.1	18.7	18.4	17.4	5.8	18.3
4th quintile	25.7	24.2	23.5	23.9	24.0	16.0	26.0
Top quintile	43.7	36.5	37.6	38.9	45.5	78.2	44.5
Top 10%	26.7	21.6	23.1	23.6	29.3	62.6	27.6
Top 5%	16.7	13.0	14.2	14.5	19.1	50.2	17.2
Gini coefficient	0.411	0.303	0.310	0.329	0.426	0.770	0.435
Coef of variation	0.72	0.51	0.55	0.59	0.74	1.26	0.76
Atkinson index ($\epsilon = 1.55$)	0.930	0.416	0.366	0.474	0.655	n.a.	n.a.
Mean income ($)	7091	11933	13881	14619	11026	2827	10354
Median income ($)	6284	11280	12969	13504	10202	1361	9727

NOTE: n.a. means not applicable because of the negative income shares.
SOURCE: See source to Table 96.

TABLE 98

Inequality measures among all family units by age of head for disposable family income, Ontario 1973

Measure	Under 25	25–34	35–44	45–54	55–64	65 & over	All ages
Shares							
Bottom 10%	0.6	2.3	2.7	2.0	1.1	1.9	1.2
Bottom quintile	3.7	7.5	8.1	6.9	4.3	5.6	4.4
2nd quintile	11.9	15.0	15.0	14.3	12.2	9.5	11.9
3rd quintile	18.4	19.6	19.1	19.1	18.6	14.6	18.9
4th quintile	26.7	24.1	23.3	24.2	24.9	23.1	25.5
Top quintile	39.4	33.9	34.5	35.5	39.9	47.3	39.3
Top 10%	22.2	19.4	20.4	20.6	23.7	29.7	23.1
Top 5%	12.2	11.1	11.9	11.8	13.6	17.9	13.4
Gini coefficient	0.361	0.262	0.260	0.284	0.354	0.413	0.352
Coef of variation	0.61	0.44	0.45	0.49	0.62	0.80	0.61
Atkinson index ($\epsilon = 1.55$)	0.484	0.247	0.209	0.284	0.467	0.380	0.422
Mean income ($)	6305	10081	11895	12430	9814	4938	9389
Median income ($)	5771	9851	11350	11873	9082	3664	8874

SOURCE: See source to Table 96.

is reduced by 14 per cent; but for the group aged 65 and over, it is reduced by 42 per cent compared to 10 per cent or less for the younger and middle-aged groups. Indeed, transfer receipts raise the incomes of family units aged 65 and over by $2655 on average, or by 94 per cent, compared to only 7 per cent for all family units. The inequality reduction also tends to be most noticeable at the bottom end of the distribution but it has a significant effect on the upper end as well. In short, direct government transfers appear to have a very substantial effect on poverty levels and inequality among the oldest age group and a more modest effect on younger and middle-aged family units.

In order to compare total family income with *disposable* family income after personal income tax has been subtracted, let us consider the effects on summary inequality measures of taking account of personal income tax payments as well. The resulting inequality figures are given in Table 98 and may be compared with those in Table 96. One notes that again there is a reduction in the Gini coefficients and coefficients of variation, but it is a rather modest reduction this time, and it is more evenly distributed across age groups. Disposable income per family unit on average is about 15 per cent less than total income, and the Gini coefficient for all age groups is about 6 per cent less. The strongest reductions in summary inequality figures occur among the age groups with peak life-cycle income (age 35–54) and among the oldest group (aged 65 and over), but for the Gini coefficient these reductions are still less than 10 per cent. And within each age group, the strongest inequality reductions occur at the top 5 or 10 per cent of the distributions, while rather mixed effects occur at the bottom of the distributions. Thus the summary measures of inequality are not always in agreement: the Gini coefficients and coefficients of variation are all lower for disposable income, while the Atkinson index does not always agree. In summary, then, the direct effect of personal taxes on aggregate inequality figures is much more modest than the effect of direct government transfers.

Let us consider now in much more disaggregated fashion what happens to inequality results for all family units together. Cumulative income shares for each 5 per cent of the population of family units from the poorest to the highest-income recipients are presented in Table 99 for primary income, total family income, and disposable income. These are the figures from which the Lorenz curves in Figure 60 are drawn. As can be seen, except for the first two vigintiles, the cumulative shares for disposable income are all above those for total income, so that for almost the whole range of the distribution the Lorenz curve for disposable income lies inside that for total income; since the former curve, however, does not lie entirely inside the

TABLE 99
Lorenz curve ordinates for all family units of primary, total, and disposable income, Ontario 1973

Vigintile	Primary income[a]	Total income	Disposable income[a]
First	−0.15(−)	0.39	0.26(−)
Second	−0.07(−)	1.23	1.23( )
Third	0.37(−)	2.37	2.56(+)
Fourth	1.30(−)	3.95	4.37(+)
Fifth	2.84(−)	5.98	6.65(+)
Sixth	5.01(−)	8.47	9.38(+)
Seventh	7.78(−)	11.47	12.60(+)
Eighth	11.13(−)	14.97	16.29(+)
Ninth	15.00(−)	18.92	20.41(+)
Tenth	19.35(−)	23.32	24.94(+)
Eleventh	24.17(−)	28.14	29.87(+)
Twelfth	29.45(−)	33.38	35.21(+)
Thirteenth	35.19(−)	39.07	40.94(+)
Fourteenth	41.41(−)	45.21	47.08(+)
Fifteenth	48.14(−)	51.83	53.67(+)
Sixteenth	55.46(−)	59.00	60.75(+)
Seventeenth	63.46(−)	66.83	68.41(+)
Eighteenth	72.35(−)	75.51	76.91(+)
Nineteenth	82.76(−)	85.63	86.64(+)
Twentieth	100.00	100.00	100.00

a Sign in parentheses shows whether figure is higher or lower than total income.
SOURCE: See source to Table 96.

latter, we cannot say unambiguously that over-all inequality is reduced by moving from total income to disposable income. Note also that the inequality reduction associated with disposable income is again rather less than the difference between total and primary income since the inward movement of the Lorenz curve in Figure 60 is not as great. The latter diagram also shows that the Lorenz curve for total income for all family units lies uniformly inside that for primary income, so that we can conclude that there is a reduction in over-all inequality in moving from the latter income measure to the former.

Similar patterns are reflected in Table 100, which shows the relative mean incomes for nineteen vigintiles, again for primary, total, and disposable incomes. The move from primary to total to disposable income results in substantially higher relative mean income measures at the lower end of the distribution and somewhat lower relative mean income figures at the top end of the distribution (see Figure 60). Thus direct personal taxes and

TABLE 100

Relative mean income of all family units for primary, total, and disposable income, Ontario 1973

Vigintile	Primary income[a]	Total income	Disposable income[a]
First	−0.014(−)	0.133	0.130(−)
Second	0.048(−)	0.196	0.229(+)
Third	0.132(−)	0.266	0.309(+)
Fourth	0.247(−)	0.362	0.414(+)
Fifth	0.384(−)	0.449	0.498(+)
Sixth	0.506(−)	0.548	0.595(+)
Seventh	0.629(−)	0.655	0.694(+)
Eighth	0.744(−)	0.746	0.782(+)
Ninth	0.842(+)	0.834	0.867(+)
Tenth	0.939(+)	0.923	0.945(+)
Eleventh	1.035(+)	1.005	1.026(+)
Twelfth	1.126(+)	1.095	1.107(+)
Thirteenth	1.223(+)	1.180	1.186(+)
Fourteenth	1.325(+)	1.275	1.273(−)
Fifteenth	1.431(+)	1.375	1.365(−)
Sixteenth	1.564(+)	1.496	1.469(−)
Seventeenth	1.712(+)	1.640	1.606(−)
Eighteenth	1.927(+)	1.849	1.799(−)
Nineteenth	2.336(+)	2.227	2.116(−)
Mean income ($)	10354	11091	9389

a Sign in parentheses shows whether figure is higher or lower than total income.
SOURCE: See source to Table 96.

transfers have a systematically reinforcing effect in the general reduction of over-all inequality figures (the over-all Gini coefficient from primary to disposable income is reduced by 19 per cent), with transfers appearing to have much the more substantial effect.

UNDER-REPORTING OF INCOMES

The income figures used in this study may not represent the real income status of family units in the population by not including all pecuniary income received. In the Survey of Consumer Finances for example, incomes appear to be systematically underreported in some respects compared to the corresponding National Accounts figures. In 1973 the total money income declared by census family units based on the Consumer Finances surveys were $76.9 billion whereas the National Accounts estimate of total Personal Income was $95.5 billion (Statistics Canada 1976b, 97). When adjustments are made to National Accounts figures to make them more comparable in definition and population coverage to those of the Survey of Consumer Finances (SCF),[1] the National Accounts total is $81.2 billion. Although the comparability of the adjusted National Accounts and SCF totals is still not perfect and the former source is also subject to errors of its own,[2] there still remains an estimated underreporting of some $4.25 billion of family income, or 5.5 per cent of the SCF total, which ought to be added to reported family income figures to make them reflect better the sums actually paid out and received.

Most of this underreporting occurs within five major income components: net income from non-farm self employment, which is under-reported by 38.2 per cent relative to the adjusted National Accounts estimate (Statistics Canada 1976b, 97); net income from farm self-employment (underreported by 21.2 per cent); net income from investment (by 37.2 per cent); Unemployment Insurance benefits (33.4 per cent); and Social Assistance benefits and other government transfer receipts (52.3 per cent).[3] The omission or under-reporting of transfer income would presum-

---

1 Statistics Canada (1976b), 83–96, discusses in some detail the difference between total family income as measured in the Survey of Consumer Finances and personal income as measured in the National Accounts. To quote a useful summary: 'The income concept used in this report is similar to the monetary income received by private households as measured in the personal income series in 'National Accounts, Income and Expenditure.' Personal income is the total current income of individuals and private non-commercial institutions, such as charitable organizations and universities ... Personal income includes imputed income as well as monetary income. Among the imputed items are labour income received in kind, imputed rents on owner-occupied houses, and imputed banking services to individuals. Furthermore, some of the income components of the personal income series are not received directly by families and individuals during the year. Among such items are employer contributions to social security and pension funds, the investment income of life insurance companies, and the investment income of industrial pension funds. The inclusion of such items in the National Accounts introduces differences in concepts between the Accounts and the income distribution estimates. On the other hand, certain income components included in the income distribution have no equivalent in the personal income series. Examples are annuity income and retirement pensions.
  'The survey estimates exclude income of families and persons whose income originates mainly in military pay and allowances and also incomes of inmates of institutions, persons residing in Indian reservations, Canadian residents temporarily abroad and families resident in the Yukon and Northwest Territories.'
  'Thus, besides differences in concepts, the two series also differ as to coverage.'
2 See, for example, the discussion in Health and Welfare Canada (1977, 50).
3 In Health and Welfare Canada (1977, 51) this figure is further subdivided into 47.3 per cent for social assistance benefits and 59 per cent for other government transfer receipts.

ably benefit most the older and poorer members of the population, whereas unreported investment income might be expected to accrue primarily to the middle and higher-income members of the population; for those reasons the net distributional effect of imputing for such unreported incomes is not clear.

The procedure that has been followed to adjust for such under-reporting is simply to multiply each of the above reported income sources for each family unit on the SCF micro file by the proportion under-reporting and then to inspect the effects of the measured inequality figures. This approach thus assumes that all family units with a given source of income under-report that income source by the same percentage. Clearly this is a rather simplistic assumption, but it reflects a number of considerations. The under-reporting factors quoted above and used in the adjustments are figures for Canada as a whole; we do not know what the corresponding figures are for Ontario alone. More important though, the shortfall of SCF family income totals from adjusted National Accounts totals reflects non-reporting of incomes as well as under-reporting. Our procedure thus handles only the latter problem and not the former; but again there is not much information on the severity of this problem in Ontario. Consequently, our adjustments for under-reporting of incomes are only rough approximations of or step toward a more complete measure of total pecuniary income receipts.

The adjustments for under-reporting are performed first in three separate steps and then in combination. The first adjustment is to government transfer receipts (including unemployment insurance benefits and social assistance benefits), which are so highly underreported. The effect of augmenting these income sources, however, is to produce a pattern of inequality change similar to that revealed for the difference between primary and total incomes in the previous section. Not unexpectedly, the over-all effect is to decrease the measured inequality figures, most markedly for the oldest age group, who (on average) are the greatest recipients of direct government transfers.

The second adjustment is to the two forms of net self-employment income (i.e., farm and non-farm). The results of the adjustments to these income sources are presented in Table 101. The general effect this time is an increase in measured income inequality compared to the conventional standard of family total income since the effect of non-farm income dominates that of farm income because there are relatively few farmers in the province. The mean increase in income varies across ages from virtually none for the youngest and oldest groups to about $600 for the highest income group aged 45–54. Inequality figures increase for each age group

TABLE 101
Inequality measures among all family units by age of head for family income adjusted for
under-reporting of self-employment income, Ontario 1973

Measure	Under 25	25–34	35–44	45–54	55–64	65 & over	All ages
Shares							
Bottom 10%	−0.3	1.8	2.3	1.5	0.6	1.1	0.7
Bottom quintile	2.5	6.6	7.3	6.2	3.5	4.5	3.3
2nd quintile	11.4	14.4	14.4	13.4	11.7	8.6	10.9
3rd quintile	18.3	19.2	18.6	18.2	18.1	13.4	18.2
4th quintile	26.7	24.2	23.2	23.5	24.7	22.0	25.2
Top quintile	41.1	35.5	36.5	38.8	42.1	51.6	42.4
Top 10%	23.6	20.6	22.2	23.8	25.6	34.0	26.1
Top 5%	13.3	12.0	13.3	15.0	15.3	21.3	16.0
Gini coefficient	0.389	0.286	0.287	0.323	0.383	0.461	0.392
Coef of variation	0.66	0.48	0.51	0.63	0.68	0.94	0.68
Atkinson index ($\epsilon = 1.55$)	n.a.	0.350	0.261	0.385	0.497	n.a.	0.552
Mean ($)	7259	12160	14533	15620	11823	5503	11339
Median ($)	6571	11638	13486	14211	10592	3725	10326

NOTE: n.a. means not applicable because of the negative income shares.
SOURCE: See source to Table 96.

TABLE 102
Inequality measures among all family units by age of head for family income adjusted for
under-reporting of net investment income, Ontario 1973

Measure	Under 25	25–34	35–44	45–54	55–64	65 & over	All ages
Shares							
Bottom 10%	1.1	2.2	2.5	1.8	1.1	1.4	1.2
Bottom quintile	3.8	7.0	7.4	6.3	4.0	4.5	4.0
2nd quintile	11.4	14.5	14.4	13.3	11.6	8.2	11.1
3rd quintile	18.2	19.4	18.9	18.1	17.9	13.2	18.3
4th quintile	26.7	24.4	23.5	23.3	24.4	22.1	25.4
Top quintile	40.0	34.6	35.8	39.0	42.1	52.1	41.3
Top 10%	22.5	19.7	21.4	24.1	25.8	34.4	24.9
Top 5%	12.2	11.1	12.6	15.3	15.4	21.6	14.8
Gini coefficient	0.366	0.274	0.281	0.323	0.377	0.467	0.375
Coef of variation	0.64	0.48	0.51	0.65	0.69	0.98	0.68
Atkinson index ($\epsilon = 1.55$)	0.437	0.251	0.231	0.312	0.435	0.462	0.422
Mean ($)	7241	12000	14318	15580	12164	5988	11401
Median ($)	6464	11598	13500	14228	10866	3982	10465

SOURCE: See source to Table 96.

TABLE 103
Inequality measures among all family units by age of head for family income:
total adjustments for under-reporting, Ontario 1973

Measure	Under 25	25–34	35–44	45–54	55–64	65 & over	All ages
Shares							
Bottom 10%	−0.2	1.9	2.3	1.7	0.7	−0.8	0.8
Bottom quintile	2.5	6.7	7.3	6.4	3.9	2.2	3.6
2nd quintile	11.5	14.4	14.3	13.3	11.9	8.2	11.2
3rd quintile	18.2	19.2	18.4	18.1	18.0	13.3	18.2
4th quintile	26.7	24.1	22.8	23.3	24.6	22.7	25.1
Top quintile	41.1	35.6	37.1	38.8	41.6	53.7	41.9
Top 10%	23.8	20.8	22.9	23.9	25.2	35.4	25.6
Top 5%	13.6	12.2	14.1	15.1	15.1	22.1	15.6
Gini coefficient	0.389	0.286	0.292	0.321	0.374	0.505	0.384
Coef of variation	0.66	0.48	0.52	0.61	0.68	1.02	0.68
Atkinson index	n.a.	0.340	0.262	0.347	0.626	n.a.	0.684
($\epsilon = 1.55$)							
Mean ($)	7436	12383	14984	16148	12460	6106	11783
Median ($)	6719	11851	13827	14648	11151	4051	10735
Mean increase ($)	173	444	709	1132	977	624	692

NOTE: n.a. means not applicable because of the negative income shares.
SOURCE: See source to Table 96.

with bottom shares declining and top shares rising. The most marked decline among bottom income shares occurs among the oldest age groups, 55 and over, while the most substantial rise among top income shares occurs in the group that already has the highest-income, those aged 45–54. Over all ages, the shares of the lower four quintiles fall while that of the top quintile rise; in other words, measured inequality increases.

The third adjustment is to net investment income (see Table 102). For groups under 45, the mean increase in family income is substantially less than $100, but it is over $500 for family units aged 45 and over. For that reason the effect on summary inequality measures for the younger groups is relatively small and in mixed directions, whereas the effect for the older groups is more marked and towards increased inequality. The reason for this increase is the rise in top income shares for the three oldest age groups. The result over all ages is to increase slightly the shares of the top income groups of family units.

Given the rather conflicting effects of the separate adjustments made so far, what are the net effects of combining all the adjustments together? The results are found in Table 103. Over-all inequality figures increase, although

TABLE 104
Lorenz curve ordinates for all family units for family income
adjusted for under-reporting

Vigintile	Total income	Adjusted total income
First	0.39	−0.04(−)
Second	1.23	0.79(−)
Third	2.37	1.96(−)
Fourth	3.95	3.60(−)
Fifth	5.98	5.68(−)
Sixth	8.47	8.24(−)
Seventh	11.47	11.31(−)
Eighth	14.97	14.83(−)
Ninth	18.92	18.78(−)
Tenth	23.32	23.15(−)
Eleventh	28.14	27.89(−)
Twelfth	33.38	33.04(−)
Thirteenth	39.07	38.61(−)
Fourteenth	45.21	44.63(−)
Fifteenth	51.83	51.12(−)
Sixteenth	59.00	58.15(−)
Seventeenth	66.83	65.82(−)
Eighteenth	75.51	74.37(−)
Nineteenth	85.63	84.42(−)
Twentieth	100.00	100.00

SOURCE: See source to Table 96.

only slightly for the Gini coefficient and coefficient of variation, which increase by only about 3 per cent compared to the original unadjusted figures in Table 96. The last line of the table indicates the average net gain per family unit by age group from the adjustment, and one can see that the middle-aged groups, which already had the highest mean incomes, ended up with the greatest dollar gains. More generally, the effect both within age groups and for all age groups together is to increase measured inequality; the most marked increases occurring for the oldest age group, where the Gini coefficient, for example, goes up by 13 per cent compared to the corresponding figure in Table 96. Evidently, the self-employment and net investment income adjustment effects have dominated the government transfer adjustment effects. For all age groups, top income shares rise, with the strongest effect for the group aged 45–54; low income shares change relatively little except for the rather marked fall for the age group 65 and older.

The effects of the combined adjustments for under-reporting on the distribution for all age groups are shown in more detail in Table 104, which presents a comparison of cumulative income shares (i.e., ordinates of a Lorenz curve) for total family income and the adjusted total income figures. As can be seen, the latter statistics lie uniformly below the former shares so that there is indeed an unambiguous outward shift of the Lorenz curve associated with this adjustment; however the shift is very small, a maximum of only 1.21 percentage points for the nineteenth vigintile level. Thus, by adjusting for under-reporting of various income sources we obtain a distribution picture that is only slightly more unequal than that suggested by the standard family total income figures reported.

IMPUTATION FOR INCOME IN KIND

Total family income estimates reported in the Consumer Finance Surveys are essentially money income figures and do not include any income-in-kind imputations. Private non-pecuniary receipts can take several forms: produce kept by farmers for their own use, 'free' meals received by domestic employees and restaurant workers, company cars and club memberships provided to business executives, and (by far the most widely spread and important) own-payment of rent for owner-occupied housing. Income-in-kind benefits can also be received through government (indirect transfer) programs such as public education, day care, and health and medical care services.[4] But because of data limitations and problems of comparability, only two imputations for private income-in-kind receipts are pursued here: for farm income-in-kind receipts, and for imputed rent for owner-occupied housing. Again, the results are not meant to be comprehensive, but only suggestive.

We turn first to the adjustment for farm income-in-kind. According to *Farm Net Income 1973*, (Statistics Canada 1974, 6, 8), total net farm income in Ontario in 1973 was $468.62 million, not including any income-in-kind, and the total estimated income-in-kind (not counting imputed

4 Adequate analysis of the distributional benefits of government in-kind transfer receipts is a very complex issue requiring substantial amounts of specialized information, as illustrated for example, in the recent study of Ontario Hospital Insurance Benefits by Manga (1977). Also, compared to the United States, there are relatively few direct in-kind government transfer programs such as food-stamp programs in Canada, and most government in-kind transfers are indirect; i.e. they are in the form of public education, health services, and so on. More general analyses of the distribution of government in-kind benefits in Canada are found in Dodge (1975), Gillespie (1976), Maslove (1972), and Reuber (1976).

house rental of owner-occupied farm houses) was $42.95 million, or 9.23 per cent of the former figure. Applying this percentage to the 167 family units on the Ontario Survey of Consumer Finances tape (whose mean farm net income receipts exclusive of income-in-kind were $7186), we estimated farm income-in-kind receipts as $663 (= 7186 × 0.0923), per farm unit. Accordingly, an imputation of $663 was added to the income of each farm family unit that reported non-zero net self-employment income from farming. This has the effect of marking up very low farm incomes by a higher rate than large farm incomes, but this is presumably exactly what one would expect.

The results of this adjustment are not presented separately in a table since the effect of the adjustment is so small. Mean income for all ages increases by only about $15 (or 0.1 per cent) with the largest dollar gains occurring in the mid and later-middle aged groups. While many inequality measures for the youngest and oldest age groups are essentially unchanged compared to those for total family income, inequality for the middle and later-middle aged groups is generally reduced very slightly.

We turn now to the adjustment for imputed income from home ownership to account for the rent that home owners in effect pay to themselves. In this case, there are no independent estimates of aggregate homeownership income benefits available. However the Statistics Canada Survey of Household Facilities and Equipment, 1972, does contain estimates of the market value of houses from which imputed rent figures could be estimated. In order to calculate such an imputation, it will be assumed that the family unit consumes only the services of its housing stock and leaves the net worth of the housing stock intact. Benefits of home ownership on asset and net worth accounts are considered separately in Chapters 11 and 12. Thus imputed rental income is estimated by the formula $r_u \cdot (\text{MV} - \text{PO})$ where r_u is the rate of housing services consumption, MV is the estimated market value of the house, and PO is the mortgage principal outstanding on the house, so that the difference MV − PO is the family's equity value in the house.[5] For empirical purposes r_u is approximated by the average mortgage rate of 9.59 per cent in 1973 (*Bank of Canada Review*, Aug. 1976, S55, Series B14024). The adjustment procedure thus consists of (1) estimating an equation for the net equity value in housing for all Ontario home

5 A different way of estimating imputed rental income that allows for consumption of the housing stock as well as annuitizing the net current market value of the house over the family's expected life horizon is suggested by Kapsalis, who found, however, that this approach yields 'practically identical results' to that followed in the present study (Kapsalis 1977, 7).

TABLE 105

Inequality measures among all family units by age of head for family income adjusted for imputed income from home ownership, Ontario 1973

Measure	Under 25	25–34	35–44	45–54	55–64	65 & over	All ages
Shares							
Bottom 10%	1.1	2.0	2.4	2.1	1.3	1.5	1.3
Bottom quintile	3.6	6.7	7.4	6.9	4.6	4.4	4.4
2nd quintile	10.6	14.1	14.6	14.1	12.0	9.4	11.2
3rd quintile	17.3	19.1	19.0	18.9	17.9	14.3	18.0
4th quintile	25.5	23.9	23.4	23.9	23.6	21.3	24.8
Top quintile	42.9	36.2	35.5	36.3	41.9	50.6	41.5
Top 10%	26.2	21.6	21.3	21.5	26.4	34.8	25.6
Top 5%	16.3	13.1	12.5	12.7	16.8	23.9	15.9
Gini coefficient	0.396	0.293	0.277	0.292	0.367	0.451	0.373
Atkinson index ($\epsilon = 1.55$)	0.442	0.272	0.240	0.274	0.369	0.359	0.397
Mean ($)	7450	12997	16068	17159	13607	6595	12543
Median ($)	6669	12510	15230	16227	12808	5334	11500
Mean increase ($)	187	1058	1793	2143	2124	1113	1452

SOURCE: See source to Table 96.

TABLE 106

Inequality measures among all family units by age of head for family income adjusted for imputed income from home ownership and income-in-kind from farming, Ontario 1973

Measure	Under 25	25–34	35–44	45–54	55–64	65 & over	All ages
Shares							
Bottom 10%	1.1	2.0	2.4	2.1	1.3	1.5	1.3
Bottom quintile	3.6	6.7	7.5	6.9	4.6	4.4	4.4
2nd quintile	10.6	14.0	14.6	14.2	12.1	9.4	11.3
3rd quintile	17.3	19.2	19.0	18.9	17.9	14.3	18.0
4th quintile	25.5	23.9	23.4	23.9	23.6	21.3	24.8
Top quintile	42.9	36.2	35.5	36.2	41.9	50.6	41.5
Top 10%	26.2	21.6	21.5	21.5	26.4	34.8	25.6
Top 5%	16.3	13.1	12.5	12.7	16.8	23.9	15.9
Gini coefficient	0.396	0.293	0.276	0.291	0.367	0.451	0.373
Atkinson index ($\epsilon = 1.55$)	0.442	0.273	0.238	0.273	0.368	0.359	0.396
Mean ($)	7452	13021	16099	17185	13622	6595	12558
Median ($)	6669	12532	15259	16253	12825	5334	11517
Mean increase ($)	189	1824	1824	2169	2139	1113	1467

SOURCE: See source to Table 96.

owners in the Household Income, Facilities, and Equipment micro data file for 1971 (Statistics Canada 1975d), (2) using this estimated equation to impute net equity value for each Ontario home owner on the SCF tape, and (3) calculating imputed rental income by the above formula and adding it to total family income. Technical and data details on estimation procedure (particularly associated with moving from one micro data file to another) are found in Appendix E.

The results of the adjustment for imputed income from home-ownership are presented in Table 105. The mean increase in income of all family units is fairly substantial (about $1450, or 13 per cent). The greatest increases occur, as one would expect, for the middle-aged groups, where the incidence of home-ownership is highest. For the groups 45–64 summary inequality figures decrease as lower income shares rise and upper income shares show mixed results. For the groups aged less than 34, however, summary inequality measures increase as bottom shares decline and upper shares rise – evidently it is the relatively high-income members among younger families that own their homes and thus gain most from the imputations. Inequality effects on the groups aged 35–44 and 65 and over are mixed with summary inequality measures indicating conflicting inferences. Over all age groups, however, the general effect is to reduce summary inequality values slightly or hardly at all as bottom and top income shares are increased and middle income shares decline slightly.

Consider now the effect of combining the farm income-in-kind and home-ownership income imputations. The results are presented in Table 106, which in fact differs hardly at all from Table 105 for the home-ownership imputation alone. Clearly, the latter dominates the farm income-in-kind adjustment since the proportion of home-owners is much greater than that of farmers and since the magnitude of the adjustment for the relevant family units is substantially greater than that for retained farm produce.

We can turn to Tables 107 and 108 to examine more closely the results for all age groups together and both imputations combined. The former table shows the cumulative income shares for our standard measure, reported total family income, as well as for the combined adjustment measure of income, and thus shows what happens to the Lorenz curve as the result of these adjustments. Though both summary inequality measures in Table 106 indicate a slight reduction in over-all inequality, this reduction is not uniform across all parts of the distribution; in fact the Lorenz curves cross twice. The very bottom few percent lose out as well as the group between the eighth and tenth vigintiles – as revealed by the relative-mean income figures in Table 108. These, however, are dominated by the general

TABLE 107
Lorenz curve ordinates for all family units for income adjusted
for imputed income from home ownership and income-in-kind
from farming, Ontario 1973

Vigintile	Total income	Adjusted total income
First	0.39	0.37(−)
Second	1.23	1.29(+)
Third	2.37	2.66(+)
Fourth	3.95	4.44(+)
Fifth	5.98	6.63(+)
Sixth	8.47	9.25(+)
Seventh	11.47	12.29(+)
Eighth	14.97	15.75(+)
Ninth	18.92	19.62(+)
Tenth	23.32	23.90(+)
Eleventh	28.14	28.61(+)
Twelfth	33.38	33.73(+)
Thirteenth	39.07	39.26(+)
Fourteenth	45.21	45.21( )
Fifteenth	51.83	51.60(−)
Sixteenth	59.00	58.52(−)
Seventeenth	66.83	66.05(−)
Eighteenth	75.51	74.42(−)
Nineteenth	85.63	84.09(−)
Twentieth	100.00	100.00

SOURCE: See source to Table 96.

relative-mean increases of the remaining below-median incomes and the
general relative-mean reductions of upper-income figures. In general the
inclusion of imputations for farm income-in-kind and rental income from
owner-occupied housing results in a rather slight and non-uniform (either
across ages or across income groups) or mixed change in measured income
inequality.

The lack of strong results from the above adjustments, however, is due
in large part to the fact that the discussion has encompassed family units of
all sizes. This aggregation hides the fact that both adjustments have been
made almost exclusively to the incomes of families – there are very few
farms or houses owned by unattached individuals. It would be informative
to analyse the effects of the two imputations under discussion upon incomes
only of family units of two or more.

TABLE 108
Relative mean income of all family units for family income adjusted for imputed income from home ownership and income-in-kind from farming, Ontario 1973

Vigintile	Total income	Adjusted total income
First	0.133	0.148(+)
Second	0.196	0.229(+)
Third	0.266	0.326(+)
Fourth	0.362	0.396(+)
Fifth	0.449	0.486(+)
Sixth	0.548	0.575(+)
Seventh	0.655	0.657(+)
Eighth	0.746	0.747(+)
Ninth	0.834	0.832(−)
Tenth	0.923	0.917(−)
Eleventh	1.005	1.000(−)
Twelfth	1.095	1.088(−)
Thirteenth	1.180	1.170(−)
Fourteenth	1.275	1.259(−)
Fifteenth	1.375	1.352(−)
Sixteenth	1.496	1.469(−)
Seventeenth	1.640	1.609(−)
Eighteenth	1.849	1.807(−)
Nineteenth	2.227	2.137(−)
Mean income ($)	11 091	12 558

SOURCE: See source to Table 96.

Before re-examining these effects, though, let us consider the basic pattern of inequality of our conventional standard, total family income, among families as presented in Table 109. Comparing these results with those for all family units in Table 96, one notes the higher mean and median incomes, particularly for the youngest and oldest age groups where unattached individuals (with their generally lower incomes) are relatively more frequent, and the markedly lower summary inequality measures associated with this rather more homogeneous population. Bottom income shares are considerably higher for families of two or more, and top income shares are slightly reduced – both contributing to the rather substantial reduction in inequality.

The inequality results that are obtained for families of two or more when both imputation adjustments are combined are presented in Table 110.

TABLE 109

Inequality measures by age of head for total family income of families of two or more, Ontario 1973

Measure	Under 25	25–34	35–44	45–54	55–64	65 & over	All ages
Shares							
Bottom 10%	2.3	2.4	2.7	2.8	2.0	2.4	2.1
Bottom quintile	7.4	7.7	8.0	8.2	6.5	6.4	6.4
2nd quintile	15.6	15.2	14.8	14.4	13.7	10.7	13.7
3rd quintile	19.8	19.4	18.8	18.7	18.2	15.0	18.7
4th quintile	24.4	23.8	23.3	23.5	23.3	22.9	23.9
Top quintile	32.8	34.0	35.2	35.2	38.3	45.1	37.3
Top 10%	18.2	19.6	21.0	20.5	23.0	28.6	22.4
Top 5%	10.1	11.3	12.3	12.0	13.7	17.5	13.3
Gini coefficient	0.251	0.260	0.268	0.268	0.312	0.382	0.306
Coef of variation	0.42	0.45	0.48	0.47	0.57	0.75	0.52
Atkinson index ($\epsilon = 1.55$)	0.234	0.229	0.207	0.211	0.284	0.309	0.275
Mean income ($)	10084	12955	14679	15922	13735	7962	13198
Median income ($)	9955	12567	13807	14849	12582	5889	12338

SOURCE: See source to Table 96.

TABLE 110

Inequality measures by age of head for family income adjusted for imputed income from both home ownership and income-in-kind from farming: families of two or more, Ontario 1973

Measure	Under 25	25–34	35–44	45–54	55–64	65 & over	All ages
Shares							
Bottom 10%	2.2	2.4	3.0	3.2	2.7	3.3	2.6
Bottom quintile	7.3	7.9	8.5	9.0	7.7	8.1	7.4
2nd quintile	15.6	15.3	15.1	15.3	14.1	12.6	14.1
3rd quintile	19.9	19.8	19.4	19.2	18.1	16.2	18.9
4th quintile	24.6	24.0	23.5	23.6	22.7	22.3	24.0
Top quintile	32.5	33.0	33.6	33.0	37.6	40.7	35.5
Top 10%	18.0	18.5	19.6	18.9	23.0	25.4	20.6
Top 5%	9.7	10.2	11.2	10.6	14.1	15.5	11.7
Gini coefficient	0.250	0.249	0.249	0.239	0.290	0.318	0.280
Atkinson index ($\epsilon = 1.55$)	0.235	0.214	0.177	0.164	0.217	0.211	0.222

SOURCE: See source to Table 96.

TABLE 111
Lorenz curve ordinates for families of two or more for income
adjusted for imputed income from home ownership and
income-in-kind from farming, Ontario 1973

Vigintile	Total income	Adjusted total income
First	0.67	0.86(+)
Second	2.08	2.57(+)
Third	3.98	4.80(+)
Fourth	6.39	7.43(+)
Fifth	9.27	10.46(+)
Sixth	12.54	13.83(+)
Seventh	16.16	17.53(+)
Eighth	20.09	21.53(+)
Ninth	24.31	25.82(+)
Tenth	28.84	30.40(+)
Eleventh	33.65	35.28(+)
Twelfth	38.77	40.43(+)
Thirteenth	44.19	45.90(+)
Fourteenth	49.95	51.70(+)
Fifteenth	56.10	57.85(+)
Sixteenth	62.69	64.45(+)
Seventeenth	67.79	71.56(+)
Eighteenth	77.63	79.36(+)
Nineteenth	86.66	88.26(+)
Twentieth	100.00	100.00

SOURCE: See source to Table 96.

Now one sees that the summary inequality statistics decline for all age groups except the youngest, where only a negligible change occurs. The largest reductions occur for age groups 45–54 and particularly for 65 and over where both bottom income shares increase and top income shares decline and the Gini coefficient, for example, decreases by 17 per cent compared to an 8.5 per cent decline for all ages. Tables 111 and 112 show that this decline in the over-all-ages inequality measures also occurs across the distribution. The first of these tables reveals that all cumulative income shares are higher for the adjusted figures than for conventional money income so that the adjusted Lorenz curve lies uniformly inside that for total family income, although by only a moderate amount. The adjustments have both raised the lower portions of the relative mean income curve as well as reduced top relative mean incomes. These results on inequality reduction

TABLE 112
Relative mean income for families of two or more for income adjusted
for imputed income from home ownership and income-in-kind from
farming, Ontario 1973

Vigintile	Total income	Adjusted total income
First	0.226	0.286(+)
Second	0.330	0.403(+)
Third	0.431	0.489(+)
Fourth	0.534	0.563(+)
Fifth	0.616	0.640(+)
Sixth	0.689	0.705(+)
Seventh	0.756	0.770(+)
Eighth	0.815	0.829(+)
Ninth	0.875	0.888(+)
Tenth	0.935	0.945(+)
Eleventh	0.992	0.997(+)
Twelfth	1.054	1.063(+)
Thirteenth	1.117	1.125(+)
Fourteenth	1.189	1.189( )
Fifteenth	1.273	1.271(−)
Sixteenth	1.362	1.360(−)
Seventeenth	1.483	1.480(−)
Eighteenth	1.663	1.643(−)
Nineteenth	1.971	1.932(−)
Mean income ($)	13 198	14 951

SOURCE: See source to Table 96.

are quite consistent, for example, with the general Canada-wide findings by
Health and Welfare Canada (1977, 77). In short, then, the two imputations
reduce moderately and uniformly the measured income inequality among
families of two or more.

SUMMARY

The three sets of adjustments to total family income figures that were
described in this chapter have resulted in three groups of empirical findings.

First, disposable income calculated by subtracting personal income taxes
shows only a modest reduction in inequality (the Gini coefficient across all
family units declines by only 6 per cent) compared to the effect of adding

direct government transfers to original factor income (where the Gini coefficient fell by 14 per cent). Nor is the reduction in inequality for tax payments unambiguous since the Lorenz curve is not entirely shifted inward, and the strongest effects occur at the top end of the distributions.

Secondly, adjustments for under-reporting of Unemployment Insurance benefits, Social Assistance benefits, other government transfer receipts, farm and non-farm self-employment income, and net investment income have, separately, rather different effects on measured income inequality figures, but when combined yield only a slight though unambiguous over-all increase in inequality (with a 3 per cent increase in the Gini coefficient).

Thirdly, adjustment for imputed income-in-kind for farm family units results only in a very slight reduction in inequality among middle-aged family units. Adjustment for imputed income from owner-occupied housing has mixed and inconclusive effects across all family units. But when the two adjustments are combined and analysis is restricted to families, there is a moderate and unambiguous reduction in inequality figures (with a Gini coefficient lower by 8½ per cent), and a fairly strong effect among families aged 65 and over (where the Gini coefficient is reduced by 17 per cent).

10
Adjustment for cost of living and size of family

INTRODUCTION

The principal objective of Part Three is to evaluate the ways in which the structure of inequality across the population changes when adjustments are made to conventional family income figures so as to reflect more accurately the distribution of economic well-being. The last chapter considered limitations to the use of reported money income as a proxy for economic well-being, limitations associated with under-reporting or non-inclusion of various forms of real income. In the present chapter we turn to another aspect of the same general issue: how well does total family income actually represent the economic well-being of the members of the family when family units differ substantially in size and location? For example, a $10 000 income for a single person in Ontario in 1973 was fairly substantial; on the other hand, for a family of eight, it would not have gone very far. Similarly, a $10 000 income would tend to go farther for a rural family than for a family living in a large urban area where food, housing, and transportation generally cost more. Thus one should recognize that the economic well-being of family members depends on family characteristics as well as family resources. Implicit in any ordering of family units according to different treatment of family members such as income per family, per family member, or per urban adult equivalent is a social welfare valuation of how individuals are being compared across the population. Consequently, an attempt should be made to evaluate the sensitivity of over-all inequality patterns to such different social valuation schemes. The present chapter examines the ways in which the income of family units varies according to family characteristics such as place of residence, family size and composition, and the age and sex of the family head.

ADJUSTMENT FOR DIFFERENCES IN PLACE OF RESIDENCE

A given bundle of goods and services can cost different amounts in different places so that a given family income might provide a higher real-valued consumption bundle in one region than in another. If one were to use total family income as an approximate index of relative family economic well-being, one ought to try to normalize for such cost-of-living differences between different areas or regions.

Canada does not have regional price indexes except for different cities. However, within a province, such as Ontario for example, one would expect cost of living differences to be more significant between urban and rural environments than between different cities. Cost-of-living differences according to the population of the place of residence have been estimated in the calculation of poverty line figures for Canada as a whole. Table 113 presents an index constructed by Statistics Canada[1] of the relative cost of maintaining a family at a standard of living corresponding to Statistics Canada's estimated poverty line in different places of residence. According to this index, the cost of maintaining a family of four, say, at the poverty line would be 10 per cent higher in very large cities than in cities of size 30000–99000, and about 20 per cent less in rural areas. It should be noted that relative cost-of-living differences are here being assumed constant

---

1 The original study on which these figures are based is contained in Statistics Canada 1973b, and the results are published in Statistics Canada 1975b, 16–17. It should also be noted that the relative cost-of-living indexes and associated poverty line figures used in this chapter were originally constructed for Statistics Canada's definition of economic family units (see footnote one of Chapter 8), while they are being applied here to the SCF micro data file of census family units (see Chapter 7). Since the census family definition is the narrower one and there are more unattached individuals among census family units than among economic family units, these smaller family units will be moved (relatively) down the real income scale by the concave cost-of-living function used in the adjustment procedure. Thus applying a cost-of-living adjustment will tend to reduce income shares and increase inequality at the lower end of the distribution somewhat more among census family units than among economic family units. Consequently, we expect the inequality effects of the cost-of-living adjustments used in this study to be slightly stronger or more accentuated (particularly among lower portions of the distributions) because the analysis is based on census family units rather than on economic family units. Similarly, we would expect the differences between census family units and economic family units to be much greater in rural areas (where family members may tend to live together longer) than in urban areas (where older and younger family members may tend to spread out more to form own family units). Consequently, in urban areas, we would expect census and economic family definitions to yield rather similar results to cost-of-living adjustments; while in rural areas, we would expect there to be some differences in the results.

TABLE 113
Poverty line indexes by area of residence

Size of area of residence	Area index
500 000 and over	1.100
100 000–499 999	1.030
30 000–99 999	1.000
Small urban	0.920
Rural	0.800

SOURCE: Statistics Canada (1975b, 17)

TABLE 114
Inequality measures by age of head of all family units for total family income adjusted for area of residence, Ontario 1973

Measure	Under 25	25–34	35–44	45–54	55–64	65 & over	All ages
Shares							
Bottom 10%	1.0	2.1	2.3	1.8	1.0	1.6	1.2
Bottom quintile	3.6	6.8	7.2	6.5	3.9	4.6	3.9
2nd quintile	10.4	14.2	14.4	13.7	11.5	7.9	10.9
3rd quintile	16.8	19.1	18.6	18.5	17.7	12.2	18.0
4th quintile	25.3	24.2	23.2	23.9	24.0	20.3	25.0
Top quintile	43.9	35.8	36.6	37.5	42.9	55.0	42.2
Top 10%	27.1	21.1	22.3	22.5	27.0	39.1	26.0
Top 5%	17.2	12.5	13.6	13.6	17.0	27.8	16.1
Gini coefficient	0.406	0.289	0.290	0.307	0.386	0.493	0.385
Atkinson index ($\epsilon = 1.55$)	0.448	0.278	0.252	0.302	0.433	0.392	0.426
Mean income ($)	7438	12447	14623	15324	11712	5207	11310
Median income ($)	6507	11683	13628	14188	10789	3765	10461

SOURCE: Based on data for Ontario from the 1973 Consumer Finance Micro Data Release Tape supplied by Statistics Canada.

across family sizes and income classes. The latter assumption is the result of a lack of information in Canada about cost-of-living differences by income class.[2] If one now uses the figures in Table 113 to normalize

2 In the United States, where there are fairly major income-in-kind transfer programs for the poor, cost-of-living adjustments may vary substantially by income class, as seen in the work of Smeeding (1977). Preliminary evidence for Canada, however, suggests that cost-of-living differences by income class are much smaller (Watts 1977).

reported family income figures on the Survey of Consumer Finances micro data file for Ontario, so that rural incomes are pushed up and incomes from large urban areas are pushed down, the results in Table 114 are obtained. These show the structure of inequality across family units in Ontario of real income adjusted solely for cost of living differences by area of residence. Comparison with the figure in Table 96 for conventional (unadjusted) family income reveals that the effect of this adjustment is a slight increase in the mean and median incomes for each age group except 65 and over; summary inequality figures are generally raised. Which age groups have the greatest change depends on the summary inequality measure used. In the case of the Gini coefficient, for example, the greatest changes occurred among the youngest and oldest age groups. Upper income shares are increased, lower income shares for those under 44 and 65 and over are decreased, and lower income shares for those under 44 and 65 and over are decreased slightly. The result across all age groups is a slight increase in aggregate inequality (3 per cent increase for the Gini coefficient and 2 per cent for the Atkinson index), which is largely due to fairly substantial increases in mid-upper income shares.

Details for the total population are shown in Table 115. As can be seen, the Lorenz curve has indeed shifted out uniformly, though only slightly. Thus adjustment for interregional cost-of-living differences generally increases the inequality figures from those for conventional (unadjusted) total family income, but by a relatively small amount.

ADJUSTMENT FOR DIFFERENCES IN SIZE OF FAMILY:
PER CAPITA FAMILY INCOME

A more important cause of differences in cost of living, however, is the differences in family size. In this and the following sections, several adjustments will be made to the family income figures to take differences in family size into account. This section provides a fairly crude adjustment by simply transforming total family income into per capita terms by dividing by the number of members in the family unit. The following sections provide for a more elaborate adjustment in terms of 'individual adult equivalents.'

The results of transforming income into per capita terms are presented in Table 116. Comparing these to the original results in Table 96 on family total income, one notes the fairly strong but mixed effects of the adjustment to per capita terms. Mean and median incomes are of course reduced – from $11091 to $4485 for all ages together. As one would expect, the largest

TABLE 115
Lorenz curve ordinates of family income for all family units adjusted for
differences in place of residence, Ontario 1973

Vigintile	Family income	Adjusted family income
First	0.39	0.33(−)
Second	1.23	1.15(−)
Third	2.37	2.30(−)
Fourth	3.95	3.86(−)
Fifth	5.98	5.89(−)
Sixth	8.47	8.36(−)
Seventh	11.47	11.32(−)
Eighth	14.97	14.75(−)
Ninth	18.92	18.64(−)
Tenth	23.32	22.95(−)
Eleventh	28.14	27.66(−)
Twelfth	33.38	32.79(−)
Thirteenth	39.07	38.33(−)
Fourteenth	45.21	44.33(−)
Fifteenth	51.83	50.81(−)
Sixteenth	59.00	57.82(−)
Seventeenth	66.83	65.49(−)
Eighteenth	75.51	74.01(−)
Nineteenth	85.63	83.91(−)
Twentieth	100.00	100.00(−)

SOURCE: See source to Table 114.

proportional decreases (to about one-third of total family income levels) occur for ages 35–54. Thus it can be seen that income differences between age groups have narrowed substantially: whereas for unadjusted family income the largest differential in mean income between age groups was 174 per cent, for per capita family income, the largest differential now is only $(5466-3289)/3289 = 66$ per cent. Inequality measures, however, show strong but mixed effects that result in much more homogeneous values across groups. For youngest and oldest age groups, the previously high aggregate inequality figures are reduced since those with highest income are also those with the largest families. For the age groups between 25 and 54, though, the aggregate inequality figures, which were previously relatively low, increase very substantially for the first two of these (the Gini coefficients rise by more than 40 per cent for the groups 25–44). Upper income shares generally increase for each age group, while lower income shares

TABLE 116
Inequality measures by age of head of all family units for per capita family total income,
Ontario 1973

Measure	Under 25	25–34	35–44	45–54	55–64	65 & over	All ages
Shares							
Bottom 10%	1.5	1.7	1.8	2.0	1.5	2.2	1.8
Bottom quintile	4.9	5.6	5.6	6.1	5.0	6.3	5.4
2nd quintile	11.4	11.0	10.8	12.1	11.7	10.9	10.6
3rd quintile	18.2	15.4	14.7	16.8	17.4	13.7	15.5
4th quintile	24.6	23.4	20.0	23.1	23.3	20.1	22.6
Top quintile	40.8	44.6	48.9	42.0	42.6	48.9	45.8
Top 10%	24.9	28.2	34.7	26.6	27.2	33.9	30.0
Top 5%	15.6	18.2	24.7	16.7	17.3	23.7	19.7
Gini coefficient	0.361	0.387	0.420	0.355	0.372	0.412	0.399
Atkinson index ($\epsilon = 1.55$)	0.385	0.351	0.311	0.316	0.364	0.285	0.343
Mean income ($)	4456	4933	3985	5043	5477	3289	4485
Median income ($)	4070	3865	3263	4263	4883	2450	3636

SOURCE: See source to Table 114.

move in different directions. Over all age groups together, bottom and top income shares increase substantially (bottom 10 per cent from 4.0 to 5.4 and top 10 per cent from 24.5 to 30.0), while middle income shares fall so that over-all inequality effects are inconclusive – the Gini coefficient indicates an increase of 6.7 per cent while the Atkinson index suggests a reduction in inequality of 18.3 per cent.

Table 117 presents more disaggregated detail about the distribution for all ages. These results are illustrated in Figure 62, which compares the Lorenz curves for total family income and per capital family income together. Obviously there is a rather substantial shift of the curve – inward over lower incomes and outward over upper ones – so that it should not be surprising that different summary inequality measures suggest different conclusions.

The relative mean income curves for all age groups together are presented in Table 118 and also illustrated in Figure 63. As can be seen, incomes over the bottom 30 per cent and top 15 per cent have increased quite substantially relative to the mean, while the middle 55 per cent have fallen markedly. In summary, then, measuring well-being across family units by per capita income rather than (conventional) total family income leads to a very different pattern of disaggregated inequality across age and income groups

TABLE 117
Lorenz curve ordinates of per capita family income for all family units,
Ontario 1973

Vigintile	Family income	Per capita family income
First	0.39	0.53(+)
Second	1.23	1.78(+)
Third	2.37	3.43(+)
Fourth	3.95	5.41(+)
Fifth	5.98	7.68(+)
Sixth	8.47	10.19(+)
Seventh	11.47	12.96(+)
Eighth	14.97	16.01(+)
Ninth	18.92	19.37(+)
Tenth	23.32	23.07(−)
Eleventh	28.14	27.12(−)
Twelfth	33.38	31.55(−)
Thirteenth	39.07	36.41(−)
Fourteenth	45.21	41.75(−)
Fifteenth	51.83	47.64(−)
Sixteenth	59.00	54.18(−)
Seventeenth	66.83	61.57(−)
Eighteenth	75.51	70.06(−)
Nineteenth	85.63	80.27(−)
Twentieth	100.00	100.00

SOURCE: See source to Table 114.

in the population, but an inconclusive change in aggregate inequality. This result should not be particularly surprising, though, because there is some evidence on number of children by family income level for Ontario that both very low-income and very high-income family units tend to have no or few children living with them (Ritchie 1977, Appendix 5). In summary then, when family income is expressed in per capita terms, both low- and high-income groups move up and middle-income groups, which are likely to include children, move down.

ADULT-EQUIVALENT INCOME ADJUSTMENT

In the previous section the adjustment in family income for differences in family size was made by simply expressing all figures in per capita terms. This adjustment ignores both the fact that the resources required to main-

Figure 62:

Lorenz curves for all family units of total and per capita family incomes, Ontario 1973

Source: Table 117

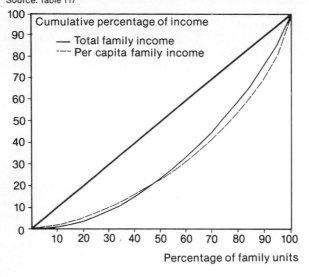

Percentage of family units

Figure 63:

Relative mean income for all family units of total and per capita family incomes, Ontario 1973

Source: Table 118

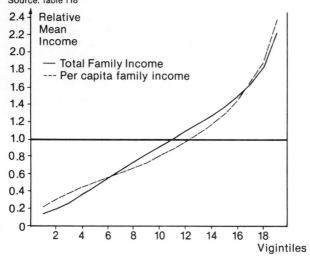

Vigintiles

TABLE 118
Relative mean per capita family income for all family units,
Ontario 1973

Vigintile	Family income	Per capita family income
First	0.133	0.217(+)
Second	0.196	0.307(+)
Third	0.266	0.382(+)
Fourth	0.362	0.449(+)
Fifth	0.449	0.501(+)
Sixth	0.548	0.552(+)
Seventh	0.655	0.610(−)
Eighth	0.746	0.668(−)
Ninth	0.834	0.738(−)
Tenth	0.923	0.811(−)
Eleventh	1.005	0.885(−)
Twelfth	1.095	0.971(−)
Thirteenth	1.180	1.065(−)
Fourteenth	1.275	1.170(−)
Fifteenth	1.375	1.295(−)
Sixteenth	1.496	1.446(−)
Seventeenth	1.640	1.648(+)
Eighteenth	1.849	1.909(+)
Nineteenth	2.227	2.369(+)
Mean income ($)	11 091	4485

SOURCE: See source to Table 114.

tain different family members at a given standard of living can vary greatly with age (compare, for example, the needs of a teenager with a younger child), and that there are economies of scale in household consumption (a family of two adults does not need twice as many resources as a single person for a given standard of living). It would make some sense, therefore, to treat individuals of different ages and sexes differently and to take account of family size before aggregating across family members to arrive at an estimate of the income needed to maintain a family at a given standard of living or level of economic well-being.

The literature on the adjustment of family income for family size and composition to reflect more accurately the level of economic well-being of the family members has become enormous; see, for example, the work of

TABLE 119
Low-income cut-offs by size of family and place of residence, Canada 1973 (dollars)

Size of family	Place of residence	500000 & over	100000– 499999	30000– 99999	Small urban areas	Rural areas
One		3116	2917	2833	2606	2265
Two		4516	4229	4106	3777	3286
Three		5763	5397	5239	4821	4191
Four		6854	6417	6230	5732	4984
Five		7661	7173	6965	6409	5573
Six		8411	7875	7646	7034	6116
Seven		9222	8633	8383	7711	6706

SOURCE: See source to Table 113.

Watts (1967), Orshansky (1965), and Kapsalis (1977).[3] In the present study, we shall not go into the actual construction of such cost-of-living indexes by family size and composition. For our purposes, it will be simplest to use the information available in Statistics Canada's estimates of low-income cut-offs, or so-called 'poverty lines,' which identify the levels of family income by family location, size, and composition that are used by Statistics Canada to distinguish families that are said to be poor from those denoted as non-poor. Table 119 reproduces the Statistics Canada 1973 poverty line estimates by family size (and composition) and area of residence.[4] It can be seen that in each column the proportionality factor of the poverty lines for different family sizes in relation to a single unattached adult runs from 1.00, 1.45, 1.85, 2.20, 2.46, and 2.70 to 2.96 for a family of seven or more. The figures of Table 119 thus reflect strong economies of scale in maintaining a family at a poverty line standard of living and embody an assumption that there are no interactions between regional effects and family-size effects in the calculation of such poverty lines. It will

3 Other relevant work in this area has been done by Friedman (1952) and Seneca and Taussig (1971) for the United States; Stark (1972) for Britain; and Podoluk (1968), Statistics Canada (1973b), and Senate Committee on Poverty (1971) for Canada.

4 The poverty-line figures in Table 119 are for Canada as a whole, but corresponding figures specifically for Ontario do not appear to be available, so that the former are used in this study. Alternative sets of figures presented by the Senate Committee on Poverty (1971) and by the Canadian Council on Social Development (Ontario Economic Council 1976) provide results that are virtually identical to those reported in this chapter. Therefore, we have reported only the results based on the Statistics Canada figures.

TABLE 120
Inequality measures by age of head of all family units: family income adjusted by
place of residence and individual-adult-equivalent, Ontario 1973

Measure	Under 25	25–34	35–44	45–54	55–64	65 & over	All ages
Shares							
Bottom 10%	1.0	1.8	2.3	2.1	1.2	1.8	1.6
Bottom quintile	3.7	5.8	6.8	6.6	4.2	4.9	4.8
2nd quintile	10.2	11.3	12.8	12.9	10.9	8.4	10.7
3rd quintile	15.0	15.0	16.7	17.0	16.1	12.0	15.6
4th quintile	21.3	20.4	21.5	22.2	23.0	19.1	21.8
Top quintile	49.8	47.6	42.2	41.2	45.8	55.7	47.2
Top 10%	34.2	32.6	27.8	26.4	30.0	40.7	31.7
Top 5%	24.0	22.7	18.4	16.8	19.7	30.0	21.4
Gini coefficient	0.447	0.403	0.343	0.337	0.409	0.493	0.414
Atkinson index ($\epsilon = 1.55$)	0.448	0.320	0.273	0.296	0.416	0.346	0.365

SOURCE: See source to Table 114.

also be assumed that the family-size effects are constant across all income
classes as well, so that the cost-of-living relatives at the poverty threshold
line are the same as at, say, an affluence threshold line.[5] Using the figures
in Table 119, we can thus compute 'welfare ratios' for each family unit on
the SCF Ontario file by dividing the family's total income by the correct
poverty-line figure. Similarly, one could create a set of poverty-line indices
(with one of the numbers in the first row of Table 119 taken as a base of
1.00), and then normalize total family income figures on the SCF Ontario

5 It should be remarked that the assumption that family-size cost-of-living effects are
treated as constant across income classes is probably not valid (Seneca and Taussig 1971)
and probably deflates too much for large family units compared to small ones at mid-
and upper-income levels. Since, as was found in Ritchie (1977, Appendix 5), large families are more prevalent in middle-upper income ranges, the result of such over-deflation
would be expected to emphasize the relative decline of the middle-upper portions of the
distribution compared to the top and bottom parts – a shift that indeed occurred rather
markedly in the text. In addition, Taussig (1973, 31) argues that the family-size deflation
adjustments may also be expected to deflate too much for large families in mid- and
upper-income ranges because families may have chosen to have larger families for their
own enjoyment and well-being. So treating family size as exogenous in our cost-of-living
deflation procedure may result in our over-adjusting and thus under-representation of
the actual well-being of a family. This argument, however, goes beyond the present
objective of trying to reflect better the status of economic well-being of a family.

TABLE 121
Lorenz curve ordinates, for all family units, of family income
adjusted for area and family size and composition, Ontario 1973

Vigintile	Family income	Adjusted family income
First	0.39	0.47(+)
Second	1.23	1.56(+)
Third	2.37	2.99(+)
Fourth	3.95	4.77(+)
Fifth	5.98	6.93(+)
Sixth	8.47	9.45(+)
Seventh	11.47	12.30(+)
Eighth	14.97	15.45(+)
Ninth	18.92	18.90(−)
Tenth	23.32	22.64(−)
Eleventh	28.14	26.69(−)
Twelfth	33.38	31.06(−)
Thirteenth	39.07	35.79(−)
Fourteenth	45.21	40.93(−)
Fifteenth	51.83	46.57(−)
Sixteenth	59.00	52.83(−)
Seventeenth	66.83	59.95(−)
Eighteenth	75.51	68.28(−)
Nineteenth	85.63	78.59(−)
Twentieth	100.00	100.00

SOURCE: See source to Table 114.

file by these indices to obtain an adjusted family income series or an 'individual adult equivalent family income' series. The inequality results for the new income series are presented in Table 120.

Again the results are fairly strong but mixed, and they have some similarities to those for the simple per capita income adjustment of the last section. Family mean income differentials between age groups are again reduced from a maximum of 174 per cent for (unadjusted) family income to a maximum of 95 per cent for the adjusted income figures. The Gini inequality measures now increase for all groups including the youngest; again the largest increases are in the 25–44 year age groups. Mixed patterns occur in the 45 and over age groups. Again, upper income shares all increase fairly substantially while bottom income shares generally decrease except for the 45–64 age groups. Over all age groups, bottom and top

TABLE 122
Relative mean income, for all family units, adjusted for area and
family size and composition, Ontario 1973

Vigintile	Family income	Adjusted family income
First	0.133	0.194(+)
Second	0.196	0.270(+)
Third	0.266	0.341(+)
Fourth	0.362	0.419(+)
Fifth	0.449	0.500(+)
Sixth	0.548	0.575(+)
Seventh	0.655	0.640(−)
Eighth	0.756	0.704(−)
Ninth	0.834	0.767(−)
Tenth	0.923	0.830(−)
Eleventh	1.005	0.895(−)
Twelfth	1.095	0.967(−)
Thirteenth	1.180	1.048(−)
Fourteenth	1.275	1.144(−)
Fifteenth	1.375	1.259(−)
Sixteenth	1.496	1.409(−)
Seventeenth	1.640	1.629(−)
Eighteenth	1.849	1.921(+)
Nineteenth	2.227	2.476(+)
Mean income ($)	11 091	7439

SOURCE: See source to Table 114.

income shares generally gain (bottom 10 per cent share rises from 4.0 to 4.8, and top 10 per cent share increases from 24.5 to 31.7) relative to the three middle-income quintiles. Over-all the Gini coefficient rises by 10.7 per cent while again the Atkinson index declines by 13.1 per cent. This is illustrated in more detail in Table 121 and Figure 64, which show the Lorenz curve for adjusted family income shifting in over its lower portion and out over the upper portion. Similarly, Table 122 and Figure 65 show the relative mean income curve for adjusted family income rising at both ends but falling off substantially in the middle. In general, then, family units in the middle 55 per cent have tended to lose out compared to those in the bottom 33 per cent and top 12 per cent. The mixed pattern of inequality change across ages and income groups is thus much the same for the present adjustment by individual adult equivalents as for the previous simpler adjustment by per capita family incomes.

Figure 64:
Lorenz curves for all family units of total family income and income
adjusted for place of residence, family size and composition, and sex of
head, Ontario 1973

Source: Table 121 and 125

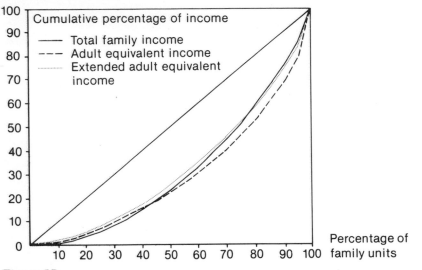

Figure 65:
Relative mean income for all family units of total family income and
income adjusted for place of residence, family size and composition, and
sex of head, Ontario 1973

Source: Table 122 and 126

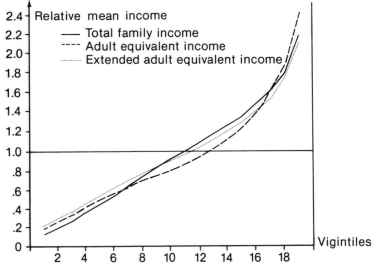

EXTENDED ADULT-EQUIVALENT INCOME ADJUSTMENT

So far, adjustments have been made for place of residence and family size. But Orshansky (1965) has shown that the income requirements for given poverty-line consumption standards of family members differ considerably among one- and two-person family units according to whether the family head is aged or not – that is, the poverty line has been estimated to be substantially lower for an older couple than for a young couple. Also the consumption needs of a family with a male head are slightly above those for one with a female head (ibid.). Therefore we have tried to combine Orshansky's results with the above poverty-line cut-off of Table 119. The resulting set of more detailed low-income cut-offs for Canada in 1973 are presented in Table 123. The figures were computed by converting the Orshansky (1965, 28) income cut-offs into indices according to family size, age of head, and sex of family head, and multiplying the figures in Table 119 by the appropriate indices.

By adjusting the family income figures on the SCF Ontario file by poverty-line indices computed from Table 123, we obtained the 'extended adult-equivalent income' summary results presented in Table 124. Comparing these to the ones originally obtained for (unadjusted) family total income in Table 96, one notes again a mixed pattern of effects similar to those found in the two preceding sections, but not so strong. Again family mean income differentials between age groups are reduced from a maximum of 174 per cent for unadjusted income to a maximum now of only 87 per cent for the adjusted series. Similarly, the aggregate inequality measures are also more homogeneous across age groups. Upper income shares for each age group again increase though not nearly as much as formerly, while lower income shares also increase but now much more than before. In contrast, then, to the results in the last two sections, the summary inequality measures now indicate a greater prevalence of inequality reduction. For all family units, for example, (see last column in Table 124) the income share of the bottom 10 per cent rises from 4.0 to 5.4 while the share of the top 10 per cent increases from 24.5 to only 25.8, so that the Gini coefficient now falls by 7 per cent while the Atkinson index falls by 23.3 per cent.

A rather marked change in the pattern of inequality has occurred between Tables 120 and 124, a change associated with the additional adjustments for sex of family head and age of head for one- and two-person family units. Every summary inequality index is lower in Table 124 than in Table 120, which shows that the two additional adjustments have had a rather marked equalizing effect within every age group. Bottom-income shares are now higher, and top-income shares substantially lower. For the whole group, the

TABLE 123
Low-income poverty lines by family size and composition, sex of head, and place of residence, Canada 1973 (dollars)

Family size	Size of area	Population			Small urban areas	Rural areas
		500 000 & over	100 000– 499 999	30 000– 99 999		
Families with male head						
One						
age ∠ 65		3256	3048	2960	2723	2367
age ⩾ 65		2935	2748	2669	2456	2134
Two						
age ∠ 65		4557	4267	4143	3811	3316
age ⩾ 65		4110	3848	3736	3437	2990
Three		5780	5413	5255	4835	4204
Four		6861	6423	6236	5738	4989
Five		7669	7180	6972	6915	5579
Six		8419	7883	7654	7041	6122
Seven		9231	8642	8391	7719	6713
Families with female head						
One						
age ∠ 65		3010	2818	2737	2517	2188
age ⩾ 65		2867	2684	2606	2398	2084
Two						
age ∠ 65		4277	4005	3888	3577	3112
age ⩾ 65		4024	3768	3658	3365	2928
Three		5602	5246	5092	4686	4074
Four		6710	6282	6099	5612	4879
Five		7531	7071	6847	6300	5478
Six		8234	7710	7485	6886	5988
Seven		9038	8460	8215	7557	6572

SOURCE: Discussion in text; Statistics Canada (1975b, 17); Orshansky (1965, 28, Table E)

income share of the bottom 10 per cent increases from 4.8 to 5.4, that of the top 10 per cent decreases from 31.7 to 25.8, and the over-all Gini coefficient falls by 16.4 per cent. These results are again quite consistent with expectations. The bottom portion of the distribution contains a relatively large proportion of aged family units and family units with a female head, and the relative position of these groups is raised up in the current adjustment procedure. On the other hand, the family units near the upper

TABLE 124

Inequality measures, by age of head, for family income adjusted for differences in area, family size and composition, and sex of head, all family units, Ontario 1973

Measure	Under 25	25–34	35–44	45–54	55–64	65 & over	All ages
Shares							
Bottom 10%	1.3	2.1	2.4	2.2	1.4	2.0	1.8
Bottom quintile	4.5	6.9	7.2	7.2	4.9	5.8	5.4
2nd quintile	12.0	13.4	13.7	14.1	12.9	9.8	12.1
3rd quintile	18.0	17.7	17.7	18.3	18.3	13.6	17.7
4th quintile	24.5	23.1	22.4	23.1	23.8	21.4	23.6
Top quintile	41.1	38.9	39.1	37.3	40.1	49.5	41.2
Top 10%	25.4	24.1	24.6	22.7	24.9	33.7	25.8
Top 5%	15.9	15.2	15.5	13.8	15.4	23.0	16.2
Gini coefficient	0.370	0.336	0.274	0.267	0.343	0.425	0.346
Atkinson index ($\epsilon = 1.55$)	0.398	0.275	0.251	0.265	0.365	0.309	0.322

SOURCE: See source to Table 114.

end of the distribution are heavily non-aged and have male heads, so that the current adjustment procedure lowers their relative position by deflating their incomes more heavily. In the case of the oldest age group, the first adjustment for place of residence resulted in increased income inequality, the second adjustment for family size yielded a mixed pattern of inequality change compared to Table 96, and now the third adjustment results in a consistent and unambiguous reduction in inequality. Clearly, the additional two factors have a substantial effect on the pattern of inequality change across age and income groups.

Over the total family population, aggregate inequality for this extended adult-equivalent income adjustment appears to have declined a fair amount relative to conventional (unadjusted) family total income for both top and bottom income shares rise while the shares of the third and fourth quintiles decline. This is illustrated in rather more detail in Tables 125 and 126. The former compares Lorenz curve ordinates (i.e., cumulative income shares) for conventional and adjusted family incomes, and one can see that the latter Lorenz curve has shifted up over most of its length except for the top income region – as illustrated in Figure 64. Indeed, the adjustments of this section and the previous one have a slightly reinforcing effect towards greater income equality over the lower portion of the distribution, while they have had conflicting effects over the upper portions of the distribu-

TABLE 125
Lorenz curve ordinates, for all family units, of family income
adjusted for differences in place of residence, family size and
composition, and sex of head, Ontario 1973

Vigintile	Family income	Adjusted family income
First	0.39	0.53(+)
Second	1.23	1.78(+)
Third	2.37	3.42(+)
Fourth	3.95	5.43(+)
Fifth	5.98	7.85(+)
Sixth	8.47	10.70(+)
Seventh	11.47	13.93(+)
Eighth	14.97	17.50(+)
Ninth	18.92	21.41(+)
Tenth	23.32	25.67(+)
Eleventh	28.14	30.25(+)
Twelfth	33.38	35.16(+)
Thirteenth	39.07	40.42(+)
Fourteenth	45.21	46.07(+)
Fifteenth	51.83	52.17(+)
Sixteenth	59.00	58.79(−)
Seventeenth	66.83	66.06(−)
Eighteenth	75.51	74.21(−)
Nineteenth	85.63	83.75(−)
Twentieth	100.00	100.00

SOURCE: See source to Table 114.

tion – the previous adjustment moved the Lorenz curve out and this adjustment moved it in again.

The same pattern is also seen in Table 126 and the associated relative mean income curves graphed in Figure 65. Compared to conventional (unadjusted) family income, the current adjusted figures have substantially higher relative-mean incomes over the lower 48 per cent or so of the distribution and somewhat reduced relative-mean incomes over the upper 52 per cent. Over the bottom third of the distribution, the adjustments of both the previous section and this one tend to raise the relative-mean incomes toward greater equality. But over the top half of the distribution the two adjustments have opposite effects. And over the top 13 per cent or so of the distribution, the current adjustment dominates the previous one and produces a greater degree of income equality at the top end of the distribution as well as at the bottom.

TABLE 126
Relative mean income, for all family units, of family income
adjusted for differences in area, family size and composition,
and sex of head, Ontario 1973

Vigintile	Family income	Adjusted family income
First	0.133	0.214(+)
Second	0.196	0.300(+)
Third	0.266	0.373(+)
Fourth	0.362	0.454(+)
Fifth	0.449	0.544(+)
Sixth	0.548	0.628(+)
Seventh	0.655	0.699(+)
Eighth	0.746	0.769(+)
Ninth	0.834	0.840(+)
Tenth	0.923	0.909(−)
Eleventh	1.005	0.976(−)
Twelfth	1.095	1.043(−)
Thirteenth	1.180	1.120(−)
Fourteenth	1.275	1.205(−)
Fifteenth	1.375	1.303(−)
Sixteenth	1.496	1.422(−)
Seventeenth	1.640	1.568(−)
Eighteenth	1.849	1.784(−)
Nineteenth	2.227	2.139(−)
Mean income ($)	11 091	6820

SOURCE: See source to Table 114.

In conclusion, then, the adjustment of family income for different location of residence, family size and composition, and sex of family head all
together results in substantially reduced inequality measures, and more particularly, works to reduce disaggregated income inequality over all portions
of the distribution for all family units except for the very middle (the 48th
to the 55th percentile) income range.

SUMMARY

This chapter has examined four adjustments to family income that may
help to reflect more accurately the distribution of economic well-being; the
adjustments were for the residential location of the family and the family
size and composition. Four sets of findings have been obtained.

First, adjustments for place of residence, i.e. urban or rural, resulted in only a slight increase in income inequality and an increase in the Gini coefficient of only 3 per cent.

Secondly, adjustment for family size differences by per capita family income reduced mean income differentials between age groups substantially and made summary inequality measures more homogeneous across age groups. The adjustment also had a very strong but mixed effect on the over-all structure of inequality in the distribution: lower-income shares rose, middle shares fell, and upper shares rose substantially so that different summary inequality measures yielded different results: the Gini coefficient rose by 7 per cent and the Atkinson index fell by 18 per cent.

Thirdly, adjustment for location and for differences in family size in terms of adult equivalents also reduced mean income differentials between age groups, yielded a roughly similar pattern of mixed changes to that obtained for (2) above, and thus caused the Gini coefficient to go up by 11 per cent and the Atkinson index to decline by 13 per cent.

Fourthly, further adjustment by adult equivalents to account also for sex of family head and whether or not the family head is aged again reduced mean-income differentials between age groups and narrowed differences in inequality statistics across age groups. The adjustment also yielded a mixed pattern of results though not as strong as in (2) or (3) above: bottom income shares rose substantially, middle shares fell, and upper shares rose, though less; both summary measures indicated a reduction in income inequality: the Gini coefficient fell by 7½ per cent, and the Atkinson index by 23 per cent.

In general the results suggest that adjustments for family size and composition have a very substantial effect on the overall structure of measured income inequality and reveal a distributional picture somewhat different from that for conventional family income. Consequently, such adjustments should be used in policy analysis of the distributional effect of various public programs, and a good deal more attention should be devoted to refining these adjustments in order to improve the evaluation of the distributional results of government policies.

11
Adjustment for capital gains

INTRODUCTION

As we have already pointed out, one objective of Part Three of this study is to measure better the distribution of economic well-being in the population. Economic well-being depends not only upon current money income and non-pecuniary receipts for a given family size and composition, but more generally upon any economic benefits that could increase one's command over available resources and thus increase the potential level of consumption attainable by family members. This theoretical concept of real personal income is very close to the classic Simons-Hicks view that 'personal income may be defined as the algebraic sum of (a) the market value of right exercised in consumption and (b) the change in the value of the store of property rights between the beginning and end of the period in question.' (Simons 1938, 50).[1] That is, real personal income may be viewed as the maximum amount of resources that could be consumed by a family in a given period (such as a year) while keeping net worth constant. This is a much broader definition than the one used in the Survey of Consumer Finances. In particular, accrued capital gains on holdings of net worth augment a family's opportunities for consumption and therefore ought also to be incorporated in our measures of adjusted family income. And since McElroy (1970) and Bhatia (1976), for example, have found fairly large differences between summary inequality measures for incomes with and without an imputation for capital gains, one would certainly wish to examine the sensitivity of our inequality results to such an adjustment.

---

1 For further discussion of this concept of real income, see also Hicks (1939, 173) and Vickrey (1947, 5–7).

Broadly speaking, there appear to be two main approaches in the literature of measuring distributional effects of a capital gains imputation. The first, which is used by McElroy (1970), Bhatia (1971, 1972, and 1976), and Stark (1972) and which may be referred to as the aggregative approach, estimates economy-wide capital gains for different types of assets and then allocates these totals to income classes in proportion to each class's holdings of that type of asset. The second method, which is used by Neil (1962) and Blauer (1971), may be referred to as the disaggregative approach; it consists of determining the asset portfolio for each age- or income-class, and the rate of inflation for each asset in the portfolios, and then working out the corresponding weighted average inflation rate of the value for each portfolio. Since for the present study we have fairly detailed portfolio breakdowns by age, income class, and family size, we shall follow the disaggregative approach.

Indeed our approach will be more disaggregative than any of the above studies save Blauer's. Both are based on an analysis of micro data, and both consider fairly detailed effects by age and income class, although the present analysis is more explicitly based on a life cycle theoretical framework. This study, of course, is restricted to Ontario families and uses asset data for 1970, whereas Blauer's work used Canada-wide asset data for 1964. Her study was also a much broader analysis of gains and losses on income and asset accounts during inflationary periods, whereas the present work concentrates on the distributional effects associated with imputing for capital gains on asset account.[2]

It should also be pointed out that the present analysis examines *accrued* capital gains whether realized or not. Studies such as Liebenberg and Fitzwilliams (1961) and David and Miller (1975) for the United States examined only realized capital gains; but, as pointed out by Bhatia (1970), this misses the greater part of total accrued gains. Secondly, it should be noted that the capital gains analysed here accrue only over a one-year period, 1973, so that the distributional effects pertain only to that year and should not be construed as representative of the pattern of capital gains benefits for any other years or for longer periods.[3] Thirdly, the following analysis is restricted to capital gains on non-human capital holdings; no attempt is made to generalize the current work to incorporate capital gains on human capital as well.

2 Other recent work on the distributional effects of inflation on real asset values as well as debt and income accounts for Canada as a whole may be found in Boyer (1976), Economic Council of Canada (1976), Manga (1978), and Love (1976).

3 This caveat also applies to the findings, for example, of Bhatia (1976) and David and Miller (1975).

Finally, the present analysis is concerned directly with nominal capital gains and how they compare in magnitude to nominal income in a given year. To translate capital gains into real terms, one can readily deflate imputed gains by the CPI inflation rate.

The general approach for imputing accrued capital gains is fairly straight-forward and is outlined in the next section; the more technical details are presented in Appendices F and G.

ADJUSTMENT PROCEDURE

The principal data source for the analysis is again the Survey of Consumer Finances 1974 micro data file of Ontario family units. However, this source contains no information on realized capital gains, assets, or net worth val-ues, all of which we obtained from the 1970 Survey of Incomes, Assets, and Indebtedness. Thus some matching up of information must be effected between these two primary data sources. In order to do so we imputed a value for total asset holdings ASSETS and a weighted average rate of capital gains RCG estimated from the latter data source for each individual family on the SCF tape on the basis of age, asset, income, and employment classifications, and then computed a variable FTIACG for family total income adjusted for capital gains as

$$\text{FTIACG} = \text{FTI} + (\text{ASSETS} \times \text{RCG}),$$

where FTI is the conventional (unadjusted) figure for family total income. We then compare the differences in inequality between the two variables FTI and FTIACG.

Thus there are two separate steps in adjustment procedure: the construc-tion of the variables ASSETS and RCG. The first is done by estimating the size of asset holdings for each family on the Ontario SCF file, and the sec-ond by estimating the portfolio composition. Although these estimates are obtained by separate procedures, it should be noted that we are not assum-ing separability of asset size and composition since the underlying theoreti-cal life-cycle effect is a principal determinant of both (directly by the age factor as well as indirectly by income class). As was pointed out in Chapter 8, both total asset holdings and composition vary markedly and systemati-cally over the life cycle, and the present capital gains adjustment procedures attempt to incorporate this fact.

The construction of an estimated value of asset holdings for each family on the SCF file consisted first of estimating an equation for total asset holdings from the Survey of Incomes, Assets, and Indebtedness. However, data from this source were not available to the authors in micro form, but rather in the form of fairly detailed cross-tabulations specially provided by Statistics Canada and described at some length in Chapter 8. The first limitation of this form of data is that detailed breakdowns of assets and net worth were available only for families of two or more and not for unattached individuals. Consequently, all further work in this chapter and the following one (which employs the net worth data from the same source) is restricted to families of two or more, or simply 'families.'

A second consequence of having asset data available in summary cross-tabular form lies in the estimation procedure itself used to impute the ASSETS figures. Technical details of the adjusted weighted regression procedure followed are provided in Appendix F. Suffice it to say that the procedure includes first, a weighted regression estimated across the individual cells of a cross-tabulation by asset holdings, age of head, and employment status of head; and secondly, use of this regression equation to impute an asset figure for each family on the SCF file.

A third limitation of using asset data from a different source is that the family unit definitions in the SCF file and Incomes, Assets, and Indebtedness Survey are not the same. The former is based on the census definition of a family unit, while the latter is based on the economic definition of a family unit, which is a somewhat broader concept. The details of definition were discussed in Chapters 7 and 8, but the most important differences pertain to family units of one person, or unattached individuals. However, since the present analysis will be restricted to family units of two or more (i.e., families) because of data limitations, the differences in definitions should not be a serious problem here.

The estimation of the average rate of capital gains on a family's portfolio, RCG proceeds along different lines. Table 86 provides a summary (aggregated across detailed asset types) of proportional asset composition according to age of head and income class for families of two or more in Canada. The important results for our purposes are reproduced in Tables 127 and 128. As can be seen from the first table, the relative importance of home and real estate ownership increases strongly with age until 35–44 and then declines as families become older and hold more of their assets in other forms, particularly liquid assets, which increase markedly in importance among older and retired groups. Table 128 shows the relatively heavy investment in non-liquid financial assets (such as stocks and mortgages) and commercial real estate holdings of the top income group. Such differences in portfolio composition would certainly be expected to result in

TABLE 127
Composition of asset holdings among Canadian families by age of head, 1970 (percentages)

Assets	Under 25	25–34	35–44	45–54	55–64	65 & over
Liquid assets	16.5	11.1	10.2	14.8	19.9	27.0
Nonliq fin assets	4.0	6.4	6.1	9.1	14.4	11.3
Total financial assets	20.5	17.5	16.3	23.9	34.3	38.3
Mkt value of home & vac home	52.7	69.2	70.5	63.0	52.7	50.6
Invmt in other real estate	5.0	4.9	8.4	8.2	8.9	8.3
Mkt value of car	21.8	8.4	4.7	4.9	4.1	2.8
Total non-financial assets	79.5	82.5	83.7	76.1	65.7	61.7

SOURCE: See source to Table 85.

TABLE 128
Composition of asset holdings among Canadian families by income class, 1970 (percentages)

Assets	Under $4000	$4000– 6999	$7000– 9999	$10000– 14999	$15000– 24999	$25000 & over
Liquid assets	19.9	20.4	14.0	13.5	17.5	18.5
Nonliq fin assets	5.7	6.5	5.3	7.9	12.1	26.3
Total financial assets	25.7	27.0	19.3	21.4	29.6	44.8
Mkt value of home & vac home	65.4	61.2	69.1	65.9	54.7	35.8
Invmt in other real estate	5.1	6.5	5.8	6.9	11.0	16.7
Mkt value of car	3.8	5.3	5.9	5.8	4.8	2.7
Total non-financial assets	74.4	73.0	80.7	78.6	70.5	55.2

SOURCE: See source to Table 86.

rather different capital gains accruals. The original data source from which these tables were constructed provided very detailed asset composition for each of the above age and income classes. Accordingly, each family on the SCF micro file within a particular age and income class is assumed to have the portfolio composition of that class. Again, technical details are provided in Appendix G.

The final set of inputs in the capital gain calculations is data on the rates of inflation in the market values of individual asset components. These data for the year 1973 are provided in Table 129. Evidently 1973 was a distinctive year from the point of view of changes in asset values. Bond prices fell

TABLE 129
Rates of inflation in the values of asset components

Assets	Change in value in 1973	Hypothetical change in value
Financial assets		
Liquid fin assets		
Cash on hand	0	0
Savings deposits	0	0
Other deposits	0	0
Can sav bonds	0	0
Other bonds	−3.18	0
Nonliq fin assets		
Stocks	−10.11	5.00
Mortgage invmt	−1.20	0
Misc invmt	−10.11	5.00
Non-financial assets		
Mkt value of home	21.50	5.00
Mkt value of vac home	21.50	5.00
Invmt in other real estate	21.50	5.00
Mkt value of car	−21.00	−20.00

SOURCE: The rate of capital gains on 'other bonds' was computed as a weighted average of outstanding Canadian federal government (non-savings) bonds across different maturities as given in the *Bank of Canada Review* (March 1974) various tables. The rate of inflation of stocks and miscellaneous investment was estimated by the percentage change in the Toronto Stock Exchange composite stock index for 1973 as reported in the *Canadian Statistical Review* (September 1974, 111). The estimate for price increases in real estate was provided by the Canadian Real Estate Association. The rate of depreciation in market (resale) value of cars was based on personal estimates of average depreciation rates by three used-car salesmen known to the authors.

somewhat in response to rising interest rates, and the stock market (as measured by the Toronto Stock Exchange composite stock index) fell very markedly in response to stagflationary conditions and investor uncertainty. By far the most successful investment was home ownership for house prices in Ontario rose an estimated 21.5 per cent in 1973 alone. Since such a pattern of capital gains appears to be so different from what one might expect in other periods, we have also considered a much more homogeneous pattern of asset inflation rates listed in the column 'hypothetical changes in value.' While it is not clear what constitutes a 'normal' year for

TABLE 130
Estimated rates of capital gains on total asset holdings
by age (percentages)

Age	1973	Hypothetical
Under 25	9.62	−0.30
25–34	14.58	2.55
35–44	16.45	3.45
45–54	13.71	2.86
55–64	11.76	2.87
65 and over	10.00	2.55
All ages	13.56	2.89

SOURCE: Based on calculations discussed in the text.

TABLE 131
Estimated rates of capital gains on total asset holdings
by income (percentages)

Income ($)	1973	Hypothetical
Less than 1000	13.93	2.72
1000–1999	15.35	3.35
2000–2999	14.86	3.17
3000–3999	13.98	2.97
4000–4999	13.33	2.68
5000–5999	13.36	2.48
6000–6999	13.86	2.74
7000–9999	15.07	2.83
10000–14999	14.34	2.89
15000–24999	12.47	2.96
25000 and over	9.09	3.10
All incomes	13.56	2.89

SOURCE: Based on calculations discussed in the text.

asset price changes, in this hypothetical case, equity, bonds, and real estate
are all assumed to inflate in value at a nominal rate of 5 per cent, and cars
to depreciate at an average of about 20 per cent a year. Subsequent analysis
in this chapter will concentrate on these two sets of asset-specific rates of
accrued capital gains.

Using the asset-specific rates of capital gains in Table 129 and the portfolio composition proportions estimated earlier, one can compute weighted average rates of capital gains, RCG, for each family on the SCF Ontario micro file. Aggregating these rates across families within particular age and income groups, one obtains the mean rates of capital gains on total asset portfolios for each age group (see Table 130) and for summary income classes (see Table 131).

One can clearly see in Table 130 the effect of home-ownership patterns on the mean rates of capital gains, which vary across ages in close association with the relative importance of home ownership. Consequently, the highest rates of return occur during peak periods of family formation. The rates of capital gains for young families are pulled down by their heavier relative investment in cars and consumer durables, and, for old families, by their heavier relative investment in stocks, bonds, and fixed-nominal-value assets. The mean rates of capital gains across income groups in Table 131 shows a more uneven pattern for 1973, although the rates fall off substantially at the top income levels, where financial asset holdings (which did not do well in 1973) were most substantial. One also notes the very different pattern of capital gains between the 1973 and hypothetical figures. The latter gains are much lower than the former, but still have much the same pattern (although less extreme) across ages. Again the youngest group loses out because of its relatively heavy investment in assets that depreciate rapidly, and the oldest age group invests (relatively) more heavily in fixed-nominal-value assets (although they now gain from their stocks and non-savings bonds as well). Across income classes, however, the hypothetical returns are again much lower but now show a markedly different pattern in which top incomes receive a relatively high rate of capital gains from their financial asset holdings. It should be noted, of course, that results for particular families may differ substantially one from another, but the present summary results are meant only as an average for various groups.

The results of multiplying the imputed total ASSETS figure for each family by its specific portfolio rate of capital gains (RCG) to obtain a family income figure adjusted for imputed accrued capital gains (FTIACG) are examined in the following section.

EMPIRICAL RESULTS

Let us consider first the empirical results for the 1973 capital gains figures, and then turn to the results for the hypothetical data. The former are pre-

TABLE 132

Inequality measures by age of head for total family income of families of two or more, Ontario 1973

Measure	Under 25	25–34	35–44	45–54	55–64	65 & over	All ages
Shares							
Bottom 10%	2.3	2.4	2.7	2.8	2.0	2.4	2.1
Bottom quintile	7.4	7.7	8.0	8.2	6.5	6.4	6.4
2nd quintile	15.6	15.2	14.8	14.4	13.7	10.7	13.7
3rd quintile	19.8	19.4	18.8	18.7	18.2	15.0	18.7
4th quintile	24.4	23.8	23.3	23.5	23.3	22.9	23.9
Top quintile	32.8	34.0	35.2	35.2	38.3	45.1	37.3
Top 10%	18.2	19.6	21.0	20.5	23.0	28.6	22.4
Top 5%	10.1	11.3	12.3	12.0	13.7	17.5	13.3
Gini coefficient	0.251	0.260	0.268	0.268	0.312	0.382	0.306
Coef of variation	0.42	0.45	0.48	0.47	0.57	0.75	0.52
Atkinson index ($\epsilon = 1.55$)	0.234	0.229	0.207	0.211	0.284	0.309	0.275
Mean income ($)	10084	12955	14679	15922	13735	7962	13198
Median income ($)	9955	12567	13807	14849	12582	5889	12338

SOURCE: See source to Table 109.

TABLE 133

Inequality measures by age for family income adjusted for accrued capital gains among families of two or more, Ontario 1973

Measure	Under 25	25–34	35–44	45–54	55–64	65 & over	All ages
Shares							
Bottom 10%	2.1	2.7	3.0	3.4	2.9	4.2	2.7
Bottom quintile	7.1	8.3	8.2	8.9	7.2	9.9	7.0
2nd quintile	14.5	15.0	13.0	13.7	12.4	13.0	12.2
3rd quintile	18.8	18.4	16.5	17.3	15.6	15.6	16.2
4th quintile	23.8	22.4	20.7	20.8	18.6	22.0	21.1
Top quintile	35.8	36.0	41.6	39.2	46.2	39.6	43.5
Top 10%	20.9	21.8	28.7	26.5	33.7	24.4	30.0
Top 5%	11.7	13.7	21.1	19.2	26.7	14.0	22.0
Gini coefficient	0.284	0.280	0.328	0.297	0.374	0.292	0.358
Coef of variation	0.54	0.76	1.15	1.05	1.37	0.61	1.31
Atkinson index ($\epsilon = 1.55$)	0.242	0.167	0.184	0.146	0.228	0.131	0.199
Mean income ($)	10330	13501	19378	21693	20508	10319	16796
Median income ($)	10338	13720	17336	20300	17652	8401	15186
Mean increase ($)	246	546	4699	5771	6773	2357	3598

SOURCE: Based on data for Ontario from the 1973 Consumer Finance Micro Data Release Tape supplied by Statistics Canada, and on calculations discussed in the text.

TABLE 134
Lorenz curve ordinates for families of two or more for
family income adjusted for accrued capital gains, Ontario 1973

Vigintile	Total income	Adjusted total income
First	0.67	0.95(+)
Second	2.08	2.65(+)
Third	3.98	4.66(+)
Fourth	6.39	6.97(+)
Fifth	9.27	9.60(+)
Sixth	12.54	12.54( )
Seventh	16.16	15.75(−)
Eighth	20.09	19.22(−)
Ninth	24.31	22.91(−)
Tenth	28.84	26.83(−)
Eleventh	33.65	30.98(−)
Twelfth	38.77	35.42(−)
Thirteenth	44.19	40.21(−)
Fourteenth	49.95	45.33(−)
Fifteenth	56.10	50.74(−)
Sixteenth	62.69	56.54(−)
Seventeenth	69.79	62.93(−)
Eighteenth	77.63	69.96(−)
Nineteenth	86.66	77.97(−)
Twentieth	100.00	100.00

SOURCE: See source to Table 133.

sented in Table 133, and one can see immediately that the adjustment is quite large for the middle- and older-age groups as compared to the results for unadjusted total family income reproduced for convenience in Table 132. Over all ages income figures are increased by 27 per cent from $13 198 to $16 796, but this increase varies across ages from only 2.4 per cent for the youngest age group to 49 per cent for the group aged 55–64, then down again to 30 per cent for the oldest group. Since the largest average increases occur for those age groups that already have relatively high incomes, differentials between age groups are increased slightly as mean income for the peak group 45–54 rises from 2.0 to 2.1 times that of the oldest age group. On the other hand, mean income for the group 65 and over is increased relative to mean incomes for the youngest two age groups, where asset holdings and home ownership are not as extensive.

The summary inequality figures in Table 133 show a strong but conflicting effect of the capital gains adjustment. The Gini coefficient over all ages increases by 17 per cent, while the Atkinson index (with $\epsilon = 1.55$) declines by 27 per cent. These strong but conflicting results occur since both bottom and top income shares go up as a result of the adjustment, while the middle income shares decline. The same pattern occurs for the family groups aged 25–64: the Gini coefficients register substantial increases, and the Atkinson indices indicate marked decreases in summary inequality. Again bottom income shares are raised slightly and upper income shares react in strongly disequalizing fashion as the higher income groups benefit heavily from their large housing investment. Among the youngest age group, however, the lower-income families tend to lose out because of their relatively heavy investment in cars and consumer durables, while upper-income groups again benefit from their housing investment. For the oldest age group, though, a quite different pattern results. Lower income shares are now raised very substantially, while higher income shares decline, with the resulting Gini coefficient reduced by 24 per cent and the Atkinson index by 57 per cent. For the oldest age group then, unlike all the other ages, inequality appears to have been dramatically and unambiguously reduced by inclusion of capital gains at least for the period 1973.

Table 134 offers a more detailed picture of the distribution for all age groups together. Again, the first column of figures shows the cumulative income shares (across all vigintiles in the distribution) for unadjusted total family income (corresponding to the last column of Table 132) and the second column shows the corresponding cumulative shares of incomes adjusted for capital gains. The figures are also graphed as Lorenz curves in Figure 66. As can be seen, the two Lorenz curves cross with the result that over the bottom 30 per cent of the distribution cumulative inequality has been reduced, while over the remaining 70 per cent of the distribution, the Lorenz curve has shifted out substantially. This pattern is further highlighted by the relative mean income results in Table 135 and Figure 67. The bottom 20 per cent of incomes have increased compared to the mean as well as the very top 5 (or less) per cent, whereas the middle 75 per cent or so have tended to lose out relatively. In general, then, the effect of imputing for accrued capital gains in 1973 over all ages has been to benefit most the bottom and very top income groups, and has resulted in dramatically differing summary inequality results. Those at the bottom end are likely to be low-income, older, and retired families that have a low current income but own their own homes; those at the very top are essentially the upper-

Figure 66:
Lorenz curves for families of two or more for family income
adjusted for accrued capital gains, Ontario 1973
Source: Table 134

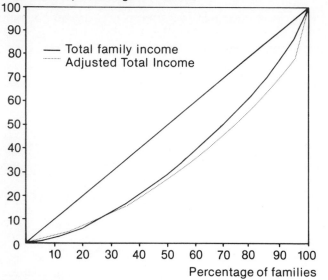

Figure 67:
Relative mean income of families of two or more for family income
adjusted for accrued capital gains, Ontario 1973

Source: Table 135

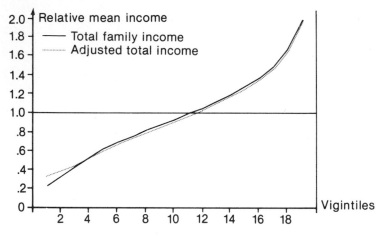

TABLE 135
Relative mean income for families of two or more for family income
adjusted for accrued capital gains, Ontario 1973

Vigintile	Total income	Adjusted total income
First	0.226	0.334(+)
Second	0.330	0.394(+)
Third	0.431	0.455(+)
Fourth	0.534	0.535(+)
Fifth	0.616	0.613(−)
Sixth	0.689	0.682(−)
Seventh	0.756	0.747(−)
Eighth	0.815	0.802(−)
Ninth	0.875	0.854(−)
Tenth	0.935	0.904(−)
Eleventh	0.992	0.958(−)
Twelfth	1.054	1.032(−)
Thirteenth	1.117	1.108(−)
Fourteenth	1.189	1.184(−)
Fifteenth	1.273	1.259(−)
Sixteenth	1.362	1.355(−)
Seventeenth	1.483	1.478(−)
Eighteenth	1.663	1.660(−)
Nineteenth	1.971	1.970(−)
Mean income ($)	13 198	16 796

SOURCE: See source to Table 133.

income recipients (who again own their own homes) at their peak income
years of middle age.

The inequality changes for the more moderate hypothetical rates of capital gains are again mixed but are not nearly so strong as for the 1973
results. From the bottom line of Table 136 one can see that the increase in
total family income from the capital gains imputation in this case is much
smaller, ranging from −1.4 per cent for the youngest age group to 21 per
cent for the group aged 55–64 and down to 8.3 per cent for the oldest group;
the average increase is $651 or 4.9 per cent. In the present case, however,
between-age-group mean income differentials are narrowed slightly by the
adjustment procedure: the ratio of mean income for the peak age group

TABLE 136
Inequality measures by age of head for family income adjusted for accrued capital gains
among families of two or more with hypothetical data

Measure	Under 25	25–34	35–44	45–54	55–64	65 & over	All ages
Shares							
Bottom 10%	2.3	2.4	2.9	3.0	2.0	3.1	2.4
Bottom quintile	7.4	7.9	8.2	8.6	6.4	7.6	6.8
2nd quintile	15.6	15.4	14.6	14.5	13.4	11.2	13.7
3rd quintile	20.0	19.6	18.7	18.7	17.7	15.0	18.5
4th quintile	24.6	23.9	23.3	23.4	22.6	22.3	23.8
Top quintile	32.4	33.3	35.2	34.8	39.9	43.8	37.2
Top 10%	17.7	18.6	20.9	20.2	24.8	27.8	22.3
Top 5%	9.5	10.3	12.3	11.6	15.6	16.6	13.2
Gini coefficient	0.249	0.251	0.267	0.261	0.328	0.357	0.302
Coef of variation	0.42	0.44	0.48	0.46	0.71	0.72	0.51
Atkinson index ($\epsilon = 1.55$)	0.232	0.211	0.190	0.183	0.291	0.251	0.253
Mean income ($)	9935	12897	15383	16857	15489	8626	13849
Median income ($)	9967	12750	14578	15866	13161	6435	12762
Mean increase ($)	−149	−58	704	935	1754	664	651

SOURCE: See source to Table 132.

45–54 to that for the lowest income group (i.e., 65 and over) declines slightly from 2.0 to 1.95.

Summary inequality measures for the whole group now indicate a weak though apparently unambiguous reduction in aggregate inequality as the Gini coefficient for all ages decreases by 1.3 per cent and the Atkinson index falls by 8.0 per cent. Across all the age groups except 55–64, inequality figures are also slightly reduced with lower income groups gaining and upper income groups losing out slightly. Again, the strongest reduction occurs for those aged 65 and over, where the Gini coefficient falls by 6.5 per cent. Clearly, the fairly broad holding of non-financial assets across family groups appears to have a fairly general though weak equalization effect on adjusted income figures. For the group aged 55–64, however, the reverse occurs with a slight increase in summary inequality figures.

Table 137 shows the general inequality reduction in more detail for all age groups, and one sees from the cumulative income shares that the Lorenz curve for capital-gains-adjusted income lies everywhere above that

TABLE 137

Lorenz curve ordinates for families of two or more for family
income adjusted for accrued capital gains with hypothetical data

Vigintile	Total income	Adjusted total income
First	0.67	0.81(+)
Second	2.08	2.35(+)
Third	3.98	4.33(+)
Fourth	6.39	6.78(+)
Fifth	9.27	9.67(+)
Sixth	12.54	12.94(+)
Seventh	16.16	16.56(+)
Eighth	20.09	20.45(+)
Ninth	24.31	24.63(+)
Tenth	28.84	29.11(+)
Eleventh	33.65	33.87(+)
Twelfth	38.77	38.94(+)
Thirteenth	44.19	44.32(+)
Fourteenth	49.95	50.02(+)
Fifteenth	56.10	56.13(+)
Sixteenth	62.69	62.75(+)
Seventeenth	69.79	69.89(+)
Eighteenth	77.63	77.70(+)
Nineteenth	86.66	86.78(+)
Twentieth	100.00	100.00

SOURCE: See source to Table 132.

for unadjusted family income, so that over-all inequality is indeed lowered
by the addition of the hypothetical capital gains imputations, although the
reduction is rather small. The corresponding relative mean income curve is
not presented because the indicated changes are so small as probably not to
be significant.

In conclusion, then, it can be seen that the two sets of imputed capital
gains adjustments yield rather different results. While the adjustment for
1973 asset price changes yielded very strong but conflicting inequality
changes, the adjustment for a more 'normal' hypothetical set of price
changes resulted in a weak but general reduction in summary inequality
figures. In both cases, however, lower income shares are increased by the
accrued capital gains adjustment.

SUMMARY

This chapter has considered an adjustment to family income figures to make them reflect more accurately the benefits of accrued capital gains incurred on family asset holdings. Two adjustments were made, one for the observed set of asset price changes during 1973, and the other for a more 'normal' set of hypothetical asset price changes. Three sets of findings have been obtained.

First, when adjustment was made for accrued capital gains incurred in 1973, mean incomes increased substantially (by 27 per cent on average) and summary inequality figures showed very strong but conflicting effects: the Gini coefficient for all age groups rose by 17 per cent and the Atkinson index fell by 27 per cent. This was the result of a rather marked increase in the shares of both bottom and top income groups and a decline in middle-income shares. The different summary measures emphasize what happened over different portions of the distribution. Within the oldest age group, however, summary inequality was reduced very substantially.

Secondly, when adjustment was made for the hypothetical set of asset price changes, mean incomes increased on average only by 5 per cent and summary inequality figures showed a weak though unambiguous reduction in inequality as the Gini coefficient, for example, fell by an average of 1.3 per cent. Lower-income groups generally gained, while upper-income shares generally declined slightly. Again, the oldest age group, 65 and over, had the strongest reduction in inequality.

Thirdly, it appears that the inequality effects of adjustments to family income for accrued capital gains can be very important in comparison to the various other adjustments considered so far in this study. However, the size of the effects and even their direction may vary greatly from one year or period to another according to the different patterns of asset price changes that may occur (particularly with respect to house prices); for that reason they constitute complex and conflicting patterns of change that can be satisfactorily captured only by a disaggregative analysis.

12
Adjustment for family wealth holdings

INTRODUCTION[1]

In the last chapter, the argument was made that economic well-being could be related to the potential consumption attainable by a family over a given period of time such as a year. Clearly, potential consumption and economic well-being of a family can be increased not only by higher income, but also by greater amounts of net worth. Consequently, some account of total net worth holdings should be included in our empirical measure of economic well-being, and it is this matter that the current chapter addresses. Indeed, according to the life cycle theories of Part One, consumption was essentially related to wealth broadly defined, so that wealth may be viewed in some circumstances as a better proxy for the long-run consumption status of a family than its current flow of income. This is particularly so for aged family units, where current income receipts may be very low, but where the family is living on its accumulated net worth and owns its own home, so that its current economic status may be much higher than would be suggested by current income alone or even adjusted for owner-occupied housing. The present chapter will attempt to integrate both income and wealth status in a common measure of family economic well-being, and then compare the distribution and inequality patterns of this new measure to those for (unadjusted) family total income. In so doing, it will also attempt to tie the present empirical analysis more closely to the basic life-cycle theory of Part One and to make explicit the importance of the time period over which potential consumption can be measured.

1 Portions of the discussion in this chapter follow the work of Beasley (1976).

Estimates of family economic well-being that reflect net worth holdings as well as income also have important policy uses in a range of different areas. In the case of means-tested public assistance or welfare programs, what is the best way to define family means? To what extent could or should a negative income tax or guaranteed annual income scheme take into account wealth holdings as well as income flows? What is the effect on the extent and structure of poverty in the population of incorporating net worth status in measures of economic well-being? How progressive is the personal tax structure looked at in terms of ability to pay as measured by net worth as well as income flow? A first step towards answering these questions is the construction of empirical proxies for economic well-being that reflect both wealth status and current income. One may recall the fairly substantial effects of adding imputed rent from owner-occupied housing (Chapter 9) and imputed capital gains (Chapter 11) to the incomes of older families, and one would perhaps expect a similar effect when adjustment is made for holdings of net worth.

How to combine a stock of wealth with an annual flow of income, however, is not initially obvious. One extreme approach would perhaps be simply to add together income and wealth holdings as an estimate of the total resources that a family ultimately has access to at any given time. Another extreme would be to include with other sources of income simply the realized returns to family wealth holdings – which has already been done in our measure of family total income – as an estimate of the benefits that actually accrue within a given year from ownership of wealth. Both of these approaches seem rather unreasonable, but they do serve to emphasize the rather important question of what the best accounting period is for measuring economic well-being. Is it a year, a decade, a lifetime? This question is addressed in more detail in the following chapter, but first we shall consider whether the benefits from net worth holdings are to be attributed all at once or spread out over time. In the first of the limiting cases above, they were to be received all in one year, while in the second, they are spread over an infinite horizon. The approach taken here is the more intermediate one of spreading them over the remaining expected lifetime of the family head.

More specifically, we first follow the approach suggested by Weisbrod and Hansen (1968) of amortizing net worth over the expected lifetime of the family head, so that by the time he can expect to die, the family's wealth would be exhausted. Details of the procedure are presented in the following section along with empirical results. The original Weisbrod-Hansen work was based on aggregate distributions without the availability of family micro data. A subsequent study by Taussig (1973), however, did apply the procedure to family micro data for the United States and found that it resulted in rather smaller and mixed effects depending on the summary measure of inequality used. Moon (1977) looked at similar questions as part of a more extensive analysis of economic status of the aged. Wolfson (1977b) used Canadian micro data to repeat the Weisbrod-Hansen analysis and found fairly similar results to Taussig for Canada. The present chapter pursues this matter in more detail by the use of much more disaggregated inequality measures and different adjustment procedures.

It is always desirable, however, when there is more than one way to make reasonable adjustments, to consider several approaches. For that reason this chapter also discusses an adjustment procedure for handling net worth that is based more closely on the theoretical discussion of Part One and compares the empirical results to those from the more standard Weisbrod-Hansen approach. As it turns out, both yield similar results and for that reason, though they are still tentative, they can be held with greater confidence. A brief summary of the empirical findings is provided in the conclusion of the chapter.

WEISBROD-HANSEN ADJUSTMENT FOR NET WORTH

The Weisbrod-Hansen approach
As already mentioned, the Weisbrod-Hansen procedure for adjusting family income for net worth holdings entails amortizing net worth so that the current stock of wealth is just exhausted by the time of the expected death of the family head, and then adding this constant-value annuity to current annual income. More specifically, the Weisbrod-Hansen measure of income is given by

$$\text{YWH} = \text{FTI} - \text{YCAP} + \text{NW} \cdot A_n,$$

where FTI $-$ YCAP is family total income net of capital or investment income,[2] and the last term is the annual lifetime annuity value of the household's current net worth NW, where A_n is the value of an n-year annuity that has a present value of one dollar. That is,

$$A_n = r/[1-(1+r)^{-n}],$$

___
2 Investment income is subtracted out before including annuity income to avoid double counting.

where r is the market rate of interest and n is the number of years of life expectancy of the family head. Taking the present value at a discount rate of r of the n-year annuity $NW \cdot A_n$ will simply yield the original stock of net worth NW. The annuity value of Weisbrod-Hansen is thus a function of total current net worth, life expectancy n and the market rate of interest r.

Implementation of this procedure with the 1974 Survey of Consumer Finance micro data file for Ontario consists of: first, imputing a net worth figure for each family on the SCF file (somewhat analogous to what was done for asset holdings in the last chapter); second, imputing a life expectancy value for each family head on the tape; and third, computing the formula for YWH for each family. Since detailed cross-tabulations of net worth data were available to the authors only for families of two or more, the present analysis is again restricted to this group.[3]

The net worth data used in the analysis come from the 1970 Survey of Incomes, Assets, and Indebtedness of Statistics Canada and are discussed in some detail in Chapter 8 above.[4] A full description of the imputation procedure for net worth is provided in Appendix H; it has three steps: estimation of a net worth equation as a function of age and family income from the 1970 net worth cross-tabulations; use of this equation to provide an estimate of net worth holdings for each family on the 1973 SCF tape; and inflation of the resulting adjusted estimates up to 1973 values.

Life expectancy figures are imputed for each family on the 1973 SCF Ontario file based on age-specific mortality rates from the Statistics Canada *Vital Statistics* (1975e). Also, since women have a longer life expectancy than men, an average was taken of the two expectancies.

For the market rate of interest, r – appearing in the formulas for the wealth annuity – two different values were used, 8 and 12 per cent, both reflecting the recent high rates of inflation and correspondingly high rates of interest in Canada. In the empirical results of this chapter, 'Index 1' values refer to calculations based on the 8 per cent interest rate figure, and 'Index 2' refers to results based on the 12 per cent figure.

Empirical results of the Weisbrod-Hansen approach
Inequality results for the Weisbrod-Hansen annuity adjustment procedure are presented in Tables 138 and 139. As can be seen from both tables,

---

3 This is in contrast to Wolfson (1977b), who looks at all family units aggregated together; for that reason his results are not really comparable to ours.
4 See also the discussion in Chapter 11 of the difference in family unit concepts between the Survey of Consumer Finances and the Survey of Incomes, Assets, and Indebtedness.

TABLE 138

Inequality measures by age of head for Weisbrod-Hansen Index 1 for families of two or more, Ontario 1973

Measure	Under 25	25–34	35–44	45–54	55–64	65 & over	All ages
Shares							
Bottom 10%	1.9	2.2	2.4	2.7	2.1	1.7	2.2
Bottom quintile	6.5	7.3	7.1	7.6	6.1	5.7	6.5
2nd quintile	14.9	14.6	13.0	12.9	12.0	11.3	13.1
3rd quintile	19.7	19.3	17.0	16.7	15.8	16.0	18.2
4th quintile	24.7	24.2	21.4	20.7	19.6	23.4	23.8
Top quintile	34.3	34.5	41.2	42.1	46.5	43.6	38.5
Top 10%	19.2	19.0	27.2	29.2	33.0	27.2	23.4
Top 5%	10.4	10.3	19.6	21.4	24.9	15.5	14.3
Gini coefficient	0.271	0.270	0.322	0.337	0.390	0.374	0.318
Coef of variation	0.52	0.51	1.06	1.23	1.33	0.76	0.54
Atkinson index ($\epsilon = 1.55$)	0.250	0.222	0.231	0.215	0.293	0.326	0.281

SOURCE: Based on data for Ontario from the 1973 Consumer Finance Micro Data Release Tape supplied by Statistics Canada, and on calculations discussed in the text.

TABLE 139

Inequality measures by age of head for Weisbrod-Hansen Index 2 for families of two or more, Ontario 1973

Measure	Under 25	25–34	35–44	45–54	55–64	65 & over	All ages
Shares							
Bottom 10%	1.7	2.1	2.4	2.9	2.3	1.7	1.9
Bottom quintile	6.2	7.1	7.1	8.0	6.4	5.6	5.8
2nd quintile	14.6	14.3	13.4	13.2	12.3	11.3	11.7
3rd quintile	19.7	19.1	17.4	17.2	16.1	16.2	16.3
4th quintile	24.9	24.3	21.9	21.2	19.9	23.6	21.6
Top quintile	34.6	35.2	40.4	40.4	45.3	43.4	44.6
Top 10%	19.3	19.5	26.8	27.3	31.5	27.0	30.9
Top 5%	10.5	10.6	18.6	19.4	23.2	15.5	22.5
Gini coefficient	0.283	0.279	0.327	0.318	0.375	0.374	0.366
Coef of variation	0.52	0.51	1.01	1.03	1.12	0.74	1.09
Atkinson index ($\epsilon = 1.55$)	0.305	0.231	0.248	0.196	0.275	0.327	0.287

SOURCE: See source to Table 138.

summary inequality measures have generally increased as compared to the corresponding figures for unadjusted family total income presented earlier in Table 132. The Gini coefficients for all age groups together, for example, increase by 3.9 per cent at the lower interest rate and 19.6 per cent at the higher one, and other summary measures increased in the same way. This general increase in summary inequality is similar to the earlier findings of Weisbrod and Hansen (1968), Taussig (1973), and Wolfson (1977b). The increases, however, are not as great as those found by Weisbrod and Hansen for aggregate data, though greater than found by the other two studies, which were based on direct access to data on individuals' wealth, although admittedly the interest rates used in the current study are higher than in the others. Also, unlike Taussig (1973, 34), we find a rather substantial difference in the magnitude of the effects for different interest rates.

Summary inequality also tends to increase across age groups though unevenly. For the youngest two age groups, where net worth holdings are usually not very large, inequality increases only mildly, as the higher-income families generally also have larger holdings of net worth. For the middle-aged groups, 35–64, where wealth holdings are greater and the annuity period shorter, inequality figures tend to go up much more substantially (with Gini coefficients rising 18–25 per cent), as again the top income shares (those with the largest net worth) markedly increase while the middle quintile shares fall and the very bottom shares show some mixed results.

For the oldest group, however, summary inequality is reduced slightly (with the Gini coefficient declining by 2.1 per cent) as bottom and top income shares (for those living mainly on government transfers and those not yet retired respectively) lose out moderately, and the middle three quintiles gain. While this reduction in summary inequality for the group 65 and over is fairly small and not unambiguous (since the corresponding Lorenz curves cross), it is in contrast to the earlier findings of Weisbrod-Hansen and Taussig, where Gini coefficients increased for this age group as well.

For the group as a whole, one notes that the middle three quintiles lose out compared to the top portion of the distribution; and in the case of the lower interest rate they also lose out slightly to the bottom portion. Tables 140 and 141 provide more detail on this pattern of adjustment for all ages of families together. The first, together with Figure 68, shows the cumulative income share for all twenty vigintile groups and for the adjusted income series compared to (unadjusted) family total income. As can be seen, the Lorenz curve for the lower rate of return lies very close to the

TABLE 140
Cumulative income shares for families of two or more for
Weisbrod-Hansen annuity indices, Ontario 1973

Vigintile	Total income	W-H 1	W-H 2
First	0.67	0.69(+)	0.55(−)
Second	2.08	2.16(+)	1.86(−)
Third	3.98	4.12(+)	3.66(−)
Fourth	6.39	6.50(+)	5.81(−)
Fifth	9.27	9.26(−)	8.29(−)
Sixth	12.54	12.37(−)	11.04(−)
Seventh	16.16	15.82(−)	14.10(−)
Eighth	20.09	19.59(−)	17.46(−)
Ninth	24.31	23.67(−)	21.11(−)
Tenth	28.84	28.09(−)	25.05(−)
Eleventh	33.65	32.78(−)	29.28(−)
Twelfth	38.77	37.75(−)	33.77(−)
Thirteenth	44.19	43.08(−)	38.61(−)
Fourteenth	49.95	48.80(−)	43.83(−)
Fifteenth	56.10	54.91(−)	49.40(−)
Sixteenth	62.69	61.50(−)	55.38(−)
Seventeenth	69.79	68.67(−)	61.91(−)
Eighteenth	77.63	76.57(−)	69.12(−)
Nineteenth	86.66	85.72(−)	77.53(−)
Twentieth	100.00	100.00	100.00

NOTE: Sign in parentheses is in relation to unadjusted income share.
SOURCE: See source to Table 138.

unadjusted income curve and crosses it between the fourth and fifth vigintiles, so we cannot say that there is a uniform or unambiguous increase in inequality. In the case of the higher rate of return, though, the Lorenz curve does lie uniformly outside that for family total income, and by a fairly substantial amount, so that in this case a rather substantial and uniform reduction in equality can unambiguously be said to have occurred.

Table 141 and the accompanying Figure 69 present some further details of where the adjustments in inequality have occurred in the distribution. Average mean income values are increased by 15 and 21 per cent from the two adjustments from a base mean income value of about 13 200 in 1973. For the adjustment with the lower rate of interest, the bottom 17 per cent or so and top 22 per cent have gained in relation to the mean at the expense of the middle 60 per cent or so. The size of the relative gains and losses is comparatively modest. For the adjustment based on the higher rate

TABLE 141
Relative mean income values for families of two or more for the
Weisbrod-Hansen annuity indices, Ontario 1973

Vigintile	Total income	W-H 1	W-H 2
First	0.226	0.240(+)	0.218(−)
Second	0.330	0.351(+)	0.327(−)
Third	0.431	0.436(+)	0.428(−)
Fourth	0.534	0.517(−)	0.511(−)
Fifth	0.616	0.587(−)	0.576(−)
Sixth	0.689	0.656(−)	0.639(−)
Seventh	0.756	0.723(−)	0.707(−)
Eighth	0.815	0.785(−)	0.772(−)
Ninth	0.875	0.850(−)	0.834(−)
Tenth	0.935	0.914(−)	0.902(−)
Eleventh	0.992	0.964(−)	0.959(−)
Twelfth	1.054	1.028(−)	1.023(−)
Thirteenth	1.117	1.105(−)	1.108(−)
Fourteenth	1.189	1.183(−)	1.189( )
Fifteenth	1.273	1.265(−)	1.275(+)
Sixteenth	1.362	1.370(+)	1.367(+)
Seventeenth	1.483	1.500(+)	1.507(+)
Eighteenth	1.663	1.671(+)	1.677(+)
Nineteenth	1.971	2.027(+)	2.055(+)
Mean value ($)	13198	15190	16022
% Increase in mean		15	21

NOTE: Sign in parentheses is in relation to unadjusted relative mean income.
SOURCE: See source to Table 138.

of return, however, the gains and losses are greater. In particular now the
bottom 70 per cent of families have lost in relation to the mean, while the
top 30 per cent or so have gained, thus yielding the more conclusive pattern of inequality change indicated by the uniform outward shift of the
corresponding Lorenz curve in Figure 69.

AN ALTERNATIVE ADJUSTMENT FOR NET WORTH

The Weisbrod-Hansen net worth adjustment that has been used in this
chapter is fairly straightforward to apply and has almost attained the status
of convention, but is certainly not the only way of adjusting the current
flow of family income to take account of the stock of family wealth hold-

Figure 68:
Lorenz curves for families of two or more for Weisbrod-Hansen annuity indices, Ontario 1973

Source: Table 140

Cumulative percentage of income

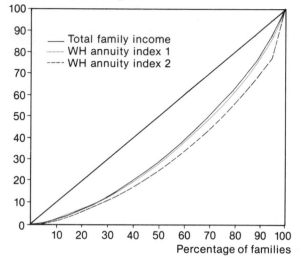

Percentage of families

Figure 69:
Relative mean index values for families of two or more for the Weisbrod-Hansen annuity index 2, Ontario 1973

Source: Table 141

Relative mean income

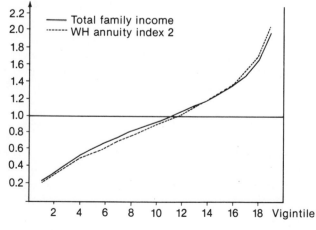

ings. Certainly the procedure has been criticized on the grounds that it ignores the earnings and savings expectations of younger families, or the sacrifices incurred by older families in accumulating their present wealth (Projector and Weiss 1969). It also associates a shorter life expectancy with a higher annuity value and a higher value for annuity-adjusted family income. These problems arise largely because the procedure is a mechanical rule for translating a stock at any given time into a flow over an expected time horizon. It does not reflect personal tastes, or represent the outcome of any choice or optimizing behaviour by the family. Therefore we are proposing a different adjustment procedure that is more strongly grounded in the life cycle theoretical framework of Part One and that attempts better to reflect simple optimal choice behaviour over time and to provide some check of the robustness of the empirical findings of the Weisbrod-Hansen procedure.

The utility-equivalent annuity approach

The framework of the alternative approach is a simple life-cycle model of optimal accumulation behaviour as discussed in Chapter 2. The approach thus attempts to move towards integrating empirical adjustment procedures with the newly developing body of theory of life-cycle family activity. It follows from the work of Nordhaus (1973) and applies his concept of a utility-equivalent annuity stream to the Ontario micro data file under study. It also allows us to interpret the rather mechanical Weisbrod-Hansen procedure in this more general behaviour framework.

While based on some fairly technical theory, the utility-equivalent annuity (UEA) approach can be explained simply in the two-period case with the aid of a simple Fisherian indifference curve diagram. Algebraic details of the more general multi-period case are presented in Appendix I. Figure 70 shows a consumer facing a two-period decision over allocation of consumption between this year ('Year 1') and next. He has a current wealth stock of W which, if unconsumed, could grow next year to a value of $W(1 + r)$, where r is the presumed market rate of interest. Thus his budget line of consumption opportunities over the two years is the straight line from W on the horizontal axis to the value $W(1 + r)$ on the vertical axis. The consumer is assumed to value both current and future consumption and thus has a set of indifference curves representing his preferences over various combinations of current and future consumption bundles. One such curve is drawn in as I. The consumer who maximizes his utility over the two periods subject to his intertemporal budget constraint will choose an optimal consumption combination such as at point A (with correspond-

Figure 70:
Illustration of utility-equivalent annuity income

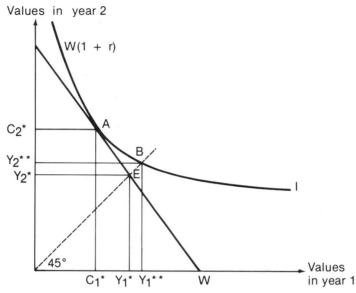

Values in year 2

ing consumption C_1^* the current period and C_2^* the second period) where he attains the highest indifference curve possible while still remaining within the consumption possibilities made available to him by the market and his current net worth resources.

In the case illustrated in Figure 70, C_2^* exceeds C_1^* as the consumer is willing to forego some current consumption to obtain greater future consumption. However, a constant value annuity stream that leaves the consumer just as well off as at point A is given by point B, where the same indifference curve through A cuts a 45° line from the origin. Since we are interested in a constant annuity value as an indicator of economic well-being, the annuity value corresponding to point B, or what will henceforth be called the utility-equivalent annuity income figure $Y_1^{**} = Y_2^{**} = Y^{**}$, would appear to be a reasonable choice. Note that again a current stock of wealth W has been translated into a constant or single-valued income annuity stream Y^{**} in a way that reflects not only market conditions and current resources (as indicated by the budget constraint), but also consumer tastes and preferences (as indicated by the indifference curves). In contrast, the Weisbrod-Hansen annuity value represented by point E in the

TABLE 142
Inequality measures by age of head for utility-equivalent annuity Index 1 for families of
two or more, Ontario 1973

Measure	Under 25	25–34	35–44	45–54	55–64	65 & over	All ages
Shares							
Bottom 10%	1.7	2.2	2.4	2.7	2.2	1.7	2.1
Bottom quintile	6.2	7.2	7.2	7.7	6.1	5.7	6.4
2nd quintile	14.6	14.3	13.4	13.0	12.0	11.3	13.0
3rd quintile	19.7	19.1	17.3	16.9	15.7	16.0	18.1
4th quintile	24.9	24.2	21.9	20.9	19.5	23.5	23.8
Top quintile	34.6	35.2	40.2	41.5	46.8	43.5	38.8
Top 10%	19.3	19.5	26.7	28.3	33.4	27.1	23.6
Top 5%	10.5	10.7	18.5	20.4	25.7	15.4	14.5
Gini coefficient	0.283	0.278	0.320	0.330	0.393	0.374	0.321
Coef of variation	0.52	0.52	1.03	1.16	1.27	0.75	0.54
Atkinson index ($\epsilon = 1.55$)	0.294	0.224	0.230	0.214	0.292	0.339	0.287

SOURCE: See source to Table 138.

TABLE 143
Inequality measures by age of head for utility-equivalent annuity Index 2 for families of
two or more, Ontario 1973

Measure	Under 25	25–34	35–44	45–54	55–64	65 & over	All ages
Shares							
Bottom 10%	1.6	2.2	2.4	3.0	2.4	1.5	1.7
Bottom quintile	5.9	7.1	7.1	8.2	6.4	5.4	5.5
2nd quintile	14.2	14.2	13.4	13.3	12.2	11.3	11.3
3rd quintile	19.5	18.8	17.2	17.5	15.9	16.4	16.3
4th quintile	24.7	24.1	21.9	21.2	19.7	23.8	22.1
Top quintile	35.7	35.9	40.5	39.9	45.7	43.0	44.9
Top 10%	20.4	20.9	27.0	26.7	32.4	26.7	30.6
Top 5%	11.3	11.4	18.7	18.7	24.4	15.3	22.0
Gini coefficient	0.291	0.285	0.327	0.311	0.378	0.373	0.373
Coef of variation	0.54	0.53	1.03	0.98	1.15	0.74	1.13
Atkinson index ($\epsilon = 1.55$)	0.384	0.270	0.253	0.171	0.276	0.364	0.298

SOURCE: See source to Table 138.

diagram (where the 45° line cuts the budget constraint) reflects only current resources and market conditions, and does not incorporate family tastes at all.

Thus the utility-equivalent annuity procedure entails the replacement of $Y^* = \text{NW} \cdot A_n$ in the formula for annuity-adjusted family income by Y^{**} with the result that now we have the adjusted income series

$$\text{YUE} = \text{FTI} - \text{YCAP} + Y^{**}.$$

The technical details of this procedure are presented in Appendix I. The computations are rather more complicated than in the Weisbrod-Hansen case, for they now include parameter values reflecting consumers' tastes that influence the curvature and position of the appropriate indifference curves. Essentially what has been done is to characterize tastes by a constant elasticity of marginal utility consumption function and provide estimates where possible of the corresponding parameters. The resulting income-adjusted inequality estimates are presented in the next section.

Empirical results with the alternative approach

Tables 142 and 143 present the inequality results of the utility-equivalent wealth annuity adjustment procedure corresponding to assumed rates of interest of 8 and 12 per cent respectively. Again the general result is an increase in inequality, this time by 4.9 and 21.9 per cent in the Gini coefficients for the group as a whole, a somewhat stronger effect than for the Weisbrod-Hansen adjustment. Again the pattern of changes differs across age groups with relatively weaker inequality adjustment at the younger end, much stronger inequality increases among the groups aged 35–64, and a slight (though ambiguous) reduction in summary inequality for the oldest age group 65 and over. And again the changes occurring at the higher rate of return are generally greater.

The general similarity between the summary empirical results here and those reported for the Weisbrod-Hansen procedure is not simply fortuitous, but has been built into the former procedure by the assumption that tastes are the same across the population. Since all families are assumed to have the same utility function (which for simplicity has been assumed to be homothetic) the ratio of Y^{**}/Y^* in Figure 70 will be constant within a given age group although not between age groups because of differing life expectancies. Therefore, in the present experiments, the Weisbrod-Hansen annuity figures for $Y^* = \text{NW} \cdot A_n$ have essentially been inflated by the constant proportion Y^{**}/Y^* within age groups before adding them to family

TABLE 144
Cumulative income shares for families of two or more for the utility-equivalent
annuity indices, Ontario 1973

Vigintile	Total income	UEA 1	UEA 2
First	0.67	0.68(+)	0.45(−)
Second	2.08	2.13(+)	1.72(−)
Third	3.98	4.08(+)	3.42(−)
Fourth	6.39	6.45(+)	5.47(−)
Fifth	9.27	9.18(−)	7.83(−)
Sixth	12.54	12.25(−)	10.48(−)
Seventh	16.16	15.67(−)	13.46(−)
Eighth	20.09	19.41(−)	16.79(−)
Ninth	24.31	23.47(−)	20.41(−)
Tenth	28.84	27.87(−)	24.32(−)
Eleventh	33.65	32.54(−)	28.52(−)
Twelfth	38.77	37.50(−)	33.04(−)
Thirteenth	44.19	42.80(−)	37.94(−)
Fourteenth	49.95	48.52(−)	43.27(−)
Fifteenth	56.10	54.64(−)	48.99(−)
Sixteenth	62.69	61.25(−)	55.15(−)
Seventeenth	69.79	68.46(−)	61.91(−)
Eighteenth	77.63	76.39(−)	69.39(−)
Nineteenth	86.66	85.51(−)	78.05(−)
Twentieth	100.00	100.00	100.00

SOURCE: See source to Table 138.

income. The resulting inequality figures for YUE should thus reflect the
same general patterns within age groups as noted already for YWH.[5]

Looking at the results for all age groups together in greater detail in
Tables 144 and 145, one notes that while details may differ somewhat from
the results for the Weisbrod-Hansen procedure, the principal findings still
hold true. At the lower rate of interest, the middle 60 per cent of families
lose out in relation to the bottom 17 per cent and top 23 per cent, so that a
slight but not completely uniform increase in inequality can be said to have
occurred. At the higher rate of interest, however, the bottom 67 per cent or
so tend to lose out relative to the more marked gains of the upper third of
the distribution, with the result that the Lorenz curve is moved out uni-

5 They will not however be exactly the *same* because Y^* and Y^{**} are added to total family
  income net of investment returns FTI − YCAP, which are clearly not distributed proportionally across members of a given age group.

TABLE 145
Relative mean income values for families of two or more for the
utility-equivalent annuity indices, Ontario 1973

Vigintile	Total income	UEA 1	UEA 2
First	0.226	0.239(+)	0.217(−)
Second	0.330	0.345(+)	0.328(−)
Third	0.431	0.434(+)	0.409(−)
Fourth	0.534	0.512(−)	0.482(−)
Fifth	0.616	0.581(−)	0.545(−)
Sixth	0.689	0.650(−)	0.608(−)
Seventh	0.756	0.718(−)	0.691(−)
Eighth	0.815	0.778(−)	0.758(−)
Ninth	0.875	0.845(−)	0.818(−)
Tenth	0.935	0.908(−)	0.883(−)
Eleventh	0.992	0.961(−)	0.947(−)
Twelfth	1.054	1.022(−)	1.020(−)
Thirteenth	1.117	1.103(−)	1.115(−)
Fourteenth	1.189	1.184(−)	1.204(+)
Fifteenth	1.273	1.272(−)	1.289(+)
Sixteenth	1.362	1.376(+)	1.393(+)
Seventeenth	1.483	1.510(+)	1.549(+)
Eighteenth	1.663	1.669(+)	1.715(+)
Nineteenth	1.971	2.021(+)	2.085(+)
Mean value ($)	13 198	15 438	17 204
% Increase in mean		17	30

SOURCE: See source to Table 138.

formly and a fairly large increase in inequality can be said to have occurred.
In summary then, inequality figures that are based only on family income
and do not take account of family wealth holdings as well may tend to
underestimate markedly the relative inequality of the distribution of economic well-being across the population.

SUMMARY

This chapter has considered two different adjustments to family income
figures in order to reflect better the economic well-being of families. The
adjustments recognize family holdings of net worth and the potential consumption this provided. Two sets of adjustments were performed: one, the
conventional Weisbrod-Hansen wealth annuity procedure; the other, a

methodological application of the utility-equivalent annuity income concept. Three series of findings were obtained.

First, for the Weisbrod-Hansen adjustment, inequality generally increased (Gini coefficients for all age groups together rose by 3.9 and 19.6 per cent depending on interest rate assumptions) because non-aged higher-income groups tend to have higher wealth holdings as well. This general pattern, however, did not occur evenly across age groups: the groups under 35 experienced relatively little change in inequality, groups 35–64 experienced a rather substantial increase in inequality, and the oldest group, aged 65 and over, had a slight reduction in summary inequality.

Secondly, for the utility-equivalent annuity adjustment, the findings are quite similar to those for Weisbrod-Hansen adjustment, but of a slightly stronger effect. Again, the middle and sometimes lower portions of the over-all distribution lose out in relation to the top portions, where net worth holdings are most substantial.

Thirdly, in general, it appears that the inequality effects of adjustments to family income for family net worth holdings can be quite important in comparison to a number of other adjustments considered so far in this study. However, they may differ substantially in magnitude according to the underlying interest rate assumptions of the adjustment. They can also constitute fairly complex patterns of change that can be adequately captured only in a fairly detailed and disaggregative analysis.

13

Toward adjustment for net social security benefits: illustration with the Canada Pension Plan

INTRODUCTION[1]

Family economic well-being can obviously be affected by the public sector as well as the private sector of the economy. So far, though, the adjustments we have made to family income figures in order to provide an improved index of economic well-being have concentrated almost entirely on various privately held resources. However, publicly provided resources such as social security and health insurance can also affect the economic well-being of families, and a disregard for this form of resources, or what may be called social security wealth, might be expected to bias inferences based solely on conventional income and private wealth figures in the direction of greater inequality than if public schemes were also accounted for (Feldstein 1974a). Such government programs would include Unemployment Insurance, Old Age Security, Family and Youth Allowances, and Guaranteed Income Supplement, as well as various other compensation and assistance schemes; and they represent a fairly large and growing proportion of the economy's product (Cloutier 1978). For that reason, there appears to be a need for extensive study of the various effects of these schemes on the economy.

Such social security programs can have a number of important effects on the private sector of the economy. On the one hand, they may have macroeconomic or aggregate effects by possibly reducing household savings and labour supplied to the market (Feldstein 1974b). On the other hand, they may also have distributional or disaggregative effects by providing net transfers of resources unevenly across families in the population. The present

1 Portions of the discussion in this chapter follow the work of Gregoire (1976).

study, because of its subject, addresses only the second of these two problems.

Within the distributional area, however, much of the theoretical analysis of household factor supplies (reviewed in Chapter 2) is rather long run in nature, based as it is on individual and family life cycle considerations. Most empirical work on distribution in this country, though, has been carried out in a rather short-run temporal framework based on annual income and wealth data collected from the census or from various Statistics Canada surveys. The study by Cloutier (1978), for example, views the distribution of social security benefits and costs in a one-year framework. The present study, however, seeks to take a step towards integrating the two streams of analysis and views social security distributional effects in an intertemporal life cycle framework. Indeed, one of the objectives of this chapter is to point out some of the intertemporal considerations involved in evaluating economic well-being even within a cross-section at one point in time. In the last chapter the time dimension played an important role in reducing wealth holdings at different stages of the life cycle to comparable annuity streams. In this chapter, taxes and social security benefits, which do not usually occur equally over the life cycle or between cohorts also occur over time and are also viewed intertemporally in comparable fashion.

The present analysis should be distinguished from the broad government tax-expenditure analyses of Gillespie (1976), Dodge (1975), Maslove (1972), and Reynolds and Smolensky (1977). Our study is much narrower in scope, concentrating on fewer tax-expenditure problems; it is based on an explicit earnings life-cycle framework and is not concerned with how aggregate distributional effects may have changed over a period of time. Indeed our analysis is much more illustrative than comprehensive, for the present analysis concentrates on only one particular (albeit important) social security program, and is meant to indicate some of the fairly complex work that is necessary in an examination of the detailed distributive aspects of even a single major social security program when viewed in a life cycle theoretical framework. Clearly, the analytical approach described here could be usefully applied to other programs as well, such as public health schemes and Old Age Security. Hence the following analysis of some of the distributional patterns associated with the Canada Pension Plan is meant to serve not as the final word, but only as a step towards more extensive distributional analysis of a range of government social security programs.

We have chosen the Canada Pension Plan for distributional analysis in this chapter for several reasons. One is the current general interest in the Plan arising from the fact that under the current combination of benefit levels, financing arrangements, and age structure of the population, the accumulated fund for the Plan is expected to be rapidly depleted in future with the result that future cohorts may have to be taxed more heavily to provide retirement benefits now promised by the Plan. The government has many options that can be considered to deal with this; and in order to understand the distributional implications of any of these, a first step is to obtain some information about the effects of the current plan.

Secondly, among the above-mentioned social security programs, the Canada Pension Plan raises most forcefully several intertemporal issues that are of some importance in distributional analysis. One is the time horizon over which economic well being should be measured. Another is the theoretical framework on which the analysis is based. While some social security programs such as unemployment insurance may be viewed simply as insurance schemes with a relatively unimportant time dimension to tax payments and receipts, a program such as the CPP has a critical time dimension that should be recognized in analysing its distributional effects. In the last chapter such considerations motivated an adjustment procedure in which consumption opportunities from current wealth holdings were spread over the remaining expected lifetimes of workers. In the present chapter we extend the life-cycle approach further by analysing expected earnings profiles over the entire working life of adults in the population. We have developed a crude earnings simulation model that permits an inquiry into the redistribution of resources between different income classes, cohorts, and families with different characteristics. This approach thus recognizes the need to incorporate not only the net worth accumulation of older families but also the earnings potential of young workers as factors affecting long-run economic well-being. We have not attempted to combine both in a simultaneous empirical analysis of life-cycle well-being, but the present work should point out the direction of framework for future empirical analysis.

Thirdly, the Canada Pension Plan is an interesting subject for analysis because of the various forms of redistribution associated with it: life-cycle or intra-cohort redistribution of resources across time from the working years to the retirement years of individuals; current or immediate redistribution across age groups in the population from younger workers who are being taxed to pay into the scheme to retired members who are receiving benefits from the scheme; and inter-cohort redistribution of resources to the older segment of the population from the young and future generations. These are three forms of redistribution that are present in differing combinations in various government programs of social security and health insurance. An examination of the Canada Pension Plan is thus a useful means of highlighting these different transfer mechanisms.

DESCRIPTION OF THE CANADA PENSION PLAN

The Canada Pension Plan was introduced in 1966 and came fully into effect after a ten-year transitional period, in 1976. The CPP is a contributory social insurance program designed to provide a basic level of support during retirement and a basic level of protection against the contingencies of disability and death by means of a graduated pension related to the level of lifetime earnings.

Since January 1966, participation in the Plan has been compulsory for all members of the labour force between the ages of 18 and 70. Employers and employees each contribute at the rate of 1.8 per cent of annual earnings between the year's basic exemption ($600 in 1973) and the year's maximum pensionable earnings ($5600 in 1973). Eligible earnings include wage and salary income and income from self-employment. Self-employed persons contribute at the rate of 3.6 per cent. Thus the maximum contributions in 1973 were applied to earnings totalling $5000 a year. The effect of the exemption is that people with low incomes make relatively smaller contributions for each dollar of pension benefits to which they will be entitled than do people with higher incomes. The exemption at the lower end of the earnings scale and the non-taxation of any earnings beyond the maximum insurable level thus render the effective average contributory tax rate progressive up to the level of the maximum earnings cut-off and then regressive beyond that.

The ceiling for pensionable earnings under the Canada Pension Plan is scheduled to increase annually by 12.5 per cent until it equals the average Industrial Composite wage and salary level (under an assumption of say, a 7 per cent annual increase in this level, maximum pensionable earnings and average industrial wages would meet in 1983). Thereafter, maximum pensionable earnings are scheduled to increase in tandem with the average industrial wage in Canada. Since 1975, the year's basic exemption has been set at approximately 10 per cent of maximum pensionable earnings.

The Canada Pension Plan provides three main types of benefits: retirement pensions, survivors' benefits (i.e., pensions for surviving spouses, orphans' benefits, and lump-sum death benefits), and disability benefits (i.e., pensions for disabled contributors, and benefits for their dependent children). The first retirement pensions became payable in 1967, and the other benefits slightly later. As the largest component of benefits by far is for retirement purposes and since the focus of our analysis is the retirement aspects of the Plan, we shall restrict our attention to retirement pension benefits under the Plan.

Retirement pensions are payable under the Plan to contributors who apply when they reach 65 years of age. The contributor's pension differs during the transitional and full-benefits period. During the first ten years of the Plan (1966–1975), less than full benefits were paid to contributors who retired during that period because of their relatively short contribution period. For each year of contribution during the transition period, benefits were increased by one-tenth of full benefits. That is, a contributor who retired in 1967 was allowed only one-tenth of full benefits; in 1968, two-tenths; and so on until full benefits were paid in 1976.

The actual retirement pension benefit formula deserves to be examined in some detail. The retirement pension is a basic monthly amount equal to 25 per cent of average adjusted monthly pensionable earnings over the contribution period of the Plan. The adjustment of monthly earnings involves calculating the ratio of each year's earnings to the year's maximum pensionable earnings for the year of retirement and the two preceding years.[2] The purpose of the adjustment is to express lifetime or career earnings of an individual in terms of current earnings levels in the economy at time of retirement. CPP pension benefits are then indexed for inflation to rise annually with the consumer price index.

Before turning to the computer simulation model incorporating these features of the Canada Pension Plan, we shall discuss briefly some of the distributional patterns associated with the Plan and some methodological issues that arise when one is trying to identify these patterns.

TYPES OF REDISTRIBUTION BUILT INTO THE CPP

The redistribution of resources resulting from social insurance schemes such as the Canada Pension Plan can take many forms; the various equity considerations have been examined in some detail by Leimer et al. (1978). I shall discuss current redistribution, life-cycle redistribution, and inter-cohort redistribution.

At any one time, a social security pension scheme redistributes resources from those who are working and earning income to those who are elderly and retired. In fact, Asimakopulos and Weldon (1968) argue that the analy-

---

2 Actually, there is some flexibility in calculating the average of the earnings ratios if one contributes for more than ten years or works beyond age 65.

sis of government pensions has little to do with the long run: 'Government pension plans are attempts not to determine the specific level of future income for any group, but to redistribute present income and provide rules intended to influence in a conditional way how later governments redistribute income.' This view considers public pensions largely as a transfer program for the aged that is financed by a payroll tax levied on the young; it is the perspective of a recent empirical study by Cloutier (1978).

Brittain (1972b, 83) and Asimakopulos and Weldon (1968) argue that contributions and benefits need not necessarily be related on an individual basis since there is no contractual obligation on the part of the present government to maintain benefits and contributions at their present level in future. They also stress the government's power of taxation and borrowing, which frees the CPP from the need to be 'actuarially sound.' The Canada Pension Plan is thus quite different in nature from a private pension or life insurance plan.

A second point of view on income redistribution through old-age insurance schemes, which is represented by Deran (1966), Prest (1970), Atkinson (1970b), and Castellino (1971), for example, abandons the one-period horizon in favour of an intertemporal one embracing the whole contributions-benefits life cycle of any individual. This is a better approach for dealing with the CPP since the benefits received are far from contemporary with the payment of the related contributions. This approach also has the merit that it does not treat each year of a person's life in isolation, but instead takes a lifetime view. The comparison between benefits and contributions must thus take place in an intertemporal or lifetime context and must incorporate important time-related factors such as growth in worker productivity and technical progress.

Thirdly, the transfer of income from the young to the elderly that results from social security programs can also be viewed in a dynamic intercohort or intergenerational context. That is, one can ask whether the support provided by one cohort for another differs through time (Browning 1973). In the case of the Canada Pension Plan, for example, benefits are related to the maximum pensionable earnings at time of retirement, and thereafter are adjusted for price changes only. This means that the elderly's pension depends on the level of earnings in the economy at time of retirement and does not reflect any changes in productivity or technical progress during his retirement. If one considers two persons with similar earnings history but from different cohorts, the younger person is likely to get a larger pension than the older one even if they both made similar contributions. Another type of inter-cohort discrimination implicit in the CPP is the exclusion of pre-1967 pensioners, who get nothing under the Plan, or the differential benefits treatment of those who retire during the transitional period 1967–1976.

In this study, redistributional characteristics of the Canada Pension Plan will be analysed in an intertemporal life-cycle context. Attention will be given to the redistributional impacts of the CPP between cohorts as well as across current income groups.

MEASURING DISTRIBUTIONAL CHARACTERISTICS OF THE CPP

There are several methodological issues that must be addressed before we can measure the extent of redistribution in a social insurance scheme such as the Canada Pension Plan. These are: how to compare benefit and contribution streams relating to different time periods; how to define the distributional neutrality of a social insurance scheme; distributional incidence of a payroll tax; and distributional incidence of pension benefits. Since the first two issues are closely related, they will be dealt with together.

Cost-benefit comparisons and distributional neutrality
In order to compare contributions and benefits relating to different time periods, one can calculate either the present value of net benefits (i.e., benefits minus contributions) at some rate of interest, or the internal rate of return (i.e., the interest rate at which the discounted actuarial value of contributions is just equal to that of benefits received). What exactly is meant by distributional neutrality in these two approaches, however, is not clear.

The present value approach has been used extensively in recent studies on the returns to social insurance schemes.[3] The principal difficulty with this approach is the necessity of choosing a discount rate for contributions and benefits; and, as is well known, different discount rates can yield rather different redistributional inferences.

In order to avoid the problem of choosing a particular discount rate, one may turn to the internal rate of return approach in which the 'real yield on net contributions' is determined endogenously. But what redistributional inferences can one draw from internal rate of return results? In calculating the internal rate of return for selected income levels, Brittain (1967) and Atkinson (1970b) conclude that the higher rate of return to low-income groups shows that the pension programs they studied were consistent with

3 See, for example, Deran (1966), Prest (1970), and Pesando and Rea (1977).

the objective of redistributing income in favour of those with low earnings. Presumably this argument also accepts the fact that an equal rate of return to all groups would mean the program is distributionally 'neutral' in the sense that it does not favour any income group. But an example from Browning (1973) shows that equal rates of return to all groups does not mean that the program is neutral because that is also consistent with larger increases in net worth for some people. More generally, it is not the rate of return on one's savings, but rather the individual's wealth that determines his command over goods and services during his lifetime. The problem of choosing a particular rate of interest to discount contributions and benefits cannot be avoided since a higher internal rate of return for low-income groups, say, does not necessarily imply redistribution in favour of low-income groups.

For that reason this study uses the discounted present value approach. Many different rates of interest have been proposed in the literature for discounting multi-period streams of contributions and benefits.[4] In the present study we use the discount rate of 6 per cent already employed in the last chapter to amortize net worth holdings. The redistributive effects of a program, however, can be gauged only by reference to some definition of redistributional neutrality. Any such definition has a certain degree of arbitrariness. Equity may refer to an equal percentage increase in wealth for all contributors. Pesando and Rea (1977) refer to programs as progressive if the amount of wealth transferred falls with higher levels of permanent income. In this study the Canada Pension Plan will be referred to as progressive if the present value of net benefits transferred falls with higher levels of family income, and neutral if net benefits remain constant across income classes.

Distributional incidence of the payroll tax
The Canada Pension Plan payroll tax, one may recall, consists of a proportional tax (levied in equal shares on employee and employer) on covered earnings from a low-income exemption level up to a statutory maximum base. This renders the structure of the payroll tax fairly regressive since: it does not allow adjustments (through personal deductions) for the personal situation of the tax payer but essentially taxes the near bottom slices of income; the marginal tax rate falls to zero for earnings above the maximum base ($5600 in 1973) so that the average effective rate declines above this

4 See, for example, the suggestions by Deran (1966), Castellino (1971), Pesando and Rea (1977), and Brittain (1967).

earnings level; and the payroll tax applies only to wages, salaries, and self-employment income, thus exempting property income, which is higher at top-income brackets (though also exempting transfer income, which is higher at bottom income brackets). Knowledge of the actual tax burden or incidence, though, is essential to an appraisal of the distributional effects of the Canada Pension Plan.

The literature on the incidence of (employers' and employees') social security contributions is large and not always in agreement. Theoretically, the payroll tax can be shifted in many ways depending on the assumptions made about market structures. Under the assumption of competitive markets, a general tax on wage income applicable in all industries tends to be borne by the wage earners because of the usually assumed inelastic supply of labour (Musgrave and Musgrave 1973, 382–7, 390–5). Moreover, in a perfectly competitive market with perfect knowledge, it is of course a matter of indifference whether the tax is collected from employers or employees (ibid., 390).

The division of the contributions between employees, employers, and consumers, however, poses problems in a non-competitive market economy. The possibility of bargaining by unions and of administered pricing by firms has resulted in some uncertainty about the extent to which the tax is shifted to consumers in the form of higher prices or borne by firms in the form of lower profits, or by workers through foregone wage increases. The outcome depends on how the various parties respond. The debate must be resolved by empirical analysis.

The main empirical work on this issue is by Brittain (1971 and 1972a), who offers evidence that the entire tax is borne by employees. A more recent study by Leuthold (1975), however, finds that on average the payroll tax in the United States is not fully shifted onto labour. Leuthold's findings, though, apply only to short-run shifting of the payroll tax and not to the longer-run possibility of substitution of other factors for labour. A study by Balfour and Beach (1979) for Canada, however, does allow for substitution and is not able to reject the full shifting hypothesis of Brittain.

In conclusion, the various attempts to test for shifting of the employers' tax component to labour yield conflicting results. However, the uncertainty about the short-run shifting of the payroll tax may disappear when one is dealing with the long run. As pointed out by Leuthold, in the short run, wages may be prevented from falling in response to a tax increase because of labour contracts, custom, or minimum wage legislation. But in the long run, the shifting of the tax to consumers or labourers is much more possible because of substitution opportunities for other factors. Since there is no agreement on the degree of shifting of the payroll tax, it is assumed in the simulation model used in this study (and outlined below) that, alternatively, there is complete shifting of the employer component of the tax onto labour and that there is no shifting at all.

Distributional incidence of CPP benefits
The standard approach adopted in empirical studies on the incidence of transfers is to impute transfer payments directly to the recipients with no shifting. However, to the extent that shifting of transfers actually occurs, the transfer recipient does not benefit by the exact amount of his transfer receipts. Theoretically, there are at least three ways in which shifting of transfer payments may occur: through changes in tax payments, through changes in product prices, and through the loss of other transfer benefits.

Taxable transfer payments, by increasing taxable income, increase tax payments, while CPP contributions reduce them. If what matters is the change in the recipient's real disposable income, then ideally one should analyse the redistributional impact of the CPP net of income taxes deducted for contributions and taxes paid on benefits. In this study, we limit our scope to the calculation of net benefits before taxation.[5]

Transfers may also cause changes in product prices if the spending patterns of the transfer recipients differ from those of the tax payers who finance the Plan. Since the introduction of variation in spending habits among different groups greatly complicates the analysis, it will not be incorporated into the present calculations of net benefits.

Loss of transfer benefits from other support programs can also occur with receipt of CPP benefits. Social security programs for the aged in Ontario include a number of related plans, and some (the Guaranteed Income Supplement and Guaranteed Annual Income System) are subject to income tests. They apply a tax rate on private income (including CPP benefits) of 50 per cent in the case of GIS and 100 per cent in the case of GAINS. There are several different approaches to the analysis of CPP benefits in relation to other income-tested programs for the aged in Ontario. CPP benefits may be analysed independently of other income-tested programs, although the analysis might be misleading because low CPP benefits render the elderly eligible for GIS and GAINS benefits. Or the CPP may be viewed as a complement to an already existing system that includes GIS and GAINS, but this further complicates an already involved framework of analysis. Thirdly, the

5 Pesando and Rea (1977) calculated net benefits before and after taxation and found them to be somewhat smaller after taxes, but identical in pattern to those before taxes.

CPP may be considered along with the distributional effects of other programs as well. Because there are no specific taxes levied to finance GIS and GAINS, this approach has the difficulty of evaluating the incidence of the general tax revenues used to finance GIS and GAINS. The present study uses the first approach for reasons of convenience, and in recognition of the fact that GIS and GAINS were legislated to supplement low CPP benefits (Bryden 1974).

A MODEL OF THE CANADA PENSION PLAN

Under the Canada Pension Plan a participant contributes a fraction of his earnings during his working life and in retirement enjoys cash benefits that are paid to him according to a formula determined by the Plan. In this context, the CPP can be regarded as a means of redistributing lifetime incomes over time, and we shall attempt to estimate the extent to which this lifetime redistribution occurs among Ontario families from the standpoint of the base year 1973 so that results will be as comparable as possible to those of other chapters in this study. The extent of life cycle redistribution will be gauged by comparing estimated present values of net CPP benefits accruing to different age and income groups in the population.

It should be recognized that, as Asimakopulos and Weldon (1968) point out, the rules of the Plan may well change in future, particularly in response to the aging of the population. However, since one cannot know exactly what changes may occur in future, the present analysis is based upon the assumption that the rules will remain unchanged for the present generation of workers. It is thus a distributional analysis of the Plan as now structured.

Because of the fairly recent implementation of the Plan, no data are yet available on lifetime payments and benefits of representative participants. Since both payments and benefits are related to earnings, one must first construct estimated individual lifetime earnings profiles, and then compute contributions and benefits under the CPP rules for each of these earnings profiles and calculate the resulting present value of the net benefits. The simulation model used to do this is explained in some detail in Appendix J.

In summary, the CPP simulation model may be outlined in four parts: estimation of cross-sectional age-earnings profiles; transformation of the cross-sectional profiles into longitudinal lifetime earnings trajectories; calculation of CPP contributions and benefits for each participant on the Survey of Consumer Finances Ontario micro data file; and computation of the present value of net benefits for each participant and aggregation across participants within family units.

The first stage in the calculation of CPP net benefits is to estimate cross-sectional age-earnings profiles for all individuals who have positive earnings. This was done by estimating fairly simple earnings equations (see Appendix K for details) separately for men and women and separately for each of nine education categories from the 1971 Census Public Use Sample Tape for individuals in Ontario. This is a particularly large micro data set that permits a fair amount of disaggregation in our regression analysis. These estimated earnings equations were then applied to individual adults on the SCF Ontario file to yield cross-sectional earnings estimates for 1973, and an adjustment was provided to ensure that earnings dispersion was not artificially reduced by the regression imputation procedure.

The second stage in the calculation is to transform the above cross-sectional profiles into longitudinal expected lifetime earnings trajectories for each adult on the tape. This essentially requires two adjustments. In the first place, various dynamic or 'time' factors such as increased worker productivity and technological progress must be taken into account. In particular it is assumed that all earnings increase uniformly over time at a constant nominal rate of 7 per cent. The resulting longitudinal age-earnings trajectories are thus steeper than the cross-sectional profiles and peak later or not at all. In the second place, adjustment is made for non-receipt of earnings. The cross-sectional earnings equations were estimated only for those labour force participants with positive earnings. But clearly some adults do not receive earnings because of non-participation or extended unemployment. This aspect is particularly important in the case of women, who tend to be absent from the labour force while raising a young family. Consequently, the longitudinal earnings trajectories are also adjusted to take account of the probability of zero earnings receipts in a given year. These probabilities have also been estimated from the 1971 Census tapes as functions of sex, age, educational attainment, and marital status. The resulting adjusted trajectories can thus be interpreted as expected earnings profiles over the life cycle of a worker.

The third stage then consists of using these expected earnings profiles to actually compute estimated CPP benefits and contribution streams for each participant on the SCF file. The formulas used have been discussed above; the calculations also incorporate various transitional aspects of the Plan. To allow for employer-shifting of the payroll tax, estimates are made under alternative assumptions of full shifting and no shifting of the tax. The expected rate of inflation according to which retirement benefits are indexed is assumed to be 2 per cent as it was also in the last chapter.

The final stage of the calculations is to aggregate the estimated CPP benefit and contribution streams over time and across participants within family units. In the first case, the discounted present value (to the year 1973) of net benefits (i.e., benefits less contributions) under the Plan is calculated for each participant based on the discount rate of 6 per cent used in the last chapter. In the second case, these figures for the present value of net benefits are then summed for the participants in each family unit. In husband-wife families, this means two potential participants; while in single-adult families, there is only one. These calculations were done for each family unit on the SCF Ontario file, and the distribution results across family units are presented in the following section.

ESTIMATED DISTRIBUTIONAL RESULTS
OF THE CANADA PENSION PLAN

This section reports the results of an empirical analysis of some of the distributional properties associated with the Canada Pension Plan based on the simulation model just described. Inequality measures for the present value of net benefits across family units by age of family head are presented in Tables 146 and 147; the first is based on the assumptions of no tax shifting, and the second on full shifting of the payroll tax.

The first thing to note in these two tables is that the mean and median present value of net benefits from the Canada Pension Plan as now constituted are positive and rather large. In the case of no shifting of the payroll tax, the mean increment of publicly provided net worth through the workings of the CPP is around $11000 per family unit in Ontario (in 1973 terms), and in the case of full shifting, it is still more than $8000. These are not trivial amounts. They show that the Plan is not actuarially sound at the assumed rate of discount of 6 per cent. This, of course, is similar to the findings of other authors[6] on the Canada Pension Plan. But it strongly supports Asimakopulos and Weldon's (1968) point that a public pension scheme such as the CPP can readily have its rules changed in mid-stream; and our findings show that some change of rules is indeed likely in the near future, otherwise the present generation of tax payers will have to foot a substantial bill to cover the expected deficits. Consequently, the present analysis should not be construed as a prediction of what the long-run distributional characteristics of the CPP will be, but rather as a description of

6 See, for example, Pesando and Rea (1977) and Rea (1978).

TABLE 146
Inequality measures by age of head for present value of net CPP benefits 1 (no shifting)
for all family units, Ontario 1973

Measure	Under 25	25–34	35–44	45–54	55–64	65 & over	All ages
Shares							
Bottom 10%	3.3	3.9	3.7	3.5	2.3	0.2	0.4
Bottom quintile	8.4	9.6	9.7	10.0	7.6	0.9	3.3
2nd quintile	12.9	15.6	14.8	15.6	16.0	2.8	13.5
3rd quintile	19.5	19.6	19.2	19.0	20.0	5.2	20.0
4th quintile	24.7	23.5	24.2	24.1	23.6	27.4	26.0
Top quintile	34.4	31.8	32.2	31.3	32.9	63.6	38.1
Top 10%	18.5	17.1	17.6	17.1	18.4	37.3	20.8
Top 5%	9.6	9.0	9.3	9.1	10.2	21.5	11.4
Gini coefficient	0.266	0.220	0.229	0.216	0.245	0.627	0.336
Coef of variation	0.46	0.38	0.39	0.37	0.43	1.25	0.75
Atkinson index ($\epsilon = 1.55$)	0.187	0.131	0.142	0.140	0.220	0.825	0.602
Mean ($)	9204	11704	13195	16192	13450	3550	11119
Median ($)	9154	11490	12683	15356	12866	852	10776

SOURCE: Based on data for Ontario from the 1973 Consumer Finance Micro Data Release Tape
supplied by Statistics Canada and on calculations discussed in the text.

TABLE 147
Inequality measures by age of head for present value of net CPP benefits 2 (full shifting)
for all family units, Ontario 1973

Measure	Under 25	25–34	35–44	45–54	55–64	65 & over	All ages
Shares							
Bottom 10%	−0.8	1.7	2.7	3.4	2.3	−2.9	−0.7
Bottom quintile	0.4	5.9	7.8	9.5	7.7	−5.2	0.9
2nd quintile	13.1	14.0	13.9	14.9	16.1	−3.1	11.2
3rd quintile	20.3	19.3	18.7	18.9	19.7	0.2	18.6
4th quintile	26.7	24.7	24.7	23.9	23.3	33.2	26.8
Top quintile	39.5	36.1	34.9	32.8	33.3	74.8	42.5
Top 10%	22.5	20.7	19.9	18.6	19.0	44.1	24.8
Top 5%	12.5	11.7	11.2	10.6	11.0	25.3	14.1
Gini coefficient	0.385	0.301	0.274	0.236	0.248	0.819	0.416
Coef of variation	0.65	0.50	0.45	0.39	0.42	1.59	0.95
Atkinson index ($\epsilon = 1.55$)	n.a.	0.328	0.222	0.161	0.236	n.a.	n.a.
Mean ($)	4285	6447	9634	14130	12532	2883	8257
Median ($)	4249	6222	9054	13383	12069	−134	7647

NOTE: n.a. means not applicable.
SOURCE: See source to Table 146.

Figure 71:
Mean present value of net CPP benefits by age of head for all
family units, Ontario 1973
Source: Tables 146 and 147

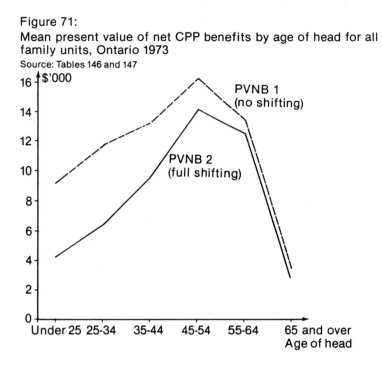

what some of the distributional characteristics of the Plan would be if no
change in the rules were to take place during the lives of the present
generation.[7]

One may also note from Tables 146 and 147 that the gains in terms of
discounted net benefits vary substantially across age groups and are greatest
for the middle-aged groups, particularly those aged 45–54 (i.e., the 1919–28
cohort), which already receive the highest incomes. The youngest workers
receive relatively less because they pay in for almost all their earning career
and receive benefits only at a distant future time. The oldest group, on the
other hand, receive very little because they have been caught in the transitional phase of the Plan and are often too old to have paid in long enough
to benefit much from it. Thus the age pattern of discounted net benefits
under the current Plan as illustrated in Figure 71 is not unlike the cross-

---

7 If the deficit were made up out of general federal government tax revenues, there would
clearly be redistributional effects associated with that as well. But since the redistributional incidence of general government revenues is so complex and distinct from that of
a particular plan such as the CPP, our analysis has been restricted to the Plan itself.

TABLE 148
Inequality measures[a] by age of head for net worth holdings for families of two or more

Measure	Under 25	25–34	35–44	45–54	55–64	65 & over	All ages
Shares							
Bottom 10%	−11.2	−3.1	−0.9	−0.3	−0.2	0.3	−1.0
Bottom quintile	−19.1	−4.1	−0.2	1.1	0.9	2.1	−0.7
2nd quintile	−5.7	2.0	7.3	8.8	9.0	8.6	5.0
3rd quintile	4.1	11.3	16.2	15.9	17.5	17.0	14.3
4th quintile	19.6	26.4	25.7	26.4	27.4	27.1	26.6
Top quintile	101.2	64.4	51.1	47.7	45.2	45.3	54.8
Top 10%	71.0	41.9	30.6	29.1	27.5	27.6	33.3
Top 5%	42.3	26.5	17.8	17.7	16.7	16.8	20.0
Gini coefficient	1.136	0.686	0.509	0.469	0.451	0.443	0.559
Coef of variation	2.33	1.31	0.81	0.81	0.77	0.76	0.99
Mean ($)	2348	11440	26538	36415	43315	42780	27986
Median ($)	530	6554	20435	27811	33202	32482	18677

a Inequality figures refer to 1970, the mean and median figures to estimates for 1973.
SOURCE: See source to Table 63.

sectional age pattern of total family income receipts that have already been studied in earlier chapters. Consequently, we find that the CPP tends to increase inequality between age groups, and that at least part of this effect is due to the way in which the CPP was phased in.

Turning to the pattern of inequality within age groups, one notes that equality in the distribution of net benefits appears greatest for the middle-aged groups 25–64, less so for the youngest age group, and much less for the oldest group, where net returns are very widely dispersed. Therefore, for the middle-aged groups, the CPP may well tend to reduce inequality in the distribution of resources while at the same time increasing it between age groups. Such an inference, however, requires a more detailed examination.

Accordingly, Table 148 presents estimated inequality results for private family net worth holdings. Since net worth estimates are not available for 1974, the summary inequality figures in Table 151 in fact refer to the year of the last net worth survey, 1970, while the mean and median figures are the corresponding 1970 figures proportionately inflated by the increase in family income levels over the period 1970–4. It should also be noted that the figures refer to families of two or more, whereas Tables 146 and 147

Figure 72:
Gini coefficients of private net worth holdings and of present value of net
CPP benefits 2 (full shifting) by age of head
Source: Tables 147 and 148

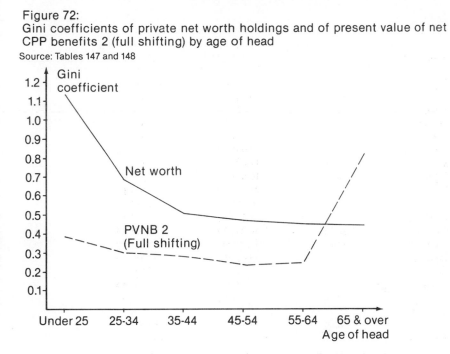

referred to all family units. Since the net worth distributions for families
of two or more (the only detailed net worth distributions available for
Ontario) are rather more equal than those for all family units, the former
are taken as a lower bound on the degree of inequality in the latter. The
summary inequality measures in these three tables show that, for all age
groups but the last, the distributions of publicly provided net worth through
expected CPP retirement net benefits are markedly more equal than the
distributions of privately held net worth. For the oldest age group, just the
reverse is true: relatively few elderly people had gained much from the CPP
by the year 1973, but many more had at least some family wealth to lean
on. These results are highlighted in Figure 72 for the case of the Gini
coefficient summary measures. Consequently, it appears that within all age
groups but the oldest, CPP net benefits have more equal distributions than
private net worth, particularly since the net worth inequality figures in
Table 148 can be thought of as lower bounds on the corresponding figures
for all family units. The reduced inequality figures also are not restricted to
particular portions of the distributions, but occur strongly at both bottom
and top ends, so that the equalization appears to be fairly widely spread.

TABLE 149
Cumulative shares for net CPP benefits and private net worth holdings

Vigintile	Net worth	Net benefits 1	Net benefits 2
First	−0.68	0.09(+)	−0.44(+)
Second	−0.97	0.38(+)	−0.67(+)
Third	−0.94	1.33(+)	−0.46(+)
Fourth	−0.73	3.32(+)	0.86(+)
Fifth	−0.22	5.91(+)	2.89(+)
Sixth	0.76	9.03(+)	5.46(+)
Seventh	2.24	12.69(+)	8.51(+)
Eighth	4.28	16.85(+)	12.02(+)
Ninth	6.91	21.41(+)	15.96(+)
Tenth	10.14	26.25(+)	20.36(+)
Eleventh	14.00	31.41(+)	25.23(+)
Twelfth	18.55	36.90(+)	30.62(+)
Thirteenth	23.80	42.76(+)	36.52(+)
Fourteenth	29.75	49.03(+)	42.89(+)
Fifteenth	36.69	55.71(+)	49.82(+)
Sixteenth	45.15	62.89(+)	57.46(+)
Seventeenth	55.16	70.68(+)	65.80(+)
Eighteenth	66.72	79.19(+)	75.15(+)
Nineteenth	80.05	88.62(+)	85.88(+)
Twentieth	100.00	100.00	100.00

SOURCE: See source to Table 146.

On comparing mean net worth and net benefit figures *between* age groups, one notes that the largest net benefit gains go to the middle-aged group, 45–54, who already have high mean wealth holdings, but the smallest gains go to the oldest age group, who have even higher mean net worth holdings. In other words, net CPP benefits tend to increase absolute differentials in mean wealth holdings between young and middle-aged workers and then slightly reduce and reverse them between middle-aged and the elderly.

Given that CPP net benefits appear to be more equally distributed within most age groups than private net worth holdings, but to accentuate in some cases mean differentials between age groups, what can one conclude about the relative inequality of net benefits over all age groups together? Table 149 presents in some detail the cumulative shares for all ages together of private net worth holdings and of the present values of net benefits from the CPP. As can be seen, both net benefit cumulative shares lie uniformly

TABLE 150
Proportion of median net benefits to median net benefits and
net worth combined, by age of head for families of two or more,
Ontario 1973

Age	Net benefits 1	Net benefits 2
Under 25	0.952	0.907
25–34	0.647	0.503
35–44	0.392	0.315
45–54	0.363	0.333
55–64	0.294	0.275
65 and over	0.052	0.023
All ages	0.398	0.307

SOURCE: See source to Table 146.

TABLE 151
Summary distribution measures by income class for present value of net CPP benefits 1
(no shifting) for all family units, Ontario 1973

Measure	Under 3000	3000–5999	6000–8999	9000–11999	12000–14999	15000–19999	20000 & over	All groups
Mean ($)	3741	6343	10070	12245	13495	15817	17808	11119
Median ($)	3073	6027	9753	12051	13323	15330	16755	10776
Gini coefficient	0.536	0.392	0.259	0.216	0.195	0.182	0.205	0.336
Coef of variation	1.00	0.91	0.73	0.71	0.73	0.70	0.71	0.75
Atkinson index ($\epsilon = 1.55$)	0.761	0.675	0.423	0.186	0.137	0.096	0.134	0.602

SOURCE: See source to Table 146.

and fairly substantially above the private net worth shares, so that both net
benefit Lorenz curves lie uniformly inside that for private wealth holdings
with net benefits 1 (i.e., with no tax shifting) being the most equal. In
general, then, one can conclude that CPP net benefits at the current rate of
discount do indeed appear to be a good deal more equally distributed than
private net worth holdings.

The relative importance of the CPP benefits compared to private net
worth holdings, however, changes quite dramatically across age groups.
Table 150 shows the ratio of median net benefits for families of two or

TABLE 152
Summary distribution measures by income class for present value of net CPP benefits 2
(full shifting) for all family units, Ontario 1973

Measure	Under 3000	3000– 5999	6000– 8999	9000– 11999	12000– 14999	15000– 19999	20000 & over	All groups
Mean ($)	2811	4945	7689	9394	10406	12534	15105	8257
Median ($)	1905	4402	6718	8214	9205	11141	13581	8647
Gini coefficient	0.745	0.543	0.408	0.365	0.324	0.294	0.291	0.416
Coef of variation	1.28	1.12	0.94	0.94	0.97	0.90	0.85	0.95
Atkinson index	n.a.	n.a.	n.a.	0.602	0.368	0.234	0.246	n.a.

NOTE: n.a. means not applicable.
SOURCE: See source to Table 146.

more to the median of CPP net benefits and private net worth combined for each age group. As can be seen, CPP net benefits constitute on average about 30 to 40 per cent of the total, but the proportion declines dramatically with age from over 90 per cent for the youngest age group to 5 per cent or less for the oldest. The CPP proportion essentially represents future expectations of gains while the net worth proportion reflects current actual wealth holdings. The youngest workers have low current holdings but relatively high expectations of future gains; the oldest age group, on the other hand, has already built up much more substantial current holdings, but has limited opportunity for expectations of future gains.

We are also interested in the distributional pattern of CPP net retirement benefits by income class. These summary inequality results are presented in Tables 151 and 152, the first again referring to the case of no tax shifting of employer contributions and the second to full shifting of the tax. Mean and median net benefits can be seen to rise steadily with income, though somewhat less than proportionally (see Figure 73 for the means); in other words, CPP net benefits do not appear to be distributionally neutral compared to family income but rather somewhat regressive.[8] That is, social security wealth provided in the form of discounted CPP net benefits tends to be greater at higher incomes though less than proportionately so. Summary inequality measures generally tend to decline with incomes since the lowest income category includes a large number of retired family units whereas the

8 Viewed in terms of the ratio PVNB/Income, however, the CPP may be seen as proportionally progressive since this ratio tends to decline somewhat with higher incomes.

Figure 73:
Mean present value of net CPP benefits by income for all family units,
Ontario 1973
Source: Tables 151 and 152

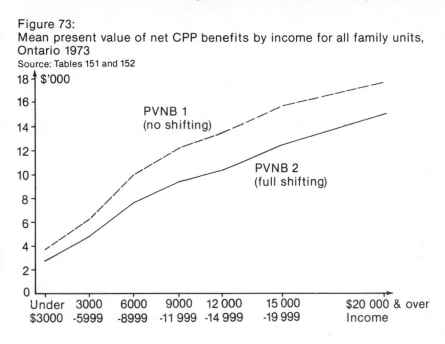

TABLE 153
Summary distribution measures by income class for private net worth holdings for
families of two or more, Ontario 1973

Measure	Under $4000	$4000–6999	$7000–9999	$10000–14999	$15000–& over	All incomes
Mean ($)	13503	14706	15674	20219	42254	20134
Median ($)	6241	8846	10174	15727	31965	13437
Gini coefficient	0.729	0.647	0.570	0.501	0.396	0.559
Coef of variation	1.29	1.18	1.02	0.88	0.68	0.99
Atkinson index ($\epsilon = 1.55$)	n.a.	n.a.	0.873	0.722	0.480	n.a.

NOTE: n.a. means not applicable.
SOURCE: See source to Table 146.

TABLE 154
Proportion of median net benefits to median net benefits and
net worth combined, by income class for families of
two or more, Ontario 1973

Income ($)	Net benefits 1	Net benefits 2
Less than 3000	0.309	0.244
3000–5999	0.617	0.517
6000–8999	0.749	0.596
9000–11 999	0.604	0.513
12 000–14 999	0.538	0.438
15 000–19 999	0.418	0.326
20 000 and over	0.322	0.258
All incomes	0.398	0.307

SOURCE: See source to Table 146.

highest has many recipients who are earning at or above the maximum pensionable earnings level over long periods of time. Corresponding results for private net worth holdings are also presented in Table 153 for families of two or more. Inequality also tends to decline with higher income levels. But mean and median net worth holdings now increase more than proportionally with income. Again it appears that CPP net benefits are more equally distributed across income classes than private net worth holdings. Table 154 also provides figures on the ratio of median net benefits to the median of the distribution of net benefits and private wealth holdings combined. As can be seen in this case, the proportion of net benefits first rises with income levels and then declines again, so that the relative importance of net benefits appears greatest for the middle income range $6000–$8999 (in 1973) and least for the lowest and very top income groups.

In general, then, the present value of net benefits not only varies systematically with age much like that of family total income and thus favours middle-aged cohorts over very young and elderly cohorts, but also appears more equally distributed than private net worth holdings in general and increases steadily with family income levels though less than proportionately.

SUMMARY

This chapter has examined the distribution of net benefits under the current rules of the Canada Pension Plan as an illustration of the use of an intertemporal life cycle framework for analysing the distribution of publicly provided social security benefits. The lifetime earnings simulation model that we developed and used incorporates the main aspects of the CPP tax and benefit structure. When it was applied to the family units on the SCF Ontario file, several important findings were obtained.

– The present value of net benefits for the CPP are generally positive and large: they average about 30 to 40 per cent of net benefits plus net worth holdings for families, so that the Plan as now constituted is not actuarially sound and will probably have to tax workers in future more heavily to maintain current benefit levels.

– Different cohorts in the population are benefiting in greatly varying degrees from the CPP; the greatest gains are going to the cohorts that were middle-aged (particularly those 45–54) in 1973 and that already received the highest incomes. The youngest and oldest workers benefited relatively little. These inter-cohort effects are at least in part attributable to the way the CPP was phased in.

– Within age groups (except the oldest) as well as over-all, summary inequality in net benefits is substantially less than that for private net worth holdings, so that, in general, CPP net benefits appear to have a fairly strong equalizing effect compared to net worth holdings.

– Across income classes in the population, the present value of CPP net benefits tend to rise with income levels (thus being regressive), though less than proportionally.

– In general it appears that the distributional effects of CPP net benefits are fairly large; however, because of the very marked transitory effect associated with the way the Plan was phased in, its effects are not as equalizing as one might have expected.

14

Summary and conclusions

SUMMARY

This study has had four objectives: (1) to review recent theoretical work in the distribution area in order to provide an analytical background for the subsequent empirical work, (2) to assemble in one place the data available on the present distribution of income and wealth for Ontario, (3) to try to evaluate the adequacy of conventional income distribution figures as proxies for the underlying distribution of economic well-being, and (4) to point out the importance of the distributional effects of government social security programs that have intertemporal characteristics.

The first objective has been addressed in Part One, which contains a background survey of some of the current work on size distribution theory with special emphasis on the theory of life-cycle income and wealth behaviour. The second objective is addressed in Part Two, where fairly extensive distributional data have been provided on incomes of individuals and family units, and assets and net worth of families in Ontario. The third objective has prompted the work in Part Three on under-reporting of income; imputation of income in kind; measurement of after-tax income; adjustments for regional cost-of-living differences and for family size, composition, and circumstances; adjustment for accrued capital gains; and adjustment for net worth holdings as well as income. The fourth objective is addressed in Chapter 13, in which a life-cycle earnings simulation model has been developed and applied to a distributional analysis of the Canada Pension Plan.

In the theoretical review in Part One, it was seen that recent theoretical models of size distribution provide a fairly elaborate framework for empirical study, particularly within the context of life-cycle behaviour. Capital income tends to become more important with age, particularly toward retirement when earnings fall off. Earned income reflects work effort, market skill acquisition, family involvement, and non-pecuniary preferences. Among men this would be expected to be manifested in a positively sloped but concave longitudinal earnings profile until a peak in later middle age, with inequality generally increasing from early middle age until retirement. In the life-cycle theories, income differences arise from opportunities and choices over the economic life cycle about expenditures and capital accumulation, education and on-the-job training, type of occupation, work effort, and time spent in the home. Thus income differences (given factor prices) are attributed to individuals' tastes on the one hand and to various background resource constraints they face in making their choices on the other.

Chapter 3 examined how demand-side factors in the labour market can affect workers' employment opportunities and earnings differentials. The main implication of the cost-minimizing behaviour surveyed lies in the incentives that firms offer and the restrictions they impose upon the labour market opportunities and earnings differentials faced by individual workers. Job access may be based on screens, and different wages paid on the basis of the particular group (sex, race, or ethnic background) that a worker happens to belong to. Promotion policies affect the level that a worker is likely to attain in his career. Chapter 4 then discussed briefly how demand- and supply-sides of the labour market can be brought together when labour is heterogeneous in order to determine a matrix of market wage rates faced by individuals and firms. Given these wage rates and corresponding life-cycle trajectories, one can then build up an over-all distribution of income and show how demographic factors and cohort effects interact to determine the observed cross-sectional structure of an income distribution.

In the chapters on empirical background in Part Two, life-cycle patterns indeed showed up very markedly in the Ontario data. Individual incomes vary significantly with age according to labour market attachment and experience, educational attainment and occupation, transfer receipts and investment benefits. Cross-sectional income profiles also tend to be concave with respect to age, first rising and then flattening or declining in later middle age. The empirical results also highlight the critical importance from a distributional point of view of individuals' labour market attachment and education-occupation opportunities. Those with very low incomes tend to have relatively weak and discontinuous labour market experience and low education and occupational skill levels; those with high incomes tend to have very strong and continuous market experience and high education and occupational skill levels.

In the case of incomes of family units, two additional dimensions are highlighted in the empirical results: family size (or the distinction between families and unattached individuals), and the number of income earners in the family. Life-cycle patterns of labour supply and income receipts differ substantially between the two types of family units and also between primary and secondary income recipients within the family unit. Consequently, the labour supply effects of different government programs should be carefully considered, particularly for secondary workers in family units. While primary earners may not change their work patterns much in response to income support or social security programs, the labour supply response of secondary earners, particularly wives, may be much more sensitive.

Turning to the wealth aspect of family economic status, one notes that asset holdings and net worth are much more unequally distributed than family income. While cross-sectional income receipts tend first to rise with age, to peak around later middle age, and then to decline markedly, family net worth holdings generally increase with age right up until retirement, and then flatten out during early retirement. Within age groups, net worth inequality tends to decline slightly with age (in the cross-section), while net worth differences between age groups widen strongly. These strong age effects on net worth reflect life-cycle patterns simultaneously in asset holdings and debts that tend to be associated with the stages of (1) family investment in housing, (2) gradual repayment of mortgage, and then (3) gradual shift toward financial assets with approaching retirement.

Part Three then considers the degree to which observed distributions of income are reasonable representations of the underlying distribution of economic well-being across the province. Accordingly, Chapters 9–13 examine a number of adjustments to the reported family income distribution figures to take account of various limitations or problems in using raw family income data as a proxy for economic well-being. In Chapter 9, adjustment for under-reporting of Unemployment Insurance benefits, Social Assistance benefits, other government transfer receipts, farm and non-farm self-employment income, and net investment income yield jointly only a slight increase in inequality: 3 per cent in the Gini coefficient for family units, compared for example, to a 14 per cent reduction in the Gini coefficient corresponding to the addition of direct government transfer income to original factor income. Adjustment for income in kind from farming and imputed income from owner-occupied housing yields a moderate reduction in inequality figures among families of 8½ per cent for the Gini coefficient and a fairly strong reduction of 17 per cent in the Gini coefficient for families aged 65 and over.

Chapter 10 adjusted family incomes to account for differences in place of residence and in family size and composition. Adjustment for differences in location of family residence as between urban and rural areas resulted in only a slight increase in income equality. Adjustment for family size differences in terms of per capita or per adult-equivalent family income had a strong but mixed effect on inequality. Further adjustment by adult equivalents to account also for sex of family head and whether or not the family head is aged also yielded a strong but mixed pattern of results. In general the results suggest that differences in family size and composition have a very substantial effect on the structure of family economic well-being, so that such adjustments ought to be incorporated into the distributional analysis of public programs.

Chapter 11 adjusted the family income to include accrued capital gains on family asset holdings. Two sets of adjustments were performed, one for the observed asset price changes in 1973, and the other for a more 'normal' set of hypothetical price changes. When adjustment was made for accrued capital gains incurred in 1973, mean incomes increased substantially, and inequality figures showed very strong but conflicting changes. Within the oldest age group, however, inequality figures were reduced very substantially. On the other hand, when adjustment was made for the hypothetical set of asset price changes, mean incomes increased moderately, and summary inequality figures showed a weak reduction in inequality with again the oldest age group experiencing the strongest inequality reduction. In general, it was found that the inequality effects of adjusting for accrued capital gains can also be rather significant and can differ very substantially in size and even direction from one period to another according to the patterns of asset price changes that occur, particularly with respect to house prices.

In Chapter 12, adjustment was made to family income figures to reflect family holdings of net worth and the potential consumption they provide. Two adjustment procedures were performed, which yielded generally similar results. For the Weisbrod-Hansen procedure, for example, inequality generally increased moderately to substantially as non-aged higher-income groups tend to have higher wealth holdings. Younger groups under the age of 35 experienced relatively little change in inequality, and the oldest group aged 65 and over had a slight reduction in summary inequality. Thus the inequality effects of adjusting for family net worth holdings can also be important, and such an adjustment should be made in distributional analysis of public programs.

Finally, Chapter 13 considered the distribution of net benefits of public-sector resources and specifically the distribution of net benefits under the Canada Pension Plan. A lifetime earnings simulation model was developed, which incorporated the main aspects of the CPP tax and benefit structure and applied to the Ontario micro data file. We found that the present values of net benefits for the CPP are generally positive and large, averaging about 30–40 per cent of net benefits plus net worth holdings for families. Consequently, the Plan as constituted is not actuarially sound and will probably have to tax workers more heavily in future to maintain current benefit levels or else reduce those levels. Different cohorts in the population, however, are benefiting in greatly varying degrees from the CPP: the greatest gains are going to the cohorts that were middle-aged (particularly those 45–54) in 1973 and that already received the highest incomes. The youngest and oldest workers benefit relatively little. Over-all, as well as within age groups (except the oldest), inequality in net benefits is substantially less than for private net worth holdings, so that in general CPP net benefits appear to have a fairly strong equalizing effect compared to private net worth holdings. The distributional effects of CPP net benefits are thus substantial, though not as equalizing as one might initially have thought because of the marked cohort effect.

CONCLUDING REMARKS

The detailed findings of the study suggest several more general conclusions that are related to policy. First, it should be remarked that the life-cycle framework is a very useful one in which to evaluate the distributional effects of some background factors and government programs, particularly the ones that are intertemporal. Social security programs, such as old-age benefits and the Canada Pension Plan, can affect not only private savings incentives but also the age of retirement and the labour supply patterns of secondary workers. Legislation affecting retirement age may have very strong distributional effects because of the steep fall-off in income at time of retirement. Medicare and other forms of health insurance may affect not only workers' health capital, but also the continuity of their employment histories, their accumulated on-the-job experience, and their age of retirement. Access to mortgage credit for prospective home buyers can affect the labour supply of secondary workers in the household. But before precise answers can be provided about the magnitudes and lag patterns of such effects, much more effort must be expended on modelling the effects of such programs in a life-cycle framework, acquiring longitudinal data files on family income, assets, and work histories, and obtaining substantially improved estimates of the critical parameters of family life-cycle behaviour.

The life-cycle framework also suggests a useful distinction for policy purposes between (1) persons with low long-run income status and little expectation of future income gains because of age, infirmity, or low market valuation of their particular skills; and (2) those with expectations of higher incomes in the future, but who have temporarily low incomes because of school attendance or employment change. The first group tends to have relatively restricted opportunities and little to fall back on in periods of low income, while the second has greater opportunities still open to it and more resources to carry it through. Accordingly, the same kinds of policies are not suitable for the two groups. For the latter, there should be more emphasis on income insurance, improved access to capital markets, and reduced employment restrictions. For the former group, however, direct transfers, categorical income-support, manpower retraining, and so on would be more suitable. That is, since low-income households are a hetero-geneous group with widely differing opportunities and expectations, what is needed is a range of programs appropriate to the different types of family units that are found near the bottom end of the distribution and not just a single transfer program such as a negative income tax.

The life-cycle framework also highlights the systematic and long-run nature of many income differences, and shows that behind the observed distribution of incomes lie more basic underlying distributions of wealth (human and non-human). These stocks of wealth represent the productive bases for market rates of remuneration and serve as vehicles for transmission of economic opportunity and status from one generation to the next. Therefore, if there are to be policies for reducing economic inequalities, they ought to recognize the source of these inequalities in wealth stocks and not just consider observed differences in current income.

The second general comment concerns the very marked patterns of income differences revealed by the data in Part Two, particularly with respect to life-cycle characteristics of households. High-income households tend to have a male head in later middle age, perhaps self-employed, and near the peak of his lifetime earnings profile. The head has a high level of education and has worked steadily in an occupation or career offering the opportunity of substantially increased earnings as greater on-the-job experience is gained. Since the family no longer has young children, the wife may also work. A fair amount of capital income may also be received from business ventures, from accumulated savings for the approaching retirement, and perhaps from inheritances. Low-income households, on the other hand, are of a more heterogeneous make-up and generally lack the above combination of attributes. They include young and old households near the beginning and end of their lifetime income profiles where the household head may not hold a full-time job because he is still completing his education or is retired from full-time employment in the labour force.

Such family units tend to be small, consisting of only one or two persons, and non-labour income in the form of transfers, pensions, and small amounts of capital income are important sources of support. Low-income households, though, also include many with family heads in the prime-age period of their working lives. Many of these households have a female head or one without sufficient productive skills to maintain steady employment at a comfortable wage. Educational attainment tends to be low and employment history discontinuous, and much of the work experience occurs in jobs in which there are few opportunities for earnings to increase with experience. These characterizations again underline the need for different types of policies to address the different types and sources of low-income problems. For young households, policies should concentrate on easing capital market restrictions, reducing employment discrimination and barriers to job entry, improving job market information, and providing opportunities for training and employment. Elderly, retired, and disabled persons, however, would be helped more by income-support, transfer payments, and social insurance, which would help even out the peak and subsequent trough of the income profile. For prime-aged families, the emphasis should instead be on improving long-run productivity, reducing the personal costs of employment (particularly for female heads with dependent children), increasing on-the-job training and information on how to acquire it, and shortening gaps in employment.

The marked patterns of income differences by age have several further implications. The substantial age/income differences imply that demographic factors affecting the age distribution of the population may have important effects on the structure of income and wealth inequality. Several recent Canadian studies in fact reveal that this indeed appears to be the case because of recent substantial increases in the proportions of young and old income recipients in the population. Life-cycle income patterns may indeed become more marked in future as a shift continues into higher-skill occupations with steeper age/income profiles.

The analysis also underlines the problem of interpreting changes in inequality measures over time. For example, consider the limiting situation where all individuals have the same opportunities and follow the same age/income profile over their careers, but do so at different times, so that at any time individuals would appear at different points along their profile. There would still be some degree of income inequality, which would be associated with individuals being different ages in the cross-section. For that reason, much research has recently been devoted to netting out average income differences by age from inequality measures in order to isolate the income inequality component not associated with changes in the age structure of the population. Yet this does not recognize the critical difference between inequality of opportunity and inequality of outcome that is inherent in the above analysis. So long as life-cycle choices exist and individuals' tastes differ, even perfect equality of background and opportunity among children may result in marked income differences. Consequently, an issue of some concern is the limiting degree to which income concentration can result from such life-cycle choices. How, then, would the upper limits of such concentration compare with observed inequality figures, and how would the residual non-choice component of income inequality (attributable roughly to differences in background and opportunities) behave over time in aggregate and for different socio-economic groups? It is obvious that matters such as these have to be kept in mind when one is evaluating inequality statistics; hence normative inferences from observed concentration figures are not usually clear-cut. At the same time, however, the analysis of possible distributional effects of government programs should consider this question of choice versus opportunities and deprivation. Again, answers to such complex questions as those above also await much more realistic and detailed theoretical models, richer sources of data, and improved parameter estimates than are now available.

A third remark arising from the study is the importance of cohort effects in the ways that different age groups are treated in the economy in both private sector and public programs. As reported in Chapter 11, for example, very substantial capital gains accrued to homeowners in 1973, a large proportion of whom were middle-aged family heads and only a small proportion of whom were young family heads. A prolonged economic depression may permanently lower the earnings profile of workers who are young at the time because of the employment experience lost. Chapter 13 explains how the structure of the Canada Pension Plan was found to benefit certain middle-aged cohorts compared to other age groups because of the way the Plan was phased in. Inequality between cohorts is thus an important aspect of distribution, and such cases illustrate the need for greater recognition of inequality of treatment and opportunity between different cohorts in the population.

The fourth principal remark is that studies like the present one omit an important dynamic aspect of the distribution of income. Incomes may suffer unexpected shocks and instability from one period to the next, thereby preventing one from making long-run plans that could improve one's economic status. Such instability of income may also be correlated with average levels of income. If so, the mean income of a group would not alone be an adequate indicator of their long-run economic opportunities. More generally, one would wish to know the patterns between incomes in a single year and average incomes over two years, five years, or even longer. That is, what is the relationship between current income levels as conventionally reported and long-run or 'permanent' income status? Again, aggregate inequality figures are uninformative about underlying inequality in long-run income status.

Individuals are also expected to experience some mobility through the income distribution, and this affects our evaluation of aggregate inequality figures as well. On the one hand, a given (cross-sectional) income distribution may result from everyone moving through the distribution along their income profile in identical fashion over their life cycle. On the other hand, a distribution of the same shape (and same associated inequality figures) may result from people remaining perfectly static at the same relative positions in the distribution over time. The normative implications of the inequality figures in the two cases, however, are clearly different. It is thus a matter of some importance to know how much opportunity, if any, individuals have to move between points in the income distribution, particularly in the case of such groups as women and immigrants. Certainly, life-cycle models suggest there is some degree of mobility through the income distribution as individuals move up and then down their lifetime income profiles. Answers to questions of income instability and income-class mobility, however, cannot be obtained from the cross-sectional data used in this study, but require longitudinal micro data on household members' income and work experience over time – data not available for Canada. There is obviously a need for standard longitudinal data if further progress is to be made on issues of income dynamics and the corresponding interpretation of (cross sectional) inequality figures.

The final general remark is that conventional income distribution figures are only very imperfect estimates of the state of inequality in the distribution of economic well-being. The life-cycle theory reviewed in Part One implies that current income is not a very good index of economic well-being, which is more closely related to the long-run or 'permanent' income and wealth status of a household. Observed current income differences reflect in part individuals' preferences for non-pecuniary benefits, future consumption opportunities, risk aversion, enterprise, leisure, and home activity. This is particularly true of young and retired households at the low end of their income histories and of prime-aged households at the peak of their earnings profiles. Consequently, current income figures alone may give a distorted view of the distribution of economic well-being across the population. Similarly, a cross section of incomes in a given year does not reflect the income dynamics and income-class mobility that may be present in the distribution. As just discussed, a high degree of immobility suggests that there should be more concern by society about income inequality figures. It may also be true that income immobility occurs in differing degrees in different regions of the distribution; for example, income mobility may be much more characteristic of middle portions of the distribution than the top or bottom, where there may be greater rigidity of income.

Conventional income statistics are very imperfect proxies for economic well-being, as the empirical analysis of Part Two also indicates, because reported total family income does not include various omitted forms of income, differences in family circumstances and composition, capital gains accruals, potential consumption benefits from private net worth holdings, and public 'wealth' benefits. Some of these have been shown to have fairly significant effects on inequality figures, particularly for specific groups in the population. Indeed, there are a number of trends that are likely to make the relationship between total family income and economic well-being even more tenuous – many people are choosing non-pecuniary job benefits or preferring leisure to income; more and more families have two, or several, wage earners; more and more people are able to choose the size of their family; an increasing number of families are being divided into two or more separate households as different generations move out and as increased separations occur. Inequality figures for family incomes reported for a given year thus need to be viewed with some care as to their normative interpretation.

Policy analysis also ought to take account of various income adjustments considered in Part Three, particularly the adjustments for family size and composition and for capital gains and wealth holdings. It should be clear, however, that our various adjustments to family income were neither exhaustive nor fully integrated and that a good deal of work still remains to be done on obtaining improved estimates of the distribution of economic well-being. Substantial work has recently been done in the related field of estimating the average 'quality of life' in Canada and elsewhere. The point of the present study is that one should also look at the parallel issue of estimating the *distribution* of participation in the quality of life or what has been called in this study economic well-being. Clearly, these two fields of inquiry should be brought together in future work, for they touch upon similar normative issues and could usefully complement each other.

APPENDICES

Measuring inequality of income

This appendix reviews in more technical fashion the inequality measures presented in Chapter 5.

SUMMARY MEASURES

In the following discussion, an income distribution is assumed to be characterized by a continuous density function $f(y)$ defined over positive values of income. The mean of the distribution is then given by

$$\mu = \int_0^\infty y f(y) \, dy$$

and the median by μ_d such that

$$\int_0^{\mu_d} f(y) \, dy = 1/2 = \int_{\mu_d}^\infty f(y) \, dy.$$

The variance is expressed as

$$\sigma^2 = \int_0^\infty (y - \mu)^2 f(y) \, dy$$

and the standard deviation by the non-negative square root of σ^2. The mean difference is given by

$$\Delta = \int_0^\infty \int_0^\infty |x - y| f(x) f(y) \, dx dy.$$

The Gini coefficient of concentration is then given by $G = \Delta/2\mu$ and the coefficient of concentration by $V = \sigma/\mu$. Sample estimates of these measures based on grouped data can be obtained, for example, from Kendall and Stuart (1969).

LORENZ CURVES AND RELATIVE MEAN INCOME CURVES

In describing the Lorenz curve, let the horizontal axis or abscissa of the curve be represented by the cumulated proportion of income recipients

$$F(y) = \int_0^y f(u)\, du,$$

where $F(y)$ clearly lies between zero and one. The vertical axis or ordinate of the curve is the corresponding proportion of total income in the distribution as expressed by

$$\phi(y) = \int_0^y \frac{u}{\mu} f(u)\, du,$$

which is also bounded by zero and one. The Lorenz curve then represents the proportion of income that the lower $100 \cdot F(y)$ per cent of the distribution receive and can be expressed symbolically as $\phi(F)$.

For the relative mean income curve, the abscissa is the same as for the Lorenz curve, while the ordinate is the derivative of the Lorenz curve:

$$\frac{d\phi}{dF} = \frac{d\phi/dy}{dF/dy} = \frac{yf(y)/\mu}{f(y)} = \frac{y}{\mu}.$$

For further details on the relationship between standard inequality measures and the underlying income density function, see Levine and Singer (1970) and Kendall and Stuart (1969, 40–51).

ATKINSON'S INEQUALITY MEASURE

In deriving his measure of inequality, Atkinson (1970) imposes certain conditions of reasonableness and convenience that he would wish such a measure to satisfy. He begins by assuming that the inequality criterion is based on a social welfare function W, which is symmetric and additively separable in the functions $U(y)$ of individual incomes:

$$W = \int_0^\infty U(y) f(y)\, dy.$$

The $U(y)$ function is a weighting function associated with each income level. Each recipient's well-being depends only on his own income, and all individuals with the same incomes are assumed to be equally well off. Y_A in Figure 22 is consequently defined by

$$U(Y_A) \int_0^\infty f(y) \, dy \; = \; \int_0^\infty U(y) f(y) \, dy,$$

so that one can see that Y_A, and thus the inequality index I, clearly depends on the weighting function $U(y)$.

Atkinson then specifies the $U(y)$ function to satisfy certain desirable properties. It is assumed to have the conventional utility-function properties of being increasing and concave (so that $U' > 0$ and $U'' \leq 0$) thus establishing the curvature of CAD in Figure 22. Finally, if the inequality index I is invariant to proportional shifts in all incomes, $U(y)$ must be homothetic (so that all indifference curves are multiples of any representative curve) of the form

$$U(y) \; = \; A + B \frac{(y/\mu)^{1-\epsilon}}{1-\epsilon}, \qquad \text{for } 1 \neq \epsilon \geq 0$$

and

$$U(y) \; = \; \ln (y/\mu), \qquad \text{for } \epsilon = 1.$$

Consequently, the resulting Atkinson inequality measure takes the form

$$I \; = \; 1 - [\int_0^\infty (\tfrac{y}{\mu})^{1-\epsilon} f(y) \, dy]^{1/(1-\epsilon)}, \qquad \text{for } \epsilon \neq 1.$$

The particular shape of the indifference curves, and thus the degree to which the population is assumed to be willing to trade off income for less inequality, is determined uniquely by the 'inequality aversion' parameter ϵ, which Atkinson argues will reasonably be assumed to take on values in the range of one to 2.5.

Definitions of terms used in Chapter 6

The following terms are arranged alphabetically. The definitions are taken from Statistics Canada (1975a).

Class of worker. This refers to the classification of employment according to whether a person, in the job reported, mainly worked for someone else for wages, salaries, tips, or commissions, or helped without pay in a 'family farm or business;' or mainly worked for himself with or without paid help. The job reported was his job in the week prior to enumeration, if employed, or his job of longest duration since 1 January 1970 if not employed in that week. The three categories are

1 Wage earners – those working for wages, salary, tips or commission, piece rates, or payment 'in kind' in non-family enterprises.

2 Self-employed persons – those fifteen years and over who had worked since 1 January 1970, and for whom the job reported consisted mainly of self employment in their own business, professional practice, or farm.

3 Others – residual category including unpaid family workers and persons who had not worked since 1 January 1970.

Education or schooling level. This refers to the highest grade or year of elementary school, secondary school, or university attended.

Income. This refers to total income received by persons fifteen years and over during 1970 from wages and salaries, business or professional practice, farm operations, family and youth allowances, government old age pensions, other government payments, retirement pensions from previous employment, bond and deposit interest and dividends, other investment sources, and other sources. Income may be either positive or negative (i.e., a loss).

Income recipient. This refers to a person who receives non-zero income.

Labour force status. This refers to a person's labour force activity in the week immediately preceding the census enumeration. The three categories are

1 Employed labour force – those who worked for pay or profit in the armed forces or civilian labour force, those who worked in unpaid family work, and those who had a job but did not work.

2 Unemployed labour force – those who were either looking for work or on temporary lay off.

3 Not in labour force – those aged fifteen years and over who are not included in either (1) or (2) above.

Major source of income. This refers to the component that constitutes the largest proportion of the total income received. The six categories are

1 Wages and salaries – all wages, salaries, tips, commissions, bonuses, and piece-rate reimbursement before deductions.

2 Non-farm self-employment income – total gross receipts less operational expenses received from the respondent's non-farm unincorporated business or professional practice including partnerships (also referred to as income from business or professional practice).

3 Farm self-employment income – total receipts from farm sales less depreciation and operational expenses during 1970.

4 Government transfer income – family and youth allowance receipts to mothers and guardians of children, Old Age Security payments, provincial Old Age Assistance payments, and all payments under the Canada or Quebec Pension Plans, unemployment insurance receipts, veterans' pensions and allowances, cash welfare payments, workmen's compensation, mothers' allowances, training allowances, and pensions to widows, blind, and disabled.

5 Investment income – interest on deposits in banks, trust companies, co-operatives, and credit unions, the yield from bonds and debentures, and dividends from stocks and shares, mortgage interest, net rents, estate income and interest or cash dividends from insurance policies.

6 Retirement pensions and other income – income received as a result of previous employment of either the respondent or a deceased relative, and such forms of income received on a regular basis as alimony, child support, payment from Children's Aid, net income from roomers and boarders, scholarships, strike pay, royalties, and pensions received from abroad.

Marital status. This includes three categories:

1 single

2 married (with spouse either present or absent)

3 other – widowed, divorced, separated.

Mother tongue. This refers to the first language learned that is still understood.

Occupations. This refers to the kind of work the person was doing, as determined by his reporting of his kind of work, his description of his most important duties, and the job title. The categories provided by the Public Use Sample Tape are:

1 Managerial, administrative, and related occupations
2 Occupations in natural sciences, engineering, and mathematics
3 Occupations in social sciences and related fields
4 Occupations in religion
5 Teaching and related occupations
6 Occupations in medicine and health
7 Artistic, literary, recreation, and related occupations
8 Clerical and related occupations
9 Sales occupations
10 Service occupations
11 Farming, horticultural, and animal husbandry occupations
12 Other primary occupations
13 Processing occupations
14 Machining and product fabrication, assembling, and repairing
15 Construction trades occupations
16 Transport equipment operating occupations
17 Other occupations
18 Occupation not stated
19 Not applicable (because persons did not work).

Definitions of asset components in Chapter 8

The following terms and definitions are taken from Statistics Canada (1973, 73–5).

Cash on hand. Currency and such 'near money' as uncashed cheques, money orders, etc.

Savings deposits. Chartered bank savings deposits and savings certificates, desposits with savings banks such as the Post Office Savings Bank and provincial and district banks, with credit unions and caisses populaires, with trust, loan, and insurance companies, and deposits held with stock brokers, investment dealers and stores; the value of deposit and guaranteed investment certificates of trust companies; and loan debentures of loan companies.

Other deposits. Deposits with chartered banks held in the form of current or personal chequing accounts.

Other than Canada Savings Bonds. Holdings of Government of Canada bonds (other than Canada Savings Bonds) including both direct issues by the Federal Government and issues of other bonds guaranteed by the Government of Canada such as the guaranteed Canadian National Railway bonds; also holdings of all other bonds and debenture issues such as provincial and municipal government bonds, public utility bonds, and industrial and other corporate bonds; also includes holdings of foreign bonds and debentures.

Stocks. Current market value of all stocks, shares in mutual funds, rights and warrants that are traded on stock exchanges or over the counter; value of shares in private investment clubs or non-traded (private) mutual funds.

Mortgage holdings. Mortgages held on residential or other types of property.

Miscellaneous non-liquid financial assets. Loans to other persons outside the family unit, assets in a trust fund or estate (provided the respondent is allowed to draw on the capital of the fund), and other assets such as oil royalties, patents, copyrights, etc.

Market value of home. Estimated market value of owner-occupied homes.

Market value of vacation home. Estimated market value of vacation home provided such a home is customarily or occasionally used by the family unit.

Investment in other real estate. Equity value (estimated market value less mortgage outstanding) in real estate other than owner-occupied homes and vacation homes.

Value of cars. Estimated market value of all cars owned by the family unit.

Not included in these measured asset components are

– equity in business or professional interests; i.e., net investment in business or professional practices in which the family unit was engaged (at the time of the survey) on the basis of sole proprietorship, partnership, or private corporation.

– insurance, pensions, and annuity savings. No data were collected in the survey on these contractual savings.

For a discussion of these and other limitations of the data, see Podoluk (1974) and Davies (1979).

Computation of measures of income and wealth inequality

The various inequality statistics used in this study were computed by means of a program developed by Beach and Andrew (1977). A copy of the FOR-TRAN code for the program can be obtained upon request from the authors. Following is a brief description of the structure of the program.

The first step in all the computations using micro data was to run a Statistical Package for the Social Sciences (SPSS) program on the micro data tapes to compute for each of several subgroup distributions (e.g. seven age-groups): a large number of histogram frequencies (usually 50–70 per distribution); and minimum, mean, and maximum figures for each distribution. These data then serve as input to the inequality program.

The inequality program takes the histogram input data for each group- (or age-) specific distribution and computes ninety-nine percentile income levels, $y(1), ..., y(99)$, which are subject to adding-up restrictions based on the computed mean income levels that have been read in. If the maximum income figures are not available, Pareto curves are fitted to the top end of the distributions and top percentile income levels are interpolated along the curves, again subject to the over-all adding-up restrictions. The percentile income levels then serve as the basis for all further calculations. They are aggregated up to provide vigintile income levels, vigintile means (from which the relative mean income curves can be calculated), vigintile income shares, and cumulative vigintile shares (from which the Lorenz curves can be plotted). Finally, the aggregate inequality measures such as the Gini coefficient, standard deviation, coefficient of variation, and Atkinson index (for several different values of ϵ) are computed and printed out.

Estimation of equity value of owner-occupied housing in Ontario

As indicated in the body of Chapter 9, the estimation of equity value of owner-occupied housing for home-owning family units in Ontario consisted of three steps: (1) estimate a regression equation for the net equity value in housing for all Ontario home-owning units in the Household Income, Facilities, and Equipment (HIFE) Micro Data File for 1971; (2) use this estimated relationship to impute net equity value for each Ontario home owner on the Survey of Consumer Finances (SCF) tape; (3) calculate the imputed rental income receipts by the formula given in the text and add it to the total family income figures on the tape. Details of the first two steps are reviewed in this appendix.

Determinants of equity value of housing in a cross-sectional micro-base equation include the critical factors of age, income, and family size. Age of head would be expected to have a positive effect on equity value of housing with perhaps a quadratic relationship called for to allow for a possible decrease in the rate of accumulation of housing equity with age. Similarly, total income would be expected to have a positive but perhaps quadratic effect on housing equity, other things being equal. Family size should also enter positively, and regional dummy variables are included as well. The equation was also specified with the dependent variable in log form in order to handle any heteroskedasticity that may be present in the error terms in level form. The equity value equation estimated by ordinary least squares from the subfile of Ontario home-owners from the HIFE micro data file for 1971 is thus

$$\log(\text{MV} - \text{PO}) = 7.80003 + \underset{(92.67)}{0.30449}\, D_1 + \underset{(74.38)}{0.30953}\, D_3$$

$$+ \underset{(2.953)}{0.01370}\, \text{NPER} + \underset{(95.02)}{0.05951}\, \text{AGE} - \underset{(54.37)}{0.00045}\, (\text{AGE})^2$$

$$- \underset{(12.26)}{0.13731}\, \log \text{FTI} + \underset{(25.89)}{0.01486}\, (\log \text{FTI})^2,$$

$$R^2 = 0.3489, \quad F_{7,3149} = 62.39, \quad \text{SEE} = 0.6622, \quad \text{NOBS} = 3157,$$

where MV — PO is the estimated equity value of housing (i.e., estimated market value of house minus mortgage principal outstanding): D_1 is a dummy variable assuming a value of 1 if the house is in an urban area with a population of 30000 or more, and zero otherwise; D_2 is a dummy variable assuming a value of 1 if the house is in an urban area with a population of 1000 to 30000, and zero otherwise (the omitted standard relative to which the coefficients on D_1 and D_3 are measured); D_3 is a dummy variable assuming a value of 1 if the house is in a rural area, and zero otherwise; NPER is the number of persons in the household; AGE is the age of the household head; and FTI is the reported total income of the household. The figures in brackets below each coefficient are the F-statistics for single-coefficient statistical tests.

The properties of this equation appear to be quite reasonable. Equity values are higher in large urban areas where market values are high and in rural areas where houses tend to be larger. Larger family size results in slightly higher equity value invested in the home. Age has the expected quadratic effect on equity value of housing, which first rises and then declines proportionally after a peak at age 66. The income elasticity of house equity η_{FTI} is in the reasonable range, increasing from 0.0678 to 0.1364 to 0.2049 as FTI increases from $1000 to $10000 to $100000. The first derivative

$$\partial(\text{MV} - \text{PO}) / \partial \text{FTI} = \eta_{\text{FTI}} \cdot [(\text{MV} - \text{PO}) / \text{FTI}],$$

which is positive, and the second derivative

$$\partial^2(\text{MV} - \text{PO}) / \partial \text{FTI}^2 = [\eta_{\text{FTI}}(\eta_{\text{FTI}} - 1) + 0.02972][(\text{MV} - \text{PO}) / \text{FTI}^2],$$

which, over the range of reasonable values for FTI, is clearly negative. So again we have a quadratic effect in income as well as age.

The above regression equation has been used to estimate imputed market value of housing for home-owning units on the SCF micro data file. But to do so raises several problems. First of all, the equation was estimated from data for 1971, but is used to impute equity value in housing in 1973 values. Consequently, the imputed figures from this equation were all multiplied up by a factor of 1.31 in accordance with an estimated increase in Ontario house values of 31 per cent between 1971 and 1973.[1]

Secondly, the underlying grouping of individuals into units is not the same in the two data files being used. For the SCF file, it is the census family unit, a fairly narrow definition ('immediate family') consisting of 'a husband and wife (with or without children who have never married) or a parent with one or more children who have never married, living together in the same dwelling' (Statistics Canada, 1975c, 8); whereas for the HIFE file, it is the household, a broader definition consisting of 'any person or group of persons occupying a dwelling ... a family group with or without servants, lodgers, etc., or a group of unrelated persons sharing a dwelling' (Statistics Canada, 1975d, Section 3, 1). How severe a problem it may be to change from one definition to another is not clear, but is likely to be reduced by our restricting our attention first to home-owners and then to family units of two or more. Since the household is the broader grouping of persons, if equity value of housing varies positively with family size, one may expect a downward bias on the coefficient on NPER in the above regression and thus an underestimate on average of the equity value of housing owned by family units. But these estimates are being used to approximate owner consumption of housing services; and if a family unit has non-family persons living with it, its own consumption of housing services ought to be reduced from what it otherwise would be. Therefore it is not certain that the difference in definitions will bias the over-all conclusions in the direction of inequality change from incorporating estimates of owner consumption of housing services.

Thirdly, it should be noted that the imputed equity value of housing figures for family units are estimated from a regression equation. These estimates, however, would have a rather smaller dispersion across the micro data family units than the true or actual values of housing equity because regression estimates are conditional means and thus have smaller variances than the true values. Therefore, so as not to reduce unnecessarily the dispersion in equity values (and imputed rental income) because of the regression technique employed, we added group-mean regression residuals back into the forecast of housing equity values. More specifically, estimated regression residuals were computed for different age, income, and area groups from the HIFE file, and these corresponding residuals were then added (algebraically) to the initial equity value forecasts from the regression equation. These adjusted estimates were then inflated up to 1973 values as already outlined.

Estimation of imputed assets

This appendix explains some of the more technical details of how the ASSETS figure described in Chapter 11 was generated for each family on the Survey of Consumer Finances Ontario micro data file. Data on assets made available to the authors by Statistics Canada in the form of cross-tabulations of total family asset holdings by age and employment status of head for families of two or more in Canada from the 1970 Survey of Incomes, Assets, and Indebtedness. Each cell in the cross-tabulation of family asset holdings by age and employment status of head contained a sample frequency and total assets figure and was treated as a single observation on the average value of assets for that cell.

Because of the restricted form in which the data were made available, a regression function on family asset holdings was limited to a relatively simple form. On the basis of life cycle considerations discussed in Parts One and Two, asset holdings are assumed to be a positive function of age of the family head with a quadratic term included as well to capture any concave effect in the cross-sectional age-assets profile because asset accumulation may tend to flatten out and even decline during the retirement period. Employment status of the head is represented by a set of 0–1 dummy variables, which shift both the intercept of the function as well as the linear coefficient on age. Since the size of the regression error on an equation for family asset holdings is likely to vary substantially with mean asset holdings across cells, particularly across age groups, the dependent variable of the equation has been specified in logarithmic form.

The estimation of an equation from cross-tabular data in which the different cells have different sample frequencies raises a weighting problem because the different 'observations' carry different weights corresponding to their sample counts. Consequently we used a weighted or heteroscedastic least-squares regression procedure in which each observation weighted by the square root of the sample count corresponding to that cell. In particular, suppose the asset equation for each individual family i in the jth cell were written in the form

$$Y_{ij} = X_{ij}\beta + u_{ij},$$

where X_{ij} is a vector of explanatory variables and β a corresponding vector of regression parameters assumed to be the same for all families in the sample. If the individual families are independently drawn in the survey, then the variance of the errors for regression equation on cell means,

$$Y_j = X_j\beta + u_j,$$

may be expressed as

$$\operatorname{var}(u_j) = \sigma^2 / \mathrm{SC}_j,$$

where SC_j is the sample count for the jth cell and σ^2 is the variance of the individual u_{ij}'s. To adjust for this heteroscedasticity, then, the equation was transformed to

$$\sqrt{(\mathrm{SC}_j)}\, Y_j = \sqrt{(\mathrm{SC}_j)}\, X_j\beta + \sqrt{(\mathrm{SC}_j)}\, u_j,$$

so that those cells with a larger frequency are weighted more heavily than those with a relatively small count.

The resulting weighted least-square regression equation was estimated as

$$\log(\mathrm{ASSETS}) = \underset{(5.532)}{5.5456\,D_{\mathrm{ER}}} + \underset{(7.574)}{4.3229\,D_{\mathrm{EE}}} + \underset{(0.001)}{0.0760\,D_{\mathrm{NLF}}}$$

$$+ (\underset{(3.356)}{0.1597\,D_{\mathrm{ER}}} + \underset{(5.669)}{0.1778\,D_{\mathrm{EE}}} + \underset{(6.807)}{0.2365\,D_{\mathrm{NLF}}}) \cdot \mathrm{AGE}$$

$$- \underset{(3.905)}{0.001525\,\mathrm{AGE}^2},$$

$$R^2 = 0.9083, \quad \mathrm{SEE} = 12.19, \quad F_{7,156} = 257.5, \quad \mathrm{NOBS} = 163,$$

where D_{ER} is a dummy variable assuming a value of 1 if the family head is an employer, and 0 otherwise; D_{EE} is a dummy variable assuming a value of 1 if the family head is an employee, and 0 otherwise; D_{NLF} is a dummy variable assuming a value of 1 if the family head is not in the labour force, and 0 otherwise; AGE is the age of the family head as represented by the mid-point of each age interval except for the youngest interval (where 22.0 was used) and the oldest (where 70.0 was used). Since the three employment categories are exhaustive, no intercept was used. The figure in brackets below each estimated coefficient is the corresponding F-statistic for the coefficient. As one can see, the equation appears to fit reasonably well, with the employment dummy coefficients following an expected pattern, and age having a quadratic or inverted-U effect on asset holdings.

The next step in the adjustment procedure is to use this equation to estimate a value for asset holdings for each family on the SCF Ontario micro file. These values, however, would have a rather smaller dispersion across families on the tape than would the corresponding true values of asset holdings because regression forecasts are essentially conditional means and thus have smaller variances than the true values. Therefore, so as not to reduce unnecessarily the dispersion in asset values (and hence the imputed capital gains) because of the regression technique employed, we added the original cell-mean regression residual back into the forecast or estimated value for asset holdings. More specifically, once a value for assets has been obtained for a particular family from the above regression equation, this value and the corresponding information on age and employment status of the head of the family jointly determine a cell from the original cross-tabulation and a regression residual corresponding to that cell. This residual is then added (algebraically) to the previously estimated assets figure. This value is then adjusted proportionally so that the mean across all families on the SCF Ontario file is the same as that given for Ontario families in the original Survey of Incomes, Assets, and Indebtedness. Finally, each figure is then inflated to estimated 1973 values by the corresponding increase in Ontario family personal income. The resulting inflated and adjusted assets figure for each family is denoted as ASSETS in the main body of the chapter. It should be noted, however, that this adjustment procedure of adding the original regression residuals back in does not fully adjust for the reduced variance in the imputed asset figures because it does not capture within-cell variation as well (see, for example, Garfinkel and Haveman 1977). However, the original Statistics Canada cross-tabulations provided no information on the latter while providing fairly detailed categorical breakdowns. So the within-cell variation has been treated as minor compared to the between-cell variation in asset holdings. Clearly, though, access to the underlying micro data on family assets would be desirable for present purposes.

Estimation of portfolio rates of capital gains

This appendix explains some of the details of estimating average rates of accrued capital gains for each family on the Survey of Consumer Finances Ontario micro file used in the present study.

Detailed percentage portfolio breakdowns by age of family head and income class were made available to the authors by Statistics Canada from the 1970 Survey of Incomes, Assets, and Indebtedness for Canadian families of two or more. They also provided similar breakdowns for Ontario families, but only for different age groups (and not income classes).

The procedure, then, entailed taking the asset-component-specific rates of capital gains for 1973 and the hypothetical rates, and using the above percentage portfolio breakdowns to compute weighted average rates of portfolio capital gains for each age and income class for the Canadian asset data and for each age group for the Ontario asset data (see Table G.1). As there is a slight difference between rates for Ontario and Canada as a whole for the first three age groups, the weighted average rates for age and income classes based on the Canadian data were adjusted by the ratio of Ontario mean rates to Canadian mean rates corresponding to each age group. The resulting 'Ontario-adjusted weighted mean rates' of portfolio capital gains used in the calculations of this chapter are presented in Table G.2; they are based on the 1973 data and in Table G.3 on the hypothetical data. Each family on the SCF tape, then, was allocated a figure from each of these two tables according to its income class and the age of the family head.

TABLE G.1
Estimated rates of capital gains on total asset holdings by age of head for Ontario and Canada (percentages)

	Under 25	25–34	35–44	45–54	55–64	65 & over	All ages
1973 capital gains							
Ontario	9.62	14.58	16.45	13.71	11.76	10.00	13.56
Canada	7.41	13.60	14.28	13.51	11.25	10.84	13.09
Hypothetical capital gains							
Ontario	−0.30	2.55	3.45	2.86	2.87	2.55	2.89
Canada	−1.31	2.20	2.92	2.86	2.63	2.62	2.73

SOURCE: See sources to Tables 127–129.

TABLE G.2
Rates of capital gains on total asset holdings by age of head and income class for 1973, adjusted for Ontario

Income ($)	Under 25	25–34	35–44	45–54	55–64	65 & over
Less than 1000	−14.65	9.24	16.02	16.57	10.94	16.22
1000–1999	−19.89	14.93	16.69	14.34	14.77	14.31
2000–2999	3.05	12.57	20.10	15.12	13.42	13.19
3000–3999	15.62	13.70	17.45	12.62	14.64	12.47
4000–4999	18.37	14.22	18.28	16.47	13.25	9.62
5000–5999	4.39	15.89	16.38	15.21	13.75	9.76
6000–6999	2.92	14.93	19.66	15.61	14.16	8.60
7000–9999	2.36	15.52	18.57	15.58	13.66	9.13
10000–14999	11.73	14.35	17.02	14.29	12.65	9.23
15000–24999	20.33	12.16	15.27	13.14	11.19	7.60
25000 and over	10.51	16.60	9.74	7.85	6.09	2.48
All incomes	9.62	14.58	16.45	13.71	11.76	10.00

SOURCE: See source to Table G.1.

TABLE G.3
Rates of capital gains on total asset holdings by age of head and income class
from hypothetical data adjusted for Ontario

Income ($)	Under 25	25–34	35–44	45–54	55–64	65 & over
Less than 1000	−2.91	0.31	3.56	3.08	2.10	3.66
1000–1999	−3.29	1.98	2.97	4.04	3.07	3.23
2000–2999	−0.82	0.52	3.80	2.84	2.46	3.17
3000–3999	0.40	1.73	3.95	2.67	2.68	2.94
4000–4999	0.39	1.94	3.39	2.99	2.67	2.47
5000–5999	−0.62	2.59	2.73	2.67	2.82	2.19
6000–6999	−0.70	2.52	3.76	2.82	2.87	2.47
7000–9999	−0.98	2.48	3.59	3.09	2.82	2.19
10000–14999	−0.15	2.72	3.48	2.76	2.87	2.15
15000–24999	0.60	2.43	3.62	2.83	2.86	2.81
25000 and over	0.78	3.80	2.63	2.84	3.12	0.91
All incomes	−0.30	2.55	3.45	2.86	2.86	2.55

The imputation procedure for net worth

This appendix explains the technical details of how net worth figures were imputed for each family on the 1974 SCF Ontario tape. Since the general procedure for imputing for net worth is similar to that for asset holdings described in Chapter 11, the present discussion roughly parallels the one in Appendix F. As mentioned in the text, the net worth data used in the analysis came from the 1970 Survey of Incomes, Assets, and Indebtedness. A detailed discussion of the characteristics of these data can be found in Chapter 8. The data were made available to the authors by Statistics Canada in the form of specially prepared cross-tabulations (for families of two or more) of family net worth by total family income and age of head for Ontario. The procedure for estimating net worth for each family on the 1974 SCF Ontario file consisted of three steps: estimation of a net worth equation as a function of age and family income from the 1970 net worth cross-tabulations; use of this equation to provide an estimate of net worth holdings for each family on the 1974 SCF tape; and inflation of the resulting adjusted estimates up to 1973 values.

Let us turn first to the estimation step. The specification of the equation is based on life-cycle considerations discussed in Part One of this study and takes into account the empirical finding of Chapter 8 that the value of family net worth holdings generally varies with age of head in a positive concave fashion (Figure 41) and with family total income in a positive convex fashion (Figure 43) and that there is a marked interaction effect between age and income as well (Tables 70 and 71). Accordingly, the regression function has been specified to be quadratic in both age and family income in the form

$$a_0 + (a_1 + a_2 \text{ AGE} + a_3 \text{ AGE}^2) \log \text{FTI}$$

$$+ (\beta_1 + \beta_2 \text{ AGE} + \beta_3 \text{ AGE}^2) (\log \text{FTI})^2,$$

where FTI represents family total income and AGE is the age of the family head. In the cross-tabular data from which the equation is estimated, FTI is in fact taken as the weighted mean income for each cell, and AGE is represented by the mid-point of each age interval except for the under 25 group, which is centred at 22, and the 65 and over group, which is represented by age 70.

A second consideration in the estimation step is that the error term of the regression equation is likely to be heteroscedastic across cells because it picks up the effect of variables that may have been omitted, particularly across ages. The conventional way of handling such heteroscedasticity is to express the dependent variable of the equation in logarithmic form. But in the case of net worth some values are in fact negative. Therefore the largest negative value across cells for each age group was calculated and represented by the variable D_a, an adjustment dummy taking the values -1200, -5600, -2700, -3200, -4400, and -500 for the six age groups employed in this study. The dependent variable was then expressed in the form log $(NW-D_a)$.

The final consideration in the estimation step is that the different cells in the cross-tabulation from which the net worth equation was estimated have very different frequencies, or sample counts. Obviously one would not wish to weight the figures in one cell equally with those in another if the former represents ten times as many families as the latter. So again a heteroscedasticity problem arises, and in this case is handled by running a weighted regression in which each observation is multiplied by the square root of the sample count for that cell. This was discussed in Appendix F. The resulting weighted regression estimates are thus

$$\log (\text{NW}-D_a) = 27.202 + (-12.267 + 0.2889 \text{ AGE} - 0.002625 \text{ AGE}^2) \log \text{FTI}$$
$$\quad (2.570) \quad (6.250) \quad (7.177) \quad (5.813)$$

$$+ (1.0827 - 0.0294 \text{ AGE} + 0.002747 \text{ AGE}^2) (\log \text{FTI})^2,$$
$$\quad (8.100) \quad (6.200) \quad (5.112)$$

$$R^2 = 0.9200, \quad F_{6,164} = 314.3, \quad \text{NOBS} = 171,$$

where F-statistics are given in brackets below each coefficient estimate.

The properties of this equation appear quite reasonable. ∂ NW∂ FTI is positive, and ∂^2NW/∂FTI^2 is also positive for reasonable values of income and age. The partial elasticity of net worth with respect to income evaluated at mean income values for ages 25, 40, and 55, for example, takes the values 3.74, 1.02, and 0.50 respectively. The age effect also has the expected quadratic pattern with peak net worth holdings occurring for an income value of $10000, for example, at age 69.

The second step in the imputation procedure is to use this equation to provide estimates of net worth holdings for each family on the 1974 SCF Ontario file. This was done by inserting particular values for age of head and family total income (deflated from 1973 to 1969 values by the proportional change in mean family total income) in the above estimated equation and generating the corresponding 1970 net worth estimates. Care was also taken to insure that the few net worth estimates outside the range corresponding to ∂NW/∂FTI $= 0$ were set at their boundary values, thereby eliminating a small number of extreme outliers. The next step in the imputation procedure is to add the regression error back in (algebraically) to these initial wealth estimates so that the new estimated net worth series will not have its dispersion across families unnecessarily reduced by the regression forecast procedure. Specifically, the initial wealth estimate along with the age and (deflated) FTI figure for each family are used to identify a particular cross-tabulation cell and associated regression residual corresponding to that family. This residual is then added algebraically to the initial wealth estimate to yield a residual-adjusted net worth estimate analogous to the procedure discussed in Appendix F for estimates of asset holdings.

The final step in the imputation procedure is to re-inflate the residual-adjusted net worth estimate by the proportional change in mean Ontario family total income from 1970 and 1973. Those figures are the ones used in the analysis in Chapter 12.

Derivation and implementation of the adjustment for utility-equivalent annuity income

In this appendix we go through an algebraic derivation of the utility-equivalent annuity income formula for the multi-period case used in the current analysis, and then explain how the different parameter values in the formulas were selected in order to implement the adjustment procedure. The following theoretical development follows the basic ideas of Nordhaus (1973).

A family is assumed to have a utility function of consumption of the form

$$V = \int_0^T U[C(t)]e^{-\rho t}dt,$$

where V is additively separable across time from the current period for the length of the family's expected life T, ρ is a subjective rate of time preference, and $U[\cdot]$ has such convenient properties as strict concavity and constant tastes over time. The family also faces constraints of the form

$$dw(t)/dt = S(t),$$
$$C(t) + S(t) = rW(t),$$
$$W(0) = W,$$
$$W(T) = 0,$$

where it is assumed that the optimization process refers to family consumption out of investment income $(rW(t))$ and the terminal capital stock is zero so that the utility equivalent annuity just exhausts the family's current stock of wealth by the time life expectancy is ended. $S(t)$ indicates savings out of investment income, r the real rate of interest, and W the current stock of family net worth.

Solution of this optimization problem by conventional procedures leads to the optimal time path of consumption of

$$dC(t)/dt = (r-\rho) U'(C)/-U''(C).$$

A useful further simplification is to represent the utility function by the isoelastic function

$$U(C) = \begin{cases} \dfrac{C^{1-\delta}}{1-\delta}, & \text{for } 0 < \delta \neq 1 \\ \log(C), & \text{for } \delta = 1, \end{cases}$$

where δ is the (constant) elasticity of marginal utility with respect to consumption. The solution can then be rewritten as

$$C^*(t) = C_0 e^{gt},$$

where $g \equiv (r - \rho)/\delta$ and $C_0 = W\int_0^T e^{(g - r)t}dt$. These optimal consumption values correspond to C_1^* and C_2^* at point A in Figure 70.

The utility-equivalent annuity income, $Y^{**}(t)$, is then defined to be the value of that constant consumption stream which gives a total utility equal to that of the optimal consumption stream. It is thus the solution of the equation

$$\int_0^T U[Y^{**}(t)]e^{-\rho t}dt = \int_0^T U[C^*(t)]e^{-\rho t}dt,$$

where $Y^{**}(t) = Y^{**}$ is constrained to be constant for all t. The resulting solution is given by

$$Y^{**} = W(r - g / 1 - e^{(g-r)T}) [\rho(1 - e^{(g(1-\delta)-\rho)T}) / (1 - e^{-\rho T})$$

$$(\rho - g(1-\delta))]^{1/1-\delta} \text{ for } \delta \neq 1,$$

which corresponds to the co-ordinates of point B in Figure 70. The expression for the Weisbrod-Hansen annuity is

$$Y^* = W[r / (1 - (1+r)^{-T})],$$

so that one can see that the two annuity values differ by a proportionality factor dependent upon tastes δ and ρ, market conditions r, and life expectancy T.

Empirical implementation of the utility-equivalent annuity procedure thus requires that particular values be assigned to the various parameters appearing in the expression for Y^{**}. For convenience and, for lack of specific estimates to the contrary, it is assumed that the parameters of the isoelastic utility function are uniform across the population.

The real rate of growth of per capita Canadian consumption g was calculated using a simple log-linear time-series regression for the period 1950–1974 as 0.028.

The real rate of return on capital for consumers was calculated following Nordhaus (1973, 497) as the weighted average of an 'equity rate' and a 'bond rate,' where the weights are the shares of 'equities' (85 per cent) and 'bonds' (15 per cent) in consumer asset portfolios. For the real rate of return on bonds, a figure of 0.025 is taken, and for the real rate of return on 'equity,' a value of 0.065 is taken from the recent findings of Helliwell, Sparks, and Frisch (1973, 281). The resulting estimate of the real rate of return on net worth is thus computed to be about 6 per cent.

Finally, Blinder (1976, 36) has pointed out that several recent independent studies have estimated the elasticity of marginal utility with respect to consumption $-\delta$ at approximately -1.5 for the isoelastic utility function used in the present analysis. Since $g = (r - \rho)/\delta$, the implicit real rate of time discount ρ indicated by the model is about 2 per cent. This value of ρ is not unreasonable and probably more realistic than the zero rate of time preference used by Nordhaus.

To calculate the Weisbrod-Hansen annuity value Y^* entails the use of market or nominal rates of return on wealth holdings, whereas the utility-equivalent annuity calculations are expressed in real terms. In order to make the latter comparable to the former, we assume two different rates of price expectations of 2 per cent and 6 per cent resulting in the same two nominal rates of interest, 8 per cent and 12 per cent, used in the Weisbrod-Hansen annuity calculation. Thus both annuity calculations have been based on the same nominal rates of interest, but in the utility-equivalent annuity approach the rates have been decomposed into real rate of interest and price expectation components.

Details of the construction of the simulation model

This appendix explains in more detail than in the main text the various computations involved in the construction of the CPP retirement benefits simulation model. There are four principal stages: estimation of cross-sectional age-earnings profiles; transformation of the cross-sectional profiles into longitudinal expected lifetime earnings trajectories; calculation of CPP benefit and contribution streams for each participant in the Plan on the Survey of Consumer Finances Ontario micro data file, and computation of the discounted present value of net benefits for each participant and aggregation across participants within family units.

The first stage in the calculations is to estimate cross-sectional age-earnings profiles for all individuals that have positive earnings. This was done by estimating semi-logarithmic earnings equations separately for men and women and separately for each of nine education categories from the 1971 Census Public Use Sample Tape for individuals in Ontario. This particular data source was used because the large number of observations available permitted a fairly substantial amount of disaggregation in the analysis. The regression estimates are presented in Appendix K.

The estimated earnings equations were then applied to records for individual adults on the Survey of Consumer Finances 1974 micro data file for Ontario to yield cross-sectional earnings estimates for 1973. However, regression estimates by their nature have a smaller dispersion across observations than the corresponding actual values, and thus could convey a very misleading impression of earnings inequality. Therefore the estimated earnings series was adjusted to conform to the actual reported earnings series on the SCF file by adding back in the (algebraic) error between the two. The adjusted estimates of earnings are thus constrained to reproduce exactly the actual earnings distribution reported for the base year of 1973.

The second stage in the calculations is the transformation of the above cross-sectional profiles into longitudinal expected lifetime earnings trajectories for each individual adult on the SCF Ontario file. This requires adjusting upward each year the cross-section profiles (illustrated in Chapter 4) to take account of expected real wage increases associated, for example, with technological and other productivity changes over time and of expected nominal wage gains associated with seniority effects, cyclical fluctuations, union pressures, and general inflation. Clearly, such dynamic or time-related changes can affect various earning groups in the population quite differently over extended periods of time, but for convenience it is assumed in this study that the impact of these effects is neutral or the same across all age groups in the population and proportionally constant over time. The rate of changes in nominal wages, salaries, and supplementary labour income per capita in Canada was estimated at 6.24 per cent (Industrial Composite Earnings series in the National Accounts, *Canadian Statistical Review*, various issues), over the period 1950–74 with an upward trend at the end of the period. So the rate of growth of nominal earnings for purposes of this study has been set at a constant 7 per cent. The resulting longitudinal age-earnings trajectories are thus steeper than the cross-sectional profiles and peak at a later age or simply keep rising until retirement.

The earnings profiles as computed so far refer, however, only to those individuals with positive earnings in 1973. They do not reflect the fact that some adults may not receive any earnings in a given year because they are students and have not yet entered the labour force; because they have retired; because they are unemployed; or because they have dropped out of the labour force owing to illness or disability or in order to have children and raise a family. This question of labour market attachment is particularly important for young and old workers and for married women. Consequently, the longitudinal earnings trajectories are also adjusted to take account of the probability of zero earnings receipts in a given year. These probabilities have also been estimated from the 1971 Census file of individuals for Ontario as functions of sex, age, educational attainment, and marital status, and are presented in summary form also in Appendix K. Since the estimated earnings profiles already incorporate the effects of part-year and part-time earnings behaviour of individuals, adjustment for zero-earnings receipts in particular years is handled by assuming that each individual has one year of zero-earnings receipts out of every N years, where

$$N = 1 / 1 - \text{AVPROB}$$

and AVPROB is the mean probability of zero-earnings for a particular age, sex, marital status, and education group averaged over potential working years beyond 1965 (when the Canada Pension Plan was legislated). Entrance into the labour force was assumed to occur at age 18 (unless delayed by higher levels of education) and final exit at age 65. The resulting adjusted earnings trajectories can thus be interpreted as expected earnings profiles over the life cycle of an earner.

The third stage of the calculations consists of using these expected earnings profiles to compute estimated CPP benefits and contributions over time for each participant of the Plan on the SCF Ontario file from 1966 on. Details of the Plan were described in Chapter 13 and need not be repeated here. To allow for employer-shifting of the payroll tax, estimates of contributions are made under two different assumptions of full shifting of the tax (i.e., a de facto proportional tax rate of 3.6 per cent on pensionable earnings) and no shifting (i.e., a proportional tax rate of 1.8 per cent). The benefit and tax rules as implemented in the model also incorporate the principal transitional aspects of the CPP with respect to the gradual phasing in of benefit entitlement and the rules for determining the basic exemption and maximum pensionable earnings levels each year from 1966 on. Nominal earnings are assumed to increase annually by a scale factor of 7 per cent, and inflation expectations (according to which retirement benefits are indexed) carry on at a constant rate of 2 per cent. Age expectations are determined in similar fashion to the description in Appendix I. The result of this phase of the calculations is a time stream of expected contributions and CPP benefits from 1966 onwards for each adult on the 1974 SCF Ontario file.

The final stage of the calculations then is the aggregation of the estimated benefit and contribution streams over time and across participants within family units. In the first step, aggregation over time for each participant is done by computing the discounted present value to the year 1973 of net benefits (i.e., benefits minus contributions) under the Plan based on a discount rate of 6 per cent described in the last chapter. The result is a figure for the estimated 'net worth' of the Plan to each participant in 1973. The second step is to sum these discounted net benefit figures for participants in each family unit on the SCF Ontario file. In the case of single-adult family units (either male or female head), there is only one participant in the unit. In the case of husband-wife families, there are two potential participants, whose net benefits are combined. The final result is an estimate of the present value of lifetime net benefits under the present rules of the CPP for each family unit on the SCF Ontario file, discounted to the year 1973. The summary inequality characteristics across age and income groups of this estimated stock of publicly provided net worth have been analysed in Chapter 13.

Earnings equations and participation proportions

The first part of the stimulation model described in Appendix J is the generation of expected lifetime earnings trajectories for adult men and women in the sample. This was done by estimating (cross-sectional) earnings equations for separate sex and education groups in the population, and then shifting the earnings equations upwards over time to incorporate average expected growth in nominal earnings, thereby generating expected longitudinal age-earnings profiles for labour force participants. The longitudinal profiles were then adjusted by a disaggregated set of age- and sex-specific labour force participation proportions to yield estimated total earnings trajectories over the expected working life of adults in 1973.

Both the cross-sectional earnings equations and the labour force participation proportions were estimated from the 1971 Census Public Use Sample Tape for individuals in Ontario in 1970. This data source was used in the construction of individual earnings profiles because the large sample size allowed a fairly disaggregated and detailed analysis of earnings patterns in Ontario, and because the Survey of Consumer Finances file on which the other calculations are done is for family units, not individuals.

Disaggregated earnings equations were run separately for each of nine education categories and separately for men and women. The education categories used are

1 No schooling
2 Schooling less than grade 5
3 Grades 5–8
4 Grades 9–11
5 Grades 12–13
6 Some university education, but no degree obtained
7 University education 3–4 years, with degree

   8 University education for 5 years or more, but without degree
   9 University education for 5 years or more, with degree.

The earnings equations were specified in fairly conventional fashion with the dependent variable in logarithmic form in order to reflect, for example, the work of Becker (1964) and Mincer (1970, 1974) and others in the human capital area and to allow for possible heteroscedasticity of the error term in a level form specification. The explanatory variables include area of residence and a quadratic function of age to reflect the concavity of cross-sectional age-earnings profiles. The earnings equations for women also included an adjustment for time spent out of the labour force for child bearing and raising a family. The particular specifications employed, then, are

$$\log(\text{YE}) = \beta_0 + \beta_1 D_1 + \beta_2 D_2 + \beta_3 D_3 + \beta_4 \text{AGE} + \beta_5 \text{AGE}^2$$

for men, and

$$\log(\text{YE}) = \beta_0 + \beta_1 D_1 + \beta_2 D_2 + \beta_3 D_3 + \beta_4 \text{AGE} + \beta_5 \text{AGE}^2 + \beta_6 \text{NC}$$

for women, where YE is the wages and salaries plus self-employment income; D_1 is a dummy variable taking a value of 1 if place of residence is an urban area of 30000 or over, and 0 otherwise; D_2 is a dummy variable taking a value of 1 if place of residence is an urban area under 30000 in population, and 0 otherwise; D_3 is a dummy variable taking a value of 1 if place of residence is a rural area but is non-farm, and 0 otherwise; AGE is the age of the individual; and NC is the number of children in a family. The omitted reference group for the area-of-residence dummies is the rural-farm category.

   The equations were estimated by least squares, and the coefficient estimates are presented in Tables K.1 and K.2. Figures in brackets corresponding to each coefficient are F-statistics for the parameter estimates. The estimated labour force proportions by age and educational attainment level are given in Tables K.3 and K.4.

TABLE K.1

Estimated earnings equations for men by education group, Ontario 1970

	1	2	3	4	5	6	7	8	9
Constant	6.3537	5.3645	5.8393	3.4977	4.1033	3.6587	4.1125	3.1584	3.6044
D_1	0.3529	0.0862	0.1251	0.0595	0.0351	0.0949	-0.6706	0.0193	-0.0046
	(2.279)	(0.648)	(18.46)	(4.943)	(1.254)	(2.657)	(3.294)	(0.066)	(0.003)
D_2	-0.5294	-0.1349	-0.0918	-0.0363	-0.0345	0.1449	-1.5959	-0.3470	-0.0862
	(3.187)	(0.957)	(6.044)	(1.004)	(0.541)	(2.653)	(11.59)	(6.310)	(0.332)
D_3	0.2420	0.6300	-0.4154	-0.3256	-0.4051	-0.2464	-1.5959	-0.4925	-0.3295
	(0.306)	(12.00)	(91.35)	(40.24)	(32.43)	(3.244)	(11.59)	(2.161)	(1.558)
AGE	0.0831	0.1365	0.1295	0.2507	0.2249	0.2366	0.2619	0.2796	0.2554
	(10.41)	(112.2)	(856.2)	(4648.0)	(2725.0)	(822.5)	(35.36)	(494.1)	(279.4)
AGE^2	-0.00092	-0.00144	-0.00144	-0.00277	-0.00243	-0.00247	-0.00293	-0.00296	-0.00258
	(12.58)	(116.2)	(918.6)	(3628.0)	(2124.0)	(570.1)	(32.80)	(400.0)	(216.8)
R^2	0.1618	0.1780	0.1785	0.4539	0.4017	0.4682	0.3989	0.4146	0.3009
SEE	0.9759	0.9452	0.7850	0.8551	0.8395	0.7933	0.7128	0.8025	0.8691
F	6.29	28.68	234.8	1211.5	729.4	283.5	11.94	126.9	83.83
NOBS	169.0	668.0	5407.0	7295.0	5437.0	1616.0	77.0	902.0	980.0

SOURCE: See source to Table 4.

TABLE K.2
Estimated earnings equations for women by education group, Ontario 1970

	1	2	3	4	5	6	7	8	9
Constant	5.3733	5.6501	6.4842	4.4261	4.9081	4.0990	2.6787	3.1750	3.4360
D_1	-0.0072	0.5005	0.1419	0.1283	0.1418	0.0314	2.7455	0.9476	0.5059
	(0.000)	(6.537)	(5.200)	(8.421)	(9.794)	(0.085)	(26.63)	(4.841)	(3.317)
D_2	-0.9187	-0.1903	-0.2298	-0.0593	-0.1305	0.0296	—	-0.1285	0.1378
	(3.182)	(0.358)	(7.341)	(0.838)	(3.781)	(0.030)	—	(0.298)	(0.094)
D_3	-3.5439	0.2139	-0.3682	-0.3651	-0.2827	-0.1731	—	-0.2146	0.1378
	(9.278)	(0.079)	(8.065)	(11.18)	(7.080)	(0.463)	—	(0.932)	(0.094)
AGE	0.1063	0.0561	0.0491	0.1541	0.1506	0.1937	0.1522	0.2086	0.2226
	(9.839)	(6.553)	(31.37)	(638.7)	(460.5)	(140.0)	(2.456)	(20.17)	(21.04)
AGE^2	-0.00102	-0.00500	-0.00047	-0.00158	-0.00157	-0.00199	-0.00189	-0.00221	-0.00230
	(9.069)	(4.617)	(25.61)	(463.5)	(340.8)	(100.3)	(2.395)	(14.03)	(15.94)
NC	-0.0562	-0.0327	-0.0586	-0.1269	-0.1935	-0.1951	-0.0200	-0.2048	-0.2267
	(1.295)	(1.048)	(26.67)	(139.2)	(239.5)	(41.08)	(0.026)	(9.534)	(11.53)
R^2	0.2123	0.0899	0.0441	0.1748	0.1362	0.1939	0.6592	0.1782	0.1632
SEE	1.083	1.002	1.031	1.132	1.095	1.101	0.7042	1.125	1.150
F	3.864	4.395	16.25	164.4	123.5	36.97	8.221	8.376	8.661
NOBS	93.0	274.0	2120.0	4664.0	4707.0	929.0	22.0	197.0	228.0

SOURCE: See source to Table 4.

TABLE K.3
Proportions of men with positive earnings, Ontario 1970

Age group	Education 1	2	3	4	5	6	7	8	9
20 or less	0.412	0.698	0.547	0.622	0.875	0.914	0.875	1.000	1.000
21–25	0.692	0.824	0.957	0.969	0.979	0.969	0.966	1.000	0.932
26–30	0.857	0.897	0.969	0.982	0.980	0.995	0.975	1.000	0.978
31–35	0.800	0.939	0.978	0.984	0.987	0.993	0.993	1.000	0.993
36–40	0.750	0.971	0.971	0.978	0.983	0.986	0.987	1.000	0.992
41–45	0.737	0.895	0.969	0.984	0.993	0.965	1.000	1.000	0.992
46–50	0.818	0.920	0.953	0.982	0.985	0.981	0.990	0.875	0.989
51–55	0.824	0.910	0.958	0.965	0.967	0.987	0.982	1.000	1.000
56–60	0.846	0.875	0.923	0.950	0.958	0.952	0.970	1.000	0.883
61–65	0.654	0.758	0.849	0.895	0.872	0.970	0.970	1.000	0.893
66 and over	0.220	0.293	0.345	0.358	0.403	0.414	0.477	0.286	0.676

SOURCE: See source to Table 4.

TABLE K.4
Proportions of women with positive earnings, Ontario 1970

Age	Education group 1	2	3	4	5	6	7	8	9
20 or less	0.000	0.503	0.409	0.628	0.817	0.744	1.000	1.000	1.000
21–25	0.571	0.222	0.508	0.643	0.784	0.798	0.859	0.750	0.846
26–30	0.222	0.500	0.384	0.464	0.596	0.673	0.750	0.750	0.733
31–35	0.545	0.389	0.416	0.515	0.544	0.593	0.532	0.500	0.650
36–40	0.545	0.565	0.443	0.543	0.551	0.596	0.500	0.500	0.778
41–45	0.529	0.484	0.419	0.535	0.581	0.639	0.405	0.500	0.818
46–50	0.611	0.547	0.439	0.541	0.547	0.609	0.556	0.500	0.222
51–55	0.455	0.435	0.425	0.502	0.561	0.481	0.542	0.667	0.600
56–60	0.188	0.186	0.310	0.410	0.438	0.581	0.357	0.000	0.889
61–65	0.053	0.158	0.186	0.333	0.365	0.435	0.100	0.000	0.375
66 and over	0.125	0.037	0.070	0.078	0.141	0.130	0.000	0.000	0.125

SOURCE: See source to Table 4.

Bibliography

Alexis, M. (1974) 'The political economy of labor market discrimination: synthesis and exploration.' In A. Horowitz and G. von Furstenberg, eds, *Patterns of Discrimination* (Lexington, Mass.: D.C. Heath-Lexington)

Ando, A. and F. Modigliani (1963) 'The life cycle hypothesis of saving: aggregate implications and tests.' *American Economic Review* 53, 109–27

Arrow, K.J. (1972a) 'Models of job discrimination' and 'Some models of race in the labor market.' In A.H. Pascal, ed., *Racial Discrimination in Economic Life* (Lexington, Mass.: D.C. Heath-Lexington)

– (1972b) 'Higher education as a filter.' *Journal of Public Economics* 2, 193–216

– (1974) 'The theory of discrimination.' In O. Ashenfelter and A. Rees, eds, *Discrimination in Labor Markets* (Princeton, NJ: Princeton University Press)

Ashenfelter, Orley (1972) 'Racial discrimination and trade unionism.' *Journal of Political Economy* 80, 435–64

– (1974) 'Discrimination and trade unions' in O. Ashenfelter and A. Rees, eds, *Discrimination in Labor Markets* (Princeton, NJ: Princeton University Press)

Ashenfelter, Orley, and J.J. Heckman (1974) 'The estimation of income and substitution effects in a model of family labor supply.' *Econometrica* 42, 73–85

Asimakopulos, A. and J.C. Weldon (1968) 'On the theory of government pension plans.' *Canadian Journal of Economics* 1, 699–717

Atkinson, A.B. (1970a) 'On the measurement of inequality.' *Journal of Economic Theory* 2, 244–63

– (1970b) 'National superannuation: redistribution and value for money.' *Bulletin of the Oxford University Institute of Economics and Statistics* 32, 171–85

Atkinson, A.B. (1971) 'The distribution of wealth and the individual life cycle.' *Oxford Economic Papers* 23, 239–54
– (1975) *The Economics of Inequality* (Oxford: Clarendon Press)
– (1976) ed., *The Personal Distribution of Incomes* (London: George Allen and Unwin)
Balfour, Frederick S. and C.M. Beach (1979) 'Towards the estimation of payroll tax incidence in Canada.' Background paper for a Conference on Canadian Incomes, Winnipeg, May 1979
Bank of Canada, *Bank of Canada Review*, Aug. 1976 and Mar. 1974
Beach, C.M. and John Andrew (1977) 'Program to compute income inequality measures.' Unpublished FORTRAN computer program. Department of Economics, Queen's University
Beasley, Thomas F. (1976) 'A proposal for measuring economic welfare.' Unpublished M.A. essay, Department of Economics, Queen's University
Becker, G.S. (1957) *The Economics of Discrimination* (Chicago: University of Chicago Press)
– (1964) *Human Capital*. National Bureau of Economic Research, General Series No. 80 (New York: Columbia University Press)
– (1965) 'A theory of the allocation of time.' *Economic Journal* 75, 493–517
– (1967) *Human Capital and the Personal Distribution of Income*. W.S. Woytinsky Lecture 1 (Ann Arbor, Mich.: University of Michigan Press)
Becker, Gary S., and H.G. Lewis (1973) 'On the interaction between the quantity and quality of children.' *Journal of Political Economy* 81, S279–88
Becker, Gary S. and Nigel Tomes (1976) 'Child endowments and the quantity and quality of children.' *Journal of Political Economy* 84, S143–62
Beckman, M.J. (1975) 'Echelle des salaires et avancement dans les organisations hiérarchiques.' *Annales de l'INSEE* 18, 45–50
– (1970) 'Management production functions and the theory of the firm.' *Journal of Economic Theory* 14, 1–18
– (1978) *Rank in Organizations*. Vol. 161 of Lecture Notes in Economics and Mathematical Systems (New York: Springer-Verlag)
Ben-Porath, Yoram (1967) 'The production of human capital and the life cycle of earnings.' *Journal of Political Economy* 75, 352–65
Bergmann, B.R. (1971) 'The effect on white incomes of discrimination in employment.' *Journal of Political Economy* 79, 294–313

Bhatia, Kul B. (1970) 'Accrued capital gains, personal income and savings in the United States, 1948–1964.' *Review of Income and Wealth* 16, 363–78
- (1971) 'The estimation and location of capital gains in Canada.' Discussion Paper 7132, Department of Economics, University of Western Ontario
- (1972) 'Capital gains and the distribution of income.' Discussion Paper 7208, Department of Economics, University of Western Ontario
- (1976) 'Capital gains and inequality of personal income: some results from survey data.' *Journal of the American Statistical Association* 71, 575–80
Bjerke, Kjeld (1970) 'Income and wage distributions: part I, a survey of the literature.' *Review of Income and Wealth* 16, 235–52
Blauer, R. (1971) 'Fixed income and asset groups in Canada.' In N. Swan and D. Wilton, eds, *Inflation and the Canadian Experience* (Kingston: Industrial Relations Centre, Queen's University)
Blaug, Mark (1976) 'The empirical status of human capital theory: a slightly jaundiced survey.' *Journal of Economic Literature* 14, 827–55
Blinder, Alan S. (1974) *Toward an Economic Theory of Income Distribution* (Cambridge, Mass.: MIT Press)
- (1976) 'Inequality and mobility in the distribution of wealth.' Princeton University Discussion Paper
Blinder, Alan S. and Yoram Weiss (1976) 'Human capital and labor supply: a synthesis.' *Journal of Political Economy* 84, 449–72
Boskin, M.J. (1972) 'Unions and relative real wages.' *American Economic Review* 62, 466–72
Bowles, S. (1972) 'Schooling and inequality from generation to generation.' *Journal of Political Economy* 80, S219–51
- (1973) 'Understanding unequal economic opportunity.' *American Economic Review* 63, 346–56
Bowles, S. and Nelson, V.I. (1974) 'The inheritance of I.Q. and inter-generational reproduction of economic inequality.' *Review of Economics and Statistics* 56, 39–51
Bowman, Mary Jean (1945) 'A graphical analysis of personal income distribution in the U.S.' *American Economic Review* 35, 607–28
Boyer, M. (1976) 'The impact of inflation on balance sheets of Canadian households.' Background Paper 3-3 (Ottawa: Economic Council of Canada)
Brittain, John A. (1967) 'The real rate of interest on lifetime contributions toward retirement under social security.' In Joint Economic Com-

mittee, 90th Congress, *Old-Age Income Assurance* (Washington, DC United States Government Printing Office)

Brittain, John A. (1972a) 'The incidence of social security payroll taxes.' *American Economic Review* 62, 739–42

– (1972b) *The Payroll Tax for Social Security* (Washington, DC: Brookings Institution)

– (1977) *The Inheritance of Economic Status* (Washington, DC: Brookings Institution)

– (1978) *Inheritance and the Inequality of Material Wealth* (Washington, DC: Brookings Institution)

Bronfenbrenner, M. (1971) *Income Distribution Theory* (Chicago: Aldine-Atherton)

Browning, Edgar K. (1973) 'Social insurance and inter-generational transfers.' *The Journal of Law and Economics* 16, 215–37

Bryden, Kenneth (1974) *Old Age Pensions and Policy-Making in Canada* (Montreal: McGill University Press)

Cain, G.G. (1966) *Married Women in the Labour Force* (Chicago: University of Chicago Press)

– (1976) 'The challenge of segmented labor market theories to orthodox theory: a survey.' *Journal of Economic Literature* 14, 1215–57

Castellino, Onorato (1971) 'Income redistribution through old-age pensions: problems of its definition and measurement.' *Public Finance* 26, 457–71

Clark, Robert, Juanita Kreps, and Joseph Spengler (1978) 'The economics of aging: a survey.' *Journal of Economic Literature* 16, 919–62

Cloutier, J.E. (1978) 'The distribution of benefits and costs of social security in Canada, 1971–1975.' Discussion Paper 108 (Ottawa: Economic Council of Canada)

Cohen, Malcolm S. and Frank P. Stafford (1974) 'A life cycle model of the household's time allocation.' *Annals of Economics and Social Measurement* 3, 447–62

Cowell, F.A. (1977) *Measuring Inequality* (Oxford: Philip Allan)

Cropper, J.L. (1977) 'Health, investment in health, and occupational choice.' *Journal of Political Economy* 85, 1273–94

Dalton, H. (1920) 'The Measurement of the inequality of incomes,' *Economic Journal* 30, 348–61

Dasgupta, P., A.K. Sen, and D. Starrett (1973) 'Notes on the measurement of inequality.' *Journal of Economic Theory* 6, 180–7

David, Martin and Roger Miller (1975) 'Capital gains and individual income – evidence on realization and persistence.' In James D. Smith, ed., *The Personal Distribution of Income and Wealth*. Studies in Income and Wealth, No. 39, National Bureau of Economic Research (New York: Columbia University Press)

Davies, J.B. (1979) 'On the size distribution of wealth in Canada.' *Review of Income and Wealth* 25, 237–59

– (1980) 'The 1970 survey of consumer finances, nonsampling error, and the personal distribution of wealth in Canada.' In Economic Council of Canada, *Reflections on Canadian Incomes* (Ottawa: ECC)

Deran, Elizabeth (1966) 'Income redistribution under the social security system.' *National Tax Journal* 19, 276–85

Diewert, W.E. (1974) 'Unions in a general equilibrium model.' *Canadian Journal of Economics* 7, 475–95

Dodge, D.A. (1975) 'Impact of tax, transfer, and expenditure policies of government on the distribution of personal income in Canada.' *Journal of Income and Wealth* 21, 1–52

Doeringer, P.B. and M.J. Piore (1971) *Internal Labor Markets and Manpower Analysis* (Lexington, Mass: Lexington Books)

Donaldson, D. and B.C. Eaton (1976) 'Firm-specific human capital: shared investment or optimal entrapment?.' *Canadian Journal of Economics* 9, 462–72

Dresh, Stephen P. (1975) 'Demography, technology, and higher education: toward a formal model of educational adaptation.' *Journal of Political Economy* 83, 535–71

Economic Council of Canada (1976) *The Inflation Dilemma*, Thirteenth Annual Review (Ottawa: ECC)

– (1980) *Reflections on Canadian Incomes* (Ottawa: ECC)

Fair, Ray C. (1971) 'The optimal distribution of income.' *Quarterly Journal of Economics* 85, 551–79

Feldstein, Martin (1974a) 'Social security and the distribution of wealth.' Harvard Institute for Economic Research Discussion Paper

– (1974b) 'Social security induced retirement and aggregate capital accumulation.' *Journal of Political Economy* 82, 905–26

Ferguson, C.E. (1969) *The Neoclassical Theory of Production and Distribution* (Cambridge: Cambridge University Press)

Fisher, Irving (1907) *The Rate of Interest* (New York: Macmillan)

– (1930) *The Theory of Interest* (New York: Macmillan)

Fleisher, Belton M. (1970) *Labor Economics: Theory and Evidence* (Englewood Cliffs, NJ: Prentice-Hall)

Freeman, R.B. (1976) *The Overeducated American* (New York: Academic Press)

Friedman, Milton (1952) 'A method of comparing incomes of families differing in composition.' In Conference on Research in Income and Wealth, Vol. 15, *Studies in Income and Wealth* (New York: National Bureau of Economic Research)

– (1953) 'Choice, chance, and the personal distribution of income.' *Journal of Political Economy* 61, 277–90

Garfinkel, Irwin and Robert Haveman (1977) 'Earnings capacity, economic status, and poverty.' *Journal of Human Resources* 12, 49–70

Ghez, Gilbert R. and Gary S. Becker (1975) *The Allocation of Time and Goods Over the Life Cycle*, National Bureau of Economic Research, Human Behaviour and Social Institutions, Vol. 6 (New York: Columbia University Press)

Gillespie, W. Irwin (1976) 'On the redistribution of income in Canada.' *Canadian Tax Journal* 24, 419–50

– (1980) 'Taxes, expenditures and the redistribution of income in Canada, 1951–1977.' In Economic Council of Canada, *Reflections on Canadian Incomes* (Ottawa: ECC)

Gintis, H., 'Education, technology and the characteristics of worker productivity.' *American Economic Review* 61, 266–79

Gramm, Wendy Lee (1975) 'Household utility maximization and the working wife.' *American Economic Review* 65, 90–100

Grégoire, Françoise (1976) 'The redistributive effects of the Canada Pension Plan in Ontario.' Unpublished M.A. essay, Department of Economics, Queen's University

Griliches, Zvi, Wilm Krelle, Hans-Jurgen Krupp, and Oldrich Kyn (1978) *Income Distribution and Economic Inequality* (New York: Halsted Press)

Griliches, Zvi and William M. Mason (1972) 'Education, income, and ability.' *Journal of Political Economy* 80, S74–103

Gronau, Reuben (1973) 'The intrafamily allocation of time: the value of the housewives' time.' *American Economic Review* 63, 634–51

– (1977) 'Leisure, home production, and work – the theory of the allocation of time revisited.' *Journal of Political Economy* 85, 1099–124

Grossman, Michael (1972) *The Demand for Health: A Theoretical and Empirical Investigation*. Bureau of Economic Research (New York: Columbia University Press, 1972)

– (1975) 'The correlation between health and schooling.' In Nestor E. Terleckyj, ed., *Household Production and Consumption*. National Bureau of Economic Research, Studies in Income and Wealth 40 (New York: Columbia University Press)

Haley, William G. (1973) 'Human capital: the choice between investment and income.' *American Economic Review* 63, 929–44
- (1976) 'Estimation of the earnings profile from optimal human capital accumulation.' *Econometrica* 44, 1223–38
Hanushek, Eric A. and John M. Quigley (1978) 'Implicit investment profiles and intertemporal adjustments of relative wages.' *American Economic Review* 68, 67–79
Harris, J., M. Wachter, and O. Williamson (1975) 'Understanding the employment relation: the analysis of idiosyncratic exchange.' *Bell Journal of Economics* 6, 250–78
Hause, John C. (1971) 'Ability and schooling as determinants of lifetime earnings, or if you're so smart, why aren't you rich?.' *American Economic Review* 61, 289–98
- (1972) 'Earnings profile: ability and schooling.' *Journal of Political Economy* 80, S108–38
Health and Welfare Canada (1977) 'The distribution of income in Canada: concepts, measures, and issues.' Social Security Research Report 04 (Ottawa: Health and Welfare Canada)
Heckman, James J. (1974) 'Life cycle consumption and labor supply: an explanation of the relationship between income and consumption over the life cycle.' *American Economic Review* 64, 188–94
- (1975) 'Estimates of a human capital production function embedded in a life-cycle model of labor supply.' In Nestor E. Terleckyj, ed., *Household Production and Consumption*. National Bureau of Economic Research, Studies in Income and Wealth 40 (New York: Columbia University Press)
- (1976) 'A life cycle model of earnings, learning, and consumption.' *Journal of Political Economy* 84, S11–44
- (1978) 'A partial survey of recent research on the labor supply of women.' *American Economic Review* 68, 200–7
Helliwell, J., G.R. Sparks, and J. Frisch (1973) 'The supply price of capital in Macroeconomic models.' In A.A. Powell and R.A. Williams, eds, *Econometric Studies of Macro and Monetary Relations* (Amsterdam: North-Holland)
Henderson, D.W. and J.C.R. Rowley (1977) 'The distribution and evolution of Canadian family incomes, 1965–1973.' Discussion Paper 91 (Ottawa: Economic Council of Canada)
Henderson, D.W. and J.C.R. Rowley (1980a) 'Socio-economic characteristics and the distribution of employment income among Canadian

families, 1967–1975.' In Economic Council of Canada, *Reflections on Canadian Incomes* (Ottawa: ECC)

– (1980b) 'The relative economic position of female-headed families in Canada, 1965–1975: some basic information.' In Economic Council of Canada, *Reflections on Canadian Incomes* (Ottawa: ECC)

Hicks, J.R. (1939) *Value and Capital* (Oxford: Clarendon Press)

Hotz, V. Joseph (1977) 'The effects of ability in a model of earnings generation.' Discussion Paper 7701, Social Systems Research Institute, University of Wisconsin

Irvine, Ian (1980) 'The distribution of economic welfare in Canada: a measurement proposal and preliminary results.' Paper presented to the Canadian Economics Association, May 1976. Since published in revised form as 'The distribution of income and wealth in Canada in a lifecycle framework.' *Canadian Journal of Economics* 13, 455–74

Ishikawa, Tsuneo (1975) 'Family structures and family values in the theory of income distribution.' *Journal of Political Economy* 83, 987–1008

Jencks, C. and Marshall Smith, Henry Acland, Mary Jo Bane, David Cohen, Herbert Gintis, Barbara Heyns, and Stephan Michelson (1972). *Inequality: A Reassessment of the Effects of Family and Schooling in America* (New York: Harper and Row)

Johnson, Harry G. (1973) *The Theory of Income Distribution*. Vol. 3 of *Lectures in Economics* (London: Gray-Mills)

Johnson, Harry G., and Peter Mieszkowski (1970) 'The effects of unionization on the distribution of income: a general equilibrium approach.' *Quarterly Journal of Economics* 84, 539–61

Johnson, William R. (1977) 'Uncertainty and the distribution of earnings.' Chapter 10 in F. Thomas Juster, ed., *The Distribution of Economic Well-Being*. National Bureau of Economic Research, Studies in Income and Wealth, No. 41 (Cambridge, Mass.: Ballinger)

Jones, R.W. (1971) 'Distortions in factor markets and the general equilibrium model of production.' *Journal of Political Economy* 79, 437–59

Kahne, Hilda (1975) 'Economic perspectives on the roles of women in the American economy.' *Journal of Economic Literature* 13, 1249–92

Kapsalis, Constantine (1977) Income security in Ontario. Mimeo. (Toronto: Ontario Economic Council)

Kendall, M.G. and A. Stuart (1969) *The Advanced Theory of Statistics*, Vol. 1 of *Distribution Theory* (2nd ed.) (London: Charles Griffen)

Kohn, M.L. (1969) *Class and Conformity: A Study of Values* (Homewood, Illinois: Richard Irwin)

Kolm, Serge-Christophe (1976a) 'Unequal inequalities I.' *Journal of Economic Theory* 12, 185–97
– (1976b) 'Unequal inequalities II.' *Journal of Economic Theory* 13, 82–111
Kuznets, Simon S. (1976) 'Demographic aspects of the size distribution of income: an exploratory essay.' *Economic Development and Cultural Change* 25, 1–94
Lacroix, R. and C. Lemelin (1980) 'Higher education and incomes.' In Economic Council of Canada, *Reflections on Canadian Incomes* (Ottawa: ECC)
Lalonde, M. (1973) 'Working paper on social security in Canada.' (Ottawa: Health and Welfare Canada)
Lazear, Edward (1977) 'Education: consumption or production?' *Journal of Political Economy* 85, 569–98
Leibowitz, Arleen (1974) 'Home investments in children.' *Journal of Political Economy* 82, S111–31
– (1975) 'Education and the allocation of women's time.' In F. Thomas Juster, ed., *Education, Income, and Human Behaviour*. National Bureau of Economic Research (New York: McGraw-Hill)
Leimer, D.R., Ronald Hoffman and Alan Freiden (1978) *A Framework for Analyzing the Equity of the Social Security Benefit Structure*, Studies in Income Distribution, No. 6, United States Department of Health, Education and Welfare, Social Security Administration (Washington)
Leuthold, Jane H. (1975) 'The incidence of the payroll tax in the United States.' *Public Finance Quarterly* 3, 3–13
Levine, D.B. and N.M. Singer (1970) 'The mathematical relation between the income density function and the measurement of income inequality.' *Econometrica* 38, 324–30
Lewis, H. Gregg (1963) *Unionism and Relative Wages in the United States* (Chicago: University of Chicago Press)
Liebenberg, Maurice and Jeanette M. Fitzwilliams (1961) 'Size distribution of personal income, 1957–1960.' *Survey of Current Business* 41, 11–21
Lillard, Lee A. (1973) 'Essay on human wealth.' National Bureau of Economic Research, Working Paper 4 (Washington)
– (1977) 'The Distribution of earnings and human wealth in a life-cycle context.' In F. Thomas Juster, ed., *The Distribution of Economic Well-Being*. National Bureau of Economic Research, Studies in Income and Wealth, No. 41 (Cambridge, Mass.: Ballinger)

Lillard, Lee A., and Robert J. Willis (1978) 'Dynamic aspects of earnings mobility.' *Econometrica* 46, 985–1012

Love, Roger (1976) 'Comparison of leverage ratios by selected socio-demographic variables, 1970.' Unpublished Statistics Canada study (Ottawa)

Love, Roger and Michael C. Wolfson (1976) 'Income inequality: statistical methodology and Canadian illustrations.' Statistics Canada 13–559 occasional (Ottawa: Statistics Canada)

Lydall, H. (1968) *The Structure of Earnings* (Oxford: Clarendon Press)

– (1976) 'Theories of the distribution of earnings.' In A.B. Atkinson, ed., *The Personal Distribution of Incomes* (London: George Allen and Unwin)

MacLeod, N. and K. Horner (1980) 'Analyzing postwar changes in Canadian income distribution.' In Economic Council of Canada, *Reflections on Canadian Incomes* (Ottawa: ECC)

Magee, S.P. (1973) 'Factor market distortions, production, and trade: a survey.' *Oxford Economic Papers* 25, 1–43

Manga, Pranlal (1977) *The Income Distribution Effect of Medical Insurance in Ontario* (Toronto: Ontario Economic Council)

Manga, Pranlal (1978) 'The distributional effects of inflation on Canadian households.' Anti-Inflation Board Discussion Paper 7803 (Ottawa)

Marshall, Ray (1974) 'The economics of racial discrimination: a survey.' *Journal of Economic Literature* 12, 849–71

Maslove, A.M. (1972) *The Pattern of Taxation in Canada* (Ottawa: Economic Council of Canada)

McElroy, Michael B. (1970) 'Capital gains and the theory and measurement of income.' Unpublished doctoral dissertation, Northwestern University

Meade, J.E. (1964) *Efficiency, Equality and the Ownership of Property* (London: Allen and Unwin)

– (1976) *The Just Economy* (London: Allen and Unwin)

Mincer, Jacob (1958) 'Investment in human capital and personal income distribution.' *Journal of Political Economy* 66, 281–302

– (1962a) 'On-the-job training: costs, returns, and some implications.' *Journal of Political Economy* 70, 50–79

– (1962b) 'Labor force participation of married women.' In Moses Abramovitz, ed., *Aspects of Labor Economics* Universities–National Bureau Committee for Economic Research (Princeton)

– (1970) 'The distribution of labor incomes: a survey with special reference to the human capital approach.' *Journal of Economic Literature* 8, 1–25

– (1974) 'Schooling, age and earnings.' In *Human Capital and Personal Income Distribution* (New York: National Bureau of Economic Research)

Mincer, Jacob (1976) 'Progress in human capital analyses of the distribution of earnings.' In A.B. Atkinson, ed., *The Personal Distribution of Income* (London: George Allen and Unwin)

Mincer, J. and Polachek, S. (1974) 'Family investments in human capital: earnings of women.' *Journal of Political Economy* 82, S76-108

Modigliani, F. and R. Brumberg (1955) 'Utility analysis and the consumption function: an interpretation of cross sectional data.' In K.K. Kurihara, ed., *Post Keynesian Economics* (New Brunswick, NJ: Allen and Unwin)

Moon, Marilyn (1977) 'The economic welfare of the aged and income security programs.' In Marilyn Moon and Eugene Smolensky, eds, *Improving Measures of Economic Well-Being*. Institute for Research on Poverty Monograph (New York: Academic Press)

Morgan, J.N. and J.D. Smith (1969) 'Measures of economic well-offness and their correlates.' *American Economic Review* 59, 450–62

Moss, Milton, 'Income distribution issues viewed in a lifetime income perspective.' *Review of Income and Wealth* 24, 119–36

Moynihan, D.P. (1967) *The Negro Family: The Case for National Action* (Cambridge, Mass.: Harvard University Press)

Muellbauer, John (1974) 'Inequality measures, prices, and household consumption.' *Review of Economic Studies* 41, 493–504

Musgrave, Richard A. and Peggy B. Musgrave (1973) *Public Finance in Theory and Practice* (New York: McGraw-Hill)

Nagatani, K. (1972) 'Life-cycle saving: theory and fact.' *American Economic Review* 62, 344–53

Neil, Herbert E. Jr (1962) 'Effects of inflation upon the incomes and asset values of consumer spending units 1949–1958.' Unpublished doctoral dissertation, University of Michigan

Nordhaus, William D. (1973) 'The effect of inflation on the distribution of economic welfare.' *Journal of Money, Credit and Banking* 5, 465–504

Oi, Walter Y. (1962) 'Labor as a quasi-fixed factor.' *Journal of Political Economy* 70, 538–55

Oja, Gail (1980) 'Inequality of the wealth distribution in Canada, 1970–1977.' In Economic Council of Canada, *Reflections on Canadian Incomes* (Ottawa: ECC)

Oniki, Hajime (1968) 'A theoretical study of the demand for education.' Unpublished Ph.D. dissertation, Stanford University

Ontario Economic Council (1976) *Social Security: Issues and Alternatives* (Toronto: OEC)

Orshansky, Mollie (1965) 'Counting the poor: another look at the poverty profile.' *Social Security Bulletin* 28, 42–81

Osman, Thomas (1977) 'The role of intergenerational wealth transfers in the distribution of wealth over the life cycle: a preliminary analysis.' In F. Thomas Juster, ed., *The Distribution of Economic Well-Being*. National Bureau of Economic Research, Studies in Income and Wealth, No. 41 (Cambridge, Mass: Ballinger)

Ostry, Sylvia and Mahmood A. Zaidi (1972) *Labour Economics in Canada* (2nd ed.) (Toronto: Macmillan)

Parsons, D. (1972) 'Specific human capital: an application to quit rates and layoff rates.' *Journal of Political Economy* 80, 1120–43

Pesando, James E. and Samuel A. Rea (1977) *Public and Private Pensions in Canada: an economic analysis* (Toronto: University of Toronto Press for the Ontario Economic Council)

Phelps, E.S. (1972) 'The statistical theory of racism and sexism.' *American Economic Review* 62, 659–62

Phelps Brown, Henry (1977) *The Inequality of Pay* (Berkeley: University of California Press)

Podoluk, J.R. (1968) *Incomes of Canadians*. 1961 Census Monograph (Ottawa: Dominion Bureau of Statistics)

– (1974) 'Measurement of the distribution of wealth in Canada.' *Review of Income and Wealth* 20, 203–18

Prest, A.R. (1970) 'Some redistributional aspects of the national superannuation fund.' *The Three Banks Review* 86, 3–22

Projector, Dorothy A. and Gertrude S. Weiss (1969) 'Income-net worth measures of economic welfare.' *Social Security Bulletin* 32, 14–17

Pyatt, Graham (1976) 'On the interpretation and disaggregation of Gini coefficients.' *Economic Journal* 86, 243–55

Ramsey, F.P. (1928) 'A mathematical theory of saving.' *Economic Journal* 38, 543–59

Rea, Samuel A. (1978) 'Redistributive effects of Canada's public pension programs.' Research report for the Economic Council of Canada (Ottawa)

Reder, Melvin W. (1962) 'Wage structure: theory and measurement.' In Moses Abramovitz, ed., *Aspects of Labor Economics*. Universities–National Bureau Committee for Economic Research (Princeton, NJ)

– (1968) 'Size distribution of earnings.' In Jean Marchal and Bernard Ducros, eds, *The Distribution of National Income* (New York: International Economic Association)

– (1969) 'A partial survey of the theory of income size distribution.' In Lee Soltow, ed., *Six Papers on the Size Distribution of Wealth and Income*. National Bureau of Economic Research (New York: Columbia University Press)

Rees, A. (1973) *The Economics of Work and Pay* (New York: Harper and Row)

Reuber, G.L. (1976) 'The impact of government policies on the distribution of income in Canada: a review.' Since published in *Canada's Political Economy: Current Issues* (Toronto: McGraw-Hill Ryerson, 1980)

Ritchie, Heather (1977) 'Family allowances: an analysis of their redistributive effects of income.' Unpublished B.A. thesis, Department of Economics, Queen's University

Rosen, Sherwin (1973) 'Income generating functions and capital accumulation,' Harvard Institute for Economic Research Discussion Paper 306, Harvard University

– (1974) 'Hedonic prices and implicit markets: product differentiation in pure competition.' *Journal of Political Economy* 82, 34–55

Rosen, Sherwin (1976) 'A theory of life earnings.' *Journal of Political Economy* 84, S45–68

– (1978) 'Substitution and division of labor.' *Economica* 45, 235–50

Rothschild, M. and J.E. Stiglitz (1973) 'Some further results on the measurement of inequality.' *Journal of Economic Theory* 6, 188–204

Ryder, Karl E., Frank P. Stafford, and Paula E. Stephan (1976) 'Labor, leisure, and training over the life cycle.' *International Economic Review* 17, 651–74

Sahota, Gian Singh (1978) 'Theories of personal income distribution: a survey.' *Journal of Economic Literature* 16, 1–55

Salop, J. and S. Salop (1976) 'Self-selection and turnover in the labor market.' *Quarterly Journal of Economics* 90, 619–27

Sattinger, Michael (1975) 'Comparative advantage and the distribution of earnings and abilities.' *Econometrica* 43, 455–68.

– (1977) 'Compensating wage differences.' *Journal of Economic Theory* 16, 112–23

Sen, A.K. (1973) *On Economic Inequality* (Oxford: Clarendon Press)

– (1974) 'Informational bases and alternative wealth approaches: aggregation and income distribution.' *Journal of Public Economics* 3, 381–403

Senate Committee on Poverty (1971) *Poverty in Canada*. Report of the Special Senate Committee on Poverty (Ottawa)

Seneca, Joseph G. and Michael K. Taussig (1971) 'Family equivalence scales and personal income tax exemption for children.' *Review of Economics and Statistics* 53, 253–62

Sheshinski, E. (1972) 'Relation between a social welfare function and the Gini index of inequality.' *Journal of Economic Theory* 4, 98–100

Simons, Henry C. (1938) *Personal Income Taxation* (Chicago: University of Chicago Press)

Smeeding, Timothy M. (1977) 'The economic well-being of low-income households: implications for income inequality and poverty.' Chapter 8 in Marilyn Moon and Eugene Smolensky, eds, *Improving Measures of Economic Well-Being*. Institute for Research on Poverty Monograph (New York: Academic Press)

Smith, James D., ed. (1975) *The Personal Distribution of Income and Wealth*. National Bureau of Economic Research, Studies in Income and Wealth, No. 39 (New York: Columbia University Press)

Smith, J.D. and J.N. Morgan (1970) 'Variability of economic well-being and its determinants.' *American Economic Review* 60, 286–95

Somermeyer, W.H. and R. Bannink (1973) *A Consumption-Savings Model and Its Applications*. Contributions to Economic Analysis, No. 79 (Amsterdam: North-Holland)

Spence, Michael (1974a) *Market Signaling* (Cambridge, Mass.: Harvard University Press)

– (1974b) 'Competitive and optimal responses to signals: an analysis of efficiency and distribution.' *Journal of Economic Theory* 7, 296–332

– (1976) 'Informational aspects of market structure: an introduction.' *Quarterly Journal of Economics* 90, 591–7

– (1977) 'Signals, contingent contracts, and the divergence of earnings from productivity: survey and extensions.' Harvard Institute of Economic Research Discussion Paper 540, Harvard University

Stark, Thomas (1972) *The Distribution of Personal Income in the United Kingdom 1949–1963* (London: Cambridge University Press)

Statistics Canada (1973a) *Income, Assets, and Indebtedness of Families in Canada, 1969* 13–547 occasional (Ottawa: Statistics Canada)

– (1973b) 'Revision of low-income cut-offs.' Unpublished study by the Consumer Income and Expenditure Division (Ottawa)

– (1974a) *Survey of Consumer Finances, Vol. 1 (Selected Reports)*. Cat. 13–550 occasional (Ottawa: Statistics Canada)

– (1974b) *Farm net income 1973*. Cat. 21–212 (Ottawa: Statistics Canada)

– (1974c) *Canadian Statistical Review*, Sept. 1974. Cat. 11–003 (Ottawa: Statistics Canada)

– (1975a) *Public Use Sample Tapes User Documentation* (Ottawa: Statistics Canada)

– (1975b) *Income Distribution by Size in Canada, 1973*. Cat. 13–207 (Ottawa: Statistics Canada)

- (1975c) *Family Incomes: Census Families, 1973.* Cat. 13–208 (Ottawa: Statistics Canada)
- (1975d) *Household Income, Facilities, and Equipment Micro Data File, 1971 Income.* User Documentation Manual, Survey of Household Facilities and Equipment 1972 (Ottawa: Statistics Canada)
- (1975e) *Vital Statistics 1974.* Cat. 84–201 (Ottawa: Statistics Canada)
- (1976a) *Micro Data File Income 1973 (Census Families).* Survey of Consumer Finances 1974 (Ottawa: Statistics Canada)
Statistics Canada (1976b) *Micro Data File Income 1973 (Census Families).* User Documentation Manual, Survey of Consumer Finances 1974 (Ottawa: Statistics Canada)
- (1977) *Survey of Consumer Finances, Vol. II (Selected Reports).* Cat. 13–551 occasional (Ottawa: Statistics Canada)
Stiglitz, Joseph E. (1973) 'Approaches to the economics of discrimination.' *American Economic Review* 63, 287–95
- (1974) 'Theories of discrimination and economic policy.' In A. Horowitz and G.M. von Furstenberg, eds, *Patterns of Racial Discrimination* (Lexington, Mass.: D.C. Heath-Lexington)
- (1975a) 'An economic analysis of labor turnover.' Stanford University Department of Economics Working Paper 53
- (1975b) 'The theory of screening, education, and the distribution of income.' *American Economic Review* 65, 283–300
Taeuber, Karl E. and James A. Sweet (1976) 'Family and work: the social life cycle of women.' In Juanita M. Kreps, ed., *Women and the American Economy* (New York: Prentice-Hall)
Taubman, Paul J. (1976) 'The determinants of earnings: genetics, family, and other environments: a study of white male twins.' *American Economic Review* 66, 858–70
- (1977a) 'Schooling, ability, nonpecuniary rewards, socioeconomic background, and the lifetime distribution of earnings.' Chapter 12 in F. Thomas Juster, ed., *The Distribution of Economic Well-Being.* National Bureau of Economic Research, Studies in Income and Wealth, No. 41 (Cambridge, Mass.: Ballinger)
Taubman, Paul J., ed. (1977b) *Kinometrics: The Determinants of Socioeconomic Success Within and Between Families* (Amsterdam: North-Holland)
Taubman, Paul J. and Terence J. Wales (1973) 'Higher education, mental ability, and screening.' *Journal of Political Economy* 81, 28–55
- (1974) *Higher Education and Earnings.* National Bureau of Economic Research, General Series, No. 101 (New York: McGraw-Hill)

Taussig, Michael K. (1973) *Alternative Measures of the Distribution of Economic Welfare*. Princeton University Industrial Relations Section Research Monograph (Princton, NJ)

Thurow, Lester C. (1969) 'The optimal lifetime distribution of consumption expenditures.' *American Economic Review* 59, 324–30

– (1970) *Investment in Human Capital* (Belmont, Cal.: Wadsworth)

– (1975) *Generating Inequality* (New York: Basic Books)

Thurow, L.C. and R.E.B. Lucas (1972) *The American Distribution of Income: A Structural Problem* (Washington, DC: US Government Printing Office)

Tinbergen, J. (1959) 'On the theory of income distribution.' *Weltwirtschaftliches Archiv*, 1956, 1155–1173. Republished in J. Tinbergen, ed., *Selected Papers* (Amsterdam: North-Holland, 1959)

– (1975) *Income Distribution: Analysis and Policies* (Amsterdam: North-Holland)

Tobin, James (1967) 'Life cycle saving and balanced growth.' In *Ten Economic Studies in the Tradition of Irving Fisher* by William Fellner, *et al.*, (New Haven: Yale University Press)

Vaillancourt, François (1980) *Differences in Earnings by Language Groups in Quebec, 1970: An Economic Analysis*. International Center for Research on Bilingualism, Publication B-90 (Quebec)

Vickrey, S. (1947) *Agenda for Progressive Taxation* (New York: Roland Press)

Wales, T.J. and A.D. Woodland (1976) 'Estimation of household utility functions and labor supply response.' *International Economic Review* 17, 397–410

– (1977) 'Estimation of the allocation of time for work, leisure, and housework.' *Econometrica* 45, 115–32

Wallace, T.D. and L.A. Ihnen (1975) 'Full-time schooling in life-cycle models of human capital accumulation.' *Journal of Political Economy* 83, 137–56

Watts, Harold W. (1967) 'The Iso-Prop index: an approach to the determination of differential poverty line thresholds.' *Journal of Human Resources* 2, 3–18

Watts, Stephen L. (1977) 'An analysis of the expenditure effect of inflation in Canada and its impact on specific consumer groups in the population.' Unpublished B.A. thesis, Department of Economics, Queen's University

Wedderburn, Dorothy, ed. (1974) *Poverty, Inequality and Class Structure* (London: Cambridge University Press)

Weisbrod, Burton A. and W. Lee Hansen (1968) 'An income-net worth approach to measuring economic welfare.' *American Economic Review* 58, 1315–29

Weiss, Y. (1971a) 'Learning by doing and occupational specialization.' *Journal of Economic Theory* 3, 189–98

– (1971b) 'Investment in graduate education.' *American Economic Review* 61, 833–52

– (1972a) 'The risk element in occupational and educational choices.' *Journal of Political Economy* 80, 1203–13

– (1972b) 'On the optimal lifetime pattern of labor supply.' *Economic Journal* 82, 1293–1315

Weiss, Yoram and Lee A. Lillard (1978) 'Experience, vintage and time effects in the growth of earnings: American scientists, 1960–1970.' *Journal of Political Economy* 86, 427–48

Welch, F. (1973) 'Black-white differences in returns to schooling.' *American Economic Review* 63, 893–907

– (1975) 'Human capital theory: education, discrimination, and life cycles.' *American Economic Review* 65, 63–73

Wilkinson, Bruce (1966) 'Present values of lifetime earnings for different occupations.' *Journal of Political Economy* 74, 556–72

Wise, David A. (1975b) 'Personal attributes, job performance, and probability of promotion.' *Econometrica* 43, 913–32

– (1975b) 'Academic achievement and job performance.' *American Economic Review* 65, 350–66

Wolfson, Michael C. (1977a) 'A real income distribution study.' Paper presented to the Canadian Economic Association

– (1977b) 'Wealth and the distribution of income, Canada 1969–70.' Research paper. Since published in *Review of Income and Wealth* 25, 129–140

Wolfson, Michael C. (1980) 'The lifetime impact of the retirement income system: a quantitative analysis' in Economic Council of Canada, *Reflections on Canadian Incomes* (Ottawa: ECC)

Yaari, M. (1964) 'On the consumer's lifetime allocation process.' *International Economic Review* 5, 304–17